Risk-sharing in the Pharmaceutical Industry

Contributions to Management Science

R.L. D'Ecclesia/S.A. Zenios (Eds.)
Operations Research Models in Quantitative Finance
1994. ISBN 3-7908-0803-2

M.S. Catalani/G.F. Clerico
Decision Making Structures
1996. ISBN 3-7908-0895-4

M. Bertocchi/E. Cavalli/S. Komlósi (Eds.)
Modelling Techniques for Financial Markets and Bank Management
1996. ISBN 3-7908-0928-4

H. Herbst
Business Rule-Oriented Conceptual Modeling
1997. ISBN 3-7908-1004-5

C. Zopounidis (Ed.)
New Operational Approaches for Financial Modelling
1997. ISBN 3-7908-1043-6

K. Zwerina
Discrete Choice Experiments in Marketing
1997. ISBN 3-7908-1045-2

G. Marseguerra
Corporate Financial Decisions and Market Value
1998. ISBN 3-7908-1047-9

WHU Koblenz – Otto Beisheim Graduate School of Management (Ed.)
Structure and Dynamics of the German Mittelstand
1999. ISBN 3-7908-1165-3

A. Scholl
Balancing and Sequencing of Assembly Lines
1999. ISBN 3-7908-1180-7

E. Canestrelli (Ed.)
Current Topics in Quantitative Finance
1999. ISBN 3-7908-1231-5

W. Bühler/H. Hax/R. Schmidt (Eds.)
Empirical Research on the German Capital Market
1999. ISBN 3-7908-1193-9

M. Bonilla/T. Casasus/R. Sala (Eds.)
Financial Modelling
2000. ISBN 3-7908-1282-X

S. Sulzmaier
Consumer-Oriented Business Design
2001. ISBN 3-7908-1366-4

C. Zopounidis (Ed.)
New Trends in Banking Management
2002. ISBN 3-7908-1488-1

U. Dorndorf
Project Scheduling with Time Windows
2002. ISBN 3-7908-1516-0

B. Rapp/P. Jackson (Eds.)
Organisation and Work Beyond 2000
2003. ISBN 3-7908-1528-4

M. Grossmann
Entrepreneurship in Biotechnology
2003. ISBN 3-7908-0033-3

H.M. Arnold
Technology Shocks
2003. ISBN 3-7908-0051-1

T. Ihde
Dynamic Alliance Auctions
2004. ISBN 3-7908-0098-8

J. Windsperger/G. Cliquet/G. Hendrikse/M. Tuunanen (Eds.)
Economics and Management of Franchising Networks
2004. ISBN 3-7908-0202-6

K. Jennewein
Intellectual Property Management
2004. ISBN 3-7908-0280-8

M.J. Thannhuber
The Intelligent Enterprise
2005. ISBN 3-7908-1555-1

C. Clarke
Automotive Production Systems and Standardisation
2005. ISBN 3-7908-1578-0

M.L. Entrup
Advanced Planning in Fresh Food Industries
2005. ISBN 3-7908-1592-6

U.M. Löwer
Interorganisational Standards
2006. ISBN 3-7908-1653-1

Gerrit Reepmeyer

Risk-sharing in the Pharmaceutical Industry

The Case of Out-licensing

Foreword by Oliver Gassmann,
University of St. Gallen, Switzerland

With 70 Figures
and 10 Tables

Physica-Verlag
A Springer Company

Series Editors
Werner A. Müller
Martina Bihn

Author
Dr. Gerrit Reepmeyer
University of St. Gallen
Institute of Technology Management
Dufourstr. 40 a
9000 St. Gallen
Switzerland
E-Mail: gerrit.reepmeyer@unisg.ch

ISSN 1431-1941
ISBN-10 3-7908-1667-1 Physica-Verlag Heidelberg New York
ISBN-13 978-3-7908-1667-9 Physica-Verlag Heidelberg New York

Physica-Verlag is a part of Springer Science+Business Media

springer.com

Printed in Germany

Cover-Design: Erich Kirchner, Heidelberg

SPIN 11571261 88/3153/DK-5 4 3 2 1 0 – Printed on acid-free and non-aging paper

Foreword

The productivity in pharmaceutical research and development faces intense pressure. R&D expenditures of the major US and European companies have topped US$ 33 billion in 2003 compared to around US$ 13 billion just a decade ago. At the same time, the number of new drug approvals has dropped from 53 in 1996 to only 35 in 2003. Moreover, the protraction of clinical trials has significantly reduced the effective time of patent protection. The consequences are devastating. Monopoly profits have started to decline and the average costs per new drug have reached a record level of close to US$ 1 billion today. As a result, any failure of a new substance in the R&D process can lead to considerable losses, and the risks of introducing a new drug to the market have grown tremendously. Particularly if a company is highly dependent on just a handful of mega-selling blockbuster drugs, the risks can be even greater. For example, Pfizer generated about 90% of its worldwide revenues in 2002 with just 8 products. Any shortfall of a promising late-stage drug candidate would have left Pfizer with a gaping hole in its product portfolio. In order to deal with these risks, many pharmaceutical companies have started to organize their R&D in partnership. In fact, more than 600 alliances in pharmaceutical R&D are signed every year. Several empirical studies confirm the rising importance of collaborations in the pharmaceutical industry, and they highlight that risk-sharing has emerged as one of the major challenges of today's collaboration management.

Mr. Reepmeyer tackles this issue by analyzing how pharmaceutical companies can share R&D risks by collaborating with external partners. He focuses on the young empirical phenomenon of out-licensing which has barely been subject to prior research. While other types of collaboration in the pharmaceutical industry, such as research alliances, co-development and in-licensing, are widely applied by practitioners and studied in great detail by scholars for several years, out-licensing has not received a similar level of attention. During the course of his investigation, Mr. Reepmeyer adopts the perspective of the pharmaceutical company that is about to sell the license to its partner company. He provides answers to the following questions: What importance does out-licensing at established pharmaceutical companies have today, and what are the main characteristics of these collaborative arrangements? How can these collaborations be managed in order to effectively and efficiently reduce R&D risks?

Mr. Reepmeyer uses a case study based research method which is well suited for the nature of this young practical phenomenon as well as the character of existing research. The insights gained are based upon comprehensive and in-depth empirical evidence. The large number of interviews (86) corresponds to the high quality of the case studies. The selected case studies all follow a clear concept and comprise profound empirical findings. Mr. Reepmeyer's work covers three major case studies of Novartis, Schering and Roche as well as several small case studies which accentuate and highlight the issue of out-licensing throughout the entire book. In order to derive managerial recommendations, Mr. Reepmeyer uses the microeconomic theory of Adverse Selection – which has only recently been awarded the Nobel Prize. The application of this theory to the case of out-licensing is not only innovative in its nature, but also allows deducing concrete and tangible recommendations for pharmaceutical R&D managers. The results of Mr. Reepmeyer's research not only provide several novel insights about risk-sharing in pharmaceutical R&D collaborations, they also include a clear framework for the manageability of out-licensing collaborations.

Prof. Dr. Oliver Gassmann
Director, Institute of Technology Management
University of St. Gallen

Preface

This book originates from my dissertation at the Institute of Technology Management at the University of St. Gallen in Switzerland, titled 'Risk-sharing in Pharmaceutical R&D Collaborations – The Case of Out-licensing'. Out-licensing represents a fairly new strategy of established pharmaceutical companies to share R&D risks via collaborations. This book as well as my thesis exemplify this young empirical phenomenon by illustrating a couple of related case studies.

For supervising my thesis and for giving me the opportunity to exploit my academic aspirations, I would like to express my deep gratitude to Professor Oliver Gassmann. His support during the entire research process was always encouraging and cordially pleasant at the same time. I would also like to thank Professor Fritz Fahrni for co-supervising my thesis. As I was allowed to conduct some part of my research at the Columbia Business School in New York, I am indebted to both Professor Atul Nerkar for being my faculty sponsor as well as to Professor Pierre Azoulay for giving insightful directions to my research work. During my time at Columbia, I gratefully acknowledged financial support by the Swiss National Science Foundation.

This book as well as my thesis would not have been possible without the input of various research interviewees in miscellaneous companies. I would like to thank them for taking the time to discuss my research questions. For contributing valuable input to this work, I am thankful to several colleagues and students at the Institute of Technology Management, especially Michael Kickuth, Christoph Kausch, Jonathan Lüthi and Stefan Keidel. Last but not least, I would like to thank Dr. Werner Müller and Barbara Feß of Springer for managing the overall publication process. Writing this book has been a great learning experience for me. I hope that the results are inspiring and helpful for pharmaceutical managers as well as students and scholars of the pharmaceutical industry respectively.

Gerrit Reepmeyer

Contents

1 Introduction

1.1 Motivation and Goal

1.1.1 Relevance of research subject

Management of research and development (R&D) at large pharmaceutical companies is facing severe conditions. The foremost concern with top management is the deteriorating R&D productivity.[1] R&D spending has arrived at a record level today, while the number of new drugs introduced to the market has been declining for several years or has remained constant at best.

In 2003, pharmaceutical companies invested more than US$ 33 billion in R&D worldwide compared to about US$ 13 billion just a decade ago. However, the number of new chemical entities (NCEs) which have been approved for market entry by the Food and Drug Administration (FDA) in the US has declined from 53 in 1996 to only 35 in 2003 (PhRMA 2004). As a response to this gap, the average R&D costs per new drug are constantly increasing. In 1976, it cost US$ 54 million to develop a new drug, US$ 231 million in 1987, and about US$ 280 million in 1991 (DiMasi 2001). This number has grown to close to US$ 1 billion by now (see Fig. 1). A recent Reuters study (2003a) supports this negative trend by concluding that the R&D performance of major pharmaceutical companies is sub-optimal. The long average development time in pharmaceutical R&D cannot be used as an excuse for the gap in R&D spending and new drug approvals, firstly because the greatest R&D expenses are in the final phases of drug development (within just a few years of market introduction), and secondly, because the observed trends in the 1990s were already present in the decades before.

Due to the escalating average R&D costs per new drug approval, the risks in pharmaceutical R&D have become paramount because any failure of a newly developed substance during the R&D process can cause significant losses. In accordance with the rising R&D input and declining output as well as the subsequently increasing R&D risks, many R&D projects are terminated at fairly early stages and long before they reach market introduction.[2] Hence, most pharmaceutical companies have built up large portfolios of patents and other forms of intellectual property, but they often

---

1 By definition, the R&D productivity describes the ratio of input in R&D versus its output.

2 Interview with McKinsey.

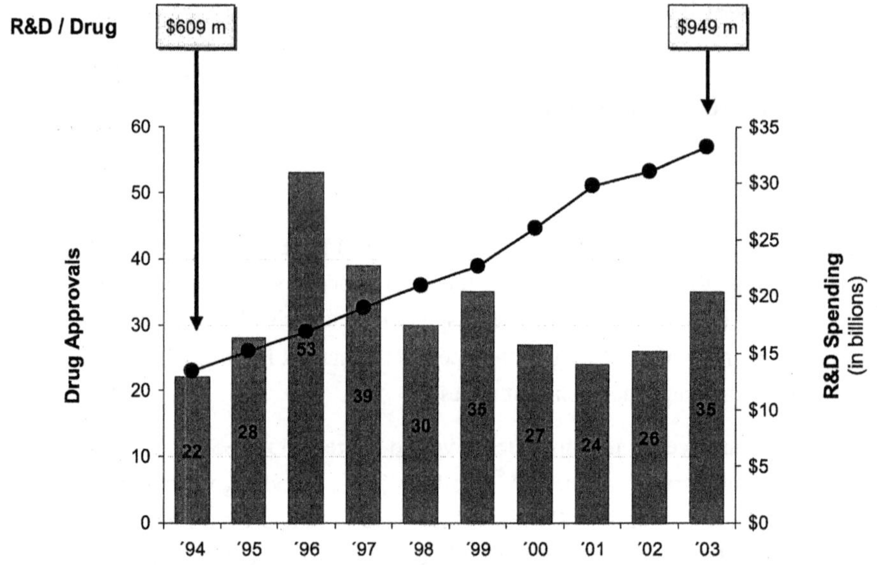

Source: PhRMA (2004)

Fig. 1. Declining productivity in pharmaceutical R&D.

use only a small portion of these intangible assets (see Festel 2004). The R&D results that have been achieved but not marketed cover valuable intellectual property, unpatented technology or interesting R&D projects across all stages of the R&D process which effectively decay in the companies' archives because their further development is oftentimes considered to be too risky. Although much idle intellectual property has little value, others could provide significant economic benefits (Festel 2004).[3]

Besides of the rise in R&D-related risks and the associated build-up of large inventories of intellectual property, most pharmaceutical companies have conceded that fundamental breakthroughs in technology or science are increasingly likely to occur outside their organizations. It has become clear today that not even the largest multinational company can hope to do all its research and development activities in-

3 In this context, Joseph Zakrzewski, Vice President of Business Development at Eli Lilly, argues that "intellectual property that is sitting on my shelf is providing no value to shareholders or to patients" (see Longman 2004).

house any more. As a response, pharmaceutical companies are increasingly compelled to access innovation activities that are conducted outside their own R&D boundaries and to rely on R&D results which do not emanate from their own R&D departments. While the first R&D collaborations in the pharmaceutical industry emerged in the late 1970s and early 1980s with the surge in biotechnology companies, today's pharmaceutical firms operate in huge networks consisting of various different organizations because the cascade of knowledge flowing from new sciences and technologies is simply far too complex for any company to handle alone. Due to the rising availability and importance of outside innovation, today's pharmaceutical R&D management is forced to look beyond their own research borders in order to improve the performance of their own R&D activities.[4]

In aggregation, pharmaceutical companies are exposed to increasing R&D risks for the development of their internally generated substances, and at the same time, a large proportion of R&D results is conducted by external entities. As a consequence, research and development collaborations which particularly consider risk management aspects have gained much attention in the recent past. Pharmaceutical companies have started to implement new collaboration vehicles which explicitly use the partner firms' resources to share some part of the R&D risks during the commercialization of their intellectual property. A fairly new type of risk-sharing collaboration that has only recently started to be applied by some established pharmaceutical companies includes out-licensing. While pharmaceutical companies are generally reluctant to out-license their most critical R&D projects because they prefer to take on the entire risk for the development of these substances in order to retain 100% of the potential profits, out-licensing represents a promising vehicle to commercialize substances which do not make it into the firms' top priority list but still have a certain value not only for other companies but also for patients. If these substances are out-licensed for further development to an external partner who is willing to take on the risks which the pharmaceutical company was not willing to carry, they could provide additional economic benefits for the pharmaceutical firm.

In summary, the out-licensing of intellectual assets to an external partner allows the pharmaceutical company to exploit originally terminated R&D projects without hav-

4 The trend towards a closer interaction with external partners in the R&D process finds additional support in a new paradigm in innovation management literature, also referred to as Open Innovation (see Chesbrough 2003). In contrast to the traditional understanding of innovation management, which Chesbrough calls Closed Innovation, Open Innovation means that valuable resources can come from inside or outside the company and places external resources on the same level of importance as that reserved for internal resources.

ing to carry the associated risks. This risk-sharing collaboration seems to be a promising approach for extracting value from internal research results and recouping some of the significant investments made in R&D which otherwise would have been sunk.[5] Therefore, out-licensing represents one of today's most prevalent vehicles for established pharmaceutical companies to improve their R&D performance.

1.1.2 Deficits in current research

'Risk-sharing in Pharmaceutical R&D Collaborations' aggregates three different groups of literature: Firstly, the term deals with R&D management in the pharmaceutical industry. Secondly, a focus is set on issues in R&D collaborations, and finally, the topic of risk management is addressed. The identification of deficits in current research thus requires a comprehensive literature review covering publications from all three literature streams: pharmaceutical R&D management, R&D collaboration management as well as risk management.

Pharmaceutical R&D management. The literature on pharmaceutical R&D management is quite extensive. Several publications deal with issues related to R&D performance. They mainly discuss success factors and strategies for producing successful new chemical entities (see Boerner 2002, Teoh 1994, Needleman 2001). Sharma and Lacey (2004) conclude that market valuations of pharmaceutical firms are responsive strongly and cleanly to the success or failure of new product development efforts. Other publications analyze the origins and drivers for competitive advantage (Cockburn et al. 2000, Yeoh and Roth 1999, Henderson 2000). Dynamics of technological innovation as well as explanatory variables of firm research intensities have been described by Achilladelis and Antonakis (2001) as well as Grabowski and Vernon (2000). Another stream of literature on pharmaceutical R&D covers issues related to resource allocation. These publications primarily deal with the distribution of internal resources to different R&D projects across different therapeutic areas and technology platforms (see Gittins 1997, Halliday et al. 1997). According to Cockburn and Henderson (1998), successful firms decentralized decision-making on the allocation of R&D resources. In addition, portfolio management approaches are discussed in the context of resource allocation as well. Blau et al. (2004) developed a portfolio management approach that selects a sequence of projects which

5 In this context, Ed Saltzman, President and CEO of Defined Health (a leading strategy consulting firm for clients in the pharmaceutical industry), claims "I think it is going to be increasingly strategic for big pharma to step up out-licensing, to better justify the ever-increasing R&D investment that they are making" (see Thiel 2004).

maximizes the expected economic returns at an acceptable level of risk for a given level of resources in a new product development pipeline. A general point of interest in the literature on pharmaceutical R&D management has also been the organizational structure of R&D departments. Cardinal and Hatfield (2000) as well as Drews (1989) discussed the embeddedness of central research activities. According to Gambardella (1992), the more basic research a pharmaceutical firm performs, the more patents it produces. Research by Cockburn and Henderson (1998) supports this fact by saying that drug discovery firms with a strong research orientation produced a greater number of important patents. According to Pisano (1997a) and Cockburn et al. (1999), the link between basic science and drug discovery at pharmaceutical companies has increased over time. A relatively small number of publications in pharmaceutical R&D covers internationalization aspects and international comparisons among pharmaceutical R&D activities (see Albertini and Butler 1995, Kuemmerle 1999, Beckmann and Fischer 1994). The role of public sciences as well as governmental and national institutional frameworks and how they affect pharmaceutical R&D also plays a negligibly small role in the literature. By far, most research on pharmaceutical R&D management deals with the emergence of the biotechnology industry over the last two decades and the subsequently increasing availability of innovation that occurs outside the boundaries of the pharmaceutical company. A detailed review of the literature in this area is provided later on.

R&D collaboration management. Literature on R&D collaboration management covers a large area of research as there has been unprecedented growth in corporate planning and reliance on various forms of external collaboration in recent decades (compare Hergert and Morris 1988, Mowery 1988, Hagedoorn 1990 and 1995, Badaracco 1991, Hagedoorn and Schakenraad 1992, Gulati 1995). While many firms historically organized R&D internally and relied on outside contract research only for relatively simple functions or products (Mowery 1983, Nelson 1990), a growing importance is now placed on collaborative projects in R&D. Several publications on R&D collaboration management deal with the description and analysis of the nature of the underlying R&D collaborations (see Kodama 1992, Hagedoorn 2002, Freeman 1991, Hagedoorn 1995). During the 1980s, a change in the nature of collaborations could have been observed. While traditional cooperative investment activities were usually tactical and passively pursued endeavors with local firms, R&D collaborations have become more strategic since the beginning of the 1980s (Porter and Fuller 1986). Regarding the business functions covered by the collaboration, the cooperative ventures are more and more directed towards jointly exploring new areas of expertise, and less towards exploiting simple economies of scale

(Gerybadze 1995). Cooperative agreements are thus increasingly molded around a very sophisticated segmentation, around functions and around specific steps within the value chain (Porter 1985 and 1990). Due to the growing importance of cooperative agreements between firms, their quantity and frequency has risen considerably since the 1970s (see Ohmae 1985, Bleicher 1987, or Dunning 1988).[6] Despite the growing importance of R&D collaborations, empirical evidence indicates that success rates of inter-firm alliances are rather low (Harrigan 1988a). Campione (2003) claims that at least half of all alliances formed over the past decade reportedly failed to meet their participants' objectives. By analyzing alliances in biotechnology companies, Niosi (2003) found out that the alliances' success (as measured by growth) is not linked to the pure existence of an alliance but rather to the financial support of venture capital and partnerships with large corporations. Further success factors for R&D collaborations include the timing of the cooperation (Katila and Mang 2003) as well as the involvement of the decision making level (De Meyer 1999). Today, companies in a wide range of industries are executing nearly every step in the value chain, from discovery to distribution, through some form of external collaboration. These various types of inter-firm alliances take on many forms, ranging from R&D partnerships to equity joint ventures to collaborative manufacturing to complex co-marketing arrangements (Powell et al. 1996).

Risk management. As R&D projects are typically considered to be high-risk projects (see Gassmann et al. 2001), risk management has become an important issue in R&D management literature over the past. Most of the relevant literature deals with different concepts of risk management and various leadership approaches. Risk management as a management issue was discussed for the first time by Oberparleiter (1930). Oberparleiter (1930) differentiates between company-risk and entrepreneur-risk. While company-risk is further broken down into market risks, organizational risks, revenue risks, and financial risks, the entrepreneur is 'putting at risk his labor and assets in order to accomplish what he/she thinks is economically feasible'. In the 1950s, the risk management aspect found acceptance as a leadership approach

[6] While all forms of cooperation seem to be increasing, there seems to be a growing tendency towards looser forms, such as project-based and non-equity partnerships. The share of equity-based R&D joint ventures in all newly established technology alliances decreased from around 80% in the early 1970s to less than 10% in 1998, and contractual arrangements radically increased both in number and share over the same period. The number of new R&D partnerships grew from around 10 per year in the 1960s to more than a few hundred per year at the end of the 1990s. Broken down by industry, the share of R&D partnerships in the pharmaceutical industry rose to about 30% of all R&D partnerships across all industries at the end of the 1990s. Only R&D partnerships in information technologies surpass pharmaceuticals by contributing to about 50% of all partnerships (Hagedoorn 2002).

in terms of insurance management. Gallagher (1952) extended the concept of risk beyond the traditional insurance thinking and emphasized risk management as a much broader issue. Risk did not only cover reimbursements of insured losses, but also capital market-driven trading as well as dealing with insurance services and premiums. Mehr and Hedges (1963) took this definition one step further and looked at insurance as only one aspect of corporate risk management. By promoting this approach, they were laying the foundation for several novel tasks and fields of activity in risk management. Despite the fact that risk management emerged from the insurance industry, the term itself should not be purely associated with insurable risks (Haller 1981). A holistic risk management covers all aspects of corporate leadership (Mensch 1991). As a result, the goals of corporate risk management must be derived from the superior goals of the corporation (Hitzig 1978, Braun 1984). Risk management has thus become a specific leadership function (Haller 1986).

In aggregation, the three major literature streams which are affected by the topic 'risk-sharing in pharmaceutical R&D collaborations' cover very extensive areas of research. However, there are some areas of literature which are right at the interfaces between pharmaceutical R&D management, R&D collaboration management and risk management (see Fig. 2). A closer discussion of the literature at these intersections is necessary not only to provide a comprehensive literature review but also to narrow down the potential deficit in current research. Therefore, the next paragraphs discuss the following areas of literature in greater detail:

- Collaborations in pharmaceutical R&D;
- Risks in pharmaceutical R&D;
- Risks in R&D collaborations.

Collaborations in pharmaceutical R&D

Today, all stages of the innovation process in the pharmaceutical industry (from discovery to marketing) are increasingly performed through some form of collaboration arrangement (see Powell et al. 1996, Tidd 1997). As already mentioned earlier, the most widely discussed collaborations in pharmaceutical R&D include the relationship between biotechnology firms and pharmaceutical companies. Several publications on pharmaceutical R&D discuss different types of these partnership agreements (see Roberts and Mizouchi 1989 and Herrling 1998). All types usually center around four general categories, each of which having its own benefits and challenges: (i) research contracts or minority investments for the purpose of gaining a window on new technologies, (ii) licensing and marketing agreements to obtain the

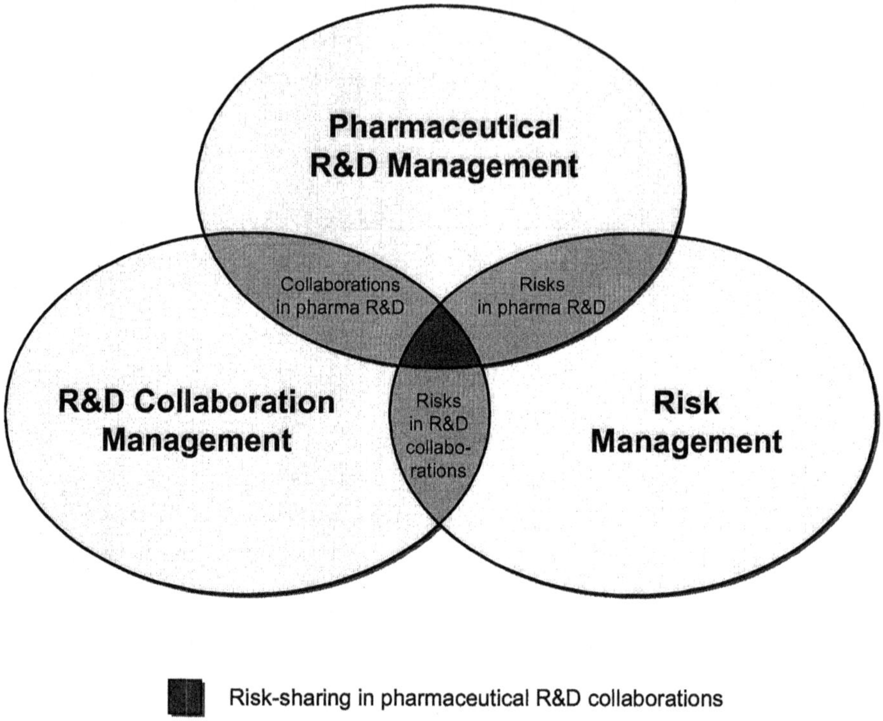

Fig. 2. Literature streams related to 'risk-sharing in pharmaceutical R&D collaborations'.

use of a particular technology, (iii) corporate alliances such as joint ventures which may or may not involve the transfer of equity, or (iv) mergers and acquisitions.

As managers in major pharmaceutical companies have generally not invested directly in novel biotechnology, they prefer to buy-in the knowledge from smaller firms (Jones 2000). Due to the fact that R&D activities are increasingly bought-in, Jones (2000) expects in the future a substantial reduction in the number of scientists directly employed by leading firms. The pharmaceutical companies then form the nodes in large-scale scientific networks, which include biotech firms as well as universities (Albertini and Butler 1995). While many external partners in novel biotechnological areas are usually small and mid-size companies (SMEs), most of these companies remain small, even those set-up several years ago (Mangematin et al.

2003). The goal of biotech firms to become large and established is thus much harder to reach. Indeed, new entrants in the pharmaceutical industry typically co-exist in a 'symbiotic' relationship with mature companies rather than replacing them (Pisano 1990, 1991). It may even not be realistic to expect the small biotech firms to become fully integrated (Tapon et al. 2001). Research by Rothaermel and Deeds (2004) involving 325 biotechnology firms that entered into 2,565 alliances over a 25-year period revealed information about the typical path of an R&D collaboration in the pharmaceutical industry. A product development path usually begins with exploration alliances predicting products in development, which in turn predict exploitation alliances. Exploitation alliances then lead to products on the market. In this context, Weisenfeld et al. (2001) identified two forms of collaboration in the biotech industry: the 'virtual company' and the 'industrial platform'. The two forms are complementary to each other in the sense that industrial platforms foster the necessary infrastructure for R&D while virtual companies facilitate the process of commercialization. Thus, when the technology lifecycle reaches the stage where technology starts being integrated into products and processes, the market orientation has to be strongly promoted. The nature of alliances between biotech and pharmaceutical companies also depends on external factors, such as the availability of funding via capital markets. Lerner et al. (2003) observed equity financing cycles between 1980 and 1995 and studied their impact on the cooperation behavior between biotech and pharmaceutical firms. They found out that in the case of diminished public market financing, small biotech firms are more likely to fund their R&D through alliances with major corporations rather than with internal funds raised through the capital markets. Agreements during periods of limited external equity financing are more likely to assign the bulk of control to the larger corporate partner, and are significantly less successful than other alliances. These agreements are also likely to be renegotiated if financial market conditions improve.

Another stream of literature regarding collaborations in pharmaceutical R&D deals with the reasons that motivate firms to enter into these alliances. According to Jones et al. (2000), there are many explanations for increased networking, including market access, speed to market, complementary assets as well as shared risks. As many of the research-oriented partner firms (mostly biotechnology start-ups) emerged over the last few years and are still comparatively small, they usually do not possess their own manufacturing and marketing capabilities and are forced to secure these complementary assets. The choices biotechnology firms make in securing these needed capabilities have been analyzed by Greis et al. (1995). The results support the shift away from upstream R&D to downstream manufacturing and marketing.

However, external partnering as a choice to complement own capabilities is not only motivated by the desire to acquire innovation assets, but also by factors in the external competitive environment, such as the regulatory climate and the dynamics of global competition. Pisano (1990) analyzed how two sources of transaction costs (small-numbers bargaining hazards and appropriability concerns) may affect established firms' choices between in-house and external sources of R&D when technological change shifts the locus of R&D expertise from established enterprises to new entrants, and established firms face a make-or-buy decision for R&D projects. While small-numbers bargaining problems motivate firms to internalize R&D, the primary drivers that affect R&D procurement decisions at established pharmaceutical firms are the firms' R&D experience, their dependence on the pharmaceutical business, and their national origin.

Besides the reasons for entering collaborations in pharmaceutical R&D, another major portion of the literature in this area discusses the performance of R&D collaborations. Rothaermel (2001) analyzed 889 different alliances and concluded that incumbents' alliances with biotech are positively associated with the incumbents' new product development and, in turn, new product development is positively associated with firm performance. Rothaermel (2001) noticed that the cooperation between incumbents and new entrants may contribute to an improvement in incumbent industry performance. Stuart (2000) showed that the success of networks is not so much influenced by the size of the network itself, but more by the characteristics of the participating companies. By analyzing 1,600 horizontal biotech alliances from 150 companies regarding the influence of the technological competence of established firms on the innovation rate of their small counterparts as measured by the number of patents of the small alliance partners, Stuart (2000) found a positive correlation between the technological position measured by patent citations of the pharmaceutical company and the innovation output of the biotechnology start-up. Research by Pisano (1997b) compared the relative performance of vertically integrated R&D projects and collaborative projects in the bio-pharmaceutical industry among 260 bio-pharmaceutical projects. The rate of termination for partnered projects is significantly higher than the failure rate of projects undertaken via vertical integration. This seems to indicate that projects with poorer prospects for reaching the market tend to be licensed to collaborative partners while those with better prospects are commercialized internally. Pisano refers to this phenomenon as the 'lemons' problem. He concludes that the higher rate of failure of partnered projects is attributable to ex-ante project selection biases rather than differences in ex-post execution of partnered vs. non-partnered projects. Deeds and Rothaermel (2003) observed the relationship between performance and age of an alliance among biotech and pharmaceutical companies. This relationship seems to be U-shaped curvilinear rather than linear, with the minimum point of alliance performance occurring after approximately 4.5 years. Strategic alliances appear to face a liability of adolescence rather than a liability of newness. It is also found that important alliances exhibit generally shorter times of duration.

Another major stream in the literature on collaborations in pharmaceutical R&D deals with trends in collaborative R&D endeavors (see Whittaker and Bower 1994). Based on research on 5,093 strategic alliances in the biotechnology industry between 1990 and 2001, Lin (2001) found out that alliances are becoming more sophisticated and mature, the drug companies are poles of alliance networks, and that the new biotech firms play a mediating role to transform scientific knowledge into patented technologies. This means that the major drug companies are becoming more dependent on external innovation. According to Jones (2000), the proportion of external R&D compared to internal R&D expenditures increased from 5% to 16% between 1989 and 1995 (in the pharmaceutical industry in UK). As a result, pharmaceutical R&D will no longer be a stand-alone activity by single companies but rather a complex web of inter-firm agreements which link the complementary assets of one firm to another. The extent of commingling in biotechnology is so extensive that the locus of innovative activity can no longer be one firm, but a network of inter-organizational relationships which are controlled by different firms (Pisano et al. 1988). The effect of these linkages will be a shift of the focus of management from that of intrafirm coordination to that of managing a complex network of inter-firm linkages. With growing complexity, a focus on the role of innovation networks will be more appropriate than the behavior of specific firms in isolation (Tidd 1997). As long as pharmaceutical companies still need help in mastering recent scientific breakthroughs, collaborations in pharmaceutical R&D will continue to grow. As abrupt innovations in biology and chemistry are serendipitous and impossible to predict, only a vast network of research relationships with university and independent labs helps get access to these serendipitous discoveries. Management of collaborations with outside innovation will thus be considered a core competence (Tapon and Thong 1999).

Risks in pharmaceutical R&D

Risk management is discussed quite extensively in the literature on pharmaceutical R&D. Grabowski and Vernon (1990) provide a very general analysis of risks in pharmaceutical R&D by looking at the relationship between risk and return from a capital market and performance-oriented perspective. Bernotat-Danielowski (2002) differentiates risks in pharmaceutical R&D between development risks and market/sales risks. While development risks are characterized by discrete probability distributions, market and sales risks can best be described by continuous probability distributions. The discrete probability distributions in development stem from the attrition rates at the different stages of the R&D process which allow the application of decision-tree or real-option models to describe the inherent risks. The continuous probability distribution in sales and market risks can best be captured by different product profiles and scenarios. This might include sensitivity analyses covering changes of variable parameters, such as treated patients, price, market share, or number of competitors.

Special attention is paid to risks in pharmaceutical R&D when the topics of project evaluation and portfolio management are addressed. In this context, different allocation models and valuation tools are widely discussed. Bunch and Schacht (2002) introduce two different models: the steady-state and dynamic model. While both models can be used to predict resource requirements at an aggregate level, the steady-state model is attractive because of its simplicity and the ability to set target resource levels to achieve a given level of R&D output. The dynamic model is useful when incorporating both current and future projects in the consideration set.

Recently, a lot of attention has been paid to real option valuation in pharmaceutical R&D. Cassimon et al. (2004) developed a methodology for valuing new drug applications (NDAs) and the R&D of pharmaceutical companies based on real options models. The R&D phase for a NDA can best be presented as a 6-fold compound option on the commercialization phase. The authors derive a closed-form solution for an n-fold compound option model, and apply it to calculate the value of an NDA using sector average figures. Brach and Paxson (2001) analyzed the Poisson real option model of a gene-to-drug venture and found that, under simple assumptions, the real option value is substantial, even if there is no intrinsic value of the venture. McGrath and Nerkar (2004) went a step further and explored firms' overall motivation to invest in a new option. Based on a study covering 45,757 patents established by the 31 major players in the pharmaceutical industry, they concluded that investments in R&D are consistent with the logic of real options reasoning. The authors found three constructs which have an influence on firms' propensity to invest in new R&D options and which could be usefully incorporated in a strategic theory of investment: scope of opportunity, prior experience, and competitive effects. Due to the limitations of real option models in practice, Loch and Bode-Greuel (2001) came up with a decision-tree model which follows option-thinking but seems to be a better tool to implement the real option approach in evaluating R&D projects. Decision-trees help provide transparency about project value and strategic options. Most importantly, carefully thinking through the tree helps identify growth options, represented by additional branches in the tree, and quantify that they not only represent different sources of risk but also major sources of value.

Risks in R&D collaborations

When risks are discussed in collaborative endeavors, the term 'risk-sharing' is frequently used. Bernstein (1996) claims that – although it is not a new phenomenon – risk-sharing has gained in importance in the recent past as a subject in research. The term risk-sharing is usually used to explain various contractual arrangements including executive compensation (see Garen 1994, Gomez-Mejia et al. 2000), franchising (see Martin 1988), insurance (see Townsend 1994), leasing (see Leland 1978), and partnerships (see Gaynor and Gertler 1995). In this context, it has to be considered that it is generally not possible to reduce a project's intrinsic risks by entering into a collaboration. However, the risks of a joint endeavor can be transferred from one entity to another which then bears the risks. These collaboration arrangements usually follow staged collaboration agreements which are linked to performance-oriented payment structures. Accordingly, each collaboration can be regarded as an investment in an option which gives both firms the opportunity to assess the value and impact of the collaboration at several different points in time, particularly after initial uncertainties are resolved. The risks are typically implied in the cooperation in terms of the price paid and the potential payoff expected.

In general, risk-sharing works as follows: In the simplest case, individuals facing independent, identically distributed risks and having identical attitudes towards risk all gain if they pool their risks and share them equally, as in an insurance cooperative. No Pareto improvement (gain for everyone) is then possible, that is, further gain for anyone must hurt someone else. The problem of efficient risk-sharing is more complicated if risks or risk attitudes differ, such as in typical R&D partnerships (see Pratt 2000). Milgrom and Roberts (1992) summarize that efficient risk-sharing contracts balance the costs of risk bearing against the incentive gains that result. Risk-sharing contracts have the benefit that they motivate parties to perform at or above contractually specified levels. That is the driving force behind the use of contingent contracts in all kinds of compensation agreements, from sales commissions to stock options (see Bazerman and Gillespie 1999). Bazerman and Gillespie

(1999) identified the following aspects which should be kept in mind for any risk-sharing contract:

- Risk-sharing contracts require continuing interaction between the parties;
- Negotiators need to think about the enforceability of contracts;
- Risk-sharing requires transparency.

Risks in R&D collaborations have been intensively discussed by Helm and Kloyer (2004). The authors claim that both suppliers and buyers of R&D results perceive two exchange risks: first, the risk of achieving a lower profitability on the innovation return than the exchange partner, and second, the risk of the partner becoming a competitor by unplanned, one-sided knowledge flows. Both risks motivate opportunistic behavior. The authors conclude that an option on later negotiation of an additional continuous innovation return-sharing which is based on contractual hostages can lower the exchange risks perceived by the supplier.

However, the risk-sharing foundation is oftentimes not limited to R&D collaborations and usually discussed in a wider context. For instance, risk-sharing has also frequently been discussed in relationships between companies and public or governmental authorities (see Dercon and Krishnan 2003).[7] A frequently cited issue describes the relationship between providers of healthcare and third-party payers (see also Leone 2002). Literature on these topics primarily discusses risk-sharing agreements from a moral hazard and collusion perspective (see Dutta and Prasad 2002, Schmidt 1999, Gaynor and Gertler 1995). In this regard, the risk aversion of the participating entities as well as the value of information become critical issues. It has generally been shown that information might have a negative impact on risk-sharing. In an economy with risk-sharing mechanisms, the release of more information may eliminate opportunities to reallocate risk through trade (see also Eckwert and Zilcha 2003, Schlee 2001).

Risk-sharing has also frequently been discussed on a country- and region-specific level comparing trade between different countries or single firms conducting business in multiple countries (see Kalemli-Ozcan et al. 2003, Schlee 2001). The companies' primary goal has usually been to better exploit comparative advantages of different countries. Risk-sharing is also a crucial part of research in the financial industry. Allen and Gale (1999) observed relationships and risk-sharing among inno-

7 Similar relationships include the interaction of companies/individuals and funding carriers, such as insurance companies (see Alger and Ma 2003).

vations in financial services. The authors argue that costly ex ante information acquisition and analysis is a major barrier to the participation of investors and firms in sophisticated markets. However, long-term relationships between intermediaries and their customers, in which intermediaries provide implicit insurance to customers, can be an effective substitute for the costly ex ante investigation. The customers know that if there is a surprise, the intermediary will share the risk. Thus, Allen and Gale (1999) conclude that such risk-sharing is only possible if both parties will benefit from the relationship in the future. This means that competition by intermediaries may be undesirable if it reduces future profits, and hence the amount of risk-sharing that can occur. Brander et al. (2002) analyzed syndicated investments (i.e. co-investments) in the venture capital industry and discussed risk-sharing and project scale as possible reasons for syndication. They found that syndicated investments have higher returns than stand-alone investments. The reason is two-fold. Firstly, the investor feels a need to obtain a second opinion. Secondly, investors pool their capital in order to reveal additional value creation potential. As co-investments have outperformed stand-alone investments, the latter explanation seems to outweigh the first, and co-investments seem to have a positive impact on overall investment performance.

Another literature stream that discusses risk-sharing is compensation-related literature. Therein, scholars usually equate risk-sharing with gain-sharing. Gain-sharing describes the relationship between companies and their employees, and points toward pay-for-performance approaches that link group-wide financial rewards to employee-created improvements in organizational performance. Thus, both employees and the firm share the risks of relative success or failure (Gross and Duncan 1998). Gomez-Mejia et al. (2000) introduced a risk-sharing framework to develop a theoretical foundation for gain-sharing. They analyzed performance-based contracts which link the firm's performance to the employees' compensation. Consequently, the employees agreed to share the risks inherent to the company. Increased risk-sharing through increased use of performance-based pay resulted in lower opportunity costs for the firm, because employees are rewarded for gains in performance that might not otherwise be forthcoming. The authors found during their research about 160 journal articles, professional publications, and books on gain-sharing until 2000, which highlights the importance of the subject in literature.

In general, there have been several attempts to formulate models and frameworks that discuss risk-sharing and try to explain this type of risk management. In summary, the foremost issues in risk-sharing include risk aversion profiles, utility functions, moral hazard issues, availability of information or the impact of intermediaries. However, almost all scholars came to the conclusion that risk-sharing is difficult to test (see Allen and Lueck 1999, Brander et al. 2002).

Conclusion: Several publications exist in all major literature streams (i.e. pharmaceutical R&D management, R&D collaboration management, and risk management) as well as at the intersections of these literature streams (i.e. collaborations in pharmaceutical R&D, risks in pharmaceutical R&D, and risks in R&D collaborations). Particularly the overlap between pharmaceutical R&D management and R&D collaboration management is very intense due to the vast quantity of literature available on outside innovation and biotechnology as input for pharmaceutical research. Risk management is also considered quite extensively in the literature on pharmaceutical R&D management. By contrast, literature at the intersection of R&D collaboration management and risk management is very scarce. Most literature on managing risks in collaborations covers areas other than R&D. Only a few selected publications mention risk management in collaborations that deal with product or service innovations (see for example Helm and Kloyer 2004, Pratt 2000, Allen and Gale 1999, Brander et al. 2002). Although there is extensive literature available across all literature streams including their respective interfaces, there is, however, no publication that covers all three literature streams in aggregation (i.e. risk-sharing in pharmaceutical R&D collaborations).

Particularly the literature regarding licensing as a means of risk-sharing is very scarce. Although licensing has been conceptually discussed for many years (see Mordhorst 1994, Ford 1985, Telesio 1979, or Taylor and Silberston 1973), there has generally been little empirical research on this topic (compare Kollmer and Dowling 2004). Only one recent study investigates the licensing agreements between young and established firms, focusing on the allocation of control rights (Lerner and Merges 1998).

Especially out-licensing at large companies is fairly underrepresented in research. There is only one recent study that compares licensing strategies at fully and not-fully integrated firms in the biopharmaceutical industry (see Kollmer and Dowling 2004). The authors come to the conclusion that there are differences in their licensing strategies. While not-fully integrated firms use licensing as their major commercialization channel and exploit their core products by licensing at their firm's maximum integration level, fully integrated firms out-license preferably non-core products because of a misfit with their overall strategy. As out-licensing brings comparable compensation in both cases, licensing also seems to be an attractive commercialization strategy for fully integrated firms. However, Kollmer and Dowling (2004) did not analyze out-licensing at fully integrated companies from a risk management perspective.

In summary, the review of current literature reveals that it is justified to assume that the intended research is about to target a white spot in management research which has not been discussed by previous scholars so far.

1.1.3 Research objective

This book addresses both a major practical issue currently under discussion in pharmaceutical R&D management as well as a corresponding gap in management research. The research intends to respond to this gap by deriving a model for structuring risk-sharing in collaborative projects in pharmaceutical R&D and developing a guideline for R&D managers which provides an answer to the following research question:

How can pharmaceutical companies share R&D risks via collaborations?

Thereby, the research focuses on out-licensing (from the perspective of the pharmaceutical company) as the underlying type of R&D collaboration due to its novelty in management practice. This raises two sub-questions:

- What means/vehicles of out-licensing as a type of risk-sharing in pharmaceutical R&D do exist today, and what are the main characteristics of these collaborative arrangements?
- How should an out-licensing collaboration be managed in order to increase the likelihood that risks can successfully be shared?

In order to provide an answer to these questions, the investigation tries to come up with results about how R&D risk-sharing decisions are made, and which criteria are used to assess the value and strategic impact of these collaborations. Overall, the research is expected to provide a guideline for pharmaceutical R&D managers regarding how to structure, organize and manage an out-licensing collaboration. The guideline is supposed to cover the following aspects:

- Which activities are predestined for out-licensing in pharmaceutical R&D?

- Which actions should be taken by pharmaceutical R&D management in order to be well prepared for executing on a successful out-licensing deal?
- What are the most important and crucial aspects when structuring the out-licensing deal?
- When and for what should external partners be used in an out-licensing collaboration, and what are the most important criteria for their selection?

1.2 Terms and Definitions

R&D Risk

There is generally no clear definition of the term 'risk' because risk differs depending on the point of view of the beholding entity and its intent of employment. The first scholars who introduced the term risk in a managerial concept have been Pratt (1964) and Arrow (1965). They defined risk in the context of absolute risk aversion, relative risk aversion and decreasing absolute risk aversion of entities making decisions under uncertainty. The extent of the entities' risk aversion is related to their utility functions. Risk aversion results in concave utility functions because it implies convex indifference curves, decreasing marginal rate of substitution, as well as 'non-specialization', which are important properties for many models in economics (see Yaari 1965, Hirshleifer 1965 and 1966).

In this context, risk can broadly be defined as 'the possibility that the result of a certain activity differs from the underlying expectations' (see also Haller 2002). The most common types of interpretation of the term risk which are relevant to business and management issues include the following (compare Hänggi 1995, Peter 2002):

- *Scientific-mathematical definition*: Risk (R) is defined as the product of the extent of a certain event (A) and the probability of its occurrence (W): $R = A * W$. Determining risk thus requires the quantification of both factors (compare Ruh and Seiler 1993, Bechmann 1993).
- *Decision-logical definition*: Risk is defined via a probability distribution function $F(x)$ of the consecutive occurrence of certain actions (compare Muschick and Müller 1987).
- *Information-theoretical definition*: Risk is defined as the information deficit of the achievement of certain targets set (see Helten 1994). Based on this definition, Mensch (1991) characterizes risk as the threat of making a wrong decision which is due to this information deficit.

- *System-theoretical definition*: Risk is defined as a holistic management issue, and is thus an undesired event, which could have a negative impact on the aspired corporate goals (compare Haller 1986).

Despite the negative connotation that is usually implied into the definition of risk, Haller (2002) argues that risk also describes the potential occurrence of a positive outcome (i.e. a chance). The relation between risk and its potentially implied return is regarded as the most appropriate criterion to assess and evaluate risk. The primary question is: which risk do we want to bear in order to achieve a certain return, or respectively, which return can be achieved at a given level of risk? (see Zimmermann et al. 1995).

The various aspects and parameters of risk help illustrate the breadth of the topic regarding the management of corporations. The most important risk topics of today's companies include quality risks, political and country-specific risks, bankruptcy and contingency reserves risks, production risks, information and data security risks, health and work safety risks, environmental and third party liability risks, as well as market and product risks (see Peter 2002). Dealing with risks in a managerial way requires as a first step the clarification of the expectations and goals of the corporation regarding its risk management (see Peter 2002). During a second step, the risk situation has to be identified, measured and assessed (Haller 2002). During the third and final step, risk management actions have to be taken. In general, there are four basic principles to handle risks: avoiding risk, reducing risk, transferring/sharing risk, and bearing risk (see Fig. 3).

This research uses a broad definition for the term risk and focuses on any risk which is related to the R&D process of pharmaceutical companies. Subsequently, any undesired outcome of the R&D process which could lead to results that do not meet the initial expectations by pharmaceutical R&D management is referred to as an R&D risk. A closer analysis and description of the particular R&D risks in the pharmaceutical industry is provided in chapter 2.1.

R&D Collaboration

A collaboration is broadly defined by Dodgson (1993) as 'any activity where two or more partners contribute differential resources and know-how to agreed complementary aims'. Gulati and Singh (1998) use a similar definition by describing a collaboration as 'any voluntarily initiated cooperative agreement between firms that involves exchange, sharing, or co-development, and it can include contributions by

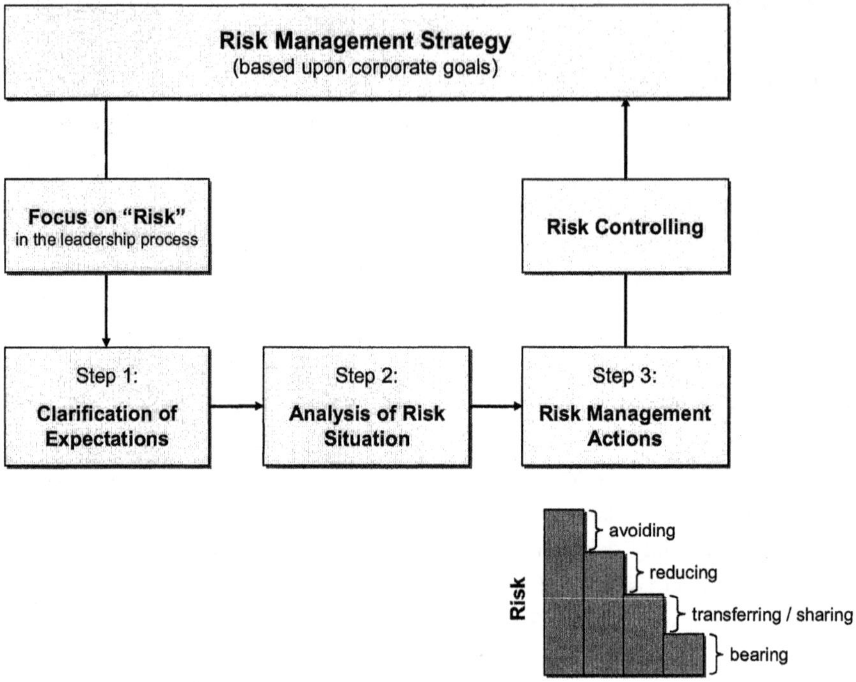

Source: Haller (2002)

Fig. 3. Basic principles to manage risks.

partners of capital, technology, or firm-specific assets'. In addition, a great variety of organizational modes can be adopted for collaborations, and several different terms are used to describe them (see also Roberts and Berry 1985, Brockhoff 1991, Chatterji 1996, Millson et al. 1996). These terms include 'cooperative agreements, networks, or alliances' (Dodgson 1993), 'strategic network' (Jarillo 1988), 'spherical firm' (Miles and Snow 1995), 'virtual company' (Chesbrough and Teece 1996), and 'industrial platform' (Cabo et al. 1998).[8]

In the case of research and development, a collaboration is more specifically defined by Hagedoorn et al. (2000) as 'an innovation-based relationship that involves, at least partly, a significant effort in research and development'. It has shown that non-

8 The term collaboration is also discussed in great detail by Harrigan (1986), Rotering (1990), Parkhe (1993), or Gulati (1998).

equity, contractual forms of R&D partnerships, such as joint R&D pacts and joint development agreements, have become very important modes of inter-firm collaboration as their numbers and share in the total of partnerships has far exceeded that of joint ventures (see Hagedoorn 1996, Narula and Hagedoorn 1999, Osborn and Baughn 1990).[9]

This research focuses on R&D collaborations in the pharmaceutical industry and uses a broad definition of the term 'collaboration' by referring to it as any activity conducted by two firms where both firms have an interest in the outcome of the joint initiative. A closer description of the relevance of R&D collaborations including their reasons and rationales is provided in chapter 2.2.

Out-licensing

Beamish (1996) defines licensing as 'a contractual arrangement whereby the selling firm (licensor) allows its technology, patents, trademarks, designs, processes, know-how, intellectual property, or other proprietary advantages to be used for a fee by the buying firm (licensee)'. According to Ehrbar (1993), most companies use licensing to lower not only costs but also risks. Smith and Parr (1993) argue that the primary forces that drive licensing of intellectual property include time savings, cost control and risk reduction. Applied to the case of the pharmaceutical industry, Roth (2004) defines licensing as 'selling the rights of a developed product or potential compound to another firm for further development, production or marketing'. From the perspective of the pharmaceutical company, licensing can be differentiated into in-licensing and out-licensing. While both concepts include the transfer of rights for a certain good from one company to another, in-licensing refers to acquiring intellectual assets whereas out-licensing refers to selling them. Strategies for buying are useful for companies that lack the intellectual assets to launch new products and businesses or for companies that want to hedge their competitive bets when they plan to do it. By contrast, strategies for selling are useful for companies that lack the resources, the capabilities, or the strategic intent to commercialize the intellectual assets they create (Torres 1999). However, the selling firm always has to consider a potential dissipation of its proprietary knowledge because the licensee always buys at least a portion of the firm's knowledge.

9 Joint ventures seem to have become gradually less popular if compared to other forms of partnering. The pharmaceutical industry in particular prefers to rely on contractual R&D partnerships primarily because of their superior flexibility (Hagedoorn 2002).

As this research analyzes out-licensing arrangements from the perspective of integrated pharmaceutical companies, out-licensing refers to the situation where an established pharmaceutical company has discovered a new research result but then decided not to pursue the idea internally any more. Hence, the pharmaceutical company is about to sell certain rights of the underlying research result to an external partner. Thereby, out-licensing deals are conducted for various objectives, can have different structures and are done because of multiple reasons. In order to define and differentiate the out-licensing collaborations which are discussed in the scope of the investigation, this research only focuses on deals which meet the following criteria:

1. The out-licensing deals under investigation purely focus on collaborations that cover *R&D-related* issues. Out-licensing deals which are signed merely for marketing or manufacturing reasons do not fall under the scope of this research. For example, out-licensing deals which transfer the rights of an already approved drug to a licensee who then simply markets the drug in a different geographical region or produces it in its own manufacturing facilities are not subject of this research.
2. The out-licensing deals under investigation are all signed with the intention to *share* R&D-related risks. This includes out-licensing deals where the seller (licensor) of the intellectual property retains an interest in the further development of the licensed product. Out-licensing deals that are done for reasons other than risk-sharing, such as licensing deals to get rid of certain assets or business units, do not fall under the scope of this research. If the licensor does not retain an interest in the further development of the exchanged product, the R&D risks are not 'shared' but rather 'disposed'.

A closer illustration of the rising prominence of out-licensing at established pharmaceutical companies including its potential, organization and limitations is provided in chapter 3.2.

1.3 Research Concept

1.3.1 Research classification

This research follows the research tradition set by Ulrich and Krieg (1974), Ulrich (1981), and Bleicher (1991), who consider organizations as 'complex, open, social systems'. The systems are influenced by the environment and its individuals, who in turn influence various transformation processes within the organizations which eventually lead to a certain output. As an applied social science, management research is impelled to remain in close contact with practice and contribute to solving practical problems.

Due to the novelty of the empirical phenomenon of risk-sharing in pharmaceutical R&D collaborations and the existence of untapped case material, this study applies an exploratory research approach. Predominantly, the emphasis is on the exploration of interesting situations, correlations and contexts in companies, and on the conceptualization of the investigated material (compare Ulrich 1981). These concepts could then be further refined in subsequent empirical research. Therefore, the underlying research aims at both generating questions and presenting propositions relevant to explaining typical phenomena (compare Kromrey 1995).

Following Kubicek (1977), Tomczak (1992) and Gassmann (1999), the research process is considered to be highly iterative (see Fig. 4). Instead of validating hypotheses created solely upon theory, the targeted new knowledge covers questions to reality which are based both upon theory and practice (Kubicek 1977). The image of reality that is created upon the initial framework and data collection is critically reflected in order to achieve differentiation, abstraction, and changes in perspective. The new theoretical understanding leads to new questions about reality. Consequently, at the time of writing a publication the research process must be frozen in a pragmatic way. All open questions at that stage in the research process have to be made explicit as part of the research results.

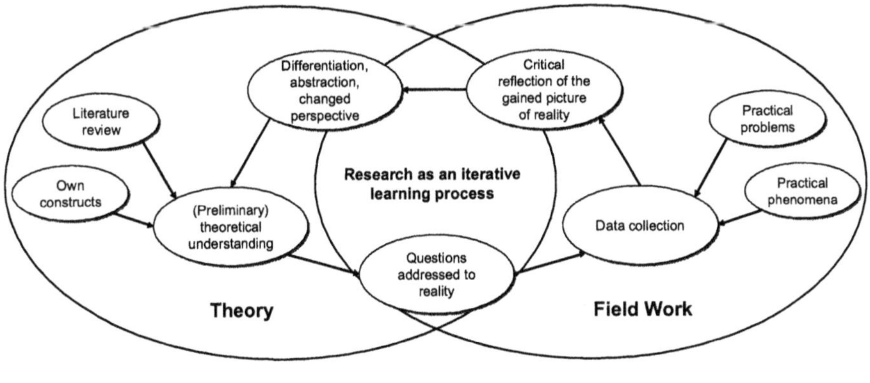

Source: following Kubicek (1977), Tomczak (1992), Gassmann (1999)

Fig. 4. Exploratory research as an iterative learning process.

Therefore, the main goal of this research is to gain practical and applicable knowledge about the research object under investigation (i.e. to derive a management model for structuring risk-sharing in pharmaceutical R&D collaborations).

1.3.2 Research methodology

As risk-sharing in pharmaceutical R&D collaborations is a very recent phenomenon, this research is about to analyze in-depth case studies following the concept of qualitative research in accordance with Eisenhardt (1989), Yin (1994) and Gassmann (1999). From the four basic types of design for case studies, this research follows a multiple-case design with the R&D collaboration (i.e. the joint project) as the single unit of analysis (see Yin 1994). The main criteria in qualitative empirical research are reliability and validity of results (see Yin 1994, Lamnek 1993, and Eisenhardt 1989). Validity and reliability is ensured during this research by combining the data from semi-structured interviews with the results of thoroughly conducted desk research, internal R&D documentation as well as presentations by R&D personnel. The interpretations are then confirmed in follow-up interviews.

After having derived a first conceptual model of R&D collaborations in the pharmaceutical industry, the research has been complemented by in-depth case studies in order to support or realign the initial findings. The companies in the case studies are primarily located in Switzerland, Germany and the USA. As the pharmaceutical industry is global in scope and reach, internationally diverse case studies are a necessity in order to derive profound research results and to deduct implications and guiding principles for pharmaceutical R&D management. Altogether, the book is building upon research carried out between Summer 2002 and Spring 2005.

The research is based upon 86 semi-structured interviews with 35 different companies primarily from the pharmaceutical/biotech industry, which are predominantly based in Switzerland, Germany and the USA. The interview partners were primarily R&D directors and senior R&D managers. 71 interviews have been conducted by the author himself, and another 15 interviews have been conducted by parties other than the author. The latter source of interviews stems from seminar works and scientific studies conducted at the Institute of Technology Management at the University of St. Gallen under the supervision of the author. Especially the work by Lüthi (2005) shall be gratefully acknowledged in this context. In addition, a survey among 60 companies has been conducted – by the order of Novartis among others – focusing on issues in strategic technology management. An overview about the empirical data collection during the research investigation is provided in Table 1.

Table 1. Overview of empirical data set.

Data Collection		
Event	**# of Interviews**	**# of Companies**
Semi-structured interviews *(Interview partners from the pharma/biotech industry)*	54	25
Contract research project *(Analysis of pharmaceutical R&D structures in CH)*	3	3
Expert workshop *(Focus on emerging trends in the pharma industry)*	14	11
Sum of own interviews	**71**	**33***
Third-party interviews *(Conducted by parties other than the author)*	15	7
Total number of interviews	**86**	**35***
Survey *(Focus on strategic technology management)*	60	60

* Number of companies is adjusted for redundancies.

1.4 Structure of the Book

The book is structured as follows (see also Fig. 5): The first section (chapter 2) illustrates the current key issues in pharmaceutical R&D. It describes the increase in R&D risks and the simultaneously increasing interaction with external innovation in pharmaceutical R&D which results in the pharmaceutical firms' desire to use collaborations in order to share R&D risks. Chapter 3 provides a brief typology of risk-sharing R&D collaborations in the pharmaceutical industry, highlighting out-licensing as a novel approach to risk-sharing.

Afterwards, chapter 4 introduces selected in-depth case studies on risk-sharing R&D collaborations placing a particular focus on out-licensing. The subsequent chapter 5 discusses the analyzed case studies and aggregates mutual characteristics which emanate from the empirical findings of the cases. Chapter 6 introduces the economic theory of adverse selection in order to help explain patterns observed during the discussion of the case studies. After the theory will have been briefly explained (it has initially been developed for insurance contracts in the insurance industry), it will be applied to out-licensing contracts in the pharmaceutical industry.

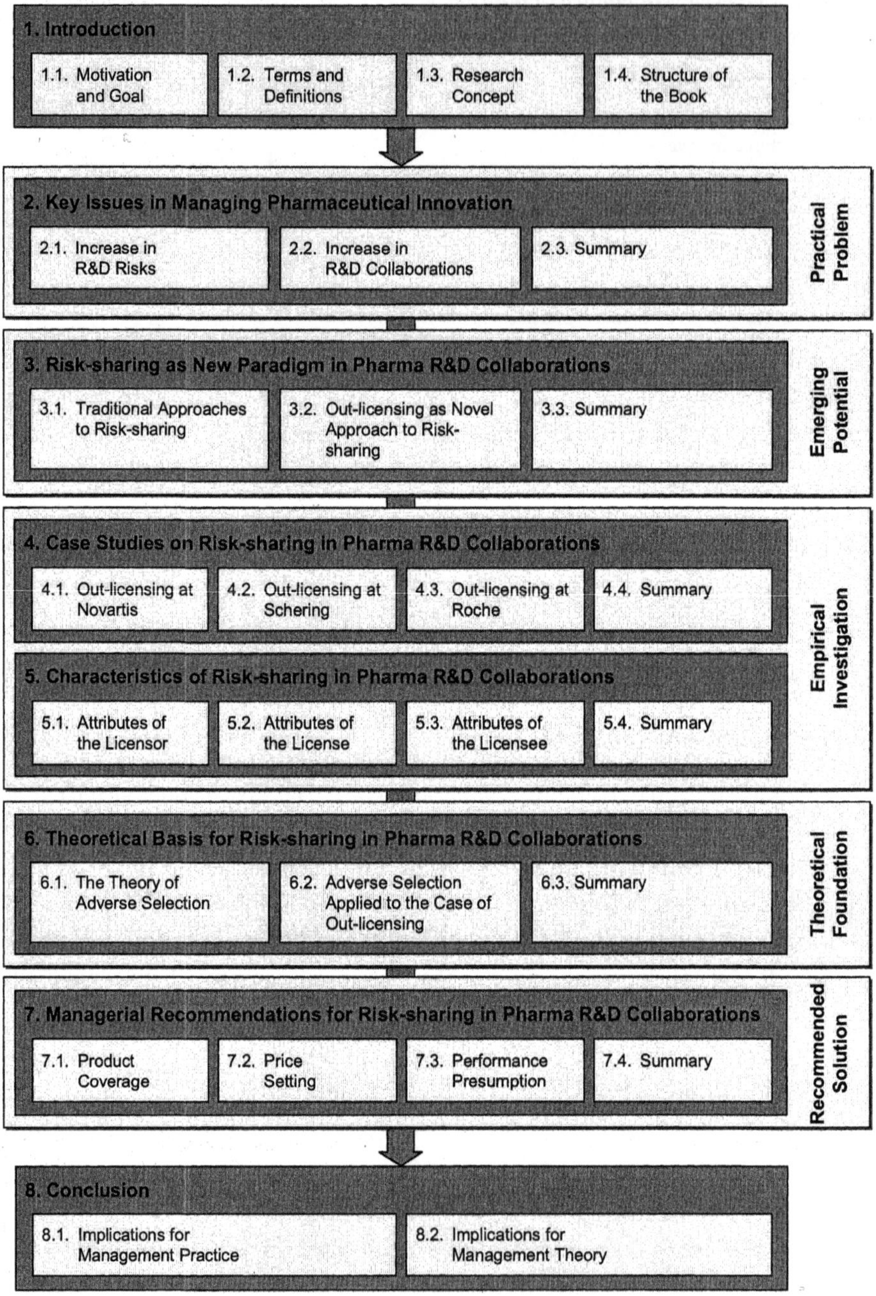

Fig. 5. Structure of the book.

Based on the insights gained from the economic theory, chapter 7 deduces recommendations for pharmaceutical companies how to manage these risk-sharing collaborations. As the theory of adverse selection highlights three different parameters which are considered to be highly relevant dimensions in managing out-licensing collaborations, chapter 7 builds upon these three parameters to derive the managerial recommendations. Applied to the case of out-licensing, the three parameters refer to the 'product coverage', 'price setting', and 'performance presumption'.

The final chapter 8 summarizes the research results and concludes with implications for management practice and theory.

2 Key Issues in Managing Pharmaceutical Innovation

2.1 Increase in R&D Risks

Due to the surge in the average R&D costs per new drug approval, the risks in pharmaceutical R&D have increased significantly. As any failure of a newly developed substance during the R&D process can cause significant losses, many R&D projects today are terminated because of risk considerations. R&D risks can be broken down into multiple separate risks. The most eminent R&D risks include:

- Risk of growth attainment;
- Risk of increasing complexity;
- Risk of technology investment;
- Risk of high attrition;
- Risk of blockbuster reliance;
- Risk of market timing;
- Risk of product differentiation;
- Risk of regulative force.

The rising importance of these risks for pharmaceutical R&D is discussed in the following chapters.

2.1.1 Risk of growth attainment

The market for pharmaceutical products belongs to the fastest growing markets in the world with an average annual growth rate of 11.1% from 1970 until 2002 (PhRMA 2003). Worldwide sales in the pharmaceutical industry reached more than US$ 466 billion in 2003 (IMS 2004). As previous success raises stakeholders' expectations of further success, these double-digit growth rates are now strictly incorporated into the industry's overall growth expectations. Today's pharmaceutical companies are forced by investors and management to at least maintain the high growth rates of the past 30 years for the foreseeable future. As a consequence, a large pharmaceutical company must introduce at least two to four new drugs on the market per year just to maintain the current growth rates (Gassmann et al. 2004). The winners in the pharmaceutical industry even have to exceed these numbers in order to deliver above-average returns to their shareholders. This growth imperative ultimately leads to a self-enforcing growth spiral which accelerates itself due to superior previous performance.

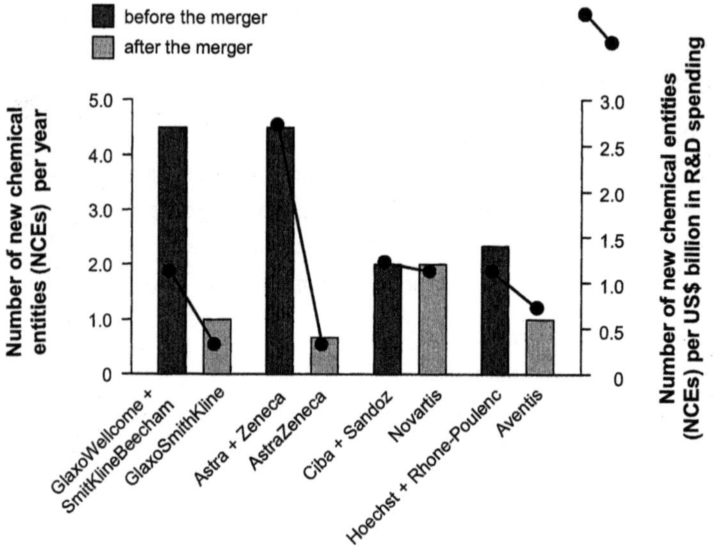

Time span: from 3 years before until 3 years after the merger.

Source: Wood Mackenzie (2003a)

Fig. 6. The failing attempt to achieve growth in the pharmaceutical industry via M&A activity.

As the pharmaceutical industry is still far from consolidation, many companies used to rely on external growth via mergers & acquisitions (M&A) to meet the required growth ratios. The most recent examples of large mergers include Pfizer & Pharmacia, Astra & Zeneca, or Aventis & Sanofi. However, mega-mergers do not necessarily result in improved performance, as illustrated by a recent study by Wood Mackenzie (2003a). Grouping the top 10 pharmaceutical companies in 'mega-merged companies' (GlaxoSmithKline, AstraZeneca, Novartis and Aventis among others) and 'non-mega-merged companies' (Merck, Johnson&Johnson, Eli Lilly and Roche among others), the study found that between 1995 and 2002, 'mega-merged companies' lost on average 2.8% of their worldwide share in the ethical drug market, while 'non-mega-merged companies' won 10%. The study also found that 'mega-merged companies' appear to produce fewer new chemical entities (NCEs) after their mergers than before. Fig. 6 illustrates this observed pattern for a few selected examples.

As a consequence, pharmaceutical R&D management is exposed to the risk that a drug candidate's target market will not be large enough to generate sufficient amounts of revenues in order to achieve the required growth rates. In most cases, pharmaceutical R&D management then terminates the respective R&D projects although the substance itself might still have a therapeutic value.[10] As the number of new drugs which have to be introduced on the market every year to attain or even exceed the aspired growth (either via internal or external growth) is constantly increasing in accordance with overall industry growth, pharmaceutical R&D management is exposed to an ever increasing risk of failing to meet these growth expectations.

2.1.2 Risk of increasing complexity

Few other industries are as driven by science, research and development as the pharmaceutical industry. R&D management thus receives a deliberate emphasis in almost any pharmaceutical company. The largest companies in the industry manage complex R&D structures funded by huge R&D budgets that cover several US$ billions (see Table 2).

Table 2. Top 10 pharmaceutical companies in R&D spending worldwide.

Company	**R&D Budget 2003** [in US $]	**R&D Budget 2002** [in US $]	**Change** [in %]
Pfizer	7.13 billion*	5.17 billion	+37.9
Johnson&Johnson	4.68 billion**	2.70 billion	+173.3
GlaxoSmithKline	4.54 billion	4.29 billion	+5.8
AstraZeneca	3.45 billion	3.06 billion	+12.7
Aventis	3.23 billion	3.67 billion	-11.9
Merck & Co.	3.17 billion	2.67 billion	+18.7
Novartis	3.07 billion	2.60 billion	+18.1
Eli Lilly	2.35 billion	2.14 billion	+9.8
Bristol-Myers Squibb	2.27 billion	2.20 billion	+3.2
Wyeth	2.09 billion	2.08 billion	+0.5

* includes the acquisition of Pharmacia in 2002.
** includes R&D expenditures not related to pharmaceuticals.

Source: Pharmaceutical Executive (2004, 2003)

10 The decline in the commercialization potential of a drug candidate can be due to a non-anticipated reduction in the number of potential patients or a decrease in the projected price of the drug.

Pharmaceutical companies are not only spending large sums on R&D in absolute terms, they are also characterized by a fairly high R&D intensity (as measured by the R&D-to-sales ratio). The R&D intensity of the major pharmaceutical companies worldwide has increased from 11.4% in 1970 to 18.5% in 2001 (PhRMA 2004, 2001). Including the money spent on in-licensing drug candidates, R&D expenditures account for the lion's share of the overall cost structure of a newly developed drug. As the effective cost structure of an original product may vary considerably from case to case, Table 3 cites ranges rather than exact figures.

Table 3. Average cost structure of a newly developed drug.

Relative Contribution	Cost Factors
20% - 40%	Research, Development, Licenses
15% - 30%	Production
5% - 15%	Technical and Administrative Costs
20% - 30%	Marketing and Distribution
20% - 35%	Margin

Source: Pharma Information (2002)

The high R&D intensity is mainly due to the complex pharmaceutical R&D process. After around 13 years of research and development time, only one of 5,000 product ideas is eventually launched on the market (Pfeiffer 2000), and more than 10,000 substances have usually been screened and analyzed for every new drug that enters

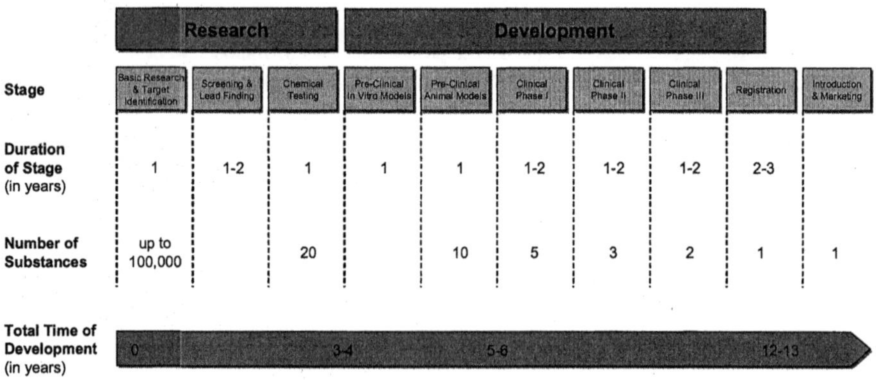

Source: adapted from Gassmann et al. (2004)

Fig. 7. R&D process in the pharmaceutical industry.

the market (Völker 2001). With today's high performance screening technologies, this number can easily reach up to 100,000 substances for each new drug. Fig. 7 illustrates an exemplary R&D process in the pharmaceutical industry.

Excursus: The different stages of the pharmaceutical R&D process

Research and development are usually strictly separated in the pharmaceutical industry. During the early stages of research, the scientists are looking for existing molecules, which could serve as a target for the substances, which are expected to have an impact on the disease that is about to be cured. During the screening stage, scientists look for a so-called lead-substance, which influences the target in the desired way. During this stage, almost 90% of all potential substances are eliminated due to the lack of desired impacts and/or effects. The remaining substances, which are on average only the few dozen most promising ones, are then handed over to development for further testing.

Pre-clinical development tests try to prove if a new substance takes effect and if it is compliant. The most important issues are to ensure that the new substance is not toxic, does not change genes and does not cause cancer or birth defects. This test-series is usually made using animal experiments. In case the pre-clinical trials are successful, the substance enters the human body for the first time during the clinical trials.

The clinical trials are separated into three different phases. During Phase I, the drug candidate is tested whether its positive animal properties can be extended to humans (compatibility and safety). During Phase II, the substance is tested to see if it is able to cure the disease. During Phase III, the substance is tried at a larger number of patients in order to establish the proper dosage and any adverse reactions to long-term use.

If the clinical trials are successful, the new product can be registered with the respective health authorities in each country where the pharmaceutical company intends to launch the product. After the registration, the new drug can finally be introduced to the market.

As pharmaceutical R&D is characterized by a high complexity, most pharmaceutical companies have started to restructure their portfolios in order to efficiently and effectively focus only on the fastest growing markets. As a result, the development of some compounds might be terminated because the substances' indication does no longer fit into the company's portfolio any more. As pharmaceutical companies can only effectively manage a certain number of high priority projects, a compound's development might even be terminated within the therapy areas served by the pharmaceutical company because other substances in the portfolio might have better prospects and deserve priority over this compound. This does not represent an impairment of the initial compound. Moreover, the compound still remains attractive, but other substances simply seem to be more promising. As a result, the increasing complexity in pharmaceutical R&D leads to the risk of dissipation of research resources: research comes up with attractive drug candidates which are then not fully exploited to their maximum potential due to strategic reasons or portfolio decisions.

2.1.3 Risk of technology investment

While the most recent scientific and technological revolution has been the biotechnology boom starting in the late 1970s and early 1980s, there are ever more complex sciences and technologies by now which affect the entire pharmaceutical R&D process (i.e. to help discover lead compounds and develop drug candidates). All novel technological approaches used today are mainly triggered by improved computing power, the rise in novel computer applications and the discovery and understanding of the human genome. All of the new sciences and technologies require tremendous investments in state-of-the-art technology platforms and infrastructure, which in turn lead to significant technology-related risks. The most prominent sciences and technologies which are expected to have the highest impact on drug discovery and development include:

- High-throughput screening;
- Combinatorial chemistry;
- Bioinformatics;
- Genomics;
- Pharmacogenomics;
- Proteomics;
- Molecular drug design;
- In-silico drug design.

High-throughput screening

Since their first application in the 1990s, high-throughput screening (HTS) or ultra high-throughput screening (UHTS) have been considered revolutionary for pharmaceutical research and discovery. Houston and Banks (1997) state that 'these new plate formats have arisen as a potential answer to the problematic question being asked at most major pharmaceutical companies: How can we screen more targets and more samples cheaply?' Today, high-throughput screening represents the major tool for lead identification. It allows large numbers of chemicals to be automatically tested for their impact on biological activity.[11] While the quantity of screened substances is increasing tremendously, the screening technologies, however, do not have an impact on the quality of the outcome. Besides screening through a vast number of substances, it is therefore equally important to have the right substances included in the pool of all substances that are to be screened. As the production of compounds did not expand at the same rate as the screening of compounds, a bottleneck in the discovery process occurred. Hence, the increasing application of high-throughput screening triggered the emergence of combinatorial chemistry.

Combinatorial chemistry

Combinatorial chemistry allows large numbers of compounds to be made by the systemic and repetitive covalent connection of a set of different 'building blocks' of varying structures to each other. According to Reuters (2002), the two technology platforms of high-throughput screening and combinatorial chemistry account for more than half of all spending on new discovery technologies in the pharmaceutical industry. This helped pharmaceutical research to be able to yield a large array of diverse molecular entities. Hence, combinatorial chemistry is a mass-production technology that synthesizes large numbers of compounds in parallel. Combinatorial chemistry has reduced experimental cycle times by more than eight hundred times and lowered costs by more than six hundred times compared to traditional methods (Booz Allen & Hamilton 1997). The subsequent availability of huge amounts of data which are generated by these new discovery technologies requires new ways to process and prepare the entailed information in order to be accessible for the overall innovation process. This need of novel information processing technologies translated into the emergence of a special discipline called bioinformatics.

Bioinformatics

Bioinformatics generally deals with the acceleration of lead discovery by providing structural data, information and knowledge. Given that a single pharmaceutical lab can generate more than 100 GB of data per day, sophisticated bioinformatics sys-

---

11 The yearly throughput of a typical lead discovery group increased from about 75,000 samples tested on about 20 targets to over a million samples tested on over 100 targets (Houston and Banks 1997). Today, UHTS allows for the simultaneous screening of more than 100,000 substances per day in a fully automated way. Some companies have achieved improvements in screening effectiveness well above a multiple of 25 by using HTS and UHTS technologies (see Reuters 2002).

tems are needed which primarily cover data management software, statistical analysis software and visualization technologies. The major tasks of bioinformatics in pharmaceutical R&D can be summarized as follows (see Gassmann et al. 2004):

- To provide and manage databases for the tremendous amount of information;
- To allow the generation of compound profiles and compound libraries for improved target identification and screening;
- To manage genome and protein sequences;
- To visualize 3D data;
- To collect data on model organisms;
- To manage the huge amount of data from the clinical tests and provide feedback to the early phases of drug discovery;
- To enable accessibility and sharing of knowledge within the corporation as well as to outside collaborators.

Genomics

Genomics is the most high profile of the many enabling technologies recently developed in pharmaceutical R&D. It describes the process of identifying genes involved in diseases through the comparison of the genomes of individuals with and without disease, and it has been heralded as having the potential to revolutionize both medicine and the entire pharmaceutical industry. The genomic revolution began in 1993 when Human Genome Sciences formed its partnership with SmithKline Beecham. However, it was not until the completion of the first draft of the human genome was announced in 2000 that the accompanying media and investor attention suggested that genomics had become an essential investment for achieving effective drug discovery in the future. No major pharmaceutical company is now without genomics capabilities, whether in-house or accessed through alliances. Genomic technologies will enable the identification of 3,000 to 10,000 new drug targets, compared with the current number of 500 (Pfeiffer 2000). The integration of genomics and other technologies will lead to a shift from broadly targeted drugs to more focused medicines with much higher therapeutic value for the target population allowing to mass-customize drugs. However, validation of the many targets generated by genomic methods is the major bottleneck today.

While genomic technologies allow for a better understanding of drug target function in genomic population subsets, or even individuals, it raises great commercial and financial concerns. Genomics-related sciences and technologies represent very capital-intensive investments. Lehman Bros. (1999) estimated that it requires a US$ 100 million annual investment to merely participate in the genomics arena. To compete more aggressively, a company might require up to US$ 300 million annually (Agarwal et al. 2001). With an average integrated pharmaceutical company spending around 25% of R&D on discovery, an aggressive investment in these new technologies would consume more than 75% of a middle-tier company such as Roche or Schering-Plough's discovery budget, and would still consume 30% of a top-tier company's budget such as GlaxoSmithKline or Pfizer (Reuters 2002). The time and resources that must be spent to develop genetic profiles and market sizes for tailored drugs are much smaller, resulting in the need for completely different portfolio management strategies. On the other hand, research by Reuters (2002) suggests that the application of disease genetics and pharmacogenetics together could, in the very best case, save as much as two-thirds on the current costs to develop a drug. Most genomics companies, however, do not usually provide full disclosure of their R&D pipelines. Hence, it is very difficult to assess the current impact of genomics on the pharmaceutical industry. In addition, some very high profile companies, including Incyte and Myriad, do not publish details of the success of their collaborations in terms of generating leads. Similarly, pharmaceutical companies with extensive in-house genomics expertise, such as Novartis and GlaxoSmithKline, do not publish details of their early stage research.[12]

Pharmacogenomics

The effect of an individual's genetic inheritance on the body's response to drugs is the object of analysis of pharmacogenomics. Pharmacogenomics integrates traditional pharmaceutical sciences such as biochemistry with annotated knowledge of genes, proteins, and single nucleotide polymorphisms, and thus combines the disciplines pharmacology and genomics. Hence, pharmacogenomics primarily deals with the production of tailor-made drugs for individuals. The drugs are then expected to be adapted to each person's own genetic makeup. Environment, diet, age, lifestyle, and health all can influence a person's response to medicines, but understanding an individual's genetic makeup is thought to be the key to creating personalized drugs

12 According to Reuters (2002), over 2,500 new targets were discovered by genomics companies by 2001, assuming no duplication. With a minimum of 49 products in pre-clinical development and at least 13 already in clinical trials, the productivity of the genomics industry seems to be strong. However, at the time of writing, the returns on investment in genomic activities are still uncertain. In addition, tremendous uncertainty about the eventual 'best play' scenario in the genomics environment acts as a 'leveler' between the established integrated pharmaceutical companies and the emerging genomics-based firms.

with greater efficacy and safety. Currently, physicians prescribe medication through a trial-and-error method of matching patients with the right drugs. If the prescribed medication does not work for the patient the first time, the physician will try a different drug or dosage, repeating the process until the patient improves. As pharmacogenomics becomes more advanced, physicians eventually will be able to prescribe medication based on an individual patient's genotype, maximizing effectiveness while minimizing side effects.

Proteomics

The term proteome refers to all the proteins expressed by a genome, and proteomics deals with proteins produced by cells and organisms. The approximately 30,000 genes defined by the Human Genome Project translate into 300,000 to 1 million proteins when alternate splicing and post-translational modifications are considered. While a genome remains unchanged to a large extent, the proteins in any particular cell change dramatically as genes are turned on and off in response to its environment. Most drugs work on proteins or protein receptors. Hence, a primary challenge of proteomics is to identify differences between the pattern of a healthy and a sick person, compare them, and identify and isolate the guilty proteins. Consequently, proteomics covers efforts to obtain complete descriptions of the gene products in a cell or organism. Proteomics includes not only the identification and quantification of proteins, but also the determination of their localization, modifications, interactions, activities, and ultimately their function.

Molecular design

While most drug discovery technologies, such as high-throughput screening or combinatorial chemistry, rely upon screening through vast inventories of naturally occurring and man-made chemicals in search of previously undiscovered substances with the desired biological activity, molecular drug design, by contrast, tries to discover new drugs by looking at the structure of the underlying proteins. Instead of eliminating the irrelevant substances in order to find the relevant ones, molecular drug design is analytically deriving the design of the target molecules. This approach seems to be far more effective and efficient than screening methods because it is based on an analytical process rather than serendipity. The basic rationale of how almost all drugs work is well known and can be systematically used for this approach: Nearly every drug works through an interaction with the target molecule or protein which causes the respective disease. The drug molecule inserts itself into a functionally important crevice of the target protein, like a key in a lock. The drug molecule is then connected to the target and either induces or, more commonly, inhibits the protein's normal function. By applying these insights, the molecular drug design methodology then consists of iterative cycles of design, simulation, synthesis, structural assessment, and redesign.

In-silico drug design

By using in-silico technologies, scientists can simulate experiments entirely in their computers which would take months or years to do in the laboratory or clinic. In-silico R&D provides a platform for testing experiments and hypotheses, predicting the results through computer simulation, and creating knowledge out of fragmented discovery and clinical data. In-silico R&D thus can increase productivity at every stage of drug discovery and development. In addition to reducing the costs associated with failure, in-silico technologies have the potential to shorten the development process by years, which allows getting new drugs to patients faster. In-silico R&D complements traditional lab-based research across the following functionalities: target identification, target validation, target prioritization, lead generation, lead optimization, and clinical development.

In summary, all of the new sciences and technologies mentioned above facilitate a faster and more effective transfer of scientific knowledge into new drug design. Trial-and-error based knowledge creation is complemented by more rational algorithms and results contributing to a more detailed understanding of the drug target function for onset, progression and chronicity of the disease. While these technologies definitely account for major improvements in pharmaceutical research, they remain relatively novel and their transition into launched products is yet to be seen. Subsequently, the implied risks of all new sciences and technologies for drug discovery and development are tremendous because of the huge investments and the lack of evidence that these investments lead to real improvements in R&D productivity. This is particularly true if the necessary technology platforms and know-how do not exist within the firm yet, and acquiring them might be too costly compared to the company's R&D budget. In addition, pharmaceutical companies do not even have the option to abandon the idea of being involved in the latest drug discovery technologies simply because they cannot afford to leave the upside potential of these developments to other companies and run the additional risk of losing substantial ground to competition over the long run.

2.1.4 Risk of high attrition

The pharmaceutical industry is characterized by unique circumstances: in most industries, the decision to terminate an R&D project is made on the basis of economic/financial considerations; in the pharmaceutical industry, however, most R&D projects are dropped due to scientific reasons, such as a lack of efficacy or safety which might only become visible at late clinical stages. Indeed, attrition rates in pharmaceutical R&D (i.e. the percentage of NCEs that drop out during a phase of testing) are fairly high, particularly at late stages of the development process. Drug development attrition rates are highest in the pre-clinical phase (60.2%) and still very high in clinical phase II (52.1%), that is after several years of development have already been conducted (see Fig. 8). Once a new drug candidate has been submitted to the regulatory authorities for approval, the attrition rate decreases to around 10%.

Translating the attrition rates into success rates provides an overview about the probability of success for a compound in the R&D pipeline. While a compound in the pre-clinical phase only has a probability of success of around 10%, this rate increases significantly once the compound passes the clinical Phase II and reaches

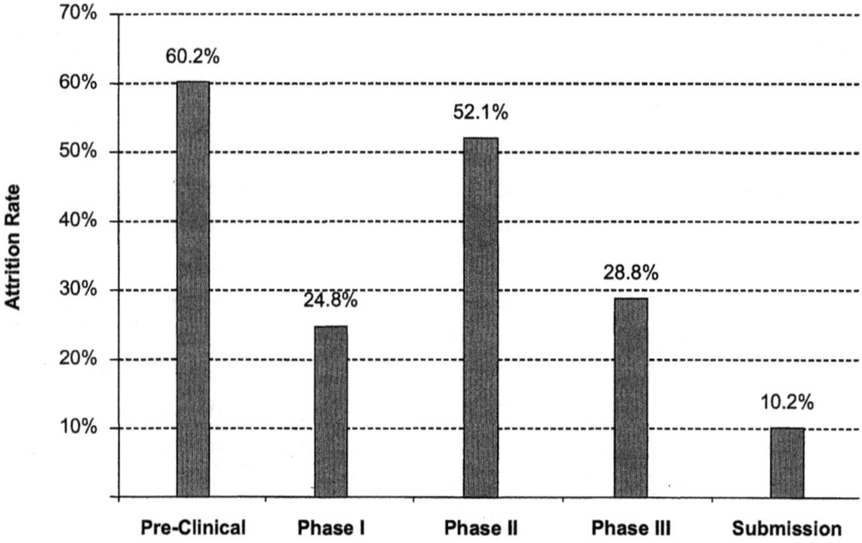

Source: Buchanan (2002) based on The Tufts Center for Drug Development data

Fig. 8. Attrition rates in pharmaceutical R&D by phase.

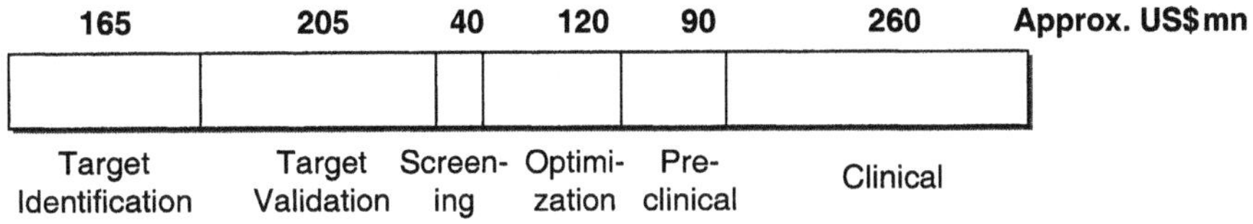

Costs include failures; target identification includes activities outsourced to academic research institutions.

Source: BCG (2001)

Fig. 9. Breakdown of drug R&D expenditures.

clinical Phase III (65.8%). Considering and comparing attrition rates and probabilities of success, the greatest potential for improvement in productivity seems to be in clinical phase II as well as just before the pre-clinical phase (i.e. lead identification and lead optimization). Particularly the high attrition rates in clinical phase II directly translate into significant R&D risks. The later a project is cancelled, the more resources have been allocated and the higher the respective financial loss. A drug candidate that reached the clinical phase II has already dissipated more than US$ 600-700 millions on average (see Fig. 9). If a drug's efficacy and safety for the desired indication cannot be assured during the late clinical stages, the compound's development usually has to be stopped, no matter if these huge research and development efforts have been made so far.

2.1.5 Risk of blockbuster reliance

Pharmaceutical companies traditionally preferred to market a few, high volume blockbuster drugs – a drug with at least US$ 1 billion in annual sales – in order to achieve their high growth rates. This becomes particularly visible by having a look at the revenue structure of most large pharmaceutical firms: according to a study by Duke University economists, only three out of ten drugs which reach the market generate revenues that meet or exceed average R&D costs, and the 20% of products with the highest returns generate 70% of total returns (see Reuters 2002).

In 2002, 58 ethical pharmaceutical products with aggregated sales of US$ 120 billion qualified as blockbuster drugs. Only two companies – GlaxoSmithKline and Pfizer – owned eight blockbuster products in 2002 (Reuters 2003a). The majority of companies owned only between one and three blockbusters (see Fig. 10). Reliance on a few blockbuster drugs has remained a largely unquestioned growth strategy of most leading pharmaceutical companies, given the strong first-mover advantages in

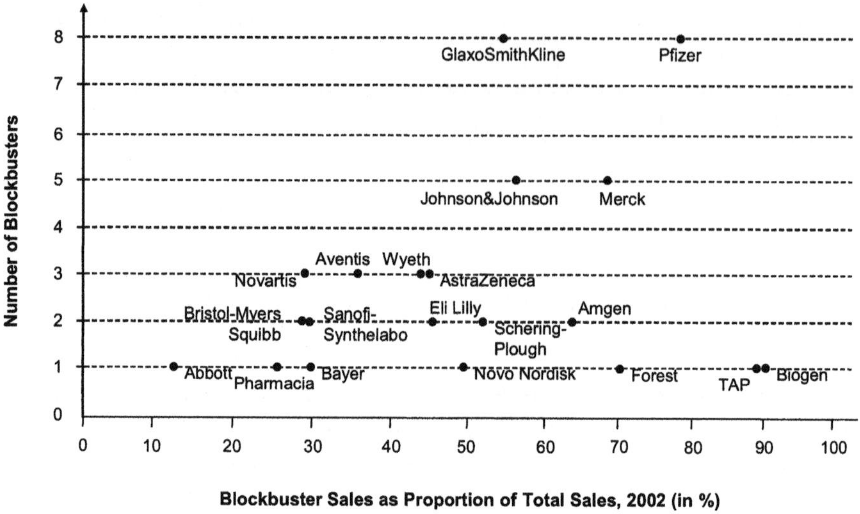

Source: Reuters (2003a)

Fig. 10. Contribution of blockbuster sales to ethical sales in 2002.

the pharmaceutical market. However, analysis conducted by Reuters (2003a) shows that blockbuster drugs worth about US$ 30 billion in revenues were due to lose US patent protection by the end of 2002. Furthermore, the blockbuster market in 2008 will be worth only 1.4 times that of the blockbuster market in 2000 and thus not be able to keep up with the 10%+ annual revenue growth expectations (Reuters 2003a). In addition, the traditional blockbuster markets are crowded with competing products launched at increasingly close intervals and targeting similar therapeutic areas. For instance, four new angiotensin products (Diovan, Teveten, Aprovel, and Atacand) were recently introduced in a period of months. This raises the question whether blockbusters can or should remain a focus of future growth. Most pharmaceutical companies have thus started to question the traditional blockbuster strategy and to balance their drug portfolios in order to compensate for declining blockbuster growth by other means.

The emergence of new drug discovery technologies, such as genomics, pharmacogenomics and proteomics, has heralded new opportunities for the pharmaceutical industry not only to generate products of higher and more selective efficacy but also to explore the opportunity of individualization and mass customization of pharmaceutical products targeting smaller patient populations with specific genotypes. Hence, it is questioned whether the mass application of a single drug to a large patient population will remain a viable strategy for the future. However, pharmacogenomics-derived products will not mean the end of the blockbuster paradigm; rather, they will help change the accepted definition of these high earning products to that of 'multi-busters', a series of personalized therapies that are able to dominate a certain targeted disease area.

Consequently, the new 'multi-buster' strategy requires targeting increasingly differentiated markets with specialized therapies. Pharmaceutical companies are expected to introduce much more products targeting these various and relatively small market segments. However, specialty markets bear higher risks as they might not allow the pharmaceutical company to recoup their R&D investments easily due to their limited market size. Novartis was one of the first companies that has recently applied this new strategy in a proactive way and came up with a successful product called Gleevec.

Novartis' Gleevec: Successful approach to target micro-segmented markets

Novartis' Gleevec is a successful example of a drug with markets that have the potential to become micro-segmented under a genomics-driven business model (see Reuters 2003a). Unlike mass-market megadrugs, Gleevec targets a chromosomal abnormality that occurs in only a small segment of the population (i.e. chronic myelogenous leukaemia, CML). The market for drugs launched for this indication was not considered sufficient in size to allow companies to recoup their R&D investment. However, Gleevec has generated lucrative revenues since its launch in 2001, and achieved blockbuster status by 2003. Its success partly reflects Novartis' aggressive, pre-launch PR strategy to drive rapid sales growth in an emerging market. With a market share of almost 100% in this specialty market, Gleevec has turned out to be the third most successful pharmaceutical launch in 2001.

If pharmaceutical companies continue to focus their attention on only a few high-volume but low-margin products, such as under the traditional blockbuster paradigm, they run not only the risk of facing intense competition but also the risk that competitors enter the small-volume but high-margin niche-markets and build up diversified and highly profitable portfolios. This exposes pharmaceutical companies to the increasing risk of missing out on new opportunities offered by novel market strategies. The risk of relying on a few blockbusters has recently been illustrated by the cases of Merck and Pfizer, where two blockbusters experienced severe safety issues by causing some major side-effects (Merck's Vioxx and Pfizer's Celebrex). Not only sales have dropped significantly but also the companies stock prices have plummeted accordingly.

2.1.6 Risk of market timing

The growth rate and market share gained in the first year after launch largely determine overall sales that can subsequently be achieved (Reuters 2003a).[13] Numerous products including Pfizer's blockbuster Lipitor illustrate this pattern. All of these products experienced above average sales growth in their first year on the market and have since continued to display strong sales performances. Although there are cases where first year market performance was good but sales did not meet long-term expectations, this is usually due to a major external event, for example the discovery of major negative side-effects.

The market dynamics during the product launch are characterized by three closely-linked determinants. To improve the probability of a new drug turning out to be a success, the product should be (see Reuters 2003a):

- Early to enter a particular therapy area or product class;
- Positioned relative to existing competition;
- Accompanied by heightened pre-launch awareness.

Notably, pre-launch promotion has become more important in recent years. A new product's rate of acceptance can be significantly boosted if the market is well prepared for it. The key focus of such investments is raising awareness among physicians and, eventually, patients. This is particularly important in new areas when a product is first to market or if there is little awareness of the disease, its symptoms and treatment options.

While the first-mover advantage along with a high awareness among key customers is crucial for a drug's successful market introduction, the right market timing is difficult to manage. The R&D process in the pharmaceutical industry lasts on average up to 13 years from the initial idea and/or the identification of a disease's symptoms

---

13 According to Gassmann et al. (2004), time-to-market is extremely important in breakthrough pharmaceuticals. The first in the market captures between 40-60% of the market, and the second only around 15%. Coming in behind third means already a negative business. Moreover, delaying market introduction of a blockbuster drug by two months not only involves the risk that a competitor seizes significant market share, it also means a net loss of US$ 100 million, or almost US$ 2 million a day.

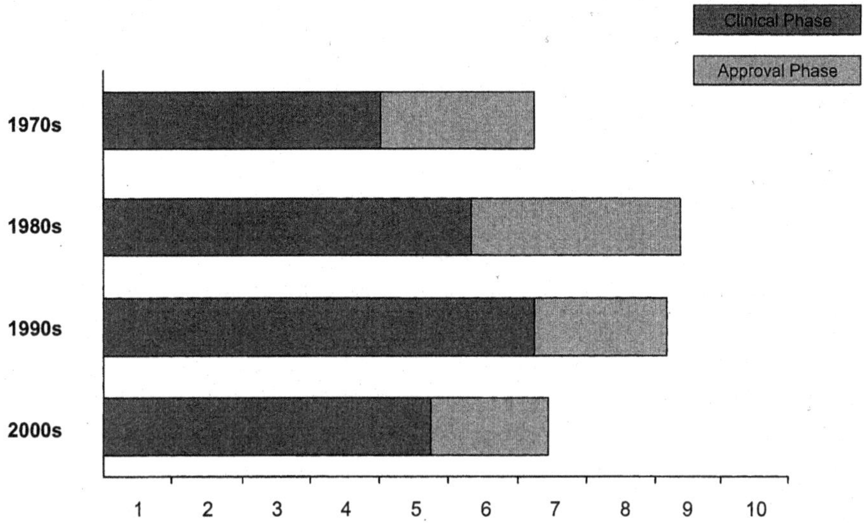

Source: PhRMA (2004)

Fig. 11. Time spent by a drug candidate in the clinical and approval phases.

to the drug's market introduction. Particularly the last phases of the process (i.e. the clinical development and approval stages) are usually characterized by a long protraction. Whereas the times necessary for research and pre-clinical phases have remained fairly constant at around 3 years each over the past decades, the average duration of the clinical development time has increased significantly since the 1970s, although it seems to have improved recently (Fig. 11). Compared to the 1980s and 1990s, modest time gains seem to have been made during the drug approval stage (i.e. after most R&D has actually been completed) and where the cooperation, speed and involvement of regulatory authorities is paramount. The average time a drug candidate spends in clinical trials could have been reduced from almost 7 years in the 1990s to a little more than 5 years in the early 2000s.

Due to the long development and approval times, pharmaceutical R&D faces the risk that a competitor might introduce a drug targeting the same market just a few months prior to the pharmaceutical company. Because of the strong first-mover advantage, the competitor will most likely capture most of the market share and profits, and will expose the pharmaceutical company to the risk of having developed a drug which will not be able to keep up with its sales and profit expectations although the drug itself has no shortcomings.

2.1.7 Risk of product differentiation

In total, there were more than 1,000 different drugs in development in the pharmaceutical industry in 2000 (PhRMA 2001). The breakdown was as follows: more than 100 for AIDS, 350 for cancer, 120 for heart diseases and strokes, 26 for Alzheimer's disease, 25 for diabetes, and more than 200 for special needs of children. However, at the beginning of 2003, all drugs on the market hit a total 120 different targets. The top 100 drugs hit only 43 targets (Zambrowicz and Sands 2003). Due to the significant increase in the number of new products that are about to enter the market, a product's differentiation from competing products becomes crucial.

The general belief that the more new chemical entities pass through the R&D pipeline and eventually enter the market the better, does not seem to be a viable strategy for the future any more. In addition, the expected mass customization and product specialization via the focus on niche-markets will amplify the trend of an increase in the number of products on the market. Successful strategies not only require a focus on the number of new chemical entities, but also a distinctive approach to target potentially attractive niche-markets and an adjustment in the way in which medicines are profiled and marketed (see Gassmann et al. 2004). Consequently, a drug's clinical profile is becoming more and more important not only to differentiate the product on the market but also to justify an FDA approval.

In general, a product's clinical profile consists of four major criteria (see Reuters 2003a): (i) efficacy, (ii) safety/side effects, (iii) dosage/administration, and (iv) costs. In other words, if a product is efficacious, has negligible side effects and can be administered with a convenient dosing mechanism, it is in a good position to compete in most markets. The product's compliance and administration become crucial if a competitor might introduce a similar drug which could be administered in a more convenient way for the patient (e.g., a 1-time per day dosage vs. a 3-times per day dosage, or an oral treatment via tablets instead of injections). The drug can only remain successful on the market if it has a unique position which provides a competitive advantage over the competing drug. The degree to which a product can be differentiated varies by therapeutic market and competitive environment. Many companies seek to differentiate a product from its major competitors through head-to-head studies. Once valuable trial data has been generated during the development phases, it is important to convey the information to key audiences, particularly opinion leaders and high prescribing physicians, in such a way that a product's benefits relative to its competitors are clear (Gassmann et al. 2004).

In general, the differentiation of a new drug is only possible by proving the drugs' superior profile in more comprehensive clinical studies. As a result, the resources invested in clinical trials are growing constantly. Whereas the purpose and the number of patients during the clinical trials varies depending on the disease area, the average number of patients needed for new drug applications has risen considerably from about 1,300 in the 1980s to about 4,000 in the early 2000s (Connolly 2001). Novartis, for instance, included 14,000 patients in the clinical studies of one of their most recent new drugs, which was introduced in the market in mid-2003 (Gassmann et al. 2004). In addition, marketing departments are working closer with their R&D counterparts to ensure that clinical trials are designed to meet specific market needs. Today, it is even common for pharmaceutical companies to conduct clinical phase IV trials after a product has been launched. Such trials typically focus on further indications and subpopulations or seek to differentiate the product from competition.

The drug's differentiation on the market also becomes critical at the time when the drug's patent protection is about to expire. Patent protection in most countries usually covers a time span of 20 years. Due to the long average development time and the desire to patent substances before the corresponding product has been launched on the market, the effecitve patent protected time in the pharmaceutical industry to market a drug is only about 8 years (BPI 1999). After a substance's patent has expired, the drug is usually exposed to competition by generic drugs. Generic drugs rely on lead substances of already marketed brand-name products where the patent protection has expired. As the generic companies can simply emulate these drugs and do not have to invest in the drug's research and development any more, generic drugs are serious substitutes for original brand-name products which can be offered at usually much lower prices. Generic drugs mount an increasing threat to profitability of large pharmaceutical companies as in extreme cases 50% or more of the value sales of a product may be eroded by generic competition within the first few months after patent expiry (Reuters 2003b). Generics have increased their share of unit volume to 47% in 2000, up from 33% in 1990 (PhRMA 2001).[14]

---

14 However, while generics capture about 50% of *unit* sales with continuous growth, they are far less profitable. Pfizer's 2001 prescription drug revenues of US$ 26.3 billion was almost five times the combined sales of the 11 leading generic drug makers covered in S&P's Industry Survey (Saftlas 2001).

The substantial increase in sample sizes and patient profiles in the clinical phases has not only led to much more comprehensive and protracted trials, but also exposes pharmaceutical companies to an increasing risk of successfully differentiating their products on the market. The most eminent risk includes that a competitor might introduce a product on the market which is characterized by a superior clinical profile. This not only makes it harder for the pharmaceutical company to justify market approval for its own drug, but also reduces the own drug's estimated sales projection. If a drug's compliance and administration turns out to be disadvantageous compared to competition, the drug's positioning in the market worsens significantly and might not even allow the pharmaceutical company to recoup the investments made in the drug's research and development.

2.1.8 Risk of regulative force

Public laws and regulations play perhaps a greater role in the pharmaceutical industry than in any other industry. The regulative force impacts pharmaceutical innovation on several levels: (i) R&D regulations and product registrations, (ii) price regulations and national healthcare systems, and (iii) intellectual property rights.

R&D regulations in experiments are mainly affected by national product registration agencies, such as the Food and Drug Administration (FDA) in the USA or Swissmedic in Switzerland. These governmental agencies stipulate authorization and registration procedures for all new drugs submitted for approval in their respective markets. Animal trials and inventions in gene technology are covered by strict authorization processes as well. New drugs must prove that they are suitable for use in human beings and the respective benefit-risk profile has to be determined prior to marketing approval. Only after a medicinal product has cleared all hurdles – and therefore fulfills regulations regarding quality, efficacy, and safety – is it granted authorization. An accelerated approval may be granted to priority drugs that show promise in the treatment of serious and life-threatening diseases for which there is no adequate therapy. For example, when the first tests of the antiviral drug AZT in 1985 showed encouraging results in 330 AIDS patients, the FDA authorized a treatment referred to as 'Investigational New Drug' for more than 4,000 people with AIDS before AZT was approved for marketing (Gassmann et al. 2004).

In most countries prices are regulated by federal authorities (directly or indirectly). In some countries the price of a product is fixed according to the social costs of the society. Yet in other countries, the price of a drug is defined by its innovativeness as measured by the number of patents in that area (e.g., Brazil). However, national healthcare systems always have the primary and most direct impact on product prices, also because they mostly decide about a drug's recommendation for reimbursement by health insurances. If a drug is not recommended by the health authorities to be reimbursed, the market potential of the drug usually declines significantly.

The overall purpose of patent law is to support research and ensure that all interests are satisfied. On the one hand, innovations should be made available in the interest of the public. On the other hand, innovators should have an incentive to innovate by being assured that their inventions are protected against unlawful imitation and replication of their knowledge. From a competitive perspective, patents are essential because it is not difficult to ascertain the respective substances of a drug and, consequently copy or imitate pharmaceutical products. Studies have shown that 65% of pharmaceutical inventions would not have been introduced without patent protection, compared to a cross-industry average of 8% (Reuters 2002). Patent protection is unclear in some key areas of pharmaceutical R&D, for instance, at the time of writing it is still unclear to what extent genes can be patented (and thus 'owned'). Sometimes, international patent law is only accepted if national interests are maintained. Brazil, for example, has threatened several times over the last ten years to suspend domestic compliance with international patent rights for malaria drugs unless certain license fees were dropped. As health authorities might prevent a drug's prospective market success, the regulative force exposes pharmaceutical companies to certain risks across several layers (i.e. approvals, patenting, and pricing among others). Moreover, the regulative force represents a fairly uncontrollable element in the entire innovation process.

Conclusion: All of the risks in pharmaceutical R&D as introduced in the previous paragraphs represent a major threat to the successful execution of any R&D project. As shown, these risks most likely increase in the foreseeable future. Simultaneously to the increase in R&D risks, pharmaceutical companies are exposed to the increasing importance of R&D collaborations which is discussed in the following chapter.

2.2 Increase in R&D Collaborations

For many decades, pharmaceutical R&D has been a fully integrated process where the pharmaceutical company owned and conducted almost every single step of the R&D value chain. Over the recent past, however, most pharmaceutical companies have started to concentrate on their core competencies centering around technology

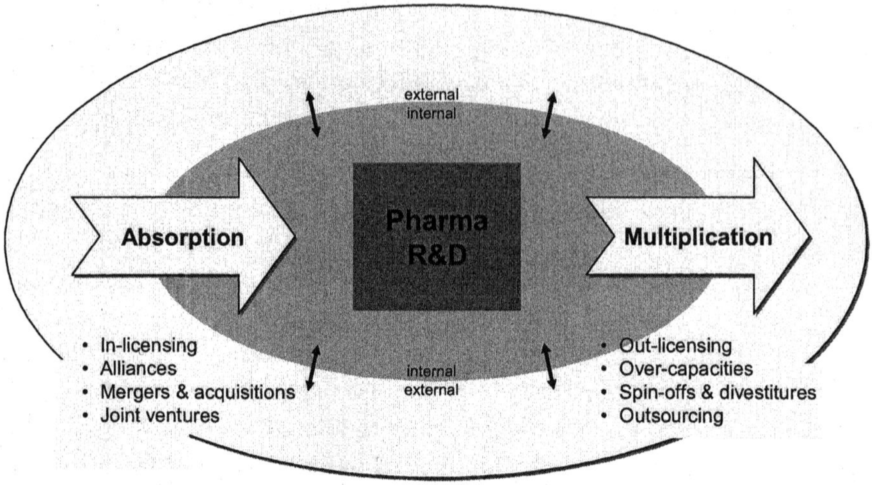

Fig. 12. Restructuring of pharmaceutical R&D departments and resulting interaction with external partners.

platforms and therapy areas. They started to streamline their R&D activities deciding which tasks had to remain inside the own boundaries, and which tasks had to be absorbed from outside entities or could be multiplied by disposing them to external partners (Fig. 12). Balancing the right size and structure of the R&D department has turned out to be one of the primary issues in pharmaceutical R&D management.

Today, all functions within the R&D department are constantly analyzed regarding their potential contribution to shareholder value creation. This also raises the question about the definition of the corporate boundaries (Gambardella 1995). Due to the increasing amount and number of interaction with outside innovation, every pharmaceutical company's R&D department today is more and more relying on some kind of interaction with external partners and organizations. Due to the rising prominence of R&D collaborations in the pharmaceutical industry, the next chapters discuss the following issues regarding R&D collaborations:

- Relevance of R&D collaborations;
- Evolution of R&D collaborations;
- Classification of R&D collaborations;
- Reasons for R&D collaborations.

2.2.1 Relevance of R&D collaborations

The trend towards the externalization of (part of) a firm's R&D activities has been discussed in recent years by several authors.[15] According to Chiesa et al. (2004), several companies have been created that provide innovators with technical and scientific services such as R&D contracts, laboratory testing services, technology consulting, industrial design, or even engineering. According to research by the OECD (2002), firms in high-technology R&D-intensive sectors, such as the pharmaceutical industry, have a high propensity to cooperate on innovation projects. The cascade of knowledge flowing from new sciences and technologies is simply far too complex for any company to handle alone. Fundamental breakthroughs are increasingly likely to occur not within a single firm's own R&D department but somewhere in an external organization's research lab. For example, Merck & Co. realized already in its 2000 annual report that their own biomedical research only contributes about 1% of worldwide biomedical research. In order to tap into the remaining 99%, the company intends to actively reach out to universities, research institutions and companies on a global scale to bring the best of technology and potential products into Merck. The firm's scientists are now challenged with the task to create a virtual lab in their research area. This means that they do not just create excellent science in their own lab, but identify and build connections to excellent science in other labs, wherever these labs may be (Chesbrough 2003). As serendipity is still considered a key success factor particularly in the early discovery phases, a network with outside innovation is highly important in pharmaceutical R&D because the likelihood that a company generates all necessary substances in-house is relatively low. Interactions with partners not only reduce the risks implied in investing in the firm's own research infrastructure, but also the risks of a lack of access to the desired substances.

Particularly the technology areas that are not yet covered by the pharmaceutical companies are subject to an analysis of how they can best be accessed outside the corporate boundaries. As illustrated in Fig. 13, more than 600 alliances between pharmaceutical and biotechnology firms worldwide have been formed annually for the last couple of years (see Recombinant Capital 2005).[16] Several large pharmaceu-

---

15 Chiesa et al. (2004) provide a good overview.

16 Of 691 new chemical entities approved by the FDA from 1963 to 1999, 38% evolved out of alliances. In accordance, the average number of biotech alliances per pharmaceutical firm grew from 1.4 per year in the period 1988 through 1990 to 5.7 in 1997 through 1998. In addition, the probability of a drug passing through human testing which has been developed jointly increases by up to 30 percentage points over drugs developed by a single firm alone (see Nicholson, Danzon and McCullough 2003).

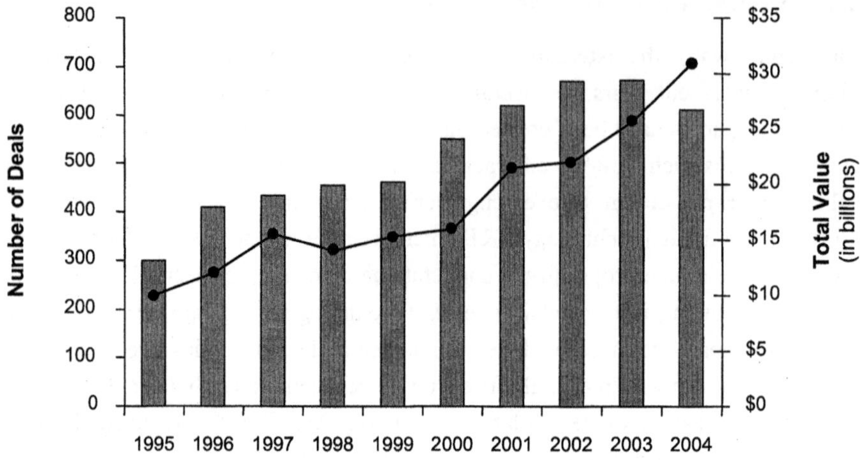

Source: Recombinant Capital (2005)

Fig. 13. Development of alliances in the pharmaceutical industry.

tical companies spend significant amounts of their R&D budgets on collaboration agreements. Aventis spends a total of 15% of its R&D budget on collaborations. One third (i.e. 5% of the total R&D budget) goes into technology partnerships in early research, discovery and screening, and two thirds (i.e. 10% of the total R&D budget) goes into development collaborations across all clinical stages, particularly Phase II.[17] Novartis has reserved about 20-25% of its research budget for extramural research and this percentage is on the rise (Herrling 1998).

2.2.2 Evolution of R&D collaborations

The first R&D collaborations in the pharmaceutical industry emerged in accordance with the rise in biotechnology companies starting in the late 1970s and early 1980s (Robbins-Roth 2001).[18] While innovation activities of established pharmaceutical

---

17 Interview with Aventis.

18 The application of biotechnology in the pharmaceutical industry initially began with the development of scientific techniques, such as genetic engineering and antibody production. The technique of genetic engineering was developed in 1973, and received its first commercial pharmaceutical application four years later when Eli Lilly started the development of recombinant human insulin in cooperation with the biotech firm Genentech. The resulting product, Humulin, became the first biotechnology product when launched in 1983 (Reuters 2002).

companies were traditionally based on organic chemistry, biochemistry and chemical engineering, biotechnology companies have built a reputation in many novel areas, such as cell biology, molecular genetics, protein chemistry and encymology (Whittaker and Bower 1994). Most biotech companies were deploying the latest approaches to drug discovery simply because they were forced to use these techniques in order to survive on the market. In turn, pharmaceutical companies were impelled to access the biotech firms' research results because of their innovativeness. As established pharmaceutical companies used to own manufacturing and distribution systems that were hard to replicate and large marketing budgets to protect their brands, they preferred to collaborate with biotech firms as a means of 'technology sourcing' strategy (see also Gambardella 1995). For many years, the traditional biotech-pharma collaboration centered around early-stage research issues, such as target identification. Over the past years, it has not been unusual for a large pharmaceutical company to have biotechnology holdings that give them a substantial piece of the action. For example, Novartis still owns about 40% of Chiron, and Roche owns about 60% of Genentech.

Reflecting the rising prominence of biotechnology companies, the industry still seems to be in its infancy.[19] Only one out of 47 biotech firms possesses a successful product (Jakob 2003). Just 24 of the 3,000 biotechnology companies worldwide were profitable in 2000 (WGZ Bank 2002). The most successful European public biotechnology firms are located in the UK. In aggregation, they had 154 products in the product pipeline that were tested at the time of writing and were expected to enter the market in the near future. Denmark and France come in second and third place with 33 and 27 products in the product pipeline respectively. Switzerland is ranked number 4 with 24 products, and German public biotechnology firms rank seventh with 11 products in the product pipeline (Ernst&Young 2002).[20] Today's collaborations between biotech and pharmaceutical companies oftentimes do not in-

19 At the end of 2000, only four biotech drugs were considered blockbuster products and generated in excess of US$ 1 billion in sales: Procrit by Johnson&Johnson (US$ 2.7 billion), Epogen by Amgen (US$ 1.9 billion), Neupogen by Amgen (US$ 1.2 billion), and Humulin by Genentech and Eli Lilly (US$ 1.1 billion).

20 By the end of 2000, a total of 76 biotechnology drugs had been approved for marketing, and 369 biotechnology drugs were in human clinical testing for more than 200 disease targets, accounting for around a third of all medicines in clinical development (Reuters 2002). A total of about 1,500 compounds were in the overall development stage around the year 2000 (Zanetti and Steiner 2001). Following their launch, these early biotechnology products accounted for an average of 13.4% of all pharmaceutical products launched between 1991 and 1995, rising to 18.2% of all products launched between 1996 and 2000 (Reuters 2002).

clude equity ownership by the pharmaceutical company any more and the deals cover sophisticated licensing agreements. Only in case a biotechnology firm seems to be a promising partner, it will most likely be acquired by the pharmaceutical firm.

Today's pharmaceutical companies operate in huge networks comprised not only of biotechnology companies, but many different organizations. This can include contract service organizations, specialized bio-pharmaceutical companies or other pharmaceutical companies. A market survey by Arthur D. Little and Solvias (2002) illustrates a radical scenario about the possible future structure of established pharmaceutical companies' R&D activities. The study reveals that the potential of collaborations for pharmaceutical companies is considered to go far beyond the traditionally known alliance structures. Only lead finding, lead optimization and marketing are seen as core activities of pharmaceutical companies that have to be provided 100% in-house (Fig. 14). All other activities can potentially be done by external

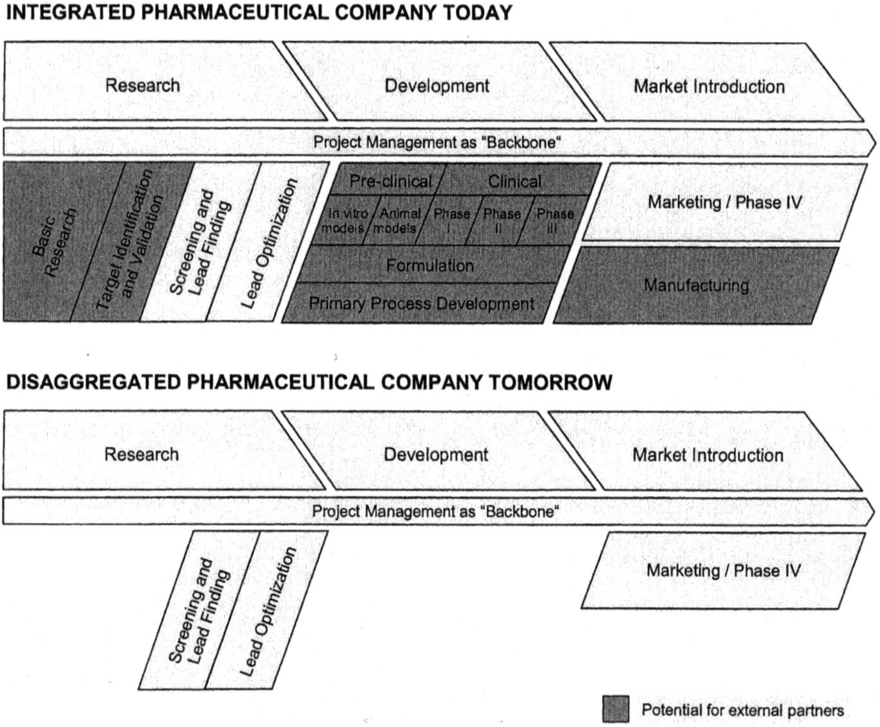

Source: Arthur D. Little and Solvias (2002)

Fig. 14. Potential of outside innovation in the pharmaceutical value chain.

parties via different types of collaboration. However, project management as a backbone process ensuring efficient know-how transfer between the different steps in pharmaceutical innovation has to remain in-house as well.

Over the recent past, a shift in collaboration behavior could have been observed in pharmaceutical R&D.[21] Until the beginning of the 2000s, most of the money spent on R&D collaborations used to be invested into early stage deals with biotech firms. Today, cooperations primarily focus on later stage deals, particularly on activities in the clinical phases. The objects of the collaborations center around substances which have already proven their efficacy in the human being and fulfill strict safety profiles. Biotech companies can no longer rely on purely communicating the intention to discover a genuinely novel compound. They must have come up with a complete substance in order to attract the pharmaceutical companies' attention. Most pharmaceutical companies are no longer willing to provide the high-risk capital to help the biotech company do basic discovery and lead identification research. As the collaboration's nature centers around more mature drug candidates, the negotiation power of the biotech firms has improved over the recent past. While it has been usual for biotech firms to receive between 5-10% of the revenues incurred in mutual projects, this number has grown in some cases to around 50% (Zanetti and Steiner 2001). Some biotech companies have been successfully negotiating for co-promotion and manufacturing rights for current and future products with big pharmaceutical companies. For example, Exelixis (in collaboration with GlaxoSmithKline) retained North-American co-promotion rights for multiple compounds under mutual development, Genta (in collaboration with Aventis) retained US co-promotion and manufacturing rights for the compound Genasense, and Neurocrine (in collaboration with Pfizer) retained US co-promotion rights for its compound Indipplon as well as co-promotion rights to the product Zoloft (Datamonitor 2003).

The increasingly rapid pace of innovation in the pharmaceutical industry calls for more flexible and looser forms of innovation agreements. In accordance, today's pharmaceutical R&D collaborations not only cover the typically technology-intensive research collaborations, but increasingly include various contractual partnership agreements, such as co-development or co-promotion agreements. Particularly the majority of the novel niche-markets can oftentimes only be entered successfully in partnership with other specialized companies. Therefore, many companies have started to engage in collaboration agreements with various partners to gain

21 Interview with Aventis.

access to the different niche-markets and to utilize an external partner's special sales force capabilities as illustrated by the case of Prometheus.

Prometheus: How a small company's sales force can be attractive to big pharma companies

Prometheus is a small specialty pharmaceutical company based in San Diego, CA. Prometheus has built a unique commercialization platform from which it launches its specialty pharmaceuticals based on providing a continuum of care in gastroenterology. Prometheus offers other technologically sophisticated diagnostic services, all geared to help gastroenterologists deliver optimal therapies for inflammatory disease (which includes Crohn's disease and ulcerative colitis). According to Windhover (2000), Prometheus' then Chairman Michael Walsh says "ultimately, this technology is part of a strategy for differentiating the sales and commercialization process. We have a field sales force of 50, calling on the 4,500 high-prescribing, high patient volume physicians. Our people end up with 20-30 minutes in the clinician's office, instead of the 2 minutes that reps in other specialties spend near the sample cabinet." Prometheus' sales representatives lead a consultative sale that doctors welcome, because they help physicians provide a continuum of care from early detection and diagnosis to drug therapy. This commercialization strategy is rarely applied by big pharmaceutical companies which solely rely on mass-marketing of high volume drugs. As a result, Prometheus positioned itself as an attractive sales partner in this specialty niche.

In addition, getting to market as soon as possible has emerged as one of the primary objectives of pharmaceutical companies. Thus, many companies decide to chose alliances not only to access new markets but also to accelerate the market diffusion of their new products. Particularly for selling new medicines on a global scale, it seems to be a promising approach to team up with a partner who has already broad expertise, deep knowledge or special access to the targeted market, and who is most likely capable to improve the product launch on the desired market. For example, many US and European companies typically introduce their new drugs on the Japanese market only in collaboration with a local pharmaceutical company. The pharmaceutical companies usually expect that the aspired higher sales generated by the collaboration will over-compensate for the loss in revenues that go to the alliance partner.

In summary, the traditionally integrated structure of pharmaceutical R&D departments is expected to further decrease, and the interaction with external partners is increasing drastically. While the internal complexity of pharmaceutical R&D can thus be reduced, the complexity of managing relationships to external partners is escalating accordingly. The increasing reliance on outside innovation requires the pharmaceutical company to think and act in a more process-oriented way. Barriers between intra-organizational units as well as to external partners are expected to diminish. Only the pharmaceutical companies that are able to manage their R&D collaborations optimally will most likely be capable to benefit from the novel developments and opportunities in the pharmaceutical industry.

Due to the quantity of different types of interaction between the pharmaceutical company and external partners, the following chapter provides a classification of R&D collaborations in the pharmaceutical industry.

2.2.3 Classification of R&D collaborations

There are many different types of potential collaboration partners in the pharmaceutical industry. Due to the still highly integrated structure and value chain in the pharmaceutical industry, the closeness of the relationship between the pharmaceutical company and the external partner can serve as a criterion for the classification of the partners' interaction with the pharmaceutical company (Fig. 15). The nature of the interaction can embrace different attributes, features and forms depending on the commitment of resources of the two parties.

The lowest degree of closeness between the pharmaceutical company and the external partner can be observed in the case of outsourcing. Many pharmaceutical companies already work together with multiple outsourcing partners during the entire

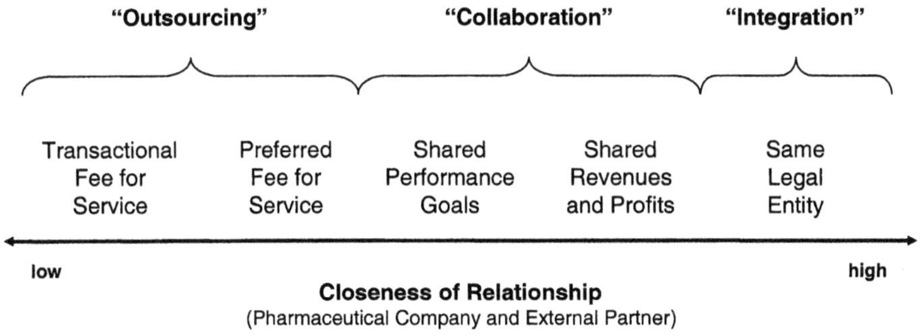

Fig. 15. Classification of partnerships in pharmaceutical R&D activities.

innovation process. These partners include a wide variety of contract service organizations (CSOs), such as contract research organizations (CROs), contract development organizations (CDOs), contract manufacturing organizations (CMOs), site management organizations (SMOs), or any other organization that provides pharmaceutical companies with a contract service. In the case of outsourcing, the external partner only provides the pharmaceutical company with a certain service. The pharmaceutical company then reimburses the service provider with a fee in return for the services received. Outsourcing thus only helps to conduct pre-defined tasks, and the interaction between the pharmaceutical company and the service provider usually centers only around clearly defined interfaces. The CRO Covidence, for example, describes outsourcing as follows: "the brain remains inside the pharmaceutical firm, only the hands are duplicated."[22]

Most of the outsourced effort is expended on non-clinical drug development, clinical trials, and manufacturing aspects of the drug development process.[23] Two different levels of outsourcing agreements can be distinguished: transactional and preferred outsourcing. If the outsourcing agreement is purely transaction-based, the price of the delivered service is the most important attribute of the collaboration, and cooperation agreements are achieved via several tenders and tactical negotiations. If the outsourcing partner has turned out to be a preferred service provider, the collaboration centers around several pre-defined, assured standards in the service package. The relationship between the pharmaceutical company and the contract service provider is characterized by conditions and qualifications which have been defined based on previous and mutually well acknowledged experiences. However, it has shown that the nature of outsourcing has changed in the past. While the outsourcing partner typically used to conduct relatively straight-forward activities such

22 While pharmaceutical companies spent US$ 9.3 billion on R&D conducted by external service providers in 2001, outsourcing is predicted to reach US$ 36 billion by 2010. This represents an annual growth rate of 16.3% compared to an average expected growth in global R&D expenditures of 9.6% during the same time period (Reuters 2003c). In addition, spending on outsourcing accounts for a significant part of the R&D budgets of most pharmaceutical companies in relative terms. In 1999, pharmaceutical companies spent about 25% of their R&D budgets for services provided by CROs. This number is expected to increase to about 40% (see Lehman Bros. 1999). In addition, research by Lehman Bros. (1999) has shown that contract research organizations are able to conduct clinical trials up to 30% faster than the average large pharmaceutical company. Today, the CRO industry consists of over 1,000 companies primarily based in the US, Europe and Asia. There are many rather small CROs which usually are regionally embedded into local market structures (see Gassmann et al. 2004).

23 Regarding the tasks that are shared in an outsourcing agreement, Azoulay (2003) analyzed project-level data for 53 firms and figured out that knowledge-intensive projects are more likely to be assigned to internal teams, while data-intensive projects are more likely to be outsourced.

as development services or the management of technology platforms, novel outsourcing agreements cover more complex tasks. The outsourcing partner's intention is thereby to extract a higher proportion of the value creation by offering improved services to the pharmaceutical company. Although outsourcing is sometimes controversially discussed in the pharmaceutical industry due to the high complexity in drug discovery, outsourcing some R&D activities to pharmaceutical service providers might lead to time and cost savings, would allow the access of new technologies and know-how and could help manage peak resource shortages.

Solvias: Spin-off as Outsourcing Partner

Solvias was created through the spin-off of a scientific competence center of Novartis in October 1999 and is a totally independent company owned by the Solvias management team. The company has around 250 highly qualified employees and offers its contracts services to many companies in the pharmaceutical, agricultural, chemical and food industries as well as to government authorities and institutes.

The company's client list is not only limited to Novartis, but covers many different firms, such as Beiersdorf, Boehringer Ingelheim, Roche, Shell or Wella among others. Solvias offers services to the pharmaceutical industry mainly in the areas of research and development, production and quality control. The company's services include a variety of chemical, physical and biological services – from synthesis to analytics.

If the relationship between the pharmaceutical company and the external partner does not only center around paying a fee in return for a service, but covers jointly conducted activities, the type of relationship is no longer referred to as outsourcing but collaboration. The level of collaboration is generally differentiated according to the collaboration's objective. On the one hand, the collaboration can revolve around shared performance goals, such as in most pharma-biotech alliances where the number of identified targets or the respective capital investment determine the base of the collaboration. On the other hand, the collaboration can be even closer if the two companies actually share the revenues and profits occurred in the joint project. In this case, the partners usually share markets and transfer rights via highly complex collaboration agreements.

The strength of the R&D collaboration model can only be exceeded by an integration of the external partner into the company's own operations. In this case, the external partner has completely been dissolved inside the pharmaceutical company, and therefore, this type of interaction cannot be called a 'joint initiative' any more. Consequently, the highest degree of collaboration in joint initiatives with external partners is represented by the collaboration model, which represents the focus of this research.

As collaborations between pharmaceutical companies and external partners are experiencing rising prominence, the following chapter provides an overview about the reasons why pharmaceutical companies engage in R&D collaborations.

2.2.4 Reasons for R&D collaborations

Firms establish alliances for many reasons (see Stuart 2000).[24] According to Greis et al. (1995), the decision to engage in collaborations is usually based on the trade-off between inter-firm cooperation and vertical integration. This trade-off is seen as a comparison of transaction costs against development costs. When the organizational efficiency gains due to shared assets are greater than the production efficiency losses, a firm will choose to cooperate. The general explanation for the overall growth pattern of newly created R&D partnerships is mostly related to the motives that 'force' companies to collaborate on R&D. Major factors mentioned in that context are related to important industrial and technological changes that have led to increased complexity of scientific and technological development, higher uncertainty surrounding R&D, increasing costs of R&D projects, and shortened innovation cycles that favor collaboration (see Contractor and Lorange 1988, Dussauge and Garette 1999, Hagedoorn 1993 and 1996, Mowery 1988, Mytelka 1991, Nooteboom 1999, OECD 1992). As a consequence, most of the research about collaboration behavior has suggested that the primary motivation for collaborating is an organization's need to secure the complementary assets necessary to support the innovation activities of the firm (Nohria and Garcia-Pont 1991, Nueno 1999, Greis et al. 1995). Campione (2003) claims that a foremost driver for R&D collaborations is a strategic business need that has been translated into a priority R&D need, which can best be realized by accessing the unique capabilities of another party. For example, two companies may discover that they have complementary technologies, intellectual property rights and/or expertise which they would like to exploit, but cannot do so on their own. Thus, the partners' aspirations are typically greater than their resources (Nueno 1999).

24 Gulati (1998) provides a good overview about firms' motives to engage in collaborations.

Another motivation for firms to enter collaborations is to defray costs and share risk when they undertake high-cost (capital- or development-intensive) projects or very speculative strategic initiatives (Hagedoorn 1993). Bayona et al. (2001) analyzed the motives that have caused industrial firms to cooperate in R&D across 1,652 Spanish firms. The authors conclude that firms' motivations for cooperative R&D are the complexity of technology and the fact that innovation is costly and uncertain. In order to undertake collaborative R&D, it is necessary to have certain internal capacities in the area of collaboration. According to Shan and Visudtibhan (1990), one of the most intuitive explanations for cooperative arrangements is their synergistic effect which includes risk reduction among other aspects. Further reasons to get involved in collaborations include some combination of obtaining access to new markets and technologies, speeding products, and pooling complementary skills (Kogut 1989, Kleinknecht and Reijnen 1992, Mowery and Teece 1993, Eisenhardt and Schoonhoven 1996). Previous success and/or failures may affect the firm's attitude towards some forms of collaboration (see Bidault and Cummings 1994, Farr and Fischer 1992). Hagedoorn et al. (2000) also analyzed why research collaborations are formed. They concluded that firms participate in research partnerships to:

- Decrease transaction costs in activities governed by incomplete contracts;
- Broaden the effective scope of activities;
- Increase efficiency, synergy, and power through the creation of networks;
- Access external complementary resources and capabilities to better exploit existing resources and develop sustained competitive advantage;
- Promote organizational learning, internalize core competencies, and enhance competitiveness;
- Create new investment options in high-opportunity, high-risk activities;
- Internalize knowledge spill-overs and enhance the appropriability of research results, while increasing information sharing among partners;
- Lower R&D costs and pool risks;
- Co-opt competition.

Additional factors relating to the technological and market forces which appear to be responsible for motivating increased collaboration among firms include the following (see also Bayona et al. 2001, Sakakibara 2001):

- Growing technological complexity;
- Rapid technological change;
- Increased competition, linked to globalization and ongoing regulatory reform;
- Increased costs and risks of innovation.

Particularly in the pharmaceutical industry, increased risks in R&D seem to have emerged as a primary driver for collaborations. A survey of strategic licensing practices in the pharmaceutical industry conducted by IBM (2003) reveals that 'more effective use of partnering to balance risk through risk-sharing' is one of the most important strategic issues in pharmaceutical R&D management. While market access was a major motivation for strategic alliances for licensors in the early 1990s in the pharmaceutical/biotech industry, empirical findings by McCutchen and Swamidass (2004) reveal that the need for 'risk reduction' is a more important reason for strategic alliances. In addition, Chakrabarti and Weisenfeld (1991) argue that a partial explanation for the increase in alliances in the pharmaceutical industry is that cooperative development of technology is less risky than internal development.

Conclusion: Collaborations are an important element of today's R&D activities in the pharmaceutical industry. While there are many different forms of collaborations, the decision to collaborate on certain R&D activities with external partners depends on various parameters. Primary drivers for the existence and further emergence of R&D collaborations with external partners include the following aspects:

- Intensive competition;
- Access to new markets;
- Scarce own resources;
- Lack of know-how;
- Use of opportunities which cannot be utilized alone;
- Cost cutting or restructuring;
- Growth aspirations (expertise, resources);
- Synergies and efficiency;
- Corporate governance and/or strategic make-or-by decision;
- Reduction of risk and/or proactive risk management.

2.3 Summary

Today's pharmaceutical R&D management is exposed to two major challenges:

- Increase in R&D-related risks;
- Increase in innovation conducted outside of the corporate boundaries.

In order to respond to both increased risks and increased outside innovation, pharmaceutical companies have started to adjust and change the nature of their collabo-

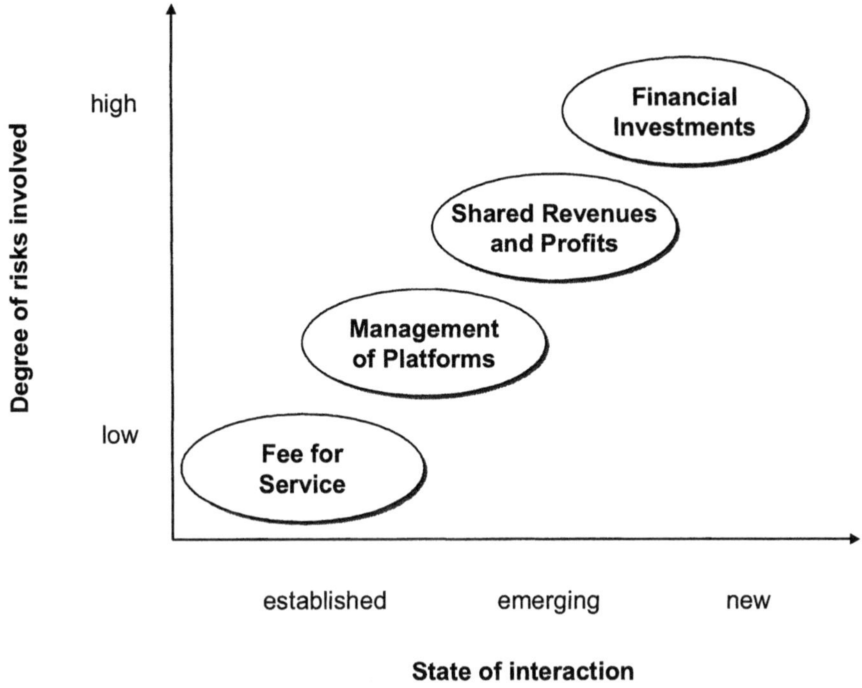

Source: adapted from Gassmann et al. (2004)

Fig. 16. Changing nature of interaction with outside innovation.

ration agreements with external partners (see Fig. 16): Instead of outsourcing relatively straight-forward activities such as development services or the management of technology platforms, pharmaceutical companies increasingly intend to use external partners to help share drug discovery and development risks (Gassmann et al. 2004). The pharmaceutical company itself could even actively support external R&D activities by making financial investments into legal entities that serve as their outside partners.

However, many companies have only recently started to proactively look at collaborations from a risk management perspective, and as a means to shift the relatively high R&D risks outside the company's own R&D department.[25] As most pharma-

25 See also interviews with Novartis and McKinsey.

ceutical companies are not willing to carry the burden of the huge risks by themselves any more, particularly in the early stages of R&D, they seek for external partners, which are expected to share some part of the R&D risk.

In summary, collaboration agreements and deal structures which proactively respond to the increasing R&D risks and explicitly cover risk-sharing aspects offer a promising vehicle for pharmaceutical companies to deal with the challenges imposed by today's industry environment. Risk-sharing arrangements have consequently become one of the most important key issues in pharmaceutical R&D management. Accordingly, the new paradigm of risk-sharing in pharmaceutical R&D collaborations is discussed in more detail in the following chapter.

3 Risk-sharing as New Paradigm in Pharma R&D Collaborations

As R&D risks are rising, many pharmaceutical companies have started to contemplate working with partners to reduce their risk exposure. Thereby, risk-sharing is only possible if both partners' success is based on the success of the joint project. The fortunes of both parties in the R&D collaboration must be inextricably linked: both companies gain or lose together, and each partner has to look at the other partner's success as their own success. Both sides of the R&D collaboration should be highly incentivized to turn the mutually developed substance into a success.

Linking the performance of both partners in the collaboration to the joint project's performance seems to represent a new paradigm in pharmaceutical R&D collaborations. It could have been observed that this type of performance-conjunction is manifested in the nature of many of today's pharmaceutical R&D collaborations. Performance-based structures are unambiguously on the rise. The amount of milestone payments in pharmaceutical R&D (i.e. payments based on the mutual achievement of certain goals) outperformed upfront payments by far over the last 10 years, reaching more than US$ 90 billion in 2004 compared to around US$ 12 billion in upfront payments for the same year (Recombinant Capital 2005). The following case example of Elitra Pharmaceuticals should help illustrate the basic nature of a risk-sharing agreement. When Elitra announced the deal, the firm explicitly said that the collaboration was signed because of risk-sharing reasons.

Risk-sharing at Elitra Pharmaceuticals

Elitra Pharmaceuticals announced in October 2002 an explicit risk-sharing collaboration agreement with bioLeads GmbH, exploiting the combination of bioLeads' natural product identification, isolation, and purification capabilities, along with bioLeads' extensive natural product library, and Elitra's antimicrobial discovery technologies. Natural products have historically been a very rich source of antimicrobials and are estimated to be the source of over 90% of currently approved antimicrobial drugs.

Under the risk-sharing agreement, Elitra will contribute an unspecified number of proprietary drug targets and related cell-based assays as well as high-throughput screening capabilities. The combination with bioLeads' natural product libraries and chemistry capabilities should help identify potential new antibacterial and antifungal drugs. Both companies will contribute to the pre-clinical development of the drug leads. Elitra retains the worldwide marketing rights for all collaboration compounds, while agreeing to pay milestones and royalty revenues to bioLeads for successful programs. "More than 99% of all soil microorganisms are still unknown and represent the biotechnological natural resource of the 21st century", said F.G. Hansske, CEO at bioLeads. "As a highly specialized company producing potential active natural compound libraries from microorganisms, bioLeads provides an extensive unexploited substance pool. Together with Elitra we achieve excellent synergies to develop and bring new drugs to the market."

As risk-sharing collaborations by their nature always center around sharing certain property rights or markets, they require both partners to contribute a certain part of the joint work. Therefore, the different types of risk-sharing collaborations in pharmaceutical R&D can be classified according to two criteria: the work that is contributed to the collaboration by the pharmaceutical company (research or development), and the work that is contributed by the external partner (research or development). Based on the perspective of the pharmaceutical company, this classification results in four different types of R&D collaboration (see Fig. 17):

- Research alliance;
- In-licensing;
- Co-development;
- Out-licensing.

All types of R&D collaboration are characterized by the fact that the two partners are highly incentivized to turn the joint effort into a success because the payout for both parties depends on the success of the mutual project. The aspired higher sales and profits generated are expected to over-compensate for the loss in revenues that go to the alliance partner. Together, the collaboration partners believe that they are able to leverage their own resources and capabilities in a way which leads to a superior performance of the project and consequently lets the R&D risks seem to decline for each partner. While the risk of the underlying R&D project remains unchanged, the synergies of the joint initiative are expected to lower the risk for both parties compared to the situation where each partner would conduct the project on its own.

Whereas research alliances, in-licensing, and co-development are quite established and traditional collaboration approaches, out-licensing has long been considered a difficult task by many established pharmaceutical companies. However, some companies have recently adopted this strategy to utilize external resources for the development of internally developed substances in order to share R&D risks. The different types of R&D collaboration are discussed in detail in the following chapters.

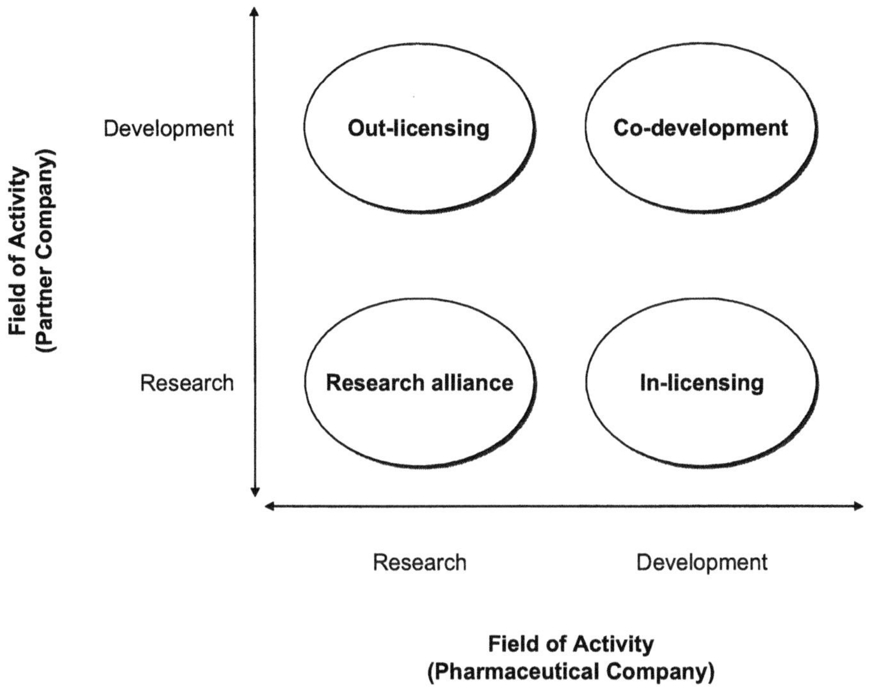

Fig. 17. Different types of collaboration in pharmaceutical R&D (perspective: pharmaceutical company).

3.1 Traditional Approaches to Risk-sharing

3.1.1 Research alliance

In case of research alliances, both partners focus on issues related to basic research and drug discovery. They usually intend to come up with new targets or compounds by leveraging their individual technology platforms, know-how or capital.

Typical research alliances of pharmaceutical companies include target identification partnerships with biotech firms. Due to the fact that most biotech firms have no product on the market yet and, hence, are heavily reliant on their research activities, they are of particular interest to established pharmaceutical companies' R&D. While biotech firms usually react very quickly to novel technology changes and deploy the latest scientific and technological equipment, pharmaceutical companies are better off in partnering rather than competing with them. Indeed, recent research has shown that new biotech firms have not replaced incumbent pharmaceutical firms, but both prefer a symbiotic coexistence (Rothaermel 2001). The incumbents have adapted to biotechnology through strategic alliances with the new entrants (Greis et al. 1995).[26]

The biotech firms' rationale to enter research alliances with large pharmaceutical companies is to access distribution channels as well as capital for the cost-intensive clinical development activities. They also seek partnerships with established pharmaceutical firms because a collaboration with a large pharmaceutical player increases the biotech firm's credibility. The technological know-how is mostly too complex to communicate to all stakeholders. A collaboration with a brand-name pharmaceutical company is a strong credential for the quality of the biotech's research (Robbins-Roth 2001). On the other hand, research alliances also provide the established pharmaceutical companies with several advantages. The two most important advantages are as follows (see Herrling 1998):

- It can acquire first-hand knowledge and expertise in a new technology;
- It has time to see whether the technology has a real therapeutic future.

If the collaboration seems to be promising, the pharmaceutical company can eventually acquire the external partner to get exclusive access to the technologies and know-how. Hence, research alliances extend the pharmaceutical companies' reach at relatively low costs and risks compared to the acquisition approach.

Today, large pharmaceutical companies typically work in huge research networks covering up to several hundreds of biotechnology firms. The relation of the collaborations is mostly bilateral with the pharmaceutical company being the hub of the network. Sometimes, a third partner enters the bilateral collaborations between the pharmaceutical and the biotech company in order to provide the necessary application environment. A network among the biotech firms mostly does not exist (see also Becker et al. 1999). Acquisitions or a majority ownership by the pharmaceutical companies are rare, even if the Swiss companies Novartis (owns a 40% stake in Chiron) and Roche (owns a 60% stake in Genentech) are examples for the latter

26 Chapter 1.1.2 provides a more detailed description of the relationship between pharmaceutical and biotech companies.

case. One of the most prominent examples of a research alliance has been the Bayer-Millennium collaboration.

Research alliance at Bayer

Between 1998 and 2003, Bayer invested a total amount of around US$ 465 million into a research partnership with Millennium. This investment included an equity investment of US$ 96.6 million for a 14% stake in Millennium. Bayer's intention was to use Millennium's genomics-related technology platform to discover 225 new genomics-based drug targets. At the end of this purely research-oriented collaboration, more than 450 drug targets could have been identified for Bayer by Millennium. In addition, Bayer was able to sell its interest in Millennium for approximately US$ 300 million which is equivalent to a multiple of 3x of the initial investment. While both parties regarded the collaboration as a success, the industry remains skeptical about the alliance's results: only one validated pre-clinical drug candidate emerged out of all drug targets that had been identified during this research alliance.

In summary, if a pharmaceutical company teams up with a partner firm for the purpose of research-related activities, this collaboration approach can serve as a vehicle for risk-sharing if the joint discovery results have a positive impact on the performance of both firms' research, such as in the example of the Bayer-Millennium alliance. The pharmaceutical firm is able to avoid heavy investments in new discovery technologies and platforms, but is able to benefit from the partner firm's resources, platforms, and know-how. The risk of making investments in novel drug discovery technologies can successfully be handed over to the partner firm who has these technologies already in place. While research alliances are a viable strategy for pharmaceutical firms to share early-stage R&D risks, they are not a new phenomenon and quite common to the industry already since the surge in biotech companies starting in the late 1970s and early 1980s.

3.1.2 In-licensing

In-licensing has emerged as a key value driver for pharmaceutical companies. Industry leaders have recognized in-licensing as a strategic mechanism through which they can achieve their corporate objectives. In the case of in-licensing, the pharmaceutical company (licensee) acquires intellectual property of a third party (licensor), and expects that this intellectual property fills a gap in its own development pipeline. Examples of tradable intellectual property rights include specific biotechnological procedures (i.e. platform technologies) or compounds. Typical applications of the intellectual property are databases or software, in which the licensor provides the respective know-how. Distinctive 'knowledge-service packages' can thus be created and actively marketed. Indeed, patents on novel biotechnological achievements are usually not used to secure the knowledge, but to purposely sell the knowledge. Even research results which are not directly related to a specific R&D activity obtain a certain value and can be marketed (Paetz and Reepmeyer 2003). In some cases, complex co-marketing agreements are signed along with the in-licensing deal.

The most important reasons why it may be desirable or necessary for a pharmaceutical company to in-license intellectual property from external third parties include:

- Quick expansion of the portfolio of potential drug candidates without the risks and costs involved in a substantial research and development program;
- Better and more flexible utilization of development capacities, which makes the financial risk more calculable.
- High complement of the in-licensed technologies with those developed in-house (e.g., a business with a promising anti-cancer drug might seek a license of a third party's drug delivery technology to enhance its own product);
- Access to rights in platform technologies and software products to assist in research and drug development. Pharmaceutical companies often prefer to focus their resources on the later stages of development and commercialization once the potential of a product or technology has been identified, where the financial rewards are clearer;
- Avoidance of infringement action by a third party. As it is not always possible to work around a patent, negotiating a license and in-licensing it can be the only way to avoid an expensive and potentially disastrous infringement claim.

The pharmaceutical companies' desire to in-license objects developed elsewhere has experienced tremendous growth. Payments for in-licensing have quadrupled for products in early and late stages of development. Average payments have increased, with the largest increase for drugs entering the mid-stage trials (Signal Magazine 1997). In addition, nine of the top ten pharmaceutical companies have in-licensed more than 40% of their marketed new molecular entities. Most of the compounds were in clinical stages I and II (Cap Gemini Ernst & Young 2001). In 2000, 14 of the top 55 drugs by sales were in-licensed (Accenture 2002). For example, all of Bristol-Myers Squibb's blockbuster products (Pravachol, Taxol, Glucophage, Plavix and Avapro) were the result of in-licensing (MedAd News 2000). GlaxoSmithKline in-licensed nine compounds in 2001 alone all of them targeting major therapy areas.

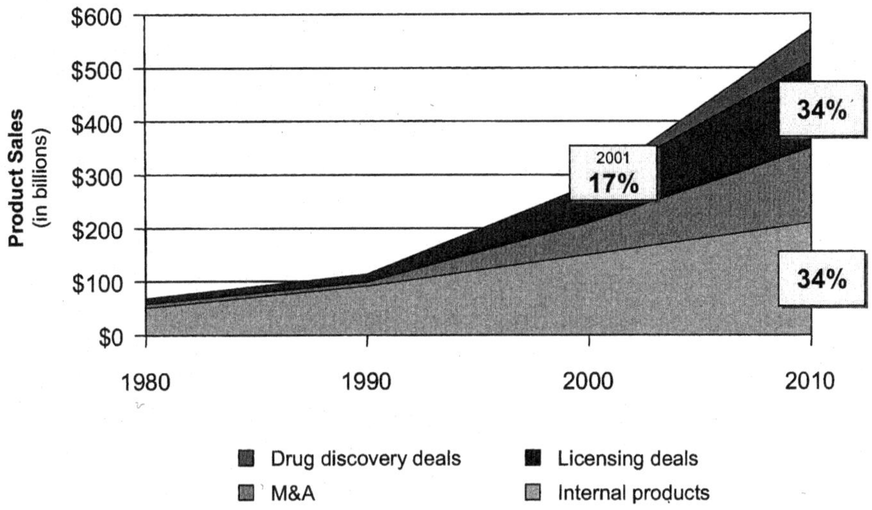

Source: Wood Mackenzie (2003b)

Fig. 18. Rising proportion of sales from in-licensed products.

In total, in-licensed products accounted for 17% of pharmaceutical sales in 2001, and this number is expected to grow to 34% by 2010 (see Fig. 18). According to research by Wood MacKenzie (2003b), sales contributed by in-licensed products will then equal sales achieved by internally developed products.

In-licensing at Pfizer

Probably the most prominent example of an in-licensed drug includes Pfizer's Lipitor. Pfizer marketed Lipitor (initially on behalf of Warner Lambert before the company had been acquired by Pfizer) to compete with drugs such as Zocor (Merck), Pravachol (Bristol-Myers Squibb), and Lipobay (Bayer) for the lucrative cholesterol-lowering drug market. Lipitor was originally in-licensed from Yamanouchi. Pfizer then used its marketing strength and sales capabilities to turn this externally sourced 'me-too' drug into the most successful blockbuster ever. In 2003, Lipitor became the first pharmaceutical product ever that topped US$ 10 billion in annual sales.

The increasing prominence of in-licensing has led to ever more complex contractual arrangements. Unidirectional one-time payments have been replaced by sophisticated and timely limited agreements, which typically cover different geographical markets. Success premiums, milestone payments, and royalty agreements oftentimes increase the contractual complexity. The extent of the performance-oriented contractual arrangement usually depends on the risk-benefit profile of the collaboration. The earlier the stage of the collaboration, the more difficult it is to calculate prospective revenue streams (Paetz and Reepmeyer 2003). Many licensors thus reserve the right to market the developed drug in certain strategically important markets by themselves (see Cap Gemini Ernst & Young 2001).

In summary, as serendipity is still considered a key success factor particularly during the discovery phases, a network with outside innovation is highly important because the likelihood of a single company generating all necessary substances in-house is relatively low. Thus, in-licensing of lead substances which have not been discovered internally provides pharmaceutical firms with a vehicle to obtain promising drug candidates while it leaves the risk of the initial discovery to an external partner. Therefore, this type of R&D collaboration not only helps the pharmaceutical firm reduce the risks implied in investments in the company's own research and discovery infrastructure, but also the risks of a lack of access to the desired substances to fill its own development pipeline. As in-licensing always includes the transfer of property rights and, therefore, links the success of the partners to the success of the joint effort, this type of collaboration is frequently used by pharmaceutical companies as a vehicle to share R&D-related risks.

3.1.3 Co-development

Co-development agreements refer to the mutual development of a drug. This approach is mostly used by companies which try to complement their development competencies and marketing capabilities. For example, a biotechnology company which already has a substance in clinical development but does not own a sales force in an important market, teams up with a larger company to mutually develop the last stages of the drug and to sell it mutually after registration. The development is usually conducted by joint teams. The origin of the used substance is of no interest in this model of collaboration. One of the earliest examples of a co-development agreement between a pharmaceutical company and a biotechnology firm is the collaboration of Eli Lilly and Genentech which entered into a joint initiative to develop the recombinant human insulin already in 1977.

For many companies, the need to collaborate in development is typically driven by a particular project need or by specific market circumstances. The increasing disintegration of the R&D process and the growing need to develop innovative drugs across various platforms and therapy areas both drive companies towards this collaborative approach. However, a few companies are now pushing beyond that point, making co-development an integral element of their business model and realizing significant gains in the effectiveness and efficiency of R&D (compare Deck and Strom 2002).

Co-development at Aventis

In 2001, Aventis Pharmaceuticals (the US subsidiary of Aventis S.A.) entered into a collaboration agreement with Altana Pharma (then known as Byk Gulden) regarding the joint development of the substance Alvesco®. The substance was initially developed by Byk Gulden. Subsequent to the agreement, Aventis was developing the drug candidate exclusively for the US market. In 2004, Aventis received market approval for Alvesco® in the US and has started to market the product. Aventis will compensate Altana Pharma in return for providing the substance by conveying a certain percentage of the drug's revenues incurred in the US. In Europe, Altana Pharma continued to develop the drug and will also market the product. Altana Pharma is expecting to reach market approval for Alvesco® for the European market by the first half of 2005.

Aventis' intention to enter the co-development with Altana Pharma was to close a gap in its product pipeline and improve the company's product portfolio. Altana Pharma's intention to enter the co-development with Aventis was to make use of Aventis' presence in the US to ensure a proper market introduction of the drug in the US market. As the story of Alvesco® is considered a success by both partners, Aventis and Altana Pharma were both able to reduce their exposure to risks – related to growth aspirations and market introduction respectively – by jointly developing the substance.

The integration of the processes by which work gets done and decisions are made are the key elements to co-development activities. For example, Aventis also engaged into a 50/50 co-development partnership with Millennium. A main aspect of this collaboration is the mutual commitment that if one company's task gets completed faster than expected, the partners may shift more tasks to that company to both equalize resource time and accelerate progress of the program (see Deck and Strom 2002). The monetary incentives for the partners to join co-development are usually upfront payments, milestone payments, as well as royalty payments after the drug successfully reached the market. Particularly revenue sharing is an important aspect of co-development agreements. Co-development is generally done to accelerate development times. The new drug is therefore able to enter the market sooner than in the case of stand-alone development which is expected to lead to higher returns even after the partner firm has received the stipulated proportion of the revenues incurred.

Co-development agreements can cover many different areas. A recent co-development agreement between Aventis and Pfizer, for example, implies that Pfizer develops a certain insulin drug and Aventis helps providing the investments necessary to build up the production capacity. In general, success factors for co-development cover the following aspects (compare Deck and Strom 2002):

- Development of a business-based co-development strategy based on each partners' strengths;
- Identification of the skill gaps relative to the resources needed for the co-development relationship;
- Definition of a process and set of criteria for evaluating and selecting development partners;
- Assignment of an active sponsor for each co-development relationship;
- Alignment of expectations of the partners and clarification how the relationship will actually work in a joint development agreement;
- Determination that each co-development deliverable has a clear, common definition across organizations;
- Establishment of explicit, direct communication linkages between development teams within and across organizations;
- Access to information tools for the development teams to enable secure, real-time information flow between companies including the establishment of processes and organizational elements that facilitate the use of those tools;
- Introduction of regular intervals to measure and assess the progress of each co-development relationship.

In summary, pharmaceutical firms prefer co-development collaborations in order to utilize the development and marketing capabilities of another firm. As biotech companies increasingly contribute late-stage compounds to their collaborations with established pharmaceutical companies, their improved negotiation power enables them to get involved in co-development agreements as well. The large pharmaceutical company can thus share development risks as the partner company has already or is about to contribute development activities to the joint project. Both firms usually share the benefits of a successful market entry via royalty revenue or profit sharing agreements.

3.2 Out-licensing as Novel Approach to Risk-sharing

While research alliances, in-licensing and co-development have been common collaboration approaches of most established pharmaceutical companies for several years, out-licensing has long been considered a difficult task for large pharmaceutical companies. While out-licensing as a phenomenon is as new as in-licensing (it is the same as in-licensing but from a reversed perspective), its utilization by large and established pharmaceutical companies, however, is fairly novel. Some large pharmaceutical companies – including Eli Lilly, Schering, Bayer, Roche or Novartis – have only recently adopted this R&D collaboration strategy.

Reasons for the pharmaceutical companies' resistance towards out-licensing

One of the most frequently mentioned reasons why pharmaceutical companies have been reluctant for so many years to apply the concept of out-licensing includes that 'no one will win any awards within a large drug company for a successful out-licensing deal that generates some upfront and modest expectations for royalties in the distant future' (see Windhover 2003). An even bigger obstacle to out-licensing by pharmaceutical companies is the realization that selling off rights to an unrecognized blockbuster could be a career-ending move for the respective executive. According to Windhover (2000), most large pharmaceutical companies are fairly uncomfortable about relinquishing control of their drugs because they fear that selling products will leave gaping holes in their revenues. In addition, R&D management also has to deal with employees' emotions affixed to killing a project which they worked on for several years. However, according to information by Merck KGaA, it is oftentimes the case that employees are even happy if another company is willing to continue a project which the out-licensing company did/could not want to pursue any further.

Another reason why many pharmaceutical companies have been reluctant to out-license their compounds has usually been that no one would consider a compound to have any value if a big pharmaceutical company – which has the necessary infrastructure to bring a compound to the market – decided to terminate the respective R&D project. Research by Kollmer and Dowling (2004) supports this perspective.

The authors figured out in a study on licensing in the biopharmaceutical industry that fully integrated firms out-license only their non-core products. The reasons are usually a misfit with their overall strategy although – considering their size – they could bring these products to the market independently. Many companies seem to fail to recognize that most R&D projects are terminated due to reasons which are not related to the compound itself. In this context, Bayer particularly highlights (when the company intends to out-license a substance) that 'this is most likely a Bayer-specific problem rather than a problem of the substance'. However, instead of acknowledging the fact that the terminated drug candidate still has a certain therapeutic value, many industry participants used to believe that the underlying compound had a negative connotation. The study by Kollmer and Dowling (2004) contradicts this belief and even highlights the potential of out-licensing at large pharmaceutical companies. The results of their research show that the out-licensing activities of fully integrated firms bring comparable compensation to that of not-fully integrated firms, even though the former mostly out-license non-core products. In both cases, licensing seems to be a profitable business.

Research by Recombinant Capital (2005) involving 2,623 alliances forged by the top 20 pharmaceutical companies with biotechnology companies between 1988 and

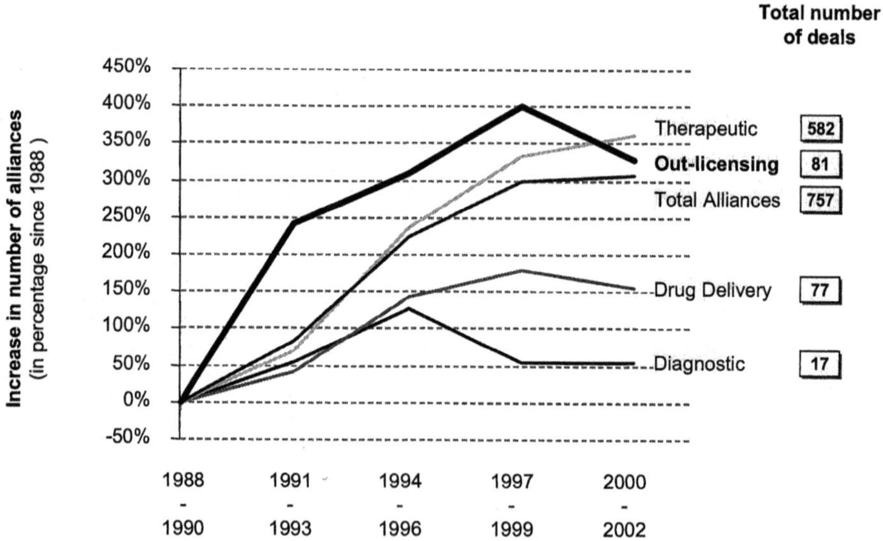

Source: Recombinant Capital (2005)

Fig. 19. Growth in alliances of top 20 pharma companies (1988 to 2002).

2002 supports the still existing resistance of large pharmaceutical companies to out-license their compounds: only 1 out of 8 alliances is an out-licensing deal by a pharmaceutical company. However, despite its fairly low contribution in absolute terms, out-licensing by pharmaceutical companies has experienced remarkable growth over the past few years (Fig. 19). While the total number of out-licensing deals between 2000 and 2002 is still small (81) compared to, for example, therapeutic alliances during the same time period (582), the growth of out-licensing deals outperformed the increase of most other types of alliances including the average of all alliances, although it has recently experienced a small slow-down. This tremendous growth is a strong indicator for the huge potential behind out-licensing.

Potential of out-licensing

As out-licensing strategies utilize external resources for the further development of internally developed substances, out-licensing always promotes the dissemination of technologies and products by integrating a company's intellectual property with

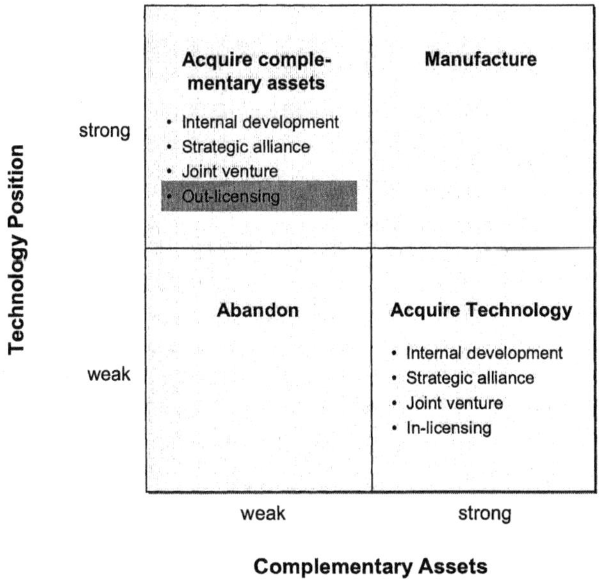

Source: Megantz (2002)

Fig. 20. Out-licensing as a strategy to gain complementary assets for the utilization of a company's own technology.

complementary assets. Therefore, out-licensing should be adopted by companies which possess a strong position in a certain technology area but lack the complementary assets necessary to exploit the technology (see Fig. 20). Successfully executed out-licensing programs provide the pharmaceutical firm with several benefits, such as additional revenue generation, cost and resource effectiveness, or mitigation of R&D related risks. Megantz (2002) states that out-licensing lowers risks because less investment and fewer resources are needed; much of the risk remains largely offloaded onto the partner company, who is responsible for the further development of the licensed product. If a product fails or a strategy changes, the pharmaceutical company can usually simply walk away without any undesirable follow-up operation. Only some usually small termination fees might occur.

A study by IBM (2003) about licensing in the pharmaceutical industry revealed that the objects that are licensed in out-licensing deals usually cover new molecular entities (see Fig. 21). The study concludes that most out-licensors are responding with their licensing offers to the needs of the current marketplace.

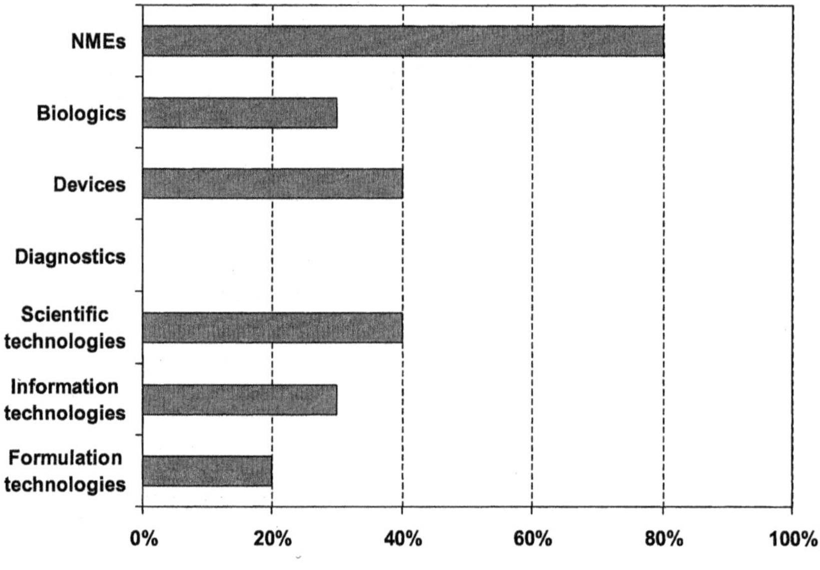

Source: IBM (2003)

Fig. 21. Product responsibility of the business development & licensing departments at pharmaceutical companies regarding out-licensing.

The most important reasons why it may be advantageous or necessary for a pharmaceutical company to out-license intellectual property to a third party relate to the risk considerations mentioned in chapter 2.1 and include the following aspects:

- No intended internal usage any more for the technology, compound, or intellectual property;
- Lack of resources and/or internal expertise for further exploitation;
- The risk profile of the substance and/or compound does not match the internal requirements;
- Specialization on certain product areas or technologies, such as a portfolio restructuring;
- Exploitation of therapy areas other than initially intended therapy areas (e.g., a pharmaceutical company only plans to develop a product or technology in one therapy area, but this product may have applications in other areas. This could even include areas which go beyond pharmaceuticals, such as cosmetics or plant breeding);
- Lack of commercialization potential (e.g., the drug's target market is considered to be insufficient in size to justify further R&D investments);
- Low-risk opportunity to move into new, complementary or unknown markets;
- Improvement of the company's revenue stream and/or market penetration by focusing on short-term income;
- Expansion of geographical reach;
- Side benefits, such as increased visibility of a brand because of advertising by the licensee or the use of improvements developed by the licensee;
- Maximization of the firm's asset utilization and value of the drug portfolio by leveraging internal R&D capacities;
- Gaining advantages in non-core markets by selling non-core technologies;
- Testing a market that might later be exploited by direct investments.

Probably the most important benefit of out-licensing includes that the pharmaceutical company could increase the utilization rate of its internal research results without using significant additional resources. As soon as the pharmaceutical company has made the decision not to continue the further development of a compound internally any more, the pharmaceutical company could find new avenues to commercialize its intellectual assets at the respective stages of the R&D process. This requires the abandonment of the traditional path of commercialization, and the creation of a new market for the compound. An external partner's R&D resources could be utilized to bring the compound to the market instead of letting the compound decay inside the pharmaceutical company's R&D boundaries (see Fig. 22).

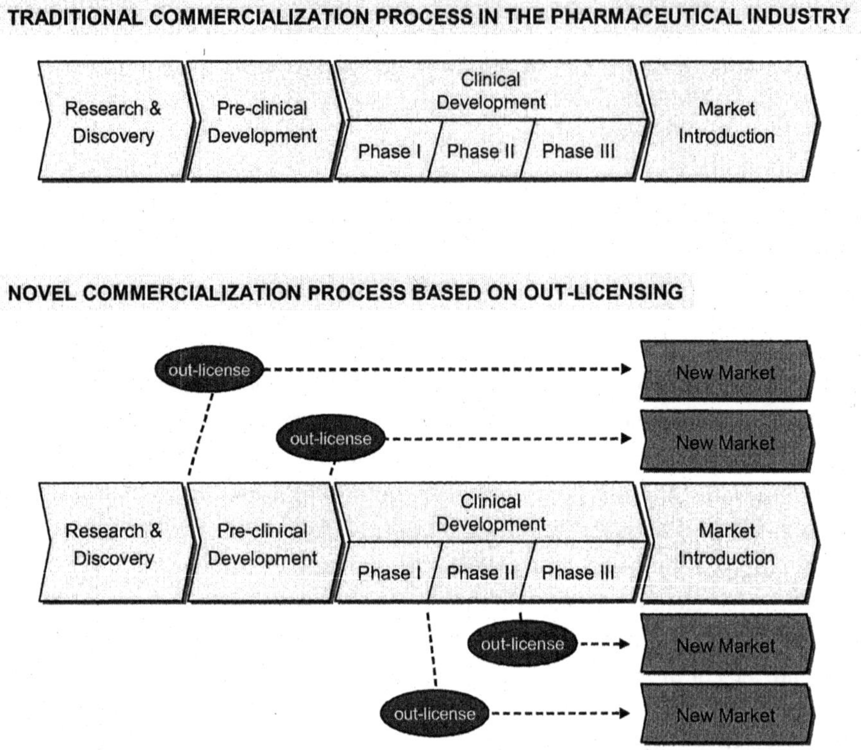

Fig. 22. Out-licensing as a way to dispose risks and open new markets.

This approach ultimately shifts the R&D risks to the outside partner. Moreover, selling the rights for further development of a compound to an external partner not only helps transfer R&D risks but also allows the generation of royalty revenues in case the licensed compound reaches the market at some point in the future. The following case example illustrates how Bayer handles out-licensing deals.

Out-licensing at Bayer

Bayer's primary intention to pursue out-licensing of compounds is to gain additional revenues for something which has already caused irreversible R&D costs and would otherwise be terminated without any further commercialization.

Bayer considers the grant of the IND (Investigational New Drug) approval to be an important milestone before a substance can be effectively licensed out. The IND approval is filed with the FDA prior to the clinical trials of a new drug (i.e. before the substance enters the human body and after it has completed the pre-clinical studies). It already gives a full and comprehensive description of the new drug. The IND is followed by the NDA (New Drug Application). As development is responsible for filing INDs at Bayer, most out-licensing agreements at Bayer are done by the development department which means that most substances are licensed out at a relatively late stage of the R&D process. However, Bayer also recently started to license out and utilize early-stage substances of its research department.

Bayer uses a four-stage process to decide if certain know-how or a certain technology should be out-licensed (see Gassmann et al. 2004). First, Bayer asks if the respective know-how/technology is a surplus product. If yes, the second stage contemplates if the know-how is strategically valuable for any core activity of Bayer's business units. If it is not, the third stage analyzes if the respective technology could be easily brought to a potentially attractive market. If this stage is answered with a yes, the final stage observes if the know-how is not strategically valuable for any other business unit at Bayer. If the intellectual property passes all four stages, it can be marketed outside of Bayer, otherwise it is retained in-house. In case the intellectual property is brought to a market, it receives its own marketing plan.

The reasons for Bayer to out-license a substance includes several aspects:

- *The number of patients that the drug candidate is expected to reach.* If the number of patients seems to turn out lower than estimated, the drug's potential is consequently less attractive. Bayer then considers out-licensing the compound hoping to find a licensing partner who finds the drug candidate attractive despite the smaller size of the target market.
- *The drug's compliance.* If a competitor is about to launch a similar product which has a better compliance, Bayer considers omitting the drug and licensing out the compound.
- *The drug's administration.* A lack of convenience for the patient might be a reason for Bayer to stop pursuing a new drug. In case a competitor introduces a similar drug which can be administered to the patient in a more convenient way (e.g., orally via tablets vs. injections), Bayer usually intends to stop the drug's development and chooses the option of out-licensing. An external partner might find a different application for the substance which could turn it into a success on a different market.
- *The price projection.* If the prospective price of the future drug drops significantly and does not fulfill the estimated sales projections any more, Bayer intends to out-license

the substance as well. Another company could have different sales channels or target markets which might make the drug attractive to them.

- *Reimbursements by the health insurance companies.* If a new drug is about to be reimbursed by health insurances, far more drugs can usually be sold than without any support by health insurances. By contrast, if the health insurances do not reimburse the patients, the new drug might not seem as attractive to Bayer any more because the projected number of sold units probably cannot be achieved. In this case, Bayer usually stops pursuing the drug candidate, but a licensing partner might still find the compound useful for its own pipeline.

Limitations of out-licensing

While out-licensing provides several benefits to the licensor, Megantz (2002) argues that it must be understood that out-licensing is not the simple, inexpensive yet highly profitable business model that many people believe it to be. The licensor must allocate resources, both financial and personnel, to perform the many tasks associated with a successful licensing effort. This includes supplying information and assistance to licensees both before and after agreements are signed, protecting intellectual property, negotiating the licenses themselves, and providing for additional expenditures required during the life of the agreement and, unfortunately, sometimes after the agreement terminates. Therefore, Megantz (2002) concludes that out-licensing must be considered as a long-term commitment which, although it offers the potential for a stable long-term revenue stream, requires substantial ongoing effort and expense. Moreover, every out-licensing agreement transfers a proportional measure of the potential reward to the licensee limiting the licensor's reward. Therefore, out-licensing also has some limitations besides its high potential. The most notable limitations are (compare also Ehrbar 1993):

- Limited income potential relative to other business alternatives;
- The possibility that a licensee might become a competitor of the licensor when the agreement expires;
- Concern that the licensee would aggressively seek to market outside its territory;
- The licensee's inability to meet acceptable business standards;
- Misunderstandings and disputes that may require prolonged discussion or even arbitration or litigation;
- The tendency of licensees to renew only on conditions more favorable to them;

- The limitations set by some countries on outwards payments for licenses;
- Potentially occurring negative image transfer from licensee to licensor;
- Exchange rate uncertainties.

Besides the limitations of out-licensing, there are also several reasons which could cause an out-licensing agreement to fail. The IBM (2003) report analyzed the different reasons of failure, and differentiates into causes of failure before the deal closure (pre-deal) and after the deal closure (after-deal).

The most significant pre-deal causes of failure for out-licensing have been the frequent occurrence of slow or unclear decision-making (reported by 80% of the respondents) as well as unequal benefit sharing between the partners (reported by 50% of the respondents). In addition, the non-compatibility of the partners' objectives is also likely to jeopardize the deal closure (see Fig. 23). However, respondents from both sides felt they would usually be able to overcome many of these issues if they were particularly interested in pursuing a deal – despite possible difficulty, such challenges would not typically lead to deal failure.

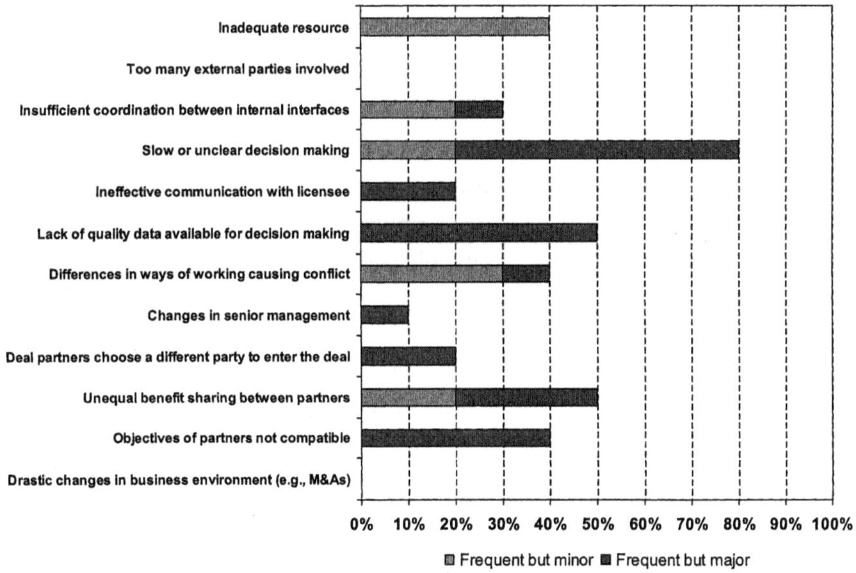

Source: IBM (2003)

Fig. 23. Causes of failure pre-deal closure for out-licensing.

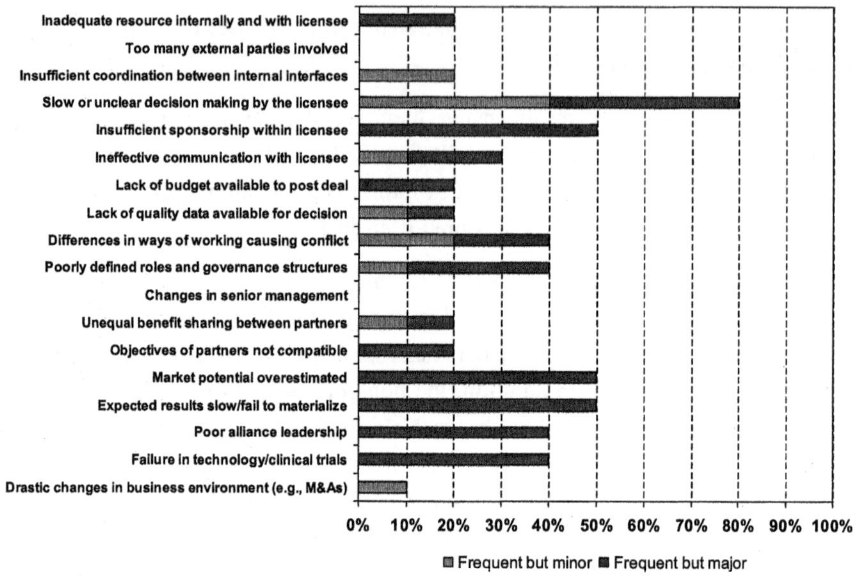

Source: IBM (2003)

Fig. 24. Causes of failure post-deal closure for out-licensing.

In contrast to the pre-deal closure, the respondents also provided a number of issues that appeared to cause difficulty after completion of the deal (see Fig. 24). Probably of most concern is the 50 percent of respondents who reported that there was insufficient sponsorship within the licensee. One insightful comment associated with this finding was 'the best deals are done with Japan, where once the company has decided to buy the product, they take it very seriously and give it the priority it deserves' (IBM 2003). According to IBM (2003), it is worth noting that similar issues are seen pre- and post-deal and many of these could be eliminated as they should be categorized as simple operational improvements.

When being asked about key reasons why expectations were not met in previous deals, most of the companies in the IBM (2003) survey responded that clinical efficacy and safety along with regulatory acceptability and size of the commercial opportunity were likely to be major causes of failure in out-licensing deals (see Fig. 25). Of particular concern is the mismatch in resources reported by both sides, where 50 percent of respondents from each group felt that either the resource levels or the resource capabilities did not meet expectations.

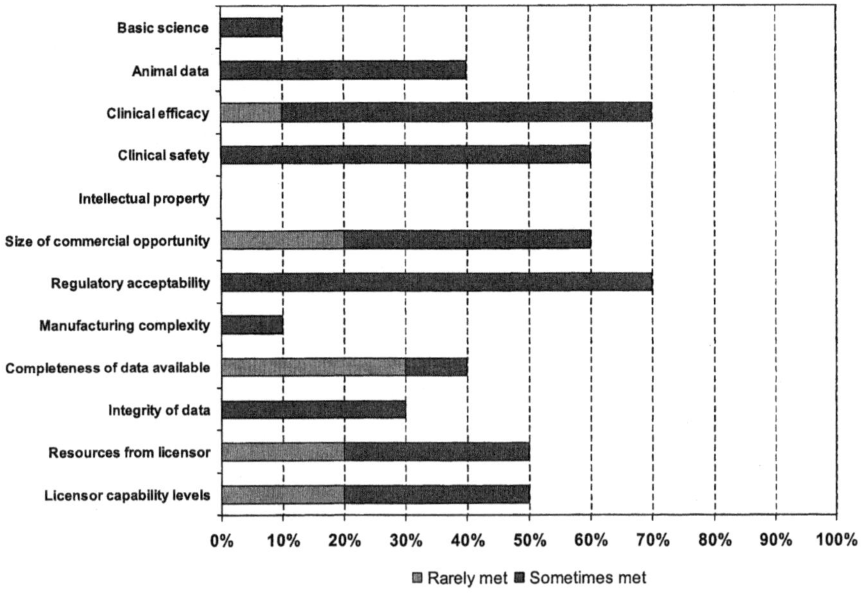

Source: IBM (2003)

Fig. 25. Expectations sometimes or rarely met with out-licensing.

Risk-transfer during out-licensing

By out-licensing a compound to an external partner, the pharmaceutical firm docs not only confer the intellectual property rights of the substance on the external partner. The partner also takes over the risks of the compound's further development. While the risk for each single market cannot be eliminated, this combined destiny of the two partners allows the transfer of risks from one partner to the other. At the same time, the out-licensing deal transfers the possible upside potential to the partner company accordingly. Out-licensing can help reduce R&D risks on an inter-company level only if the cooperation partner has superior competencies and capabilities regarding the particular substance than the pharmaceutical company. Otherwise, the risk can only be relocated but not reduced.

The only way how a pharmaceutical company can effectively share risks in an out-licensing deal is if it has the chance to get the compound back at a later stage of its development process and when the remaining risk is lower than before. If a pharmaceutical company cannot recall the compound, the risks are purely disposed and not shared (based on the perspective of the pharmaceutical company). Re-licensing rights are usually executed via call-back options. These options allow the pharmaceutical company to license the substance back at a certain stage in the R&D process. In general, call-back options are controversially discussed (see also Brockhoff 1999, Zürcher and Blaser 2004). While the pharmaceutical company normally has strong interests to buy back the substance after initial uncertainties and risks have been reduced, the licensee has no incentive to give back the substance particularly if it seems to become a market success. Thus, the call-back option usually limits the licensee's potential upside. If the compound would not be out-licensed by an established pharmaceutical company but would be on the open licensing market, the licensee would most likely be able to get a licensing deal at better terms. While a call-back option is the most effective way to recall a compound from an external partner, other vehicles of retaining an interest in the compound could include preferred re-licensing negotiation rights or exclusive co-promotion rights.

As the estimation of a drug's potential is very complex and characterized by a high uncertainty, mistakes in evaluating the potential of a substance could have a high price in terms of opportunity costs if the pharmaceutical firm is unable to benefit from the drug's upside potential any more. For instance, Aventis failed to recognize the potential of one of its products when the firm sold it for a relatively low price to King Pharmaceuticals without retaining any stakes in the drug's future potential.

Aventis: Call-back options would prevent missing out on a compound's upside

The specialty pharma company King Pharmaceuticals acquired the drug Ramipril (Altace), an angiotensin-converting enzyme (ACE) inhibitor, in 1998 from Aventis as part of a package of three drugs costing US$ 363 million (see Thiel 2004). Aventis sold the drug because it was not clearly differentiated from other products in this crowded therapeutic field. After a subsequent study conducted by King Pharmaceuticals, which proved that the drug reduced risk of death from stroke and heart attack in certain populations, the drug got additional labeling that certified its uniqueness. King Pharmaceuticals generated US$ 527 million in sales with the drug Altace in 2003 alone. Because Aventis did not have any stakes in the drug any more, the company missed out on this great opportunity just because its judgment about the drug's potential was wrong. King's management only faced marketing risks – the prospect that they would never be able to get the expected sales out of what looked like a me-too ACE inhibitor – but they did not have to worry about getting the product into the pharmacies because it had already been in the US market for seven years.

As illustrated by the case of Aventis, most pharmaceutical companies are afraid to miss out on the opportunity of participating in a drug's upside potential. Therefore, pharmaceutical companies typically do not get involved in an out-licensing deal if they do not retain certain re-licensing rights, such as call-back options. By contrast, pharmaceutical companies get involved in out-licensing deals with no re-licensing rights if they simply want to dispose certain intellectual assets. However, this out-licensing apporach is usually not conducted as a means to share R&D-related risks. As the call-back option gives the pharmaceutical companies the right (but not the obligation) to license the substance back at a later stage of the R&D process, the call-back option is a necessity for pharmaceutical firms to transfer risks during an out-licensing agreement.

3.3 Summary

This chapter has introduced four different types of R&D collaborations which allow a pharmaceutical company to share risks during the R&D process. These R&D collaborations include:

- Research alliances;
- In-licensing;
- Co-development;
- Out-licensing.

All of these collaboration approaches differ along several aspects. Although research alliances and co-development refer to arrangements where the two parties are conducting joint activities, in-licensing and out-licensing typically center around the grant of intellectual property rights. However, as the former is likely to involve cross-licensing of intellectual property rights and the latter often includes an element of collaboration between the parties, such as co-marketing activities, the boundaries between the two types of collaboration are blurred. Using a risk-sharing contract often has another important benefit: it creates significant goodwill. On the one hand, the contract provides a safety net, limiting each company's losses should an agreement unexpectedly fail. On the other hand, it reduces the possibility of one company earning a large and unexpected gain at the other's expense. A risk-sharing contract thus tends to enhance the trust between the parties, setting the stage for mutually beneficial negotiations in the future.

While research alliances, in-licensing and co-development represent fairly common collaboration approaches, out-licensing has only recently been regarded by established pharmaceutical companies as a vehicle to share R&D-related risks. Many pharmaceutical firms have started to realize that there are much more opportunities for the commercialization of internally developed compounds than the traditional in-house development. Particularly if the pharmaceutical company has decided to terminate a project, this does not mean any longer that this project cannot create value for the firm's shareholders and patients any more. As the pharmaceutical companies are restructuring their portfolios in favor of high-revenue products and prune away non-important products, many more commercializable products should become available for out-licensing than ever before (Windhover 2000). Most of these compounds still have a certain value although they have been terminated by the pharmaceutical companies.

Out-licensing these products not only allows the pharmaceutical companies to increase their 'shots on goal' in R&D which is expected to increase the odds of success for new drug candidates, but also requires them to create new markets for the respective compounds. This way, the research results can be utilized and generate additional revenues at almost no additional costs. The pharmaceutical company has to find a buyer for the compound and it also has to find a collaboration structure which allows the firm to benefit from the compound's upside potential while it simultaneously lets the deal seem attractive for the buyer. The following chapter introduces different case studies on out-licensing as an opportunity to share risks in pharmaceutical R&D and illustrates the nature of this new collaboration model.

4 Case Studies on Risk-sharing in Pharma R&D Collaborations

This chapter discusses three case studies on risk-sharing in pharmaceutical R&D collaborations. The case studies all focus on out-licensing at large pharmaceutical companies.[27] The goal of the case study analysis is to identify patterns and schemes regarding the management of out-licensing collaborations from the perspective of a large pharmaceutical company. These insights should provide the empirical basis for the managerial recommendations which are given later in chapter 7. The cases cover out-licensing deals at Novartis, Schering and Roche. All cases pursued the following questions: How does the pharmaceutical company organize and implement out-licensing? How is the out-licensing collaboration structured? Why was the partner company able to take on the risks which the pharmaceutical company could not or did not want to take?

The case study analysis covered only companies in the biopharmaceutical industry. It can subsequently be assumed that R&D management at all companies in the case studies is subject to the same industry conditions. As the environment for all companies is very similar, the firms' actions and performance primarily depend on firm-specific characteristics. Although the analyzed companies are domiciled in three different countries (Switzerland, Germany and the USA), all companies are located in Western economies. According to von Zedtwitz, Gassmann, and Reepmeyer (2003) as well as Gassmann and von Zedtwitz (1998), the pharmaceutical industry is considered to be highly internationalized for several years. Thus, it can be argued that R&D management at these companies follows related principles and shares similar values and beliefs. The reason why these cases have been selected for the case study analysis are multifold. All cases illustrate out-licensing collaborations at large and integrated pharmaceutical companies. In addition, the partner companies in the out-licensing deals were all relatively small compared to the pharmaceutical companies. Another reason why these case studies have been selected includes that the cases all describe licensing deals which seem to have turned out to be a success. In one case (Roche), the licensed substance has even achieved market approval already and is generating revenues for both partners. The other licensing deals are still under development but made significant positive progress since the closure of the licensing deals.

27 As long as not otherwise mentioned, the information provided in the case studies are based upon interviews with representatives of the respective companies as well as information that is taken from the companies' websites.

4.1 Out-licensing at Novartis

In 1998, researchers at Novartis came up with a new substance which was about to enter development, but Novartis' R&D management decided to stop this project. However, some of Novartis' employees strongly believed in the substance and were interested in pursuing this opportunity further. Subsequently, they started to set up their own company called Speedel and in-licensed the substance from Novartis. Novartis also looked at this novel partnership model with Speedel as an opportunity to transfer the development risks to an outside partner, but simultaneously retain the opportunity to participate in the compound's potential upside.

Chapter 4.1.1 will first provide a brief overview about the two companies (Novartis and Speedel). Afterwards, the out-licensing strategy of Novartis is described in greater detail in chapter 4.1.2. Special attention is paid to the integration of out-licensing within Novartis as well as the reasons and rationale for out-licensing. Chapter 4.1.3 discusses the details of the out-licensing collaboration. Finally, chapter 4.1.4 describes the special capabilities of Speedel which enabled the firm to take a compound into development which Novartis did not want to pursue any more.

4.1.1 Company profiles

Novartis

Novartis was formed in 1996 through the merger of Ciba Geigy and Sandoz. After several divestments and consolidations pursuant to the merger, Novartis now operates its core businesses in two divisions: pharmaceuticals and consumer health. Headquartered in Basel, Switzerland, Novartis employs more than 81,000 people worldwide and operates in over 140 countries around the globe. In 2004, Novartis achieved overall sales of US$ 28.2 billion and a net income of US$ 4.8. billion. The pharmaceutical division accounted for 65% of Novartis' 2004 revenues, which is equivalent to US$ 18.3 billion. The consumer health division accounted for the remaining 35% of sales covering over-the-counter (OTC) self-medication, animal health, medical nutrition, infant and baby foods, eyecare products as well as generics, which operate under the brand name Sandoz.

The pharmaceuticals business posted double-digit sales growth in 2004, gaining total market share during the year. Sales growth has primarily been due to the key therapy areas cardiovascular and oncology. Novartis owned 5 blockbuster products by 2004. The best selling products include the hypertensive product Diovan,

Gleevec against chronic myelogenous leukemia, and Zometa against cancer-related bone complications. Novartis has a solid history of successful drug discovery and one of the best pipelines in the industry. In 2001 and 2002, Novartis achieved the highest number of key-market approvals in the pharmaceutical industry, with 20 registrations and 22 major submissions in the United States, the European Union and Japan. As measured by the number of new product approvals, Novartis was the most effective generator of innovation quality worldwide in 2000 and 2001. Novartis introduced 5 new products in 2000 and 4 new products in 2001. According to Reuters (2002), Novartis owned 172 patents at the end of 2001.

Novartis invested approximately US$ 4.2 billion in R&D in 2004, resulting in a R&D-to-sales ratio of 14.9% for the entire group. Only the pharmaceutical division reported a R&D-to-sales ratio of 18.8%. The pharmaceuticals division is organized into five business units: primary care, oncology, transplantation, ophthalmics and mature products. Novartis' product pipeline comprises a total of 75 projects in clinical development as of the end of 2004. This includes both new molecular entities and additional indications or formulations for marketed products. Overall, there are 52 projects in advanced, late-stage development or registration. Novartis has introduced 13 new drugs on the market since 2000, more than any other pharmaceutical company during the same time.

Key to Novartis' success will be the company's efforts to increase its presence in the US, the largest and fastest growing market in the world. Novartis has almost doubled the size of its US sales force since 1998. At the end of 2002, Novartis had a US sales team of close to 5,000 sales representatives. In addition, Novartis launched in 2002 its corporate 'Institute for BioMedical Research' in close proximity to MIT in Cambridge/Massachusetts, which takes the lead in worldwide corporate R&D activities. The Cambridge facility currently houses over 400 scientists and technology experts and is expected to expand to approximately 1,000 employees in the near future. The Cambridge headquarters will continue to grow, with a US$ 4 billion investment planned over the next 10 years.

Speedel

Speedel is an independent biopharmaceutical company with core competence in drug development, particularly in cardiovascular and metabolic diseases. Speedel is headquartered in Basel and deploys further locations in New Jersey and Tokyo. The company was founded in 1998 by Dr. Alice Huxley, a global project manager for Novartis. By now, Speedel employs around 60 people. Speedel initially received seed money from the Novartis Venture Fund, and has secured several other follow-on investments from private-sector investors including the Dutch venture capital firm DSM Ventures and private individuals. As of today, Speedel has secured about CHF 180 million since its foundation; one third of the money comes from operating revenues, one third from equity and one third from a convertible loan.

Speedel's business model initially relied heavily on partnering. Speedel supplements its partners' R&D by in-licensing molecules at the late research/early development stages (Phase 0/I) from fully integrated pharmaceutical companies as well as biotechnology companies and universities. Speedel then develops the drug candidates through to completion of proof-of-concept in man at clinical phase II, after which stage Speedel may partner with leading pharmaceutical companies for Phase III development and commercialization for large-scale indications or it may continue Phase II development itself for specialist indications. In 2002, Speedel set up its own late-stage research unit, Speedel Experimenta, which is expected to provide the company with in-house compounds for development and intellectual property. Its first success case from this unit was announced in February 2005 with early Phase I data from a new series of renin inhibitors. However, Speedel intends never to enter early discovery research or manufacturing. Speedel's business model thus differs significantly from that of a traditional integrated pharmaceutical company in the way that Speedel's R&D process principally covers the stages between lead identification/optimization and clinical phase II. Therefore, Speedel's contribution to the pharmaceutical industry are consequently Phase II/III molecules for partnering with established pharmaceutical companies.

During its development activities, Speedel fully owns the respective molecules, and is thus taking on all the development risk itself. The pharmaceutical partner company usually retains a 'call-back' option on the licensed substance. If Speedel is successful in establishing proof-of-concept in man, the pharmaceutical company may license the compound back and proceed to full development in Phase III as well as commercialization, activities that big pharmaceutical companies typically perform exceptionally well. However, if Speedel is successful, and for whatever reason, the pharmaceutical company would choose not to call back the compound, Speedel would be free to continue development and commercialization or to offer the asset to another third party licensee. An example of this is SPP301, an endothelin respetor antagonist which Speedel in-licensed from Roche in 2002 under a call-back and then subsequently acquired the full rights in 2003. At the time of writing, Speedel's pipeline comprised 6 substances under development spread across different phases of the development cycle and across 3 modes of action.

4.1.2 Description of the out-licensing strategy

Integration of out-licensing within the corporation

Out-licensing at Novartis is organizationally embedded in the firm's Business Development & Licensing department (BD&L). This department deploys 80 employees whereas 3 persons are responsible for out-licensing. Compared to in-licensing, the importance of out-licensing seems to be fairly low. However, Novartis considers out-licensing as an important issue in order to add economic value to idle substances. The decision to out-license certain substances is based on various reasons. Novartis usually decides to license out a substance due to one of the following rationales:

- The substance is not strategically relevant any more;
- The substance does not fulfill the required performance potential;
- New substances arise which cannot be pursued any further within the scope of Novartis and without making significant upfront investments in infrastructure and know-how.

The primary objective of out-licensing is to at least recoup the costs which have been incurred for the respective substances so far. In addition, Novartis expects to achieve additional benefits and royalty revenues in case the collaboration partner successfully introduces the new substance on the market. For this reason, Novartis always includes revenue participation clauses in any out-licensing contracts.

Regarding the decision which substance should be out-licensed, Novartis conducts market dynamics analyses including the observation of competitors' activities. In case a Novartis product reaches the market shortly after a competitor has introduced a similar product, the product usually does not meet the initially aspired sales projections any more (which is about US$ 500 million per drug for a peak-year). If a drug candidate might not be able to reach these sales levels any more, an external partner firm which is satisfied with lower sales projections could still be interested in the drug candidate although Novartis does not want to pursue this opportunity any further. Every product in the Novartis pipeline is evaluated according to key success factors. If a substance does not meet the go-criteria in the periodically occurring portfolio decision-meetings, the substance will be stopped; no matter how much financial resources have already been invested into the substance's development. Particularly the substances which have already dissipated significant resources are of interest for out-licensing because this could be the only way to at least generate some kind of payback. Therefore, it is not unusual within Novartis that the project teams themselves suggest to out-license a stopped substance in order to see at least some kind of success for the huge amount of work they have already put into the substance's development.

Novartis sees particular benefits in licensing out to smaller companies. These firms are usually very interested in Novartis' substances; in addition to the substance, they also receive the reputation of Novartis, which in turn enables them to secure funding from investors more easily. Other big pharmaceutical companies usually do not show a lot of interest in Novartis substances. They are mostly not satisfied by Novartis' deal terms, because Novartis typically intends to keep some kind of ownership in any further discovery of the out-licensed substance. As a consequence, it is not surprising that Novartis signs most out-licensing deals with smaller companies. Sometimes, Novartis out-licenses substances to partner firms which are just about to be founded. Adequate competencies of the partner as well mutual trust are the necessary conditions for these licensing deals.

Out-licensing as a 10-step process

Novartis uses a standardized out-licensing process (see Fig. 26). First, a cross-functionally staffed committee decides which substance might potentially be out-licensed. The head of the Business Development & Licensing department is always participating during this step. While the decision committee based in Basel decides about out-licensing of all global development projects, there are also local teams which might evaluate and decide about licensing out a substance targetting a relatively small local market. After the decision committee has come to the conclusion to license out a substance, a team around the Head of Drug Delivery Licensing & Out-licensing comes into play. This team creates a product profile (2-3 pages) aggregating the most important non-confidential product information. This product profile contains the already conducted development activities as well as data about projected potentials.

During a next step, Novartis identifies possible licensing partners. This search is done by screening through all sorts of information (publicly available as well as internally available) about other bio-pharmaceutical companies and their respective R&D activities. The possible licensing partners are evaluated and assessed according to their competencies and capabilities to pursue the further development of the drug candidate which mainly includes financial aspects.

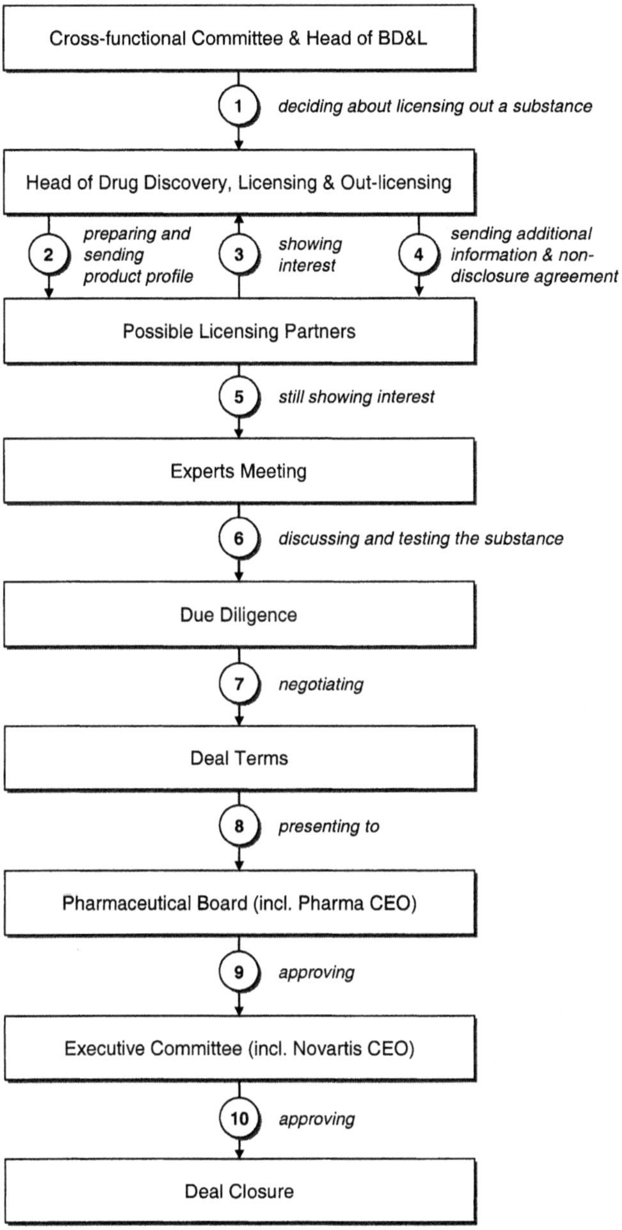

Fig. 26. Out-licensing process at Novartis.

After the identification of some possible licensing partners, the potential licensees receive the previously prepared product profile with a non-binding inquiry about the out-licensing opportunity. While some substances usually attract statements of interest within a relatively short period of time, other substances might be available for out-licensing for several years. In case no partner can be found, these substances are withdrawn and the projects are terminated. If a possible licensing partner shows a first interest in a certain substance, Novartis signs a non-disclosure agreement with this company. It can be the case that Novartis signs different non-disclosure agreements with multiple partners. After having signed these agreements, Novartis sends a confidential and detailed documentation about the substance to each partner. If a partner is still interested after having read the additional documentation, the first personal interaction between Novartis and the potential partner takes place. Experts of both firms meet and discuss the substance including the chances and risks associated with the drug's development. In some cases, Novartis might also send small probations of the substance (a few milligrams or grams) to the partner. This allows the partner to practically proof the substance with in-vitro or in-vivo trials.[28]

If there are still several partners interested in the substance after this stage of the out-licensing process, the more powerful partners are invited for due diligence negotiations. The typical due diligence takes place at Novartis and lasts about 1 or 2 days. It can be the case that Novartis negotiates with two partners simultaneously at the same time. After this step, Novartis and the potential partner discuss the key terms of the licensing agreement. If the partners agree on the terms, the Head of Drug Delivery Licensing & Out-licensing gives an internal presentation of the entire process to the pharmaceutical board including the CEO of the pharmaceutical division at Novartis. If the pharmaceutical board approves the deal, the pharma CEO presents the deal towards the Novartis Executive Committee under the supervision of Novartis' CEO Dr. Daniel Vasella. This gremium ultimately approves the deal. However, the Executive Committee reserved the right to retrospectively stop or terminate any out-licensing project.

Characteristics of an out-licensing contract

The actual contract is then prepared by the Head of Drug Delivery Licensing & Out-licensing, a corporate lawyer, a person from the patent department as well as a key scientist. A contract usually covers 50-60 pages. Novartis generally differentiates

28 While in-vitro trials analyze a substance in test-tubes, in-vivo experiments use living organisms.

between two types of contracts. Firstly, the option-licensing-agreement, which gives the partner an option for a product license. In this scenario, the partner can proof if it can successfully pursue the further development of the underlying substance and decides at a later point in time about the definite purchase of the license. Secondly, the licensing-agreement, which includes a traditional licensing contract right from the beginning. The contract typically covers upfront payments, milestone payments and royalty revenues. The highest milestone payments occur if the substance finally reaches the market.

The link between Novartis and the partner throughout the collaboration is formed by a so-called Key Contact Person. For some larger deals, Novartis creates a Steering Committee comprised of BD&L employees which follows the same purpose as the Key Contact Person in observing the progress of the substance at the licensing partner. The Key Contact Person or Steering Committee respectively observe in semi-annual and annual analyses if the contractual agreements are still met. Typically, Novartis is contractually allowed to withdraw from a licensing deal if certain targets and milestones are not met.

Risk considerations play a crucial role for out-licensing at Novartis. While out-licensing represents the risk that an initially internally developed substance might generate significant revenues for an external partner at some point in time, Novartis is exposed to the risk of not being able to participate in this upside potential. In order to manage this risk of a potentially wrong projection of the drug's potential, Novartis usually retains a call-back option in any out-licensing contract. The point in time when Novartis would like to use its call-back option is usually stated in the contract. The call-back option differs across different substances depending on product-specific development risks, the substance's market potential, or the performance potential of the licensee. The call-back will usually occur if the risks for further development of the substance are low enough in order to justify the call-back and further internal development. This point in time is usually somewhere between Phase II and the end of the development process. In case the point in time for the call-back is not part of the contract, Novartis reserves the right to start re-licensing negotiations depending on the individual situation of the substance's development.

The entire out-licensing process from the initial negotiations of the key terms through the deal closure usually lasts between 6 to 9 months. Searching and screening for the partner is not included in this time period. Novartis' stakeholders are also included throughout the entire out-licensing process. The units which are affected by the out-licensing deal can give their comments and critics at any time.

4.1.3 Structure of the out-licensing collaboration

In 1999 (after Speedel had been set up and started operations), Novartis out-licensed to Speedel the substance Aliskiren (SPP100), which targets cardiovascular indications. Aliskiren is an oral renin inhibitor that has demonstrated exciting potential for the treatment of hypertension. Today's market for antihypertensives represents approximately US$ 40 billion or about 40% of the entire cardiovascular market. It is expected to reach US$ 50 billion by 2009 (Speedel 2004). Hypertension affects more than 135 million people in the developed world. It is a major cause of strokes, chronic renal disease, congestive heart failure and myocardial infarction. Renin inhibitors, such as Aliskiren, work by regulating the kidney's production of renin. Renin, an enzyme, is associated with the release of a second substance that narrows blood vessels, making it harder for blood to flow through the arteries and raising blood pressure. Aliskiren suppresses the release of renin – and thus keeps blood pressure in a normal range.

After Novartis had out-licensed the substance Aliskiren, Speedel started performing the respective development activities for Aliskiren's clinical phases I and II. In total, Speedel conducted 18 clinical studies comprising about 500 patients and healthy volunteers. In addition to pilot studies in chronic renal failure and heart failure, Speedel ran a 4-week, 220-patient Phase II study that compared the compound to Merck & Co.'s Losartan (Cozaar); the two substances showed similar blood-pressure lowering effects. Crucially, Speedel was the first company to establish clinical proof of concept in Phase II and to have developed and patented a commercially viable manufacturing process for a renin inhibitor, an area of industry research for over 20 years.

Throughout the duration of the collaboration, Novartis retained a call-back option to license the substance back at any stage of development. As Novartis was pleased by the positive development results, the company exercised the call-back option for the compound in September 2002 (see Fig. 27). In November 2003, Novartis announced that its was moving Aliskiren into clinical phase III trials, which were initiated in March 2004. This left Speedel with significant milestone payments due to the successful development in Phase I and II. The amount of the milestone payments, which Speedel received from Novartis in July 2004 was not disclosed. However, they included a cash element and an equity participation. In January 2005, Novartis announced positive data from the Phase III study of Aliskiren as a monotherapy for the treatment of hypertension, and positive Phase II data from a combination study of Aliskiren with Diovan, another anti-hypertensive compound which is Novartis'

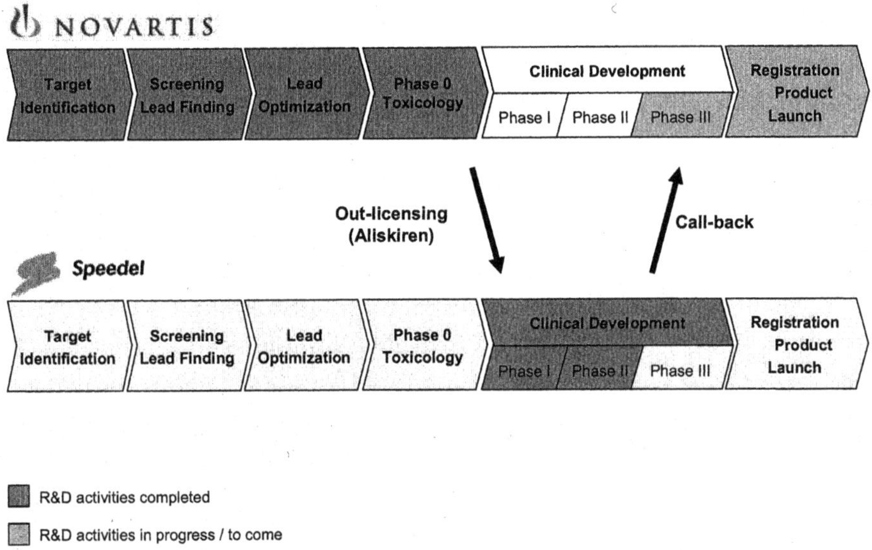

Fig. 27. Out-licensing collaboration between Novartis and Speedel.

leading drug. Novartis is expected to file for regulatory approval in early 2006. In addition, Speedel might profit by additional royalty payments once the compound enters the market. The drug's market launch would then benefit both Novartis and Speedel by generating revenues for the two companies starting in fiscal year 2007.

By taking full control over the licensed compound, Speedel thus relieved Novartis of the full burden of risk at this critical juncture in the development cycle, utilizing its own human, operational, and financial resources. Konrad Wirz, Speedel's CFO is quoted saying "We take the entire risk for Phase I and Phase II" (Sheridan 2003). Accordingly, Novartis avoided the risks in Phase I and II, and enjoyed the downstream opportunity of licensing back the drug candidate.

4.1.4 Capabilities of the out-licensing partner

Speedel was able to take a substance into development which Novartis did not want to pursue any further. Therefore, Speedel must have certain capabilities and competencies that enable the firm to develop the drug candidate, and which differentiate Speedel from Novartis along certain specific aspects.

There are several factors which are responsible for Speedel's success, primarily the firm's development efficiency. This efficiency and single-mindedness would have been almost impossible inside Novartis, particularly because Novartis was then still in post-merger flux and without serious interest in what was at the time perceived as a doomed area of development. According to company information, Speedel needed only around 30 weeks for Phase I and another 40 weeks for Phase II development. By contrast, a large pharmaceutical company alone (i.e. without the assistance of a contract research organization, CRO) would need on average around 85 and 140 weeks respectively (Fig. 28). If the large pharmaceutical company relies on support by a CRO, it is most likely able to reduce its development time. However, the big pharma firm will on average not be able to match Speedel's development efficiency (the clinical development time covers the weeks from final protocol synopsis to final clinical study report excluding treatment period). According to Speedel, the reasons behind its clinical development efficiency have been:

- Vision and a clear strategic direction;
- Clear focus on a single therapy area, which results in specialized know-how and expertise;

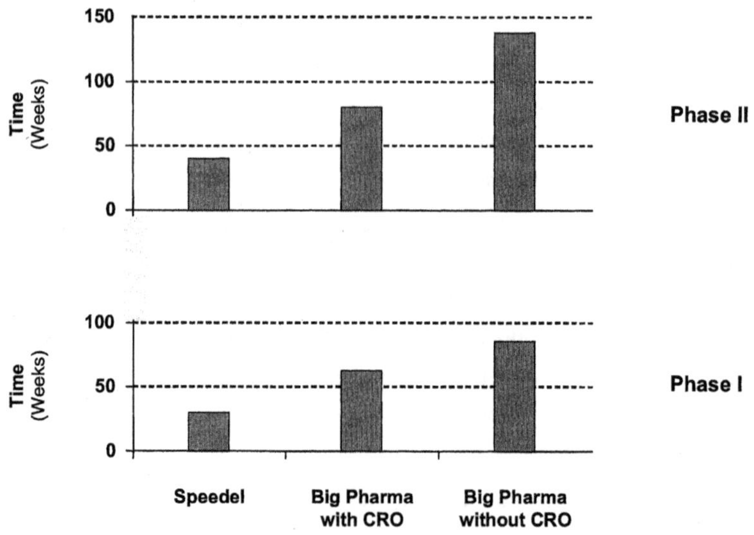

Source: Speedel (2004)

Fig. 28. Comparison of clinical development time: Speedel (substance: Aliskiren), big pharma with CRO, and big pharma without CRO.

- Tight project management and strict milestones (performance management via management-by-objectives: clear, quantifiable goals for every single employee);
- Cost-effective business model without investing in cash-intensive in-house facilities, while relying on a network with external partners, such as CROs, for non-core experimental activities;
- Out-standing management team;
- Entrepreneurial culture;
- Future-orientation of employees (once a decision has been made, employees have to look ahead what is coming next);
- Endurance and a never-give-up mentality;
- Strong financial discipline.

Particularly the financial discipline played a critical role for Speedel's success. Obtaining the capital necessary for the firm's operations represented by far the most important challenge during the evolution of Speedel. According to Alice Huxley, CEO of Speedel, this task was 'a whole new world, language and way of doing business' (Huxley 2004). While still at Novartis, Speedel's R&D managers never had to discuss where their money is coming from. It was always at management's disposal, although rather virtually than in real terms. Due to Speedel's independence, the firm's status allows the exploitation of opportunities throughout the pharmaceutical industry to optimum effect, without restrictions.

Another advantage of Speedel's business model compared to other pharmaceutical companies includes that due to Speedel's size, the firm can utilize an optimum of drug development capacity – either operational or financial. Such opportunities abound, especially after corporate mergers, portfolio restructuring or strategic refocusing by large and medium-sized pharmaceutical companies. In case of biotechnology or research start-up companies, many do not have the technical, clinical, or financial assets required for success in drug development and commercialization. To maximize manpower resources, Speedel has established a Medical as well as a Scientific/Technical Advisory Board. Speedel collaborates with opinion leaders from Boston University and Brookdale University Hospital, Brooklyn (USA), the Nagoya University (Japan), the University of Montpellier (France), and the Universities of Lausanne, Fribourg, Basel and Zurich (Switzerland). Speedel believes that this wealth of knowledge and experience is instrumental to efficient drug development.

The evaluation made by Speedel for potential drug candidates which are about to be taken into development depend on stringent selection criteria, such as innovative compounds or a new mode of action. Speedel readily accepts the technical challenges posed by complex chemical structures, and is especially interested in compounds that are potentially first on the market in a specific therapeutic class.

When being asked, what Speedel did differently than any other pharmaceutical company would have done in the development of the drug candidate Aliskiren, the answer by Alice Huxley is simple: 'It was a combination of a deep belief that renin inhibitors can work as a drug and the fact that we were concentrated entirely on this project. [...] We'd put our careers, our money, our professional reputations at stake to make this a success' (WSJE 2003).

Despite its specific competencies and capabilities which allowed Speedel to perform the development of Aliskiren, the underlying business model also has some disadvantages for Speedel, which is particularly due to the call-back option. It can be assumed that Speedel would have benefited much more from the compound if the firm could have been the sole company which brings the compound through Phase III trials to the market. Speedel is aware that an out-licensed substance is still of strategic value to the licensor. Another potential downside intrinsic to Speedel's model is that the licensor may fail to exercise its call-back option, damaging the compound's reputation as a result: if the originator doesn't recoup the drug, others may assume there are inherent limitations to the compound. Ultimately the call-back option allows both the 'Big Pharma' originator and Speedel to achieve a win-win situation, with both parties sharing risk and reward. Certainly without this type of deal, it would be very difficult for a company like Speedel to acquire compounds and take them all the way to market in large-scale indications such as hypertension.

Conclusion: The out-licensing approach as seen at Novartis enables large pharmaceutical companies to increase their 'shots on goal' without simply enlarging their already significant in-house R&D budgets. The success of the collaboration with Speedel demonstrates how the continuing disintegration of the pharmaceutical value chain creates new partnership models which allow the pharmaceutical company to leverage not only its own core competencies, but also the strengths of its partners.

One of the most notable issues during this collaboration was the fact that Speedel had been a relatively young company which did not have a track record regarding the execution of drug development projects at the time of the deal closure. Thus, Novartis sold the compound Aliskiren to a company for further development although it was not sure whether the partner firm would be able to successfully execute the compound's development. The fact that Speedel's management team had previously been with Novartis was one of the main reasons why Novartis trusted Speedel to be able to turn the substance into a success. In contrast to traditional licensing deals, however, this out-licensing deal has been characterized by a fairly high information asymmetry between the licensor and the licensee regarding the further execution of the compound's development.

4.2 Out-licensing at Schering

In 1999, Schering was in clinical phase II trials for its substance Atamestane which was expected to target prostate cancer in men. During the clinical phase II, Schering decided that the substance should no longer be a part of its portfolio and terminated the project. During the same time, the company Intarcia had identified an unmet medical need in the area of hormonal-based therapies against breast cancer in postmenopausal women. Thus, Intarcia was actively looking for a new substance which could be used for this treatment. As the profile of Schering's substance Atamestane seemed to meet all requirements demanded by Intarcia, Intarcia approached Schering with the request to license the compound. As Schering did not want to miss out on the compound's potential upside, the department for Corporate Business Development at Schering decided to out-license the substance Atamestane to Intarcia. Now, the compound is in Phase III clinical studies at Intarcia and has strong prospects to successfully enter the market in the foreseeable future.

The following chapter 4.2.1 provides a brief overview about the two companies (Schering and Intarcia). Then, Schering's out-licensing strategy is described in more detail in chapter 4.2.2. Chapter 4.2.3 discusses the details of the out-licensing collaboration, and chapter 4.2.4 finally describes the special capabilities of Intarcia which allowed the company to develop the compound while Schering decided to stop its further development.

4.2.1 Company profiles

Schering

Schering, founded in 1851, is engaged in the discovery, development, manufacture, marketing and sale of pharmaceutical products. Headquartered in Berlin, Germany, Schering employs around 26,000 people and has more than 140 subsidiaries worldwide. By reporting revenues of € 4.9 billion for 2004, and a net income of € 500 million, Schering belongs to the large players in the pharmaceutical industry.

The company's revenues in 2004 are split as follows: Schering posted about € 2.5 billion (50%) of sales in Europe, € 1.2 billion (25%) in the USA, and another € 468 million (10%) in Japan. Schering spent about € 0.9 billion on R&D during the same year, and deploys research and development activities in 9 locations in Europe, USA, and Japan.

Schering has four core business areas: gynecology and andrology, specialized therapeutics, diagnostics and radiopharmaceuticals as well as dermatology. In its gynecology and andrology business, Schering offers products for fertility control in women and men, hormone replacement therapy in menopausal women, testosterone therapy in men and the treatment of selected gynecological and andrological diseases. The specialized therapeutics segment offers pharmaceuticals for selected disabling and life-threatening conditions. The diagnostics and radiopharmaceuticals segment offers contrast media for x-ray, magnetic resonance imaging and ultrasound, as well as radiopharmaceuticals for use in nuclear medicine. The dermatology segment provides treatment for severe skin disorders, such as eczema, mycoses, acne, psoriasis and hemorrhoids.

The most successful business areas in 2004 have been the gynecology and andrology business with € 1.8 billion in sales, followed by the specialized therapeutics with € 1.5 billion in sales. The diagnostics and radiopharmaceuticals business was responsible for about € 1.3 billion in revenues, and dermatology accounted for about € 200 million. Schering's best selling products include Betaferon (therapeutics), Yasmin (fertility control), and Magnevist (diagnostics).

Intarcia Therapeutics

Intarcia Therapeutics is a biopharmaceutical company located in Emeryville, California. The company was initally founded in 1995 under the name BioMedicines and started operations in 1997. Today, Intarcia has 35 full-time employees, 25 of whom are engaged in research and development activities or direct support thereof.

Intarcia applies an innovative and targeted approach to the acquisition, development and commercialization of novel therapeutic products for the treatment of cancer and infectious diseases. The company uses its expertise in clinical medicine, pharmaceutical development and regulatory affairs to discover alternate clinical applications or development pathways for clinical stage products with validated mechanisms of action and existing clinical safety and activity data. Intarcia then frequently combines these products with other products or technologies to create new therapeutic products that address significant market needs. In order to execute its business strategy, Intarcia intends to:

- *Acquire products with significant market potential*: This includes the identification, evaluation and purchase of product candidates which can be developed into therapeutics with superior characteristics compared to existing therapies. Intarcia expects that there is usually less competition for product candidates for which alternate clinical applications could have been discovered or development pathways could not have been identified by their originators. This translates in both lower acquisition costs and future financial obligations. In addition, when the company acquires product candidates with validated mechanisms of action and significant existing safety and clinical data, the firm's early clinical development risk is reduced.
- *Advance programs through development*: Intarcia's management team has distinctive expertise in drug development covering biology and clinical medicine, clinical development and regulatory affairs, pharmacology, as well as formulation and drug delivery.
- *Maximize the commercial potential of product candidates*: After product approval, Intarcia intends to maximize the commercial opportunity for the product by either (i) building an own US sales and marketing organization, (ii) establishing strategic collaborations to market products, or (iii) increasing market opportunity by expanding the indications for the firm's therapeutics.

So far, Intarcia has applied its business approach to create and advance two lead clinical programs: Atamestane and omega DUROS®. While Atamestane targets the treatment of hormone-dependent breast cancer in postmenopausal women, omega DUROS® is expected to become a treatment of hepatitis C. In addition to the two programs, Intarcia has two earlier stage programs in development for the treatment of cancer.

Intarcia's management executes the strategies of redirected and expanded development by forming partnerships with multiple partners. Besides the licensing deal with Schering, Intarcia signed different development and/or commercialization agreements with ALZA, Boehringer Ingelheim, and the G.D. Searle subsidiary of Pharmacia (now Pfizer). During its own development activities, Intarcia also relies on third party service providers to conduct the clinical trials for its product candidates. The clinical trials for the development of Atamestane are currently conducted by PAREXEL International Corporation, PRA International and PSI Pharma Support International.

Since the company's inception, Intarcia has principally been funded through the sale of more than $195 million of the company's stock. Investors in the firm include several venture capital firms. First-round investors in 1997 included Brentwood Venture Capital and Delphi Ventures. The second financing round closed in 1999 and included Alta Partners and InterWest Partners in addition to the previous investors. In 2000, Intarcia secured a US$ 38 million mezzanine round of funding. All previous investors participated including the new investors Bay City Capital, Lombard Odie & Cie, as well as Pictet & Cie. In June 2003, the company closed on another financing round where all previous investors participated including Alta BioPharma Partners, NEA and Venrock Associates as new investors. In December 2004, Intarcia raised another US$ 50 million in a Series E financing. The investors included Alta Partners, NEA, Granite Global Venture and Venrock Associates. While Alta Partners, NEA and Venrock had been existing investors, Granite Global Venture made its initial investment into Intarcia. In February 2005, Intarcia filed its S-1 with the Securities and Exchange Commission (SEC) in the US and expects its IPO during fiscal year 2005.

4.2.2 Description of the out-licensing strategy

Integration of out-licensing within the corporation

Out-licensing at Schering is organizationally handled at the department for Corporate Business Development which employs 21 people in total. The department is structured along three functions: (i) Licensing, (ii) Out-licensing, and (iii) the Office of Technology. Most of the department is located in Berlin, Germany. However, the head of Corporate Business Development is based in the US. The Licensing group is mainly dealing with substances in the clinical development stages. The Office of Technology is working primarily with research-related technologies. While both of these groups (Licensing and the Office of Technology) almost exclusively deal with in-licensing activities, there is one expert working on out-licensing issues. However, as out-licensing deals at Schering have significantly increased over the recent past, employees from the other two functions support this group in its out-licensing activities.

Schering's first out-licensing deal ever was the agreement with Intarcia which was reported in 1999 (compared to 13 in-licensing deals during the same year). In 2001, Schering reported its second out-licensing deal (compared to 8 in-licensing deals), and in 2002 the company already posted 3 out-licensing deals (compared to 9 in-licensing deals). This development goes along with Schering's new perspective on out-licensing which has also been presented at the company's 2003 'R&D Day'. Dr. Hubertus Erlen, CEO of Schering, announced that 'an increased strategic focus will be set on out-licensing activities in order to optimize the utilization of the company's assets'. In order to indicate the strategic importance of out-licensing, Schering usually refers to out-licensing as 'out-partnering'. This terminology is expected to highlight that the substance is not merely sold but still remains a joint development initiative.

The major reasons for the decision to proactively pursue out-licensing of drug candidates are mainly strategy-driven or budget-driven. Schering actively supports a strong out-licensing mentality within its R&D department. It is clear to every R&D manager that a substance which cannot be developed in-house any more, should optimally be further pursued by an external partner. The reason is simple: if a drug candidate is not pursued any further, its value immediately drops to zero. Thus, Schering follows the motto 'to take the chance of out-licensing because the company cannot lose anything'. Schering has recognized that the time is over where data are simply archived somewhere in the firm's basement or are kept secret without any potential to create value any more just to keep third parties away from the data. Then, the company misses out on a possible financial participation in case these data might generate some value any time in the future. The cultural change at Schering towards creating a positive mentality for out-licensing was not easy. A few successful examples had to be established in order that the employees started to accept this new policy. Over the past three years, Schering's employees became more open towards the idea that an external partner can complete the development of one of Schering's substances in a very efficient and profitable way. In fiscal year 2004, out-licensing has become – for the first time ever – an own item in the company's budget calculations.

There are generally no restrictions, when a substance should best be out-licensed. The only criteria is the profitable completion of the project. However, Schering determines already at quite early stages of each project's lifecycle if a product should be pursued internally, terminated or licensed out. Thereby, Schering bases its projections on risk-adjusted NPV calculations. At the time of writing, about 70% of the out-licensing projects did stem from the company's research, whereas the remaining 30% derived from development, production, or marketing. This focus on an early stage classification tries to minimize development costs as well as other resources as soon as possible. The risks of rising costs at later stages of development are consequently the primary reason of the desire to license out. At the time of writing,

Schering was involved in 6 out-licensing deals. However, as there have not been up-front or milestone payments involved in any of these out-licensing collaborations but royalty revenue payments instead, it cannot be determined by now how successful these collaborations have been because the respective substances have not entered the market yet.

Out-licensing as a 9-step process

Schering's out-licensing process is structured into three phases (presentation, transaction, and implementation). Each phase again consists of different steps. In total, the out-licensing process at Schering comprises nine steps (see Fig. 29).

After the portfolio management board has made the decision to out-license a substance to an external partner, the first phase of the out-licensing process begins. During this phase (presentation phase), Schering identifies potential partner firms by giving non-confidential presentations about the opportunities of potential out-licensing candidates. The company also proactively publishes a list with out-licensing offerings on its website (compare Table 4). After a potential interesting partner could be found for a substance, Schering signs confidentiality agreements which lay the foundation for further negotiations and the presentation of confidential project information. The presentation phase usually ends with some kind of mutual understanding of the two partners about the substance, so that the first steps of the transaction can be started.

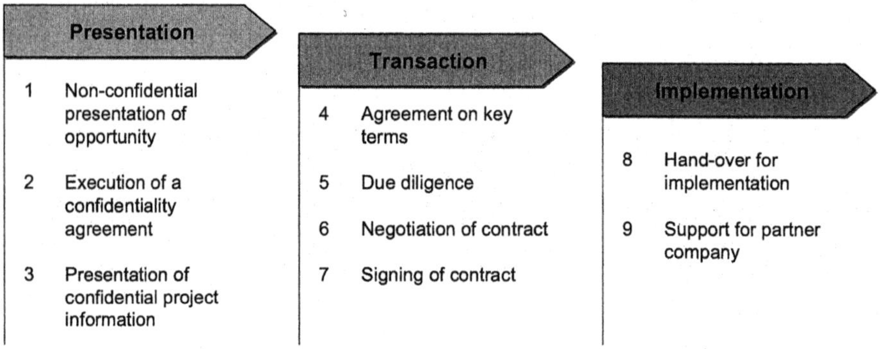

Fig. 29. Out-licensing process at Schering.

Table 4. Out-licensing offerings at Schering (as of November 2004).

Project	Targeted Indication	Territory
Project status: Phase III / in registration		
Abecarnil, β-carboline BDZ partial agonist, oral	Anxiety disorders	Worldwide excl. Scandinavia
Nebido™, testosterone undecanoate, i.m.	Primary and secondary hypogonadism	USA
Project status: Phase II		
Iloprost, prostacyclin derivate, oral	Osteonecrosis and other bone and joint diseases	Worldwide
Project status: Pre-clinical		
4-thio-FAC, deoxycytidine analog, i.v.	Pancreatic and non-small cell lung cancer	Worldwide
Antiestrogen, selective estrogen receptor downregulator, oral	Breast cancer	Worldwide
ADP (adenosine diphosphate), receptor antagonist, oral	Prevention and treatment of atrial thrombosis	Worldwide
MS-377, sigma-1 opioid antagonist, oral	Schizophrenia	Worldwide
Project status: Technology		
Target-specific ultrasound contrast agent technology	Diagnosis of disease on molecular level	Worldwide
Ultrasound contrast agent quantification technology	In-vivo sono-immunohistology in conjunction with target-specific ultrasound contrast agent	Worldwide

The first task during the transaction phase is then to find an agreement around key terms of the deal. Afterwards, the actual due diligence process can start. The two partners meet to discuss the exact utilization opportunities of the substance including its chances and risks. If the licensee still shows interest in the substance, the contract is usually elaborated and finalized before it can ultimately be signed by both partners.

During the implementation phase the substance including all relevant documentation is handed over and Schering ensures active support for the partner company. The latter is a very important step of the out-licensing process because Schering knows that it can only benefit from the out-licensing deal itself if the substance enters the market successfully. For this reason, Schering deploys a steering committee which supervises the collaborations' progress on a periodical basis.

The out-licensing process at Schering takes about 10 months, whereas the due diligence requires most of the time. As the due diligence also requires significant resources from Schering, the company tries to define the key terms of the deal as soon as possible. In order to justify the costs for the out-licensing process, Schering does not get involved in deals with a deal size of less than € 500.000.

4.2.3 Structure of the out-licensing collaboration

In February 1999, Schering and Intarcia entered into a license agreement for the exclusive worldwide license rights to Atamestane for the treatment of hormone-dependent breast cancer. Atamestane is an aromatase inhibitor which is now being developed in combination with toremifene, an approved estrogen receptor blocker, for the treatment of hormone-dependent breast cancer in postmenopausal women.[29] At the time of the licensing deal, Atamestane had passed the IND (investigational new drug) approval by the FDA already. Intarcia's current US intellectual property protection relating to the Atamestane combination program consists primarily of the US patent licensed from Schering relating to Atamestane. However, this patent is due to expire on June 18, 2005, having been extended by one year from its original expiration date. In order to utilize the exclusivity provided by the Atamestane patent, Intarcia must obtain FDA approval of the combination product candidate before the Atamestane patent expires. Intarcia has already filed US and foreign patent applications relating to the Atamestane combination program but the patents have not been granted yet.

The licensing agreement between Schering and Intarcia is also subject to Schering's options to co-promote Atamestane in the United States and to market Atamestane outside the United States exclusively. Schering agreed to provide Intarcia with access to historical data and its remaining bulk drug inventory, to collaborate with Intarcia to improve manufacturing processes and to develop a source of commercial supply. In addition, Schering has agreed to become the commercial manufacturer of Atamestane. Pursuant to the license agreement, Intarcia paid Schering an upfront cash fee and agreed to make milestone payments of up to $5.25 million based on the

29 Breast cancer is the most common cancer in women. In the US, there are an estimated two million patients diagnosed with breast cancer. There are approximately one million postmenopausal women in the US diagnosed with hormone-dependent breast cancer. Approximately 130,000 postmenopausal women in the United States are diagnosed each year with hormone-dependent breast cancer, where estrogen is the primary driver of tumor growth, and an estimated 40,000 US patients are diagnosed with advanced breast cancer annually. Worldwide sales of hormonal therapies for breast cancer exceeded US$1.2 billion in 2004 and is projected to grow to more than US$2.5 billion by 2007.

success of the development program. While Intarcia has the right to make the final decision on all matters pertaining to the development program other than matters related to human safety, Intarcia periodically updates Schering on the substance's development progress. With respect to matters relating to human safety during clinical testing of Atamestane, decisions are made jointly. As part of the deal, Intarcia was also able to acquire sufficient clinical drug supplies of the product candidate to efficiently proceed into clinical trials. The structure of the out-licensing deal is illustrated in Fig. 30.

While Atamestane was still in development at Schering, it targeted prostate cancer in men. During that time, Schering had already generated significant clinical activity and safety data across several disease indications. Schering had conducted clinical trials of Atamestane in approximately 900 patients for the treatment of benign prostatic hyperplasia, an enlargement of the prostate gland in men. Since the estrogen production pathway in men is identical to the estrogen production pathway in postmenopausal women, Intarcia utilized the existing data to change the targeted indication from prostate cancer in men to breast cancer in women, because the entire safety database could have been used for Intarcia's clinical development. Schering

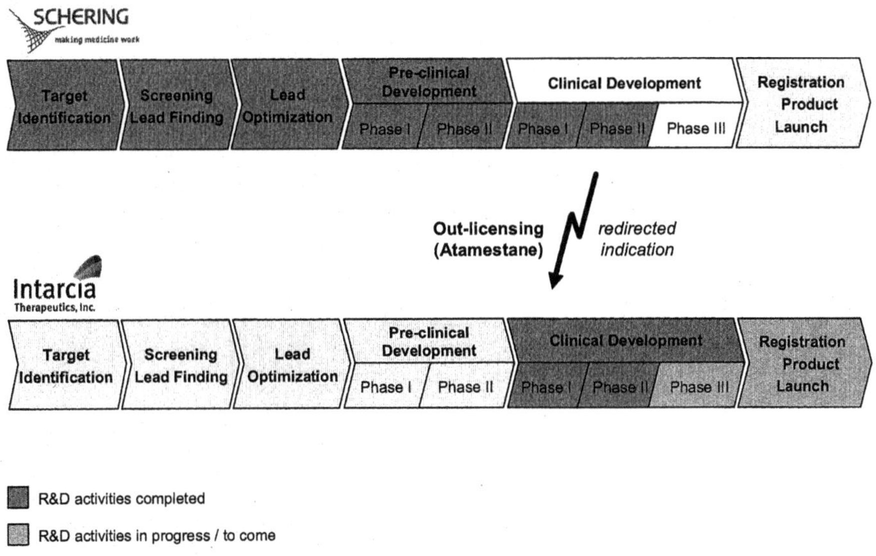

Fig. 30. Out-licensing collaboration between Schering and Intarcia.

also had performed a Phase II multi-center clinical trial evaluating Atamestane in women with recurrent advanced breast cancer who had progressed while on Tamoxifen and showed that Atamestane is active as second line hormonal therapy in women with recurrent hormone dependent advanced breast cancer. In this trial, Atamestane significantly lowered estrogen levels and delayed tumor growth for a median of seven months, suggesting anti-tumor activity.

After having in-licensed the compound, Intarcia started to redirect the indication of Atamestane to an orally bioavailable endocrine treatment for breast cancer. While Schering had already conducted clinical Phase II trials for Atamestane, Intarcia still had to conduct a number of preclinical studies and a Phase Ia clinical trial evaluating the combination in healthy postmenopausal women due to the compound's changed indication. Intarcia completed the clinical Phase I testing in normal volunteers. Phase II clinical testing has also been successfully completed with a multicenter trial conducted in Germany in women with breast cancer recurring despite prior treatment with a different anti-breast cancer drug (Tamoxifen).

Intarcia is currently conducting Phase III clinical development of Atamestane. The company expects to have data from the first of two ongoing Phase III clinical trials in the first half of 2006. Both of the Phase III clinical trials cover 840 patients and compare this novel combination of Atamestane and toremifene to Femara (letrozole), an already approved aromatase inhibitor. The patients in Phase III are being treated with the combined therapy for 9-18 months in 60 different centers across 4 different countries. If the Phase III trials are successful, Intarcia intends to file a New Drug Application (NDA) for approval of Atamestane in combination with toremifene. In addition, if data from the first Phase III trial are positive, the company intends to initiate additional clinical trials to evaluate the combination therapy in the adjuvant breast cancer setting.

Regarding the commercialization of the substance, Intarcia intends to build its own sales and marketing organization in order to co-promote the combination therapy in the United States with a major pharmaceutical or biotechnology partner. The company believes that it can effectively market the combination therapy in the United States with an 80 to 100 person sales force targeting medical oncologists in the United States. Intarcia plans to seek a partner to exclusively market the combination therapy outside the United States. However, Schering has options to co-promote the combination therapy with Intarcia in the United States and to market it exclusively outside the United States. Schering may exercise either or both of its options at any time prior to 90 days after Intarcia has delivered to Schering the audited final clinical study report for the first Phase III trial. If Schering elects to exercise both of these options, it will assume full financial and decision-making responsibility for all further development activities, reimburse Intarcia for development costs that have incurred to Intarcia prior to exercise and make additional payments to Intarcia upon product approval. In addition, Intarcia will receive a royalty from Schering on sales outside the United States and expects to share equally in the profits from joint commercialization in the United States. If Schering chooses not to exercise one or both of the options, Intarcia will be required to pay Schering royalties on commercial sales by Intarcia or its affiliated marketing partners in the applicable territory.

4.2.4 Capabilities of the out-licensing partner

As Intarcia took a substance into development which Schering decided to terminate, Intarcia must be characterized by some capabilities and competencies regarding the compound's further development which Schering, in turn, does not seem to possess.

Intarcia claims that one of the most important characteristics that differentiate the company from larger pharmaceutical companies includes its high flexibility. Due to its small size and mission to redirect the indication of licensed compounds, the company is much better able to analyze and determine the maximum value potential of a compound. Intarcia can be more creative in finding delivery techniques in concert with other state-of-the-art technology platforms. According to Intarcia, the approach to 'think outside of the box' allows for more innovative ways to bring new drug candidates to market and, therefore, to commercialize research results. The commitment towards innovation at Intarcia is also expressed by the company's entrepreneurial culture which is highlighted by its highly venture-capital funded ownership structure as well as several equity incentive plans which entitle the employees to participate in the company's – and therefore Atamestane's – future success.

In addition, Intarcia believes that its ability to identify opportunities for its licensed drug candidates yield valuable insights that permit the firm to acquire, develop and commercialize its product candidates more rapidly and with significantly lower costs than traditional approaches to drug development. Moreover, the strategy of redirected development is often the most efficient and cost-effective means of advancing drugs rapidly into late stage development and commercialization. Therefore, Intarcia's strategy is not only innovative but also cost-effective.

Another characteristic which allows Intarcia to pursue the further development of Atamestane even after Schering decided to cancel the project is Intarcia's relatively small size. As a result, Intarcia is able to focus on much smaller markets which might be considered too small by some larger firms, such as Schering. Due to Intarcia's highly venture capital-backed ownership structure and its denotation as a biotechnology company, all shareholders and stakeholders expect the company to take on higher risks than in the case of a traditionally integrated pharmaceutical company. Although Intarcia slightly reduced its overall risk exposure via diversification by filling its pipeline with four projects, the company remains a high-risk business.

Conclusion: Intarcia took over full control over Atamestane by licensing the compound from Schering which also includes the burden of carrying the risks associated with the compound's further development. At the same time, Schering retained an interest in the compound's further development and will benefit accordingly if the drug might enter the market in the future. However, by out-licensing the compound, Schering did not have to carry the respective R&D risks any more.

Compared to Schering, Intarcia is a young and small company. At the time of the licensing deal, the company had just been set up and the firm still only employs around 35 people today. However, Intarcia in-licensed a compound from Schering that was supposed to enter the clinical phases which are usually very cost-intensive and require comprehensive trials. This raised the question at the time of the deal closure if Intarcia would be able to conduct the required development activities despite its small size and the lack of a respective track record. Regarding the further development, this out-licensing collaboration has thus been characterized by a comparatively high degree of asymmetric information between the licensor and licensee.

4.3 Out-licensing at Roche

In 1997, Roche was restructuring its cardiovascular therapy area following the takeover of Boehringer Mannheim. During the restructuring, Roche decided to terminate the further development of some compounds because of strategic reasons. This included the substance Bosentan which still had prospects to become a market success but did not fit into Roche's portfolio strategy any more because the substance's indication was considered to be too small (Brunner 2002). A number of Roche managers around Jean-Paul Clozel – then Vice President in Roche's cardiovascular department – approached Roche's CEO Dr. Franz Humer about spinning off the research project into a separate company. Humer gave his blessing but made clear that Roche would not put up any money and would retain the intellectual property of the substance Bosentan. Clozel and three other Roche managers set up the company Actelion, secured venture funding and in-licensed the substance Bosentan from Roche. Today, the substance Bosentan is approved and marketed in most major markets in the world under the brand Tracleer®. Both Actelion and Roche were able to benefit from the revenues incurred from a compound which might still be languishing in Roche's lab if the company would not have out-licensed it to Actelion.

Chapter 4.3.1 provides a brief overview about the two companies (Roche and Actelion). Then, the out-licensing strategy of Roche is described in more detail in chapter 4.3.2. Afterwards, chapter 4.3.3 discusses the details of the out-licensing agreement.[30] Finally, chapter 4.3.4 describes the special competencies of Actelion which enabled the firm to successfully bring the substance Bosentan to market approval while Roche did not want to pursue this opportunity any more.

4.3.1 Company profiles

Roche

Founded in 1896 in Basel, Switzerland, by Fritz Hoffmann, Roche was one of the world's first pharmaceutical manufacturers. Today, Roche is a leading healthcare company that is active in the discovery, development, manufacture and marketing of novel healthcare solutions in two core businesses: pharmaceuticals and diagnostics. In 2004, Roche sold its consumer health business for CHF 3.7 billion to Bayer. Roche employs around 65,000 people and has operations in approximately 150 countries. In 2004, Roche posted total revenues of CHF 29.5 billion. The pharmaceutical business accounted for CHF 21.7 billion whereas the diagnostics business contributed the remaining CHF 7.8 billion. Roche's net income for fiscal year 2004 was CHF 4.3 billion.

Roche deploys research centers worldwide including the following locations: Basel (Switzerland), Penzberg (Germany), Nutley and Palo Alto (USA). In addition, Roche participates in the research conducted by the pharmaceutical company Chugai (Japan) and the biotech firm Genentech (USA) through significant equity interests. In 2004, Roche invested around CHF 4.4 billion in research and development (including R&D investments of Genentech and Chugai).

30 As some information about the licensing agreement were not authorized for disclosure by the parties involved in the licensing deal, the case study only refers to authorized data as well as publicly available information.

Roche's pharmaceutical division offers a portfolio of medicines in various therapeutic areas, including anemia, cardiovascular diseases, central nervous system, dermatology, infectious diseases, inflammatory and autoimmune diseases, metabolic disorders, oncology, respiratory diseases, transplantation, and virology. In 2004, the pharmaceuticals division posted four major product launches (Avastin, Tarceva, Boniva, and Xeloda), and had 64 new molecular entities in the pipeline. The key brands of Roche's pharmaceuticals division in 2004 (including their respective product sales) have been MabThera/Rituxan (CHF 3.4 billion), NeoRecormon/Epogin (CHF 2.1 billion), Pegasys/Copegus (CHF 1.6 billion), Herceptin (CHF 1.4 billion), CellCept (CHF 1.4 billion), and Rocephin (CHF 1.3 billion).

The company's diagnostic division supplies an array of testing products and services to researchers, physicians, patients, hospitals and laboratories worldwide. Its products and services address prevention, diagnosis, treatment and the monitoring of diseases. Roche is the global market leader in diagnostics having a market share of 21%. Major competitors including their market share include Abbott (12%), Johnson&Johnson (11%), Bayer (8%), Beckman C. (8%), and Dade Behring (6%).

At the end of 2004, Roche's R&D pipeline comprised 107 research projects and 79 development projects across all targeted therapy areas.

Actelion

Actelion is an independent biopharmaceutical company with its corporate headquarters in Allschwil/Basel, Switzerland. The company was founded in late 1997 by four previous Roche managers. Actelion's vision centers around the principle to combine the best attributes of both the biotech and pharmaceutical industries by blending biotech innovation, speed and flexibility with pharma discipline in drug development, regulatory and marketing.

Actelion focuses on the discovery, development and marketing of innovative drugs for significant unmet medical needs. The company is a leading player in innovative science related to the endothelium – the single layer of cells separating every blood vessel from the blood stream. Actelion employs around 840 people and recorded CHF 471.9 million in sales and an operating income of CHF 85.6 million in 2004. Actelion has global subsidiaries in key markets in Europe (Austria, France, Germany, Greece, Italy, Spain, Switzerland, UK and Ireland, Nordic countries and the Netherlands), North America (USA and Canada), Latin America (Brazil) and Asia Pacific (Australia and Japan). Actelion's strategy centers around three key elements:

- Maximization of research and development efforts by either discovering or in-licensing a steady stream of new products. Actelion also aims to maximize the value of its products, for example, by seeking additional indications for existing drugs.
- Retention of significant share of value by maintaining substantial market rights to Actelion's products in selected markets which might include partnering with other pharmaceutical or biopharmaceutical companies.
- Maintenance of a culture focused on innovation.

A few months after its inception, Actelion secured its first round of funding. In May 1998, Actelion announced the closing of a CHF 18 million (US$ 12 million) round of equity financing. Provided by an international syndicate of several of the leading venture capital firms in the area of lifescience investments in Europe, the transaction constituted one of the largest early stage private equity financings ever to occur on the continent in this area at that time. Under the co-leadership of Atlas Venture (NL, F, D, US, UK) and Sofinnova (F, US), the investor consortium comprised 3i (UK, D), TVM Techno Venture Management (D), Genevest (CH) as well as a few Swiss private investors.

Only ten months after announcing its initial financing, Actelion disclosed in March 1999 the conclusion of a new major financing round. The funding amounts to CHF 48 million (US$ 34 million) and is structured as a CHF 38 million equity investment and a CHF 10 million bank credit facility. With this operation, Actelion had raised financing of nearly CHF 70 million (US$ 50 million) in its first operating year. This represents one of the largest funding amounts ever obtained by a new lifescience company in such a short period. The first round investors provided one third of the new equity, the rest being raised from new investors from six countries. TVM Techno Venture Management GmbH, Munich, coordinated the round. BKB Basler Kantonalbank, Basel, provided the credit facility. Proceeds from the new funding had mainly been used to finance the clinical development of the compounds Bosentan and Ro 61-0612, and also supported work on Actelion's own discovery projects.

In April 2000, Actelion took advantage of favorable market conditions in the public equity markets, and offered its stock in an IPO on the Swiss Stock Exchange (SWX) (ticker symbol: ATLN). With an issue price of CHF 260, Actelion managed to gather a strong book, the offering being 19 times oversubscribed. Under the lead management of Credit Suisse First Boston, Actelion offered 900,000 registered shares with a par value of CHF 10. A further 100,000 registered shares are reserved for issuance subject to the exercise of an overallotment option. In total, there are 4,633,860 outstanding shares in Actelion. The IPO resulted in net proceeds for Actelion of around CHF 200 million (US$ 148 million).

4.3.2 Description of the out-licensing strategy

Integration of out-licensing within the corporation

Out-licensing at Roche is organizationally embedded into the Pharma-Partnering department which directly reports to the head of the pharmaceutical division at Roche. Within the Pharma-Partnering department there are three groups responsible for (i) licensing, (ii) business development and (iii) alliance management. The out-licensing activities are located within the licensing group (see Fig. 31).

The out-licensing process at Roche is straightforward. The Product Development Meeting (PDM) – which is one of three major committees at Roche responsible for

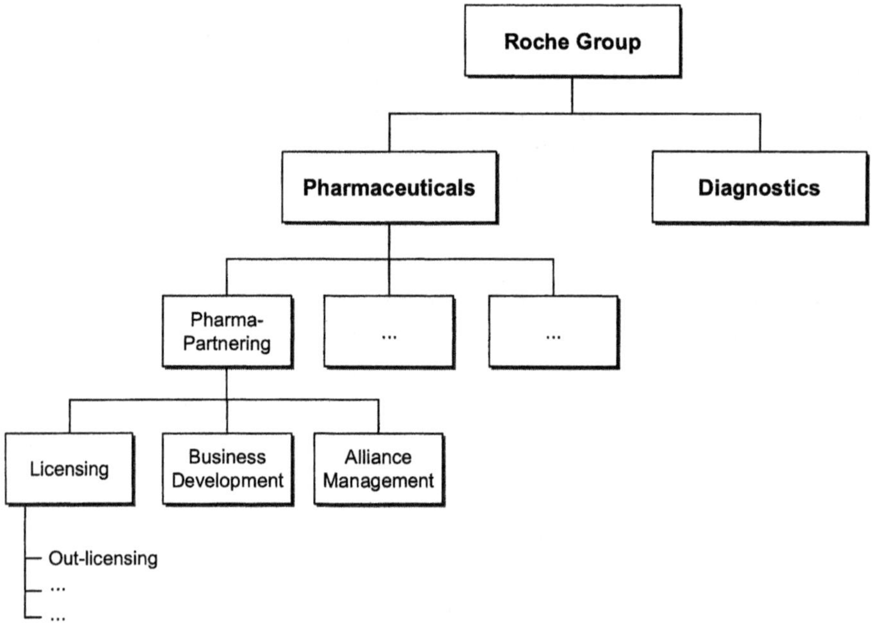

Fig. 31. Organizational integration of out-licensing within Roche.

all major portfolio decisions – determines the substances in Roche's portfolio which might potentially be out-licensed. The PDM hands over the information about potential licensing candidates to the out-licensing team which consists of two persons who are exclusively working on out-licensing and directly report to the Global Head of Licensing & Alliances who is located in Basel, Switzerland. The job of the two out-licensing specialists is to manage all out-licensing projects at Roche which includes to decide about the type and structure of the out-licensing deal. After having received the decision from the PDM that a substance could be out-licensed, the out-licensing experts start to develop strategies, performance criteria and collaboration structures for each out-licensing deal.

The team of out-licensing experts is also responsible to find potential licensing partners. In order to identify partners, the team relies on publicly available databases as well as internal administration systems. If a potential partner has been found, a so-called negotiator joins the team who organizationally belongs to the licensing group as well. The negotiator escorts the entire negotiation process until the deal is closed. During the due diligence, another expert from the alliance management group joins the out-licensing team and the negotiator. This alliance manager supports during the integration of the out-licensing project into the external company, and will remain the point of contact for the partner company after the deal has been closed. The alliance manager coordinates the flow of information and other services related to the licensed compound from Roche to the external partner. This ensures not only the contact to the partner firm and control over the outflowing information, but also allows the observation of the progress of the compound's development at the licensee.

The entire out-licensing process (from the decision of the PDM to the closing of the deal) usually takes up to 9 months. The time per deal that is devoted to out-licensing is about as high as the time devoted to in-licensing. As the employees who are involved in the out-licensing project are usually blocked for any other activity within Roche, Roche only out-licenses substances which are expected to have a high potential for value creation. In 2004, Roche closed five out-licensing deals.

Rationale and decision for out-licensing

As described earlier, the decision which substances should be out-licensed is made in accordance with general strategic portfolio decisions made by the Product Development Meeting (PDM). The PDM uses extensive NPV calculations and warranted value models to concretize a compound's expected performance and profit estimates. Another key figure used by Roche to analyze the value of a substance is the operating profit after capital charges (OPAC). This analysis illustrates the strategic positioning of every compound in the portfolio which allows the justification of an out-licensing decision. Only if a compound is considered to be non-critical and does not need to be developed completely internally, Roche is about to get involved in an out-licensing deal. Consequently, Roche uses out-licensing in a rather short-term and tactial way.

As a result of the decisions made by the PDM, Roche considers to out-license substances which target markets that might be too small to be explored by Roche itself, or where the drug's potential is too insecure. However, Roche usually does not consider very late stage projects to be attractive for out-licensing because the investments already made in the drug's development are not in a favorable relation to the potential profits. Another reason for out-licensing includes that the development time might be too long, and the drug is expected to face intensive competition at the time it enters the market. Last but not least, a rationale for out-licensing could be the fact that other substances in the portfolio simply have a larger sales potential even if the substance which is about to be out-licensed also has good prospects to become a market success.

In general, Roche's portfolio of out-licensing deals comprises projects with call-back option, without a call-back option, or out-licensing collaborations which are similar to traditional alliances. Roche usually applies call-back options only for projects which are done with smaller partners. Larger partners are mostly not willing to give a substance back after they successfully completed its development. Besides the call-back option, another advantage of out-licensing to a smaller firm is that the partner firm is very dedicated to the substance's development and usually devotes most of its resources to the licensed compound. Roche expects that this type of focus can lead to a significant reduction in development time. However, the amount of upfront payments flowing from the licensee to Roche is usually smaller due to the limited financial capacity of the partner firm.

4.3.3 Structure of the out-licensing collaboration

In November 1998, Actelion announced that it had obtained the exclusive license from Roche for the clinical development of the compound Bosentan (Ro 47-0203), the first orally active endothelin receptor antagonist. At the time of licensing, Bosentan was in Phase III clinical development at Roche for congestive heart failure and had been tested at more than 800 subjects with various diseases. Phase II results had shown impressive hemodynamic effects with the compound in patients with

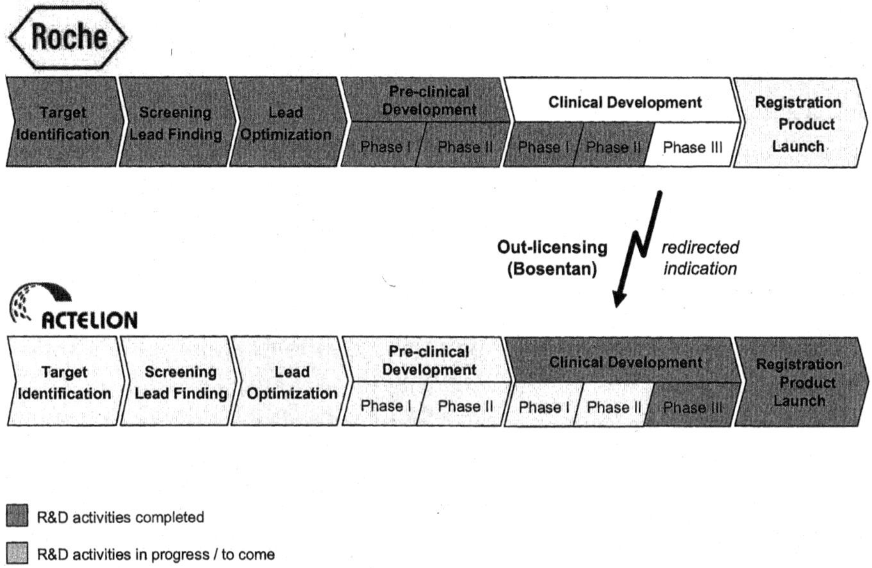

Fig. 32. Out-licensing collaboration between Roche and Actelion.

moderate to severe heart failure. In 1999, Actelion started Phase III clinical development of Bosentan (see Fig. 32). However, Actelion changed the compound's initial indication. Instead of still targeting congestive heart failure, Actelion started trials with patients suffering from pulmonary hypertension. As pulmonary hypertension represents a more severe disease than congestive heart failure, potential side effects are considered relatively less important, which in turn could increase the drug's probability of receiving market approval. Under the licensing agreement, Roche had the option to take back the compound upon completion of Phase III (see Actelion 2004a).

The substance Bosentan is an orally active dual endothelin receptor antagonist (ERA). The compound works by blocking the binding of endothelin (ET) to both of its receptors, ET_A and ET_B, thereby preventing the deleterious effects of ET. As a dual ERA, blocking both ET receptors, this treatment has a unique potential compared to selective agents currently in development, which only block receptor type ET_A. ET is produced and secreted by the endothelium, a single layer of cells covering the inner surface of blood vessels. ET not only regulates blood flow by causing blood vessels to narrow (vasoconstriction), but also causes other deleterious effects, such as stiffening blood vessels (fibrosis), changing their shape (remodeling) and size (hypertrophy), and predisposing them to inflammation. The over-production of ET as a key pathogenic mediator plays a critical role in chronic diseases such as connective tissue diseases (e.g. scleroderma), pulmonary fibrosis, acute heart failure, and pulmonary arterial hypertension (PAH).

Particularly pulmonary arterial hypertension (PAH) represents a chronic, life-threatening disorder, which severely compromises the function of the lungs and heart. Patients diagnosed with pulmonary hypertension have only a 50% chance to be alive 5 years after the diagnosis. Bosentan improves the PAH patient's exercise capacity, such as the ability to perform daily activities without becoming short of breath, and reduces clinical worsening, improving the patient's quality of life. PAH is a progressive disease, characterized by abnormally high blood pressure in the blood vessels which supply the lungs. The first signs of PAH, such as mild shortness of breath (dyspnea), fatigue and difficulty exercising, are so subtle that the disease is often either misdiagnosed or not diagnosed until the patient's condition is far advanced. Approximately 100,000 people in Europe and the United States are afflicted with either primary pulmonary arterial hypertension or secondary forms of the disease related to tissue disorders or other conditions that affect the lungs, such as scleroderma, lupus, HIV/AIDS or congenital heart disease (Actelion 2004b).

In 2000, Actelion received orphan drug designation for Bosentan in the treatment of pulmonary arterial hypertension by the FDA in the US. In the same year, Actelion filed the New Drug Application (NDA) for Bosentan with the FDA. The approval by the FDA for Bosentan has been granted in 2001, and the drug has subsequently been marketed under the brand name Tracleer® (Bosentan) for the oral treatment of pulmonary arterial hypertension (PAH). After Tracleer® had been introduced on the US market, Actelion started to file for market approval in other countries including Switzerland, and the European Union. Approval by the EU has been granted in 2002. The marketing authorization was valid for all of the then 15 EU member states and has also been recognized by Norway and Iceland. At the time of writing, additional approvals had been granted in Australia and Japan. The fact that Actelion filed for Bosentan's market approvals on its own implies that Roche did not make use of its call-back option after the successful completion of Phase III.

The drug Tracleer® has turned out to be a market success. Sales for Tracleer® in 2004 have been CHF 449.2 million, and no competitor from the same class of drugs is close to launching a similar competing product. As PAH is a rapidly progressing disease, Actelion estimates the drug's peak sales to reach between US$ 400 – 500 million by 2006 (Actelion 2005). Due to the success of Tracleer®, Actelion has chosen not only to expand Tracleer®'s use in PAH, but also to evaluate Tracleer®'s potential beyond PAH. Actelion launched additional development programs to establish the effect of Bosentan in scleroderma, an autoimmune disease afflicting up to 200,000 patients worldwide, and in complications of this disease such as pulmonary fibrosis and digital ulcerations. A preliminary safety analysis of a first pilot study evaluating Bosentan's efficacy and safety in patients with an advanced form of spreading skin cancer (metastatic melanoma) seems to indicate that Bosentan is well tolerated. Efficacy analysis is ongoing. With these new orphan indications, the peak sales of Tracleer® could potentially be doubled or tripled. While the initially targeted indication of Tracleer® (i.e. PAH) would never allow the drug to become a blockbuster because of the fairly small market size of PAH, the drug's new indications might enable the substance Bosentan to surpass the US$ 1 billion mark in total revenues achieved. Phase III results of the digital ulcers indication are expected to be completed in the second half of 2005, whereas Phase II/III results for idiopathic pulmonary fibrosis and pulmonary fibrosis related to scleroderma are expected to be completed by the end of 2005 or beginning of 2006 (Actelion 2004c).

The licensing deal has not only paid off for Actelion but also for Roche, because Roche is participating in Tracleer®'s success as well. While Roche would have stopped the substance's further development, Bosentan is now creating value for both Roche and its partner Actelion as well as patients suffering from PAH. According to Business Week (2002), the licensing deal entitles Roche to a nearly 10% cut of sales. Based on Tracleer®'s sales in 2004, this equates to around CHF 45 million in additional royalty revenues which would not have incurred if the substance would have never been out-licensed.

4.3.4 Capabilities of the out-licensing partner

As Actelion was able to successfully bring the substance Bosentan to market approval and launch, the company must be characterized by some special capabilities and competencies which enabled the firm to execute the compound's development while Roche decided not to pursue the compound's development any more.

Compared to Roche, Actelion is a fairly small and entrepreneurial company. At the time when the out-licensing deal was closed, Actelion was just a few months old and had only secured its first round of venture capital funding which consisted of a CHF 18 million equity investment. Another indicator of Actelion's entrepreneurial culture includes that the management's compensation is strictly tied to the company's success. As of June 2004, Actelion's management was holding 13.1% of the outstanding shares (see Actelion 2004c). Despite the company's comparatively small size, Actelion has built a unique platform with a global reach in key areas of regulatory affairs and sales and marketing. The company has created an opportunistic yet scientific corporate culture of 'drug hunters' with the ability to aggressively apply resources while managing risk (Sovereign 2005).

Actelion itself claims that speed and efficiency have been the major success factors of the development of Bosentan (see Actelion 2004d). It took Actelion only 26 months from the first trials to market approval. A major element of efficiency has been the company's disciplined financial management which was responsible for moving Actelion towards the biotech industry average of generating net margins in the range of 20% to 25% (Sovereign 2005). Actelion's performance in the development of Bosentan reflects the company's vision to marry the best attributes of the biotech and pharmaceutical industries by blending biotech innovation, speed and flexibility with pharma discipline in drug development, regulatory and marketing (Actelion 2004d).

The efficiency in drug development has translated into a unique price differentiation of the drug Tracleer® compared to its nearest rival, GlaxoSmithKline's Flolan. While a year's supply of Flolan costs around US$ 100,000, Tracleer® costs only US$ 28,000 (compare Business Week 2002). In addition, Tracleer® does not only differ from Flolan in terms of the price, but also in terms of administration. While Flolan must be administered through a catheter, Tracleer is the first PAH drug to be taken orally.

Conclusion: Out-licensing at Roche has a clear mission and position inside the company. The out-licensing deal with Actelion gave Roche the opportunity to bring a substance to the market which the company had initially stopped. Actelion used its special development capabilities, changed the substance's indication and turned the compound into a marketed product. Tracleer® (Bosentan) is now creating value not only for Actelion but also for Roche although Roche did not have to face any additional operating risks regarding the substance's further development.

Although Actelion is on its way to become a fairly established biopharmaceutical company, the firm was in its infancy at the time when the out-licensing deal had been closed. Due to the lack of a track record, it was fairly difficult for Roche to determine Actelion's likelihood of being able to successfully develop the substance Bosentan. While it was helpful that Actelion's founders and most of the initial management team had been working with Roche before setting up Actelion, the partner firm's newness led to the situation that the out-licensing deal was characterized by an asymmetric distribution of information between the licensor and the licensee regarding the probability that the licensee will be able to execute the compound's further development.

4.4 Summary

This chapter aggregates the commonalities and differences of the analyzed out-licensing collaborations which represent the basis for further discussion including the derivation of the managerial recommendations. Table 5 illustrates the most relevant characteristics of the analyzed out-licensing collaborations. The table has been classified into characteristics that are related to the pharmaceutical company, the collaboration and the partner company respectively.

Table 5. Characteristics of the analyzed out-licensing collaborations.

	Novartis – Speedel (Aliskiren)	**Schering – Intarcia (Atamestane)**	**Roche – Actelion (Bosentan)**
Pharma Company			
Out-licensing concept	tactical	strategic	tactical
Out-licensing responsibility	BD&L department	BD&L department	Pharma-Partnering
Out-licensing impetus	external (from prev. Novartis managers)	external (from partner company)	external (from prev. Roche managers)
Out-licensing proceeding	clearly defined	clearly defined	clearly defined
Collaboration			
Stage of the out-licensing deal	before clinical phases	after IND approval	after Phase II
Indication of the substance after closure of licensing deal	same indication	changed indication	changed indication

Table 5. (continued).

Existence of call-back options	yes	yes, for marketing outside the US, and for co-promotion inside the US	yes
Status of call-back option today	call-back option exercised after Phase II	substance still in development at licensee	call-back option not exercised
Partner Company			
Special characteristics	highly focused on few selected therapy areas	highly focused on few selected therapy areas	focus on one system (endothelin)
Partner's size relative to pharma firm's size	small	small	small
Year of inception	1998	1997 (orig. under the name BioMedicines)	1997
Ownership structure	venture capital funded (appr. CHF 120 mn.)	venture capital funded (US$ 195 mn.; IPO expected during 2005)	venture capital funded (CHF 66 mn.; further CHF 200 mn. from IPO in 2000)

Characteristics of the pharmaceutical companies

The case studies revealed that out-licensing seems to be a rather need- and occasion-driven activity than a strategic and high-priority task. Most large pharmaceutical companies typically place much more emphasis and efforts on in-licensing in order to fill potential gaps in their development pipeline instead of commercializing terminated R&D projects. While out-licensing at Novartis and Roche could be considered rather tactical, only Schering adopted a proactive and strategic out-licensing concept. Schering's CEO even declared on the company's 2003 'R&D Day' that out-licensing will become an important strategic task at Schering.

The out-licensing activities at the analyzed pharmaceutical companies are organizationally well handled. All companies assign dedicated resources to out-licensing and set up a distinct group of people who are responsible for out-licensing. However, the licensing impetus still seems to be rather passive. All companies have been approached by the external partners with the request to get involved in the out-licensing deal. In the case of Novartis and Roche, the companies have been approached by previous executives. The out-licensing process at all three analyzed companies is clearly defined.

Characteristics of the collaboration

All out-licensing deals have been signed at particularly late stages, that is during the development stages. The most important criterion that has to be passed by the substance in order to become an attractive out-licensing object seems to be the IND (Investigational New Drug) approval. The IND approval is filed with the FDA prior to the clinical trials of a new drug (i.e. before the substance enters the human body and after it has completed the pre-clinical studies). It gives already a full and comprehensive description of the new drug.

In two out of the three cases, the substance's indication has been changed. Changing a substance's indication can have a significant impact on its development potential. If a substance is applied for a different indication which is expected to treat a more severe disease, the change will most likely allow for more severe side-effects. As a consequence, side-effects which might not have been acceptable for the old indication might be acceptable under the new indication. Only Speedel continued to target the same indication as the substance Aliskiren had already targeted when it was still inside Novartis.

The licensing agreements all included call-back options by the pharmaceutical companies. While Novartis exercised its call-back option after the successful completion of Phase II, Roche seems to have its option let expired. Actelion introduced the substance Bosentan on the market by itself. Schering has a structured 2-fold re-licensing option giving it the right to market the developed drug exclusively outside the US and to decide if it would like to co-promote the drug within the US, together with Intarcia. However, Schering did not exercise any of its two options yet. The substance Atamestane is still under development at Intarcia.

Characteristics of the partner companies

All partner companies deploy a very focused strategy centering only around certain R&D activities and a few selected therapy areas. Actelion pursues a special strategy by focusing on the potential of just one system (the endothelin). In addition, the partners in the out-licensing agreements are all characterized by a small size when being compared to their licensing counterparts. With around 60 employees, Speedel is about 1,350-times smaller than its licensing partner Novartis which employs about 81,000 people. Intarcia (35 employees) is about 740-times smaller than its licensing partner Schering (26,000 employees). Among the group of partner companies, Actelion represents by far the largest company with around 840 employees. However, Actelion is still about 80-times smaller than its licensing partner Roche with 65,000 employees.

The partner companies were all comparatively young and newly incepted. At the time of writing, the partner companies were on average only between seven and eight years old. All partner firms were significantly funded by venture capital investors. Speedel has secured around CHF 120 million in venture funding since its inception, and Intarcia closed on US$ 195 million in four different financing rounds. During 2005, Intarcia is expecting to go public via an IPO. Actelion has successfully completed its IPO already in 2000 before having secured around CHF 66 million in venture capital in the three years prior to its IPO.

It seems that the companies which are most likely preferred by large pharmaceutical companies as out-licensing partners during the R&D process in order to share R&D-related risks are comparatively small and highly specialized biopharmaceutical companies. This group of companies belongs to a group of so-called 'specialty pharma' firms. Specialty pharma companies typically focus on only a few development activities, such as pre-clinical development and/or clinical phase I and II trials. As these companies are usually not conducting any research activities, their business is fundamentally dependent upon getting compounds from the outside, for instance, via in-licensing (see also DeGiralamo 2004).[31]

Out-licensing agreements with other large pharmaceutical companies for the purpose of sharing certain R&D risks are very rare. Although there are several out-licensing agreements between two large pharmaceutical companies, no collaboration could have been identified during the course of the research which refers to a risk-sharing contract where one big pharmaceutical company out-licenses a compound with the right to buy it back at a later stage. Most of the out-licensing agreements between two large firms focus on commercialization aspects of compounds which

31 There are several well-established specialty pharma companies, such as Forest Laboratories, King Pharmaceuticals, Allergan, or MGI Pharma, which have achieved varying degrees of success and profitability over the recent years. Their business model was largely based upon combing through the unwanted and underappreciated drugs in the portfolios of discovery-based large pharmaceutical companies, then making savvy in-licensing deals, often augmented by new studies aimed at extending labels or markets (Thiel 2004).

are already fully developed and approved. During this type of out-licensing arrangement, the out-licensing company usually does not have the required market presence in a certain market, and therefore sells the marketing rights to another pharmaceutical company which then sells and distributes the drug on that particular market. As the in-licensing firm might have to conduct a few additional studies (bridge-studies) in order to get market approval for the respective target market, the two established pharmaceutical companies usually agree not only on out-licensing but also include other aspects into the collaboration, such as co-development, co-promotion or co-marketing activities. Co-development collaborations are also increasingly signed with biotech companies. While biotech companies have traditionally been the most favorite collaboration partner for research alliances and in-licensing, they have recently become a preferred partner for co-development activities, particularly for compounds developed by the biotech company.

In summary, all of the analyzed case studies are characterized by the same situation: The established pharmaceutical companies (Novartis, Schering and Roche) always out-licensed their substances (Aliskiren, Atamestane and Bosentan) to fairly small and young companies (Speedel, Intarcia and Actelion). At the time of the deals closing, the small partner companies did not possess most of the downstream resources needed for drug development. Moreover, the partner firms did not have a track record of successful execution of development projects in the respective therapy areas. As a result, the pharmaceutical companies did not have much information to presume the partner's ability to successfully develop the licensed compounds. In two cases (Novartis and Roche), this lack of information could have been reduced to a certain extent because the partner firms' management teams were previously working with Novartis and Roche respectively. Thus, Novartis and Roche could deduce some more information about the likelihood of the licensing deal to eventually become a success. Nevertheless, one of the main aspects of all analyzed case studies was the existence of a comparatively high degree of asymmetric information between the licensor and the licensee.

The more specific characteristics of the out-licensing collaborations are subject to a detailed discussion in the following chapter.

5 Characteristics of Risk-sharing in Pharma R&D Collaborations

Based upon the case study analysis in the previous chapter, this chapter investigates different aspects of the observed out-licensing arrangements which have shown to enable the pharmaceutical companies to share R&D risks with their external partners. As pharmaceutical companies use risk-sharing collaborations in order to transfer risks from their own operations to the operations of an external partner firm, the success of the collaboration thus depends on the degree of the risks that can be transferred including the likelihood with which the risk transfer occurs. The most appropriate criterion to describe the success of a risk-sharing collaboration is consequently the risk transferability of the underlying collaboration.

In general, there are three entities involved in any out-licensing arrangement: the seller of the license (i.e. the pharmaceutical company), the buyer of the license (i.e. the partner company), and the license itself (the product exchanged). Accordingly, the subsequent chapters analyze various attributes of the following three entities regarding their impact on the risk transferability in the out-licensing collaboration:

- Licensor;
- License;
- Licensee.

5.1 Attributes of the Licensor

The case study analysis illustrates several attributes of the licensors which are essential prerequisites for the transfer of risks. The attributes which have shown to be the most important determinants for the risk transferability from the perspective of the pharmaceutical company include:

- Out-licensing approach;
- Out-licensing organization;
- Out-licensing process.

These three attributes, including their specifications, are described in more detail in the following paragraphs.

5.1.1 Out-licensing approach

As almost no other industry is as driven by science, research and development as the pharmaceutical industry, a pharmaceutical company's research results are usually regarded as the firm's most important assets. Sometimes, the research results of pharmaceutical companies are even referred to be the firm's 'crown jewels' (see Adam 2003). Therefore, pharmaceutical companies place a great emphasis on bringing their own research results to the market and have traditionally been very reluctant to sell their research results before they reach market approval by the FDA. Subsequently, out-licensing at big pharmaceutical companies does not have a great tradition, and the companies' mindset is usually not prepared for out-licensing. As most pharmaceutical companies are typically focusing on in-licensing instead of out-licensing, a first and significant step for a successful implementation of out-licensing includes a change in the pharmaceutical company's mindset about out-licensing. Merck KgaA has recognized the potential of out-licensing and has recently started to change its perception of out-licensing with the intention to improve its R&D performance.

Merck KgaA: Changing the mindset about the perception of out-licensing

For many years, Merck treated undesired and secondary substances by terminating the underlying R&D projects. Recently, the company's licensing department has started to realize that this seems to be a very inefficient way of economic thinking. In addition, the success of a few out-licensing deals, such as of the product Glucophage which was out-licensed to Bristol-Myers Squibb due to portfolio restructuring reasons, has started to change the general mindset about out-licensing at Merck. The royalty revenues of deals like this, which had initially never been considered to be possible, have made the company aware of both the intrinsic value of any compound in the R&D pipeline as well as the relevance of intellectual property. According to Merck, this trend is today reflected in the strategy of the licensing & business development department, particularly in the area of the firm's high potential products.[32] Today's mission of the licensing & business development department at Merck includes seeking to increase the market potential of any substance in Merck's portfolio, which intentionally covers out-licensing.

Once a pharmaceutical company decided to adopt the concept of out-licensing, the company can generally select between two types of out-licensing (see Parr and Sul-

32 High potential products at Merck include products which do not belong to the company's core products but possess certain attributes which make them attractive to be further developed in collaboration with an external partner.

livan 1996): strategic and tactical. While strategic out-licensing proactively pursues selling intellectual assets, tactical out-licensing is passively waiting for a potential opportunity to sell licenses to third parties. In addition, strategic out-licensors are typically willing to sell any kind of intellectual property, whereas tactical out-licensors usually intend to keep their most important intellectual assets in-house (Megantz 2002). However, when it comes to out-licensing stalled or failed compounds, very few big pharmaceutical companies have adopted so far the philosophy of 'keeping assets moving'. The majority believes that they cannot make enough money from the endeavor to warrant the investment in resources (Windhover 2003). As a result, most pharmaceutical companies – with a few exceptions – do not have a dedicated out-licensing infrastructure yet or a commitment to it. Instead, the task usually falls to otherwise-engaged business development executives who can make more of a name for themselves from their in-licensing responsibilities.

Due to the deteriorating productivity in R&D pharmaceutical companies need to think about different ways to judge their R&D performance, which means to have more eyes looking for value within the R&D department that the companies themselves may not perceive. According to Windhover (2003), the problem is that pharmaceutical companies assume they know the value of their portfolios. This is oftentimes a self-defeating posture, because what's worthwhile should not be determined by the owner of the intellectual property. The real value of any intellectual property in a pharmaceutical company's portfolio can only be determined accurately by its value perceived by a potential buyer. Not only the value of an invention might not be judged accurately by the inventor in many cases, but also its commercialization potential. Joseph Zakrzewski, VP Business Development at Eli Lilly, who is responsible for the company's out-licensing activities, claims after having completed several successful out-licensing deals: "If I didn't put them in our partners' hands I can tell you exactly where these assets [the compounds, G.R.] would be sitting – our shelves. But they've now created lots of value for us, for our partners, and for our patients." Over the last five years, Eli Lilly generated approximately US$ 2 billion in additional revenues due to out-licensing activities (see Longman 2004).[33]

---

[33] Companies in industries other than pharmaceuticals achieve large revenue streams by selling licenses for several years. Texas Instruments is one of the companies that pioneered the idea that licensing should be treated as a profit center. The firm has collected more than US$ 2.5 billion in royalties from 1994 to 1999 (Torres 1999). Another example includes Philips and Sony which developed the CD in the early 1980s and, to make the CD a new standard, they licensed the technology in order to enhance the diffusion of their new product. Since the mid-1980s, Philips and Sony have collected an estimated US$ 2 billion in royalty revenues. IBM is reporting an estimated US$ 1.5 billion in annual sales due to licensing.

In this context, the pharmaceutical company should also determine the scope of its out-licensing program. This includes to clarify if out-licensing should only cover compounds in development stages (i.e. they have passed all necessary research activities and have consequently received IND approval), or if substances should be out-licensed which are still in quite early stages of the research process. The characteristics of the compounds including their stage in the R&D process are critical because they determine the responsibilities of the out-licensing officers. According to Hastbacka and McCarthy (1997), a growing number of licensing organizations is getting involved in licensing activities early in the research and development process. They argue that this pattern is a key factor in the transition from tactical to strategic licensing.

After having decided to adopt a strong commitment towards out-licensing, the pharmaceutical company should pursue the vision of becoming a 'partner of choice' for external partners who might buy the license. This significantly increases the likelihood of finding the most promising out-licensing deals. Pharmaceutical companies should look at several key factors to position their own out-licensing offers and to meet the partner firm's expectations accordingly – such as potential partners' product portfolios, potential sales and the ability to replicate a partner's technology. No licensing deal is worth undertaking unless it meets both parties' needs. Companies must structure their relationships to reflect each partners' differences and encourage them to focus on their areas of competitive advantage, increasing the total value of the collaboration. Once the pharmaceutical company has built its 'partner of choice' strengths, it could build its reputation through traditional media channels, sales forces, corporate web sites and co-branding. The pharmaceutical and biotechnology industries judge the success of licensing deals both on financial merits and on intangibles, such as goodwill and admiration. In discovering and pursuing future opportunities, companies that meet those criteria have a strong competitive advantage over companies that do not meet them. In addition to public buzz, successful companies leverage their strength and expertise as a selling point in negotiations. Out-licensing teams could promote their strengths and past successes alongside their marketing, sales and scientific expertise and capabilities.

In summary, a pharmaceutical company can either adopt a proactive or passive approach to out-licensing (see Fig. 33). A proactive approach is characterized by the firm's willingness to commercialize its internal research results before they reach market approval by the FDA as a fully developed new chemical entity. This implies that the pharmaceutical firm has adopted the mindset of an out-licensor which does not exist at many companies yet. The implementation of a proactive approach to

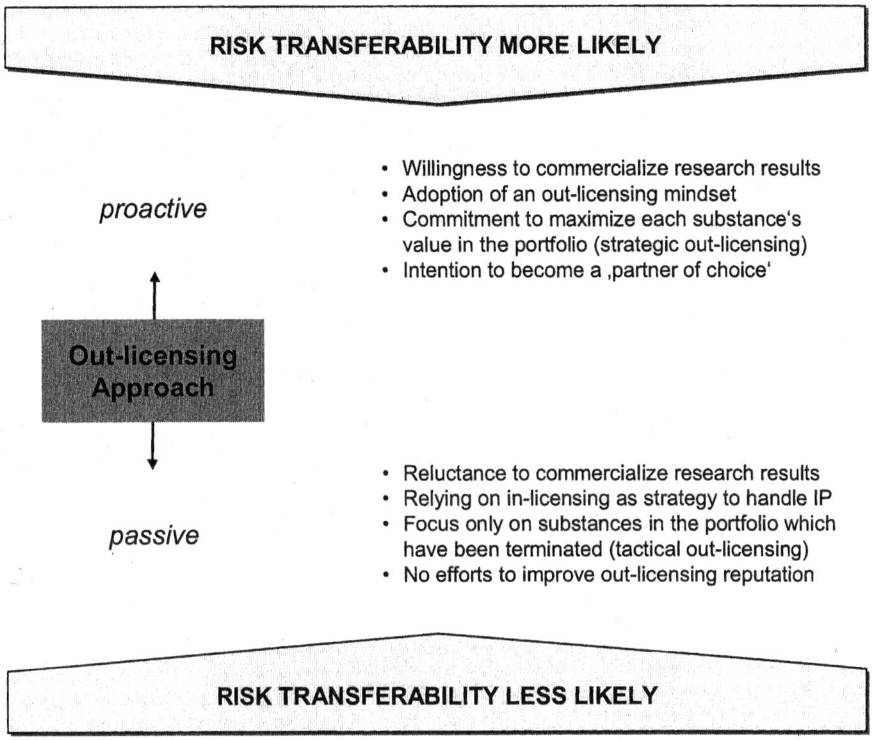

Fig. 33. Proactive vs. passive out-licensing approach of the licensor.

out-licensing shows a strong commitment to maximize the value of each substance in the company's R&D department, no matter if this substance is currently under development internally or if it is sitting on the shelf. A proactive out-licensing approach also includes that the pharmaceutical company intends to become a 'partner of choice' for out-licensing deals which is expected to increase the firm's ability to get access to the best out-licensing deals. Due to the higher commitment and the more vivid actions and activities, a proactive approach to out-licensing seems to be more suitable to allow the pharmaceutical company to close an out-licensing deal, and, thus share risks with external partners than a passive approach. As a result, implementing a proactive out-licensing approach is expected to increase the transferability of R&D risks.

5.1.2 Out-licensing organization

When the general commitment towards out-licensing has been determined and the approach to out-licensing is defined, the next step of a successful implementation of out-licensing covers the organization of the out-licensing activities. The case studies have shown that out-licensing needs significant top management support because the concept itself is fairly novel and the decision to out-license a compound could have far-reaching consequences. For example, in the case of Novartis, every out-licensing deal has to be approved – and therefore receives the support – by the company's CEO. In the case of Schering, it has been the company's CEO who declared out-licensing as 'a new strategic issue with highest priority'. This helps giving all out-licensing activities the motivation and trust needed to get accepted within the entire organization. Hence, internal sponsorship has shown to be an important success factor of any out-licensing activity.[34]

Besides management support, out-licensing activities also have to be incorporated via some organizational framework. According to Megantz (2002), a company's out-licensing strategy has shown to be a major factor in how its licensing program is organized. Out-licensors who pursue a proactive out-licensing approach tend to have either a stand-alone department or devoted dedicated resources to the out-licensing effort, while out-licensors who pursue a passive out-licensing approach tend to treat it as a function of another department, such as legal or finance, and did not provide dedicated resources. Megantz (2002) also believes that licensing activity, rather than strategy, is the major factor in the organization of a licensing program. If licensing activity is significant, regardless of company size, then it is advantageous to set up a separate formal licensing organization.

The companies in the case studies generally organized their out-licensing activities within their Business Development & Licensing (BD&L) departments. While these departments are primarily dealing with in-licensing activities, there are some experts who are responsible exclusively for out-licensing. In some cases, such as in the case

34 From an organizational perspective, Schon (1963) was one of the first researchers who discussed the importance of support and sponsorship within the organization for the success of any corporate activity. Therefore, the success of any activity is likely to be higher if it is backed by a champion and a sponsor. On the one hand, the champion – oftentimes referred to as 'the manager' – is responsible to convince higher management that the endeavor is feasible, economically attractive and worthy of significant investment. On the other hand, the sponsor is responsible to provide the funding and a formal hierarchical linkage between the new initiative and the corporation. Burgelman and Sayles (1986) came to the conclusion that the existence of a positive relation between the champion and the sponsor has a critical impact on the success of any corporate activity.

of Schering, employees from other functions within the BD&L department are increasingly expected to support the out-licensing efforts because the importance of out-licensing has grown rapidly inside of Schering.

A stand-alone licensing organization, such as the BD&L department, provides companies with a number of benefits including the demonstration of a commitment to licensing and licensees, creating well-defined lines of communication, and the development of licensing professionals. Hastbacka and McCarthy (1997) argue that if the licensing department is part of the corporate function, without dedicated resources and without influence on the company's research and development efforts, then it will not have the people resources to convert the technologies into revenue streams, a process in place to identify technologies to license, to handle negotiation or to support the technology after the fact. The authors identified a variety of organizational structures for the licensing function. In their cross-industry analysis, half of the licensing departments reported to corporate officers. Others reported to the business units, while very few reported to the legal department. Large companies in mature industries often had a corporate licensing function. A large pharmaceutical company which is known for managing their out-licensing activities for many years in a well organized way is Eli Lilly.

Organization of out-licensing at Eli Lilly

Within Eli Lilly there is a team of 4-6 people working on out-licensing. The team reports to the Vice President Business Development, Joseph Zakrzewski. The team was formed already in 1998, and has since then out-licensed between 55 and 60 products (Thiel 2004). The vision of Eli Lilly's out-licensing activities is to be always prepared to out-license any substance which does not fulfill Eli Lilly's strategic or performance-related requirements any more. Out-licensing at Eli Lilly is also motivated by the desire to help patients. An out-licensed compound that has been brought to the market by a partner firm and then starts treating patients justifies any out-licensing decision. Eli Lilly promotes the philosophy of out-licensing internally, and employees at Eli Lilly convey the flexibility and openness which is necessary for closing out-licensing deals.

Based on probability-adjusted NPV calculations, Eli Lilly evaluates the potential of its substances and is subsequently willing to out-license any compound which is considered to be non-strategic for Eli Lilly. According to Zakrzewski, it does not make any sense if assets which have a certain value on the market, decay in the company's basement after the decision has been made to stop their further development. A committee comprised of members of three different departments including the out-licensing team decides about potential out-licensing candidates.

An important aspect of any out-licensing collaboration is the trust to the external partner. Although the contracts are quite comprehensive, an out-licensing deal can only be successful if both partners trust each other and bring the necessary commitment to the table. In this context, Eli Lilly intends to engage in out-licensing deals for the long-term instead of quickly cashing out. Key relations to key partners are central. Out-licensing deals at Eli Lilly are evaluated by using a dynamic methodology. In case a deal delivers negative experiences, these experiences are used to evaluate future projects.

Eli Lilly out-licenses any compound, no matter at which phase of the pre-clinical or clinical stages of the R&D process. The payments usually include upfront and milestone payments as well as royalties. The metric to determine the success of an out-licensing deal is a positive cash-flow. According to information by Eli Lilly, 75-80% of all out-licensing deals can be classified as successful.

Besides setting up a stand-alone organization for out-licensing, another type of organizational structure that can be used for companies with a low number of licensing deals is to form a committee for each licensing project. Novartis uses this approach in the early stages of its out-licensing process. Whereas this approach does not allow for a specialization of the licensing function, it is a way to leverage a variety of individual backgrounds and strengths (see White 1997). Another organizational model includes the usage of outside agents to handle the licensing function. This model has the advantage of using licensing professionals who are experienced and dedicated to the task which reduces the risk of making failures. However, the drawbacks to outsourcing the licensing function are that the agent typically gets a large portion of the revenue and the company gives up control of the overall administration of its intellectual property (see Battersby and Grimes 1996).

After determining whether licensing should be a stand-alone activity or part of another group or business unit, a company must also decide if the licensing program will have its own profit and loss responsibilities and where it reports the revenues incurred. The revenues derived from licensing can be retained by the licensing program or returned to the business units that produced the technology. Megantz (2002) believes that having profit and loss responsibility allows a licensing program to measure its performance. Companies engaged in strategic licensing usually will put someone with profit and loss experience in charge. Hastbacka and McCarthy (1997) figured out in their cross-industry study that half of the companies surveyed had licensing programs with profit and loss responsibility, and most of them returned the generated revenues back to the business units that produced the technology. Dennis (2004) argues that giving back revenues to the business units ensures their cooperation and ongoing enthusiastic support for further licensing activity. In this context, Schering was the only company in the case study analysis which has declared that out-licensing had become – for the first time ever – an own item in the company's budget calculations for fiscal year 2004.

In summary, the probability of success of any out-licensing deal seems to improve if the out-licensing activities are organizationally well embedded into the corporation (see Fig. 34). This requires sufficient sponsorship and management support within the company. Due to the novel nature of out-licensing, mentoring and nurturing

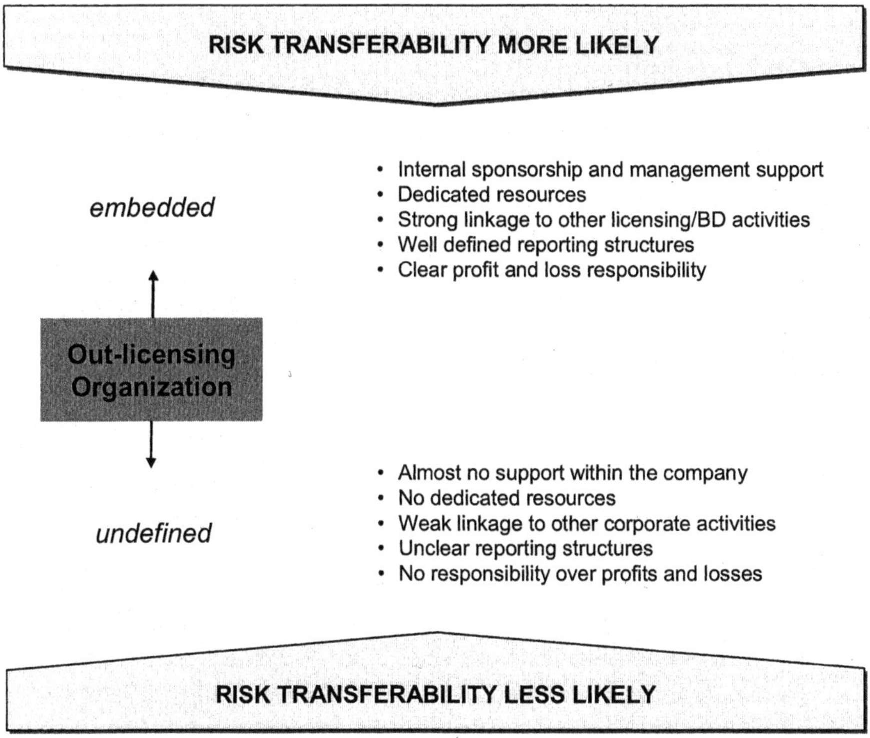

Fig. 34. Embedded vs. undefined out-licensing organization of the licensor.

these activities is critical to their success. Moreover, it is expected to be helpful if the pharmaceutical company provides dedicated resources for the out-licensing efforts in terms of money and/or people. A strong linkage to other business development and licensing activities helps achieve synergies and knowledge transfer between executives. A solid out-licensing organization requires clearly defined reporting structures. In some cases, profit and loss responsibility for the out-licensing officers increases the impact of out-licensing from an organizational perspective. A well embedded out-licensing organization seems to be more likely to enable the pharmaceutical company to close on promising out-licensing deals than an undefined out-licensing organization. Consequently, a well embedded out-licensing organization is expected to increase the transferability of risks.

5.1.3 Out-licensing process

Out-licensing requires a range of activities, including strategic planning, targeting of potential opportunities, preparation of supporting material, evaluation of the product and partner, contact with potential partners, negotiation, due diligence and the management of the deal after it has been closed. The IBM (2003) study about licensing in the pharmaceutical industry reveals that ownership of the different activities of out-licensing changes over the course of the process. The business development & licensing (BD&L) departments exhibit proportionally more ownership when defining the strategy, finding the buyer, assessing the product, and closing the deal (see Fig. 35). During the transition and ongoing development of a product with a licensee, ownership tends to return to the project team, scientists or clinicians. The BD&L function may have some influence during these stages, but in general, its level of responsibility is waning.

A successful out-licensing process depends on applying a methodological approach. Based on the case study analysis, Fig. 36 illustrates an exemplary out-licensing process which could generically be applied by any pharmaceutical company. After choosing the product which could potentially be out-licensed, the next step includes to determine the product's potential. This implies the preparation of a comprehensive prospectus outlining the product's characteristics, intellectual property status and commercial positioning. This prospectus should be critically reviewed internally to ascertain the product's strengths and weaknesses, and to identify any likely questions or gaps in the available data (compare Scott 2001). In addition, the team should be identified which would be necessary to close on this licensing deal. This step is predominantly expected to help the pharmaceutical company itself gain a

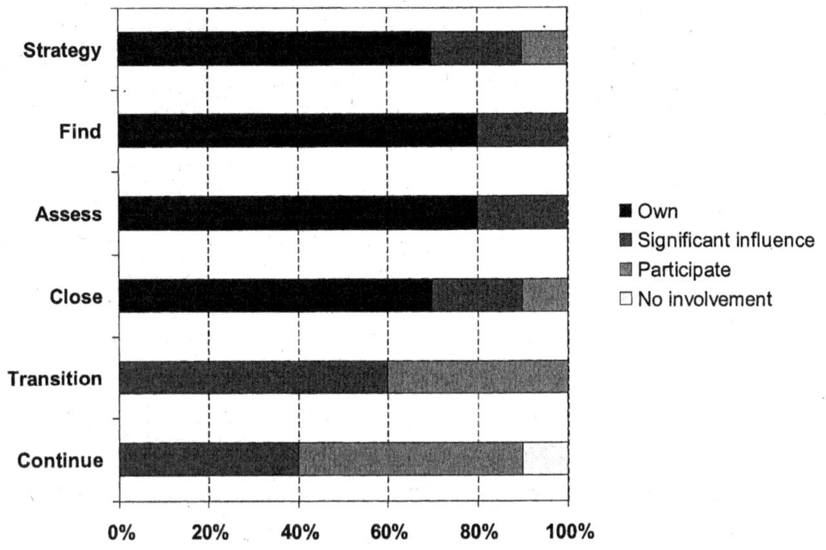

Source: IBM (2003)

Fig. 35. Process responsibilities of the business development & licensing departments at pharmaceutical companies regarding out-licensing.

closer understanding of the product and the resources required for the out-licensing deal. Eventually, the out-licensing aspirations could be stopped at this stage if the analysis reveals that the product should best be kept inside the firm without any further activity.

After having assessed the product's potential, it should be asked 'how' and 'when' the product could best be out-licensed? This primarily deals with setting the ideal profile for target partners, agreeing on target terms and fall-back positions, as well as analyzing the product's potential market. Megantz (2002) argues that market information is the most important factor in developing a successful licensing strategy. Only accurate and reliable information about size, growth, technology and competitors will allow the licensor to evaluate its product's value properly. In case of early-stage compounds or technology licenses, however, Razgaitis (1999) argues that market analysis is less important as it tends to involve intellectual property at the beginning of the technology lifecycle where little market data is usually available. The next steps will be to identify a list of up to 20 potential target companies, and to

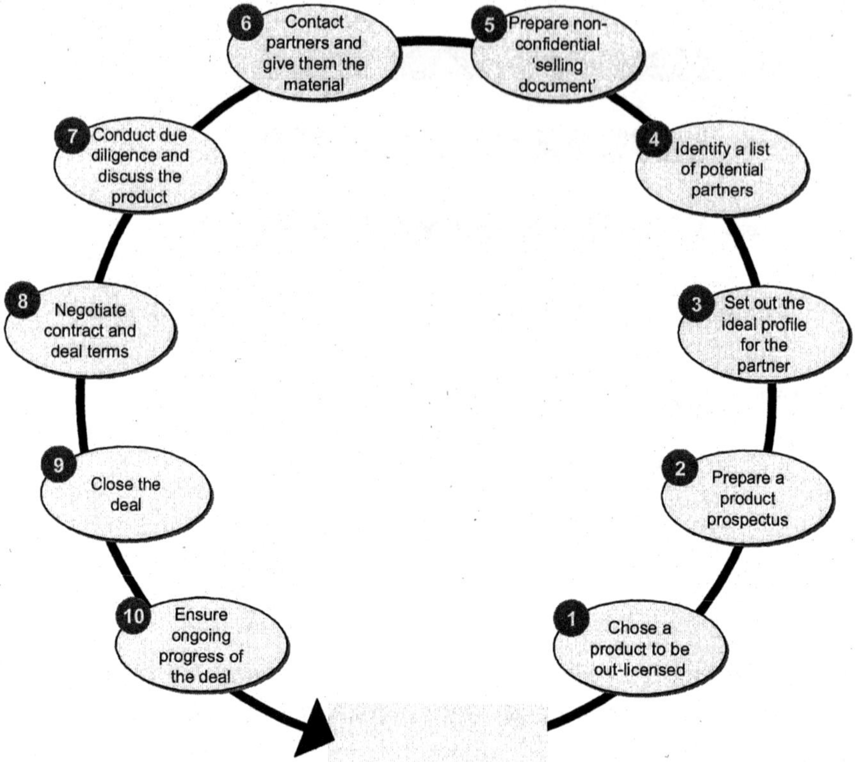

Fig. 36. Exemplary out-licensing process.

prepare a short non-confidential 'selling document'. This document can be presented to the potential licensees at the first contact to attract their attention. Although only non-confidential information shall be provided in the selling document, it should be considered that a key element in any out-licensing activity is the quality and format of data to be supplied to prospective partners.

After having raised first interest at the partner firm, the pharmaceutical company could provide more information about the product – even confidential data after having signed a non-disclosure agreement. The product prospectus could ideally be structured to provide detailed outlines for confidential as well as non-confidential aspects covering all the types of information that will be sought by any potential licensee. Getting a company to review the confidential material is one of the most vital steps of the out-licensing process. If the target licensing managers cannot be persuaded to take a new opportunity seriously during the first contact, then it will be difficult if not impossible to interest them later. After a target company has shown interest in the compound, the confidential material including additional sensitive data can be exchanged, and the actual due diligence can start. This includes close communication and the exchange of critical information and knowledge between the firms. Site visits and mutual test trials of the substance under discussion are quite common approaches to help the partner firm decide about acquiring the license. If the partner firm is still interested in buying the substance, the contractual details have to be negotiated and the deal terms defined. This includes agreements on draft secrecy and/or material supply agreements. In addition, the term sheets of the collaboration have to be prepared describing the deal structure regarding further development, production, marketing, distribution as well as the split-up of potential revenues and profits. Only if this step is completed, the deal can finally be closed. After the deal has been closed, there are still several activities to be done in order to turn the licensing deal into a success. In the case studies that have been discussed in chapter 4, the licenses were all straight licenses. This means that the partner firms took over full responsibility of the project. While the pharmaceutical firms have retained an interest in the compounds via call-back options, they did not conduct any further development activities. However, in case of bottleneck situations at the partner firm, the pharmaceutical company might provide some additional assistance in order to turn the joint project into a success.

In summary, the out-licensing process of the licensor can either be well structured or fairly fuzzy (see Fig. 37). A structured process starts with the licensor's awareness of the different tasks that have to be completed. The ownership of every tasks is clearly assigned. Successful out-licensors then usually apply very methodological approaches to out-licensing and follow clear procedures that cover every aspect of the out-licensing process. It is helpful to possess well-elaborated policies and guidelines to interact and negotiate with the partner firms at any stage during the out-licensing process. Therefore, a structured out-licensing process seems to be the basis for any successful out-licensing deal. A well structured process is thus expected to be an important enabler for a high risk transferability from the perspective of the pharmaceutical company.

Conclusion: This chapter has analyzed the case studies from chapter 4 regarding the attributes of the licensor and their contribution towards the risk transferability dur-

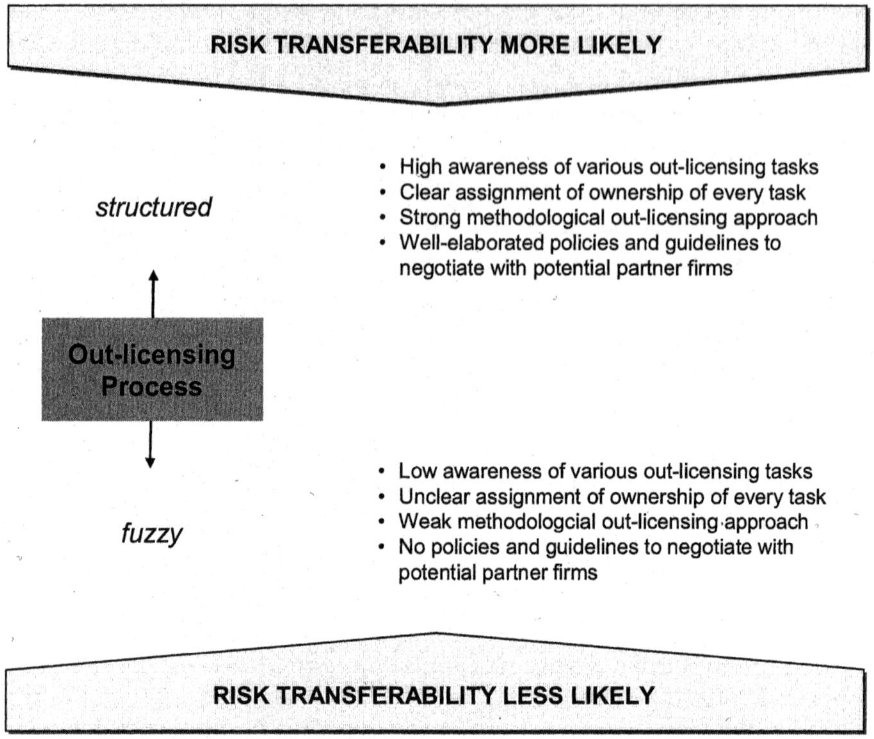

Fig. 37. Structured vs. fuzzy out-licensing process of the licensor.

ing the collaboration. The following three attributes of the licensor could have been identified which are considered to have an impact on the risk transferability:

- Out-licensing approach;
- Out-licensing organization;
- Out-licensing process.

The risk transferability is more likely to be high if the attributes of the licensor meet the following criteria (Fig. 38):

- The out-licensing approach should be proactive;
- The out-licensing organization should be well embedded into the corporation;
- The out-licensing process should be structured.

The risk transferability is likely to be low for the opposite specifications.

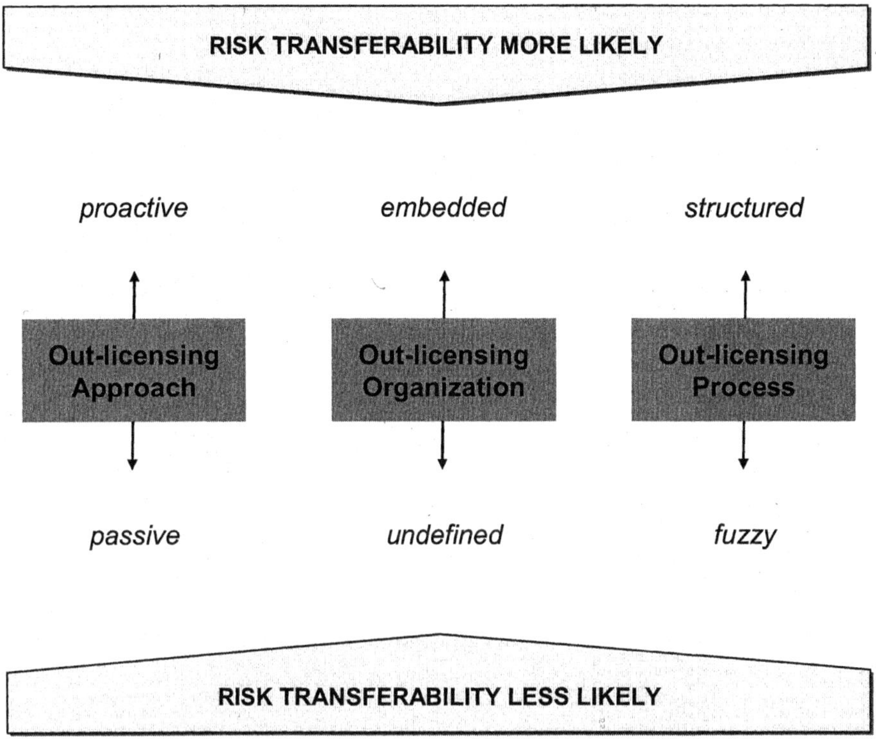

Fig. 38. Attributes of the licensor and their impact on risk transferability.

5.2 Attributes of the License

The case study analysis also provides insights about the attributes of the license itself which help explain when the risk transferability in the observed collaborations is most likely to be high or low. The most important attributes related to the license which are expected to determine the risk transferability during the out-licensing collaboration include:

- Appropriability regime;
- Bargaining range;
- Compensation structure.

These three attributes, including their specifications, are described in more detail in the following paragraphs.

5.2.1 Appropriability regime

Innovations are expensive to produce but inexpensive to imitate. As a consequence, the problem arises that firms in competitive markets might not be able to fully appropriate the fruits of their innovations. This particularly applies in industries which are characterized by high R&D intensities (see Vinod and Rao 2000). One factor that determines the degree to which any research can be applied is the appropriability of the results obtained. The more general the nature of the research, the less applied it is, the more difficult it will be to appropriate the results and the less incentive there will be for firms to engage in it (Bayona et al. 2004, Chen 1997, Link and Bauer 1989, Link and Tassey 1989, Sakakibara 1995, Scott 1989, Sinha and Cusumano 1991). For this reason, it is argued that basic research requires government backing and should take place in universities and research centers (Kostoff 1996, Ouchi and Bolton 1988).

While it is generally difficult to measure appropriability, an indicator which best describes appropriability is the ratio of private returns to social returns resulting from innovations (see Harabi 1995). This ratio varies between 0 and 100%, and the closer it is to 100%, the better is the appropriability from the perspective of the innovator.[35] Arrow (1962) was the first scholar who described the phenomenon of appropriability faced by innovating firms that invest heavily in research and development. He argues that innovative firms often realize but a fraction of the total benefits accrued to the society from their R&D investments. Outside firms might benefit from the R&D conducted by the innovating firm due to spillover effects or technological externalities. As a result, Arrow (1962) concludes that privately owned firms are likely to underinvest in R&D because they are unable to fully appropriate returns from their innovation activities.[36]

---

35 In general, there is a difference between appropriability ex ante and appropriability ex post (see Trajtenberg et al. 1992). The ex ante notion emphasizes the potential capability of an innovator (or the organization which owns the innovation), to fully, or at least, partially, appropriate the returns from the innovation. The ex post concept of appropriability, on the other hand, defines the proportion of social returns that can be privately appropriated by the innovator after the innovation has been introduced.

36 Since then, the role of appropriability in technological innovations has gained much attention in management literature, and empirical support for the existence of appropriability concerns has been well documented in management research (see Vinod and Rao 2000). Astebro (2004) observed the impact of 36 innovation, technology and market characteristics on the probability that early-stage R&D pro-

According to Gulati (1998), the level of appropriation concerns is oftentimes influenced by the appropriability regime of the entire industry. As the appropriability regime of an industry is the degree to which firms are able to capture the rents generated by their innovations (see Anand and Khanna 1997), firms are more likely to retain the profits they earn from their proprietary resources in a tight appropriability regime. In a loose regime, by contrast, these profits are subject to involuntary leakage or spillovers to other firms.

Particularly when firms intend to engage in technology-related collaborations, appropriability becomes a critical issue. A firm's concerns about appropriation will generally vary depending on the industry in which the alliance occurs and, accordingly, the degree to which the appropriability regime in the industry is tight or loose (see Teece 1986). If participants in a collaboration believe that the appropriability regime is strong, because patent protection is significant, that they can keep trade secrets or that their first-mover advantage is sufficiently large, they are likely to be less concerned about appropriation in an alliance, and this will be reflected in the formal governance structure used for the alliance (Gulati 1998). In this context, Cassiman and Veugelers (2002) examined the effects of knowledge flows on R&D cooperation highlighting two measures of knowledge flows, namely, spillovers and appropriability. They conclude that there is a significant relation between external information flows and the decision to cooperate in R&D. Firms that rate generally available external information sources as more important inputs to their innovation process are more likely to be actively engaged in R&D agreements. In the case of a strong appropriability regime, Teece (1986) claims that contractual modes such as licensing agreements are recommended in order to profit from technological innovation. The impact of appropriability on licensing as a type of cooperation with rising prominence in technology-related industries was analyzed by Kim (2004). He investigated the validity of potential factors that might affect the incentives of companies to license out their technology. The results have shown that besides transaction costs and market competition, appropriability considerations weigh in heavily in explaining the licensing behavior. Kim (2004) summarizes that the best-known obstacle to an efficient market for out-licensing is the appropriability problem.

jects will reach the market. His analysis among 561 R&D projects identified appropriability conditions to be one of the four characteristics which stand out as most predictive for future commercial success. In addition, a study by Mansfield et al. (1981) figured out that 60 percent of the patented innovations in their sample were imitated within 4 years. Brockhoff (2003) found that securing appropriability belongs to one of the most important strategic R&D success factors for organizations that produce R&D results for proprietary use. The appropriability of a new technology also depends on the charactersitics of the innovation itself.

Appropriability plays a critical role particularly in the pharmaceutical industry: drugs can easily be copied because it is not difficult to analyze an already developed pharmaceutical product regarding its respective ingredients and substances. As a result, intellectual property protection receives a strong emphasis in the pharmaceutical industry. Patents on pharmaceutical discoveries are usually applied to medical devices, such as drug delivery mechanisms, since few manufacturers would want to wait until they perform clinical trials on a compound to apply for patent protection. In general, appropriability is considered to be very high in the pharmaceutical industry because patent protection is extremely effective (Levin et al. 1987), and the rate of imitation is slower for ethical drugs than for other products (Mansfield et al. 1981). The strong patent protection results in relatively little appropriation concerns in the pharmaceutical industry, which corresponds to a tight appropriability regime. In addition, Levin et al. (1987) figured out in a survey among 650 R&D managements, 130 lines of business in 18 industries that firms in only two industries (one of them pharmaceuticals) considered patents as the highest ranked method for protecting gains from product innovation.

As patented drugs consequently appear to enjoy a high degree of appropriability over the patent life in the US and most other industrialized countries (see Tylecote 2004, Vinod and Rao 2000), imitation around a patent becomes difficult because of the exacting nature of a compound claim that covers the chemical entity, including any and all formulations or uses of the chemical entity (Winter 1987). This is despite the fact that the chemical entity itself becomes public knowledge by the time the drug is approved for sale. Thus, the pharmaceutical industry is generally shaped by a combination of a strong appropriability regime during the life of the patent offset by a short effective patent life, intense post-patent competition from the generics and the absence of any patent protection or only a weak protection in much of the developing world's markets. The following case example illustrates how Bayer differentiates its intellectual property according to its applicability at the partner firm.

Differentiation of intellectual property at Bayer

The technological innovations which might be out-licensed at Bayer can have different attributes. Bayer differentiates its intellectual property in 'white-space' developments or other technologies, such as devices or methods that are no longer used by Bayer's business units. Bayer looks at every intellectual property as a product of its own which could be sold on a respective market. Thereby, Bayer strictly follows the rule, 'don't try to sell any leftovers'. Regarding the commercialization of the licenses, Bayer differentiates between three different types of licenses which have different characteristics regarding their applicability at the partner firm. The three types of licenses include business licenses, product licenses, and technology licenses. While business and product licenses deal with entire businesses and/or products and thus have a fairly concrete application potential, the technology licenses usually cover very broadly defined technology-related issues. The applicability of technology licenses is typically very fuzzy which also results in complications regarding the license's valuation (see Gassmann et al. 2004).

The case studies have shown that the applicability of the licensed substances has always been comparatively strong for the partner companies. After having acquired the license, the partner firms could have applied and used the substances in their development programs without any fear of spill-overs or a lack of protection which would have benefited one party in the collaboration at the expense of the other party. The strong appropriability regime in the analyzed out-licensing agreements becomes particularly apparent as in two out of three cases, the partner firms even changed the substance's indication which would not have been easily possible under weak appropriability conditions.

In summary, a tight appropriability regime offers a solid protection of intellectual property and guarantees the inventor (the pharmaceutical firm in the case of out-licensing) to receive the fruits of its research and development activities (the private returns are greater than the social returns). A tight appropriability regime reduces the unwanted outflow of information before the licensing deal closes. In case of a weak appropriability regime, it would be possible for the licensee to use information gained during the due diligence without paying for it once an idea is disclosed to the licensee. Because of this concern, a potential licensor would be reluctant to disclose the core of the technology, depriving a potential licensee of the chance to evaluate it. The same is true for the licensee vice versa after the deal closure. Therefore, a tight appropriability regime increases the likelihood of the licensing deal to happen. In addition, a tight appropriability regime also creates a direct application potential for the partner firm which is about to license the intellectual property from the pharmaceutical company. Only if the partner firm anticipates immediate appropriation of a licensed compound, it is willing to buy a substance from a pharmaceutical company (see Fig. 39). Therefore, a tight appropriability regime increases the likelihood that a partner firm agrees to take a substance under development, and therefore, it increases the possibility that the pharmaceutical company is able to transfer risks to the external partner.

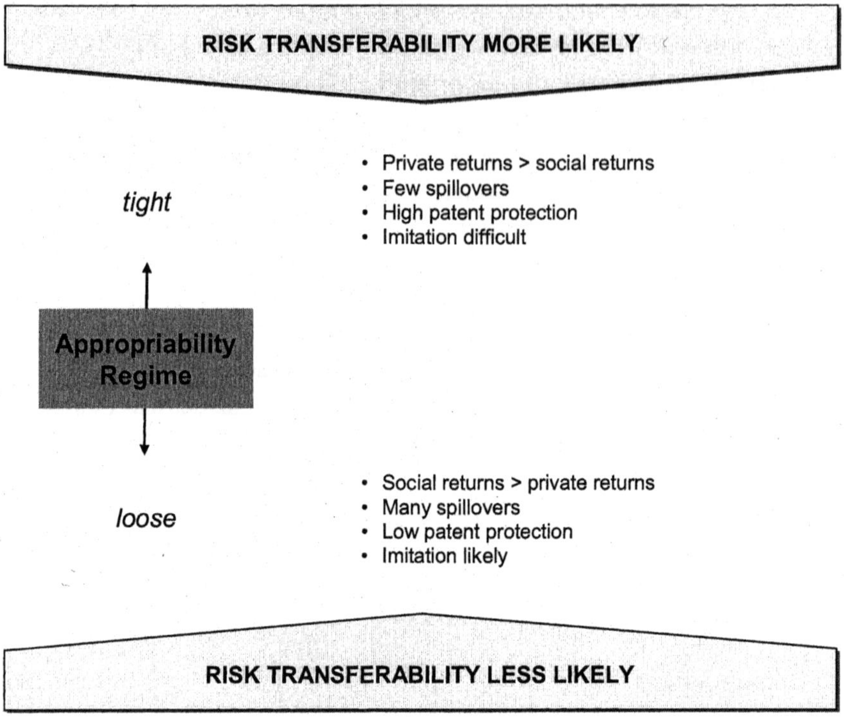

Fig. 39. Tight vs. loose appropriability regime of the license.

5.2.2 Bargaining range

The likelihood of a licensing deal to happen is usually dependent upon its worth to both the licensor and the licensee. Pharmaceutical firms evaluate the worth of a compound via various valuation methodologies (see Gassmann et al. 2004). The majority of pharmaceutical companies relies on the probability-adjusted expected net-present-value (eNPV) method in order to select projects. This method projects future cash in-flows and out-flows and discounts the balance of each year's probability-adjusted net cash-flow to the present date by the relative costs thereby incurred. Some firms combine NPV calculations with decision-tree analyses. Novartis, for instance, evaluates projects by comparing the potential value and expected performance of the projects. The potential value includes considerations about the market, competitiveness and/or feasibility. Performance parameters relate to the capabilities of the team, overall project objectives and the patent position among others. This approach can be applied to technology platforms as well.

In general, pharmaceutical companies' project valuation methods usually center around two different types of unknowns (compare Cook 2004): risks and uncertainties. While risks usually have a few, discrete outcomes (such as failure rates at each R&D phase), most unknowns have a continuous range of uncertainty (such as forecasts on market sizes and growth rates). In general, risks are considered explicitly in decision tress, while uncertainties are measured through Monte-Carlo simulations and then applied to decision trees.

Depending on the two types of unknowns that need to be considered, four valuation methods are applied in the pharmaceutical industry (see Cook 2004): (i) basic decision tree analysis, (ii) advanced real option valuation, (iii) basic real option valuation, (iv) discounted cash flow valuation. In some cases, R&D projects offer options that go beyond the actual project. For example, the development of a new product could be tied to the development of a new process, which has a certain probability to be used for the development of other products in the future. In situations like these, option-values have to be added to the direct value of a particular project. In this context, the real option valuation method has been widely discussed. In 1994, Merck & Co. was the first pharmaceutical company that reported to use real options for the evaluation of strategic investments in biotechnology firms. However, in the following time period, the real option concept was primarily discussed by academia and less by industry (compare Hartmann and Hassan 2004).

One of the specific characteristics of a licensing deal is that not only one but two firms are conducting a valuation of the underlying project. As the valuation techniques of both partners usually cover sophisticated and very complex mechanisms, both companies typically have different preferences regarding their project evaluation and use different parameters as input for their valuation models. As a result, both firms will normally come up with different values for the same project (i.e. the same license in the licensing deal). Subsequently, a licensing deal will only occur if the perceptions of the value of the potential drug differ between the licensor and the licensee in a way where the licensee concedes the project to have a higher value than the licensor. As a consequence, an external partner is only willing to purchase a compound from a pharmaceutical firm if its expected NPV projection of the compound is higher than the pharmaceutical firm's expected NPV projection of the same compound:

$$eNPV\ (compound\ X)^{\ Partner\ Firm} > eNPV\ (compound\ X)^{\ Pharmaceutical\ Firm}$$

As the underlying compound is the same for both NPV calculations, a difference in NPV projections is only possible, if the two parties have different perceptions about the compound's potential or their own ability to execute the compound's further development. Distinctive factors thus include synergies, beliefs, experiences, or risk assessments.

The most appropriate measure to describe the value potential of a substance that is to be out-licensed is the bargaining range which describes the range between the minimum price possible that the licensor expects to receive and the maximum price possible that the licensee is willing to pay for the license (see Fig. 40). To estimate the bargaining range, the pharmaceutical firm's NPV of the underlying project has to be determined as well as the partner firm's NPV for the same project. However, the factors and parameters that would differ between the two firms have to be changed. The value potential of the license (i.e. the bargaining range) is consequently represented by the value to the licensee minus the value to the licensor. This is equivalent to the maximum value that is capturable in the license. In order to figure out a fair price for the license and to compare the NPV calculations, the NPVs for both parties are set equal to zero. The variable that determines the differences for both projections is consequently the price of the license. Thus, the two prices which enable the two NPVs to become zero consequently represent the minimum price and maximum price possible respectively. After the bargaining range has been

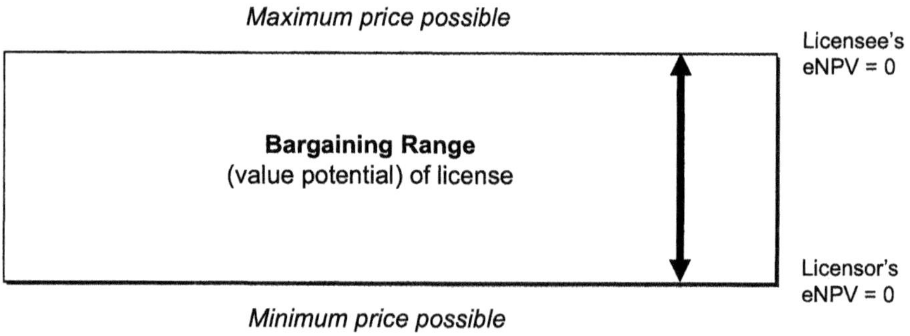

Source: Cook (2004)

Fig. 40. Bargaining range of the license.

determined, an initial offer price can be deduced, and bargaining simulations can be made in order to optimize the price. A large bargaining range illustrates that the two partners differ substantially in their preferences for the valuation of the underlying project (i.e. the license). In addition, the revenue forecasting scenarios of the two partners diverge significantly because they seem to assess the chance/opportunity profile of the license in a different way. The following example which refers to the Schering-Intarcia collaboration should help illustrate the meaning of the bargaining range.

The size of the bargaining range determines the licensing opportunity

In the licensing collaboration with Schering, the licensee Intarcia seemed to be able to see a higher value potential in Schering's substance Atamestane as Schering was able to see itself. Although the substance was identical for both partners, Intarcia's business strategy deliberately allowed the firm to alternate the clinical application and/or the development pathway of in-licensed compounds. The company justified this strategy with the belief that redirected substances face less competition because the originator(s) disregarded these development opportunities. As a result, Intarcia believed to have been able to reduce its licensing costs and future financial obligations for the substance Atamestane. As Schering did not seem to have the same opinion about the value potential of Atamestane, this discrepancy apparently translated into a sufficiently large bargaining range which justified Intarcia's decision to acquire the substance.

The size of the bargaining range, and therefore the value of the licensing deal, also depends on the timing of the licensing deal (i.e. the stage at which the compound is licensed). As the expected net present value (eNPV) approach also takes into account the amount of investment still required to bring a compound to the market, a compound that is entering clinical phase I has a much lower value for the partner firm than a compound that has completed clinical phase III. The reason is that the licensor has usually invested very little in a compound which is just about to enter clinical trials compared to the large amounts that will be invested by the licensee for the clinical development and market introduction. Therefore, the more advanced the compound is in the development process, the more equal will be the investments and rewards that are shared in the licensing deal (see Fig. 41). Thus, it can be assumed that the value distribution of a licensing deal is tightly linked to the distribution of the expected net present value.

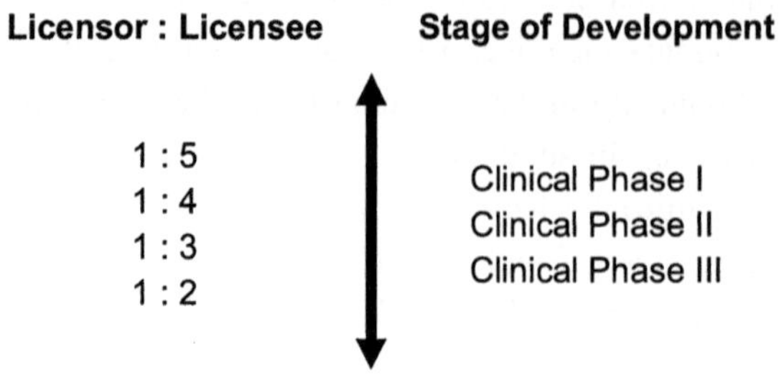

Source: Walton (2004)

Fig. 41. Share of expected NPV in a traditional licensing deal.

According to Walton (2004), the relative split of value between licensor and licensee has tended to converge the later the licensing deal has been signed during the R&D process. While the licensee was able to retain around four to five times more than the licensor if the deal has been signed during the clinical phase I, this ratio goes down to just around two if the deal is signed during the clinical phase III. Thus, the later the compound is out-licensed, the greater will be the relative share of the expected NPV for the licensor. However, the licensor also has to carry the burden of the development costs and risks to bring the compound to these late stages. Therefore, an ideal stage of out-licensing does generally not exist. It will always be a trade-off between the development costs to bring a compound to a certain stage which makes it attractive to the licensee and the potential value that can be generated for the licensor during the deal.

In summary, the larger the bargaining range, the higher the difference in the license's perception by the partner firm compared to the perception by the pharmaceutical company. If the partner firm believes to generate a higher value for the substance, the partner seems to evaluate the risks inherent in the substance's development to be lower than the pharmaceutical firm, or the partner is able to carry a higher risk burden (Fig. 42). As a consequence, the likelihood of the out-licensing deal to be closed is fairly high because the partner company seems to be willing to take on the risks that the pharmaceutical company intends to hand over, and is still able to come up with a positive net present value of the underlying project. Therefore, a large bargaining range increases the opportunity that the pharmaceutical firm is able to out-license a compound to an external partner, and the transferability of R&D risks increases as well.

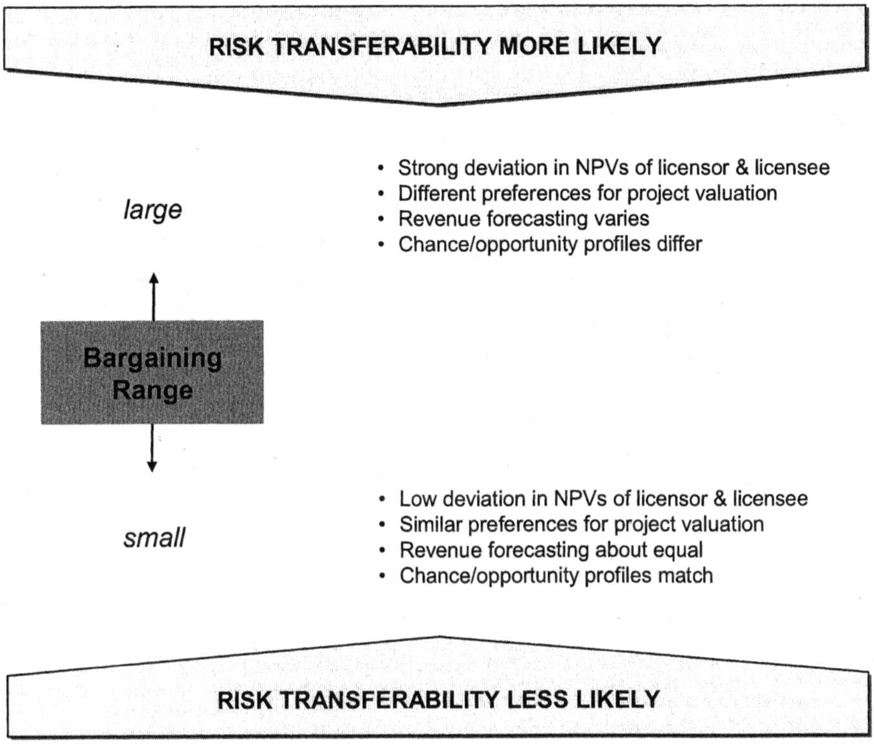

Fig. 42. Large vs. small bargaining range of the license.

5.2.3 Compensation structure

Licensing deals between pharmaceutical companies and external partners, such as the traditionally known deals with biotech firms, have been applied in the industry for several years. In general, when a drug is passed from one company to another for further development, the compensation structure defines the payments that have to be made including further obligations which have an impact on the firms' financial compensation. Market forces and negotiating ability will affect the proportion of the overall value that each party is able to retain. According to Walton (2004), benchmarking studies reveal that deals relating to similar products at similar stages of development tend to broadly have similar compensation structures. Two similar products, licensed at the same stage of development, will have similar risk-reward profiles and, therefore, similar deal structures are likely to emerge. Differences in early-stage, mid-stage, and late-stage payments between the deals reflect the differing needs and priorities of each partner of the deal.

While the compensation structure of the deal generally reflects the negotiated balance of the conflicting desires of the two partners, both partners will try to maximize their rewards and minimize their risks when structuring the deal. To illustrate the possible effects, two extreme scenarios are introduced (see Walton 2004):

- At one extreme, a company could in-license a drug for a one-time cash payment payable immediately after the deal has closed. The amount paid would be equal to the current eNPV of the project. Although the company would end up with huge gains if the drug will succeed (because it will receive 100% of the revenues incurred and would not have to provide any royalty revenues to the licensing partner), the risk is tremendous because the attrition rates in pharmaceutical R&D are comparatively high. No company would typically put a large amount of cash at risk for something which is much more likely to fail than to succeed. On the other hand, the partner who would receive the cash payment would try to avoid foregoing the participation in the compound's upside potential, although the large cash amount might be tempting.
- At the other extreme, the agreement could contain no payments until the drug is on the market. The then incurring royalty payments would consequently have to be large in order to provide a reasonable eNPV for the licensor. However, if the drug turns out to fail during some stage of the development process, the licensor might end up with no payments at all although it had to come up for the entire costs of the compound's development by itself. This compensation structure is particularly dangerous for small biotech firms which do not have a large and diversified development portfolio in order to compensate for potentially occurring losses during the development process.

Due to the experience of both partners with licensing, the deal structures today have become highly complex as both parties increasingly ask for a higher contribution in the overall value of a given product or deal. In addition, the deal sizes are getting bigger. In 1995/96, the average total payment coming to biotech companies from their alliance partners was US$ 32.7 million. By 2003/04, the average total payment had jumped to US$ 75.1 million – an increase of 130 percent (see McCully and van Brunt 2004). The rise in the average deal valuation over time has largely been due to the substantial increase in milestone payments (Fig. 43). Although some pay-

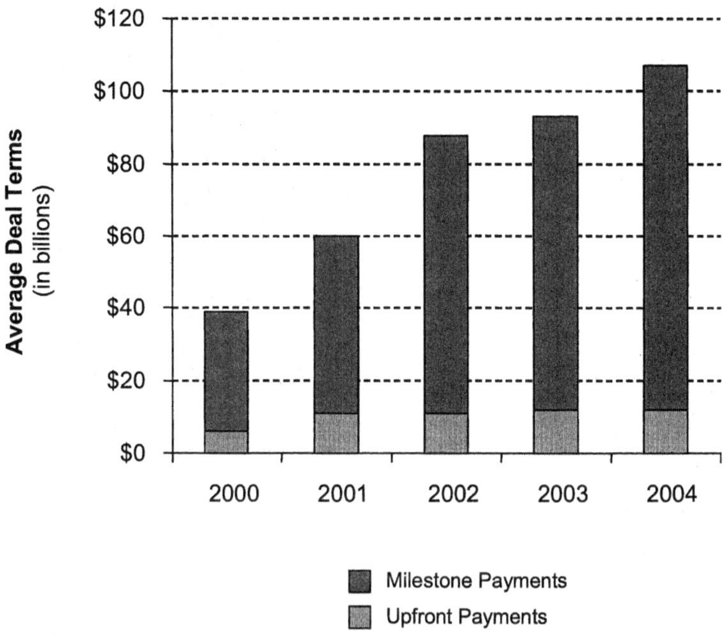

Source: Recombinant Capital (2005)

Fig. 43. Average deal terms regarding upfront and milestone payments in pharmaceutical R&D collaborations.

ments in a pharmaceutical licensing deal can be guaranteed and may occur on specific points in time, the majority of the payments today – both in terms of number and nominal value – are contingent on some measure of future success, and only become payable at some future point in time, that is if certain milestones and gates have been achieved by the partner firms. The increasing relative proportion of milestone payments compared to upfront payments illustrates the desire of the licensing partners to tie their success to the joint project and simultaneously share the R&D-related risks.

Table 6 provides an overview about the compensation and deal structure of some selected key licensing deals in 2002. All of these deals were in-licensing deals (from the perspective of the pharmaceutical company). As illustrated by the case of Aventis (in cooperation with Genta), the milestone payments might out-number the upfront payments by up to 28-times. Therefore, the pharmaceutical company only pays when value is actually created.

Table 6. Compensation and deal structure of key licensing deals in 2002.

Companies	**Product**	**Deal Structure**					
(Licensee / Licensor)		*Deal Value**	*Upfront Payment*	*Milestone Payment*	*R&D Costs*	*Equity Investment*	*Loan Facility*
GSK / Exelixis	Multi-prod. (Phase II)	$ 569M	$ 30M	$ 350M	$ 90M	$ 14M	$ 85M
Aventis / Genta	Genasense (Phase III)	$ 477M	$ 10M	$ 280M		$ 72M	$ 75M
Eli Lilly / Amylin	AC 2993 (Phase III)	$ 435M	$ 80M	$ 215M		$ 30M	
Pfizer / Neurocrine	Indipplon (Phase III)	$ 400M	$ 100M	$ 300M			

* Deal value describes the total value of all payments but could include certain other compensation values.

Source: Datamonitor (2003)

As an increase in the ratio of milestone payments vs. upfront payments primarily reduces the risks for the licensee, this compensation structure would not benefit the pharmaceutical company's desire to reduce risks in the case of out-licensing. According to Windhover (2000), a big pharmaceutical company is also not necessarily looking to out-license products for large, upfront cash payments on the balance sheet. For one thing, it wants to avoid a sudden revenue hole on its income statement, a problem that cannot be alleviated by a large one-time payment. At the same time, especially the smaller licensing companies that in-license from the pharmaceutical companies don't want to spend hundreds of millions of dollars up front (Windhover 2000). In most cases, the smaller partner firms do not even have the financial resources for making significant upfront payments. As a result, out-licensing deals at large pharmaceutical companies are usually structured in a way which gives the pharmaceutical firm the opportunity to participate in the substance's further development via some type of re-licensing rights or royalty revenues.

A re-licensing right which is frequently used in out-licensing deals by large pharmaceutical companies and could also be observed in all of the analyzed case studies is the 'call-back option'. Without the call-back option, most pharmaceutical companies would never have entered into an out-licensing agreement at the first place. However, call-back options only seem to appear in out-licensing deals by established pharmaceutical companies with smaller partner companies as supported by the following example of Roche.

Handling of call-back options at Roche

Roche uses call-back options in out-licensing deals only for deals that are forged with smaller partners. If the partner is a large firm itself with a global market presence and sales force, it is very unlikely for Roche to be able to secure the right to buy back a compound after it has been granted market approval. The large partners typically only agree for licensing deals if they gain full control over the entire compound. Thus, large pharmaceutical firms are preferred partners for out-licensing deals where Roche has no interest in the compound's future development any more. However, as a large partner firm might be able to generate higher revenue streams than a small partner firm, the potential royalty revenues attributable to Roche might be higher. This might overcompensate for the lack of the call-back option. Risk considerations seem to rank secondary in these deals.

A possible reason for the existence of call-back options between large pharmaceutical companies and smaller partner firms could be the different negotiation power of the pharmaceutical company compared to the small partner. As illustrated by the case studies, the partners mostly did not possess any product before the licensing agreement was closed, and they were very dependent on in-licensing drug candidates which would match their specialized therapeutic focus. Without the call-back option, gaining access to the project in the first place would have been much more complicated for the licensee if not impossible. In addition, if the out-licensing partners are small companies, such as Speedel, Intarcia or then Actelion, these firms might not even be able to make significant milestone payments related to the compound's development success due to their financial constraints.

Other means which would tie the success of the joint project to the success of both partners in an out-licensing deal would be royalty revenue agreements. However, royalty revenues only occur if the compound successfully enters the market. Depending on the substance's position in the R&D process, the probability of the compound reaching the market might be fairly low, which could significantly reduce the likelihood of any royalty revenues. Besides royalty revenues, co-promotion and co-marketing arrangements also tie the success of a joint project to the success of each partner in a licensing agreement. Another method used by the pharmaceutical company for sharing the success and risks of a joint project in an out-licensing collaboration is to include a right of first refusal regarding re-licensing negotiations into the licensing contract. This might give the pharmaceutical company special rights in discussing a potential re-licensing. Other than a call-back option, which definitely allows for licensing a substance back, these rights do not grant the right to re-license the substance but place the pharmaceutical company in a superior negotiation position over other competitors who might be interested in the substance.

In summary, if an out-licensing deal primarily involves paying pre-defined fees, each partner gains or loses on its own depending on their respective valuation of the deal. Only a higher proportion of success-based payment elements in the compensation structure of the licensing deal is an appropriate means to link the success and failure of each partner to the result of the joint project (see Fig. 44). In the case of out-licensing, the call-back option represents the most widely used vehicle which allows the pharmaceutical company to share risks by retaining an interest in the substance's further development and to license it back when the risks might be lower. Other approaches to consolidate the performance of the partners' joint project in an out-licensing deal include special rights for re-licensing negotiations, royalty reve-

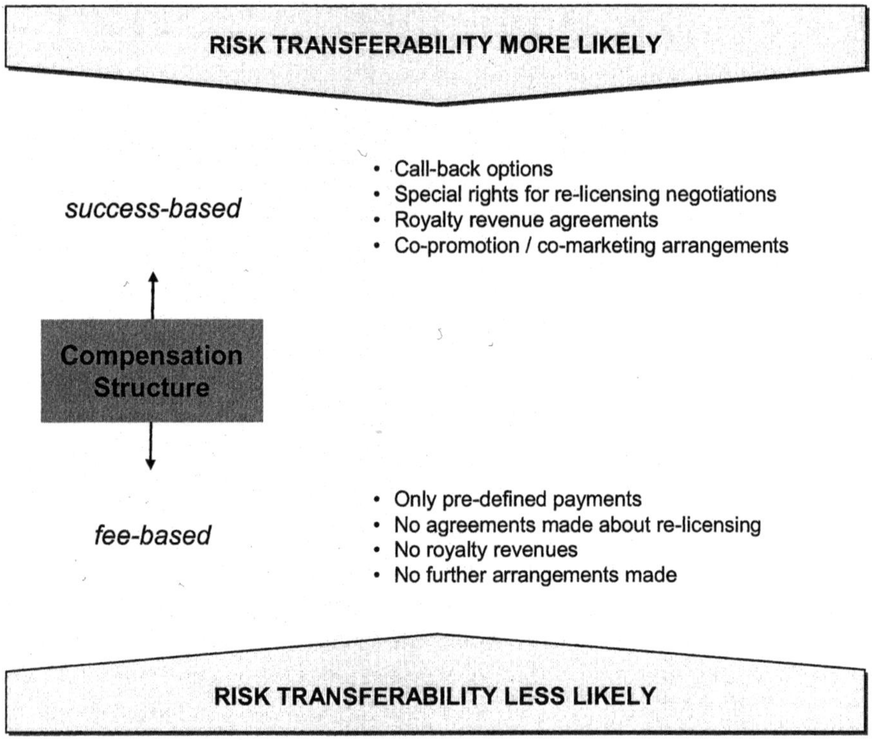

Fig. 44. Success-based vs. fee-based compensation structure of the license.

nues or co-promotion and co-marketing arrangements. Only if the compensation structure allows both partners in the out-licensing collaboration to share the rewards and benefits of the deal, they will be able to share the risks of the joint activities which subsequently increases the transferability of risks in the R&D collaboration.

Conclusion: This chapter has discussed the attributes of the licenses of the case studies regarding their contribution towards the risk transferability. The following three attributes could have been identified, which are considered to have an impact on the risk transferability:

- Appropriability regime;
- Bargaining range;
- Compensation structure.

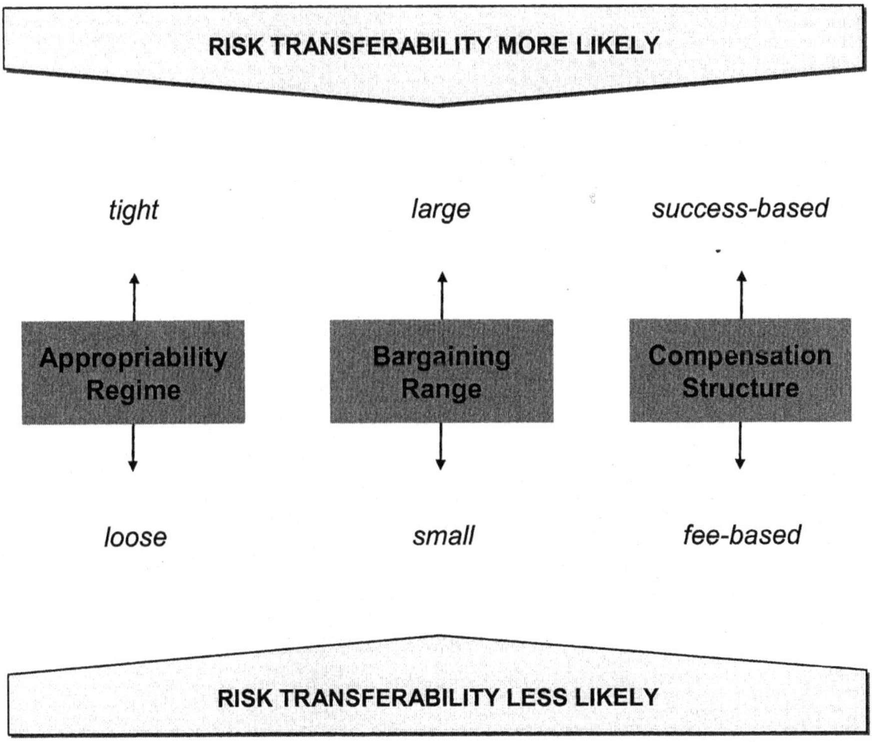

Fig. 45. Attributes of the license and their impact on risk transferability.

The risk transferability is more likely to be high if the attributes of the license meet the following criteria (Fig. 45):

- The appropriability regime should be tight;
- The bargaining range should be large;
- The compensation structure should be success-based.

By contrast, the risk transferability is more likely to be low if the attributes are denoted by the opposite characteristics.

5.3 Attributes of the Licensee

The case studies in chapter 4 have illustrated that the partner firm in the out-licensing collaboration plays a particularly important role because it is the legal entity that ultimately carries the risks which the pharmaceutical company did not want to bear. The most important attributes of the licensees which could be identified during the case study analysis to have an impact on the risk transferability of the out-licensing arrangements include:

- Business strategy;
- Corporate flexibility;
- Entrepreneurial setting.

These three attributes, including their specifications, are discussed in more detail in the following paragraphs.

5.3.1 Business strategy

In all out-licensing collaborations, the licensee takes over full ownership and responsibility of the licensed compound. Then, the licensee starts to conduct the R&D activities which the pharmaceutical firm would have originally been conducting but considered too risky. As a result, the business strategy of the licensee must be similar to the business strategy of the pharmaceutical firm, at least regarding the R&D activities that are to be conducted during the collaboration. Although in the case of Schering and Roche, the indication of the substance had been changed after the closure of the licensing deal, the new indications always belonged to the same therapy area as the substance's initial indication. This allowed the licensee to make use of already available clinical trial data. Therefore, it seems that pharmaceutical companies prefer to out-license their compounds to companies that are direct competitors – at least for some part of the conducted R&D activities. Collaborations between competing firms – which is sometimes also referred to as 'co-opetition' – has been widely discussed in management research.[37] According to the OECD (2002), it is generally believed that competition fosters innovation. The innovation system in industries with a growing demand for cooperation is shifting towards more complex linkages among knowledge production activities. On balance, such cooperation appears to improve the innovative capacity of firms and the efficiency of their innovation activities. Moreover, competition and cooperation are not necessarily opposing forces, given that cooperation in R&D may enable the creation of new markets, and technology licensing may increase the number of competitors in a market.

The partner firms in the case studies (Speedel, Intarcia and Actelion) are directly competing with their traditional pharmaceutical counterparts, however, only on certain selected activities during the entire R&D process. Speedel, Intarcia and Actelion are characterized by a very focused development portfolio targeting just a few selected development activities across a few therapy areas (see Table 7). Actelion does not limit itself to therapy areas but chose a focus on the endothelin system, which represents treatment options for various diseases. Due to the strong focus, the companies are able to aggregate highly condensed expertise in these areas, which allows them to outperform other companies on the respective development tasks in the same areas. Christensen et al. (2004) support the opportunity offered by specialized companies to help large and integrated companies to focus their R&D activities on the pieces that add the most value. The authors claim that companies which continue to integrate their research activities across the entire value chain face the possibility of research 'leaking' to specialist companies. Thus, companies should not employ a one-size-fits-all-forever strategy for capturing value across the lifecycles of their technologics. Rather, the right strategy will depend on finding the decoupling point, for each technology, at each point in time.

---

37 According to Lado et al. (1997), success in today's business world often requires that firms pursue both competitive and cooperative strategies simultaneously. However, collaborations between competitors have been facing considerable criticism. While some scholars have regarded the pursuit of both competitive and cooperative strategies as a paradox (Cameron 1986, Poole and Van de Ven 1989, Quinn and Cameron 1988), Bleeke and Ernst (1995) have even shown that collaborations between competitors with similar core businesses, markets, and skills tend to fail. Contrary to the negative downside, other researchers claim that strategic managers have recognized that striking a balance between competition and cooperation is vital to the performance and survival of business enterprises (Perlmutter and Heenan 1986, Teece 1989). On the one hand, it is argued that firms may need to adopt repertoires of behavior that support cooperation and trust (Hill 1990). On the other hand, it has been suggested that firms may need to compete for competencies generated through strategic alliances (Hamel 1991). It is further asserted that the best partner in a strategic alliance is a strong competitor (Deming 1993). By pooling complementary resources and capabilities, firms can initiate and perform competitively on projects that they could not have done alone (Harrigan 1985).

Table 7. Therapeutic focus of the analyzed partner firms.

Company	Therapy Areas / Focus	# of Projects under Development
Speedel	Cardiovascular Metabolic diseases	6
Intarcia	Oncology Infectious diseases	4
Actelion	Focus on the endothelin system targeting various indications	10

In contrast to the high focus of the specialty pharma companies, the entire pharmaceutical market consists of several different therapeutic areas. Fig. 46 illustrates the largest segments.[38] Although most of the major pharmaceutical companies have started to reorganize their activities and narrow down their therapeutic focus, they still serve multiple therapy areas simultaneously.

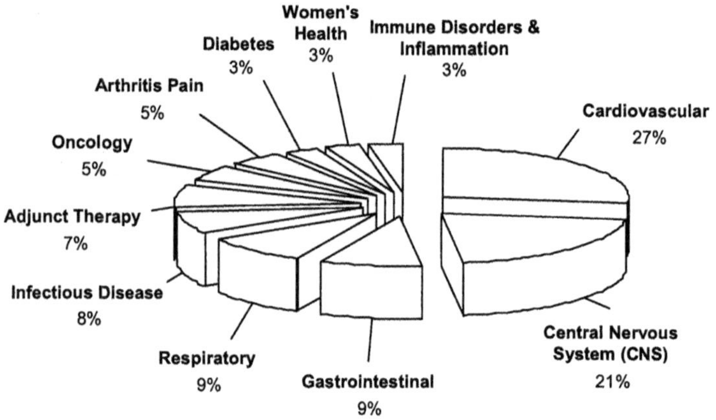

Source: Reuters (2003a)

Fig. 46. Segmentation of the global blockbuster market in 2002.

38 The blockbuster market is dominated by cardiovascular and central nervous system (CNS) therapies. With combined sales of more than US$ 57 billion in 2002, they represent nearly half of all blockbuster sales. More than 300 million people in the seven major national markets (US, UK, Japan, France, Germany, Italy, Spain) suffer from the most common form of dyslipidemia, hypercholesterolemia, making it one of the most prevalent conditions in the Western world (Reuters 2003a). Three of the top five cardiovascular blockbusters are anti-dyslipidemics: Pfizer's Lipitor (atorvastatin), Merck's Zocor (simvastatin), and Bristol-Myers Squibb's Pravachol (pravastatin).

In addition, each of the licensees works on no more than 10 projects simultaneously. By contrast, large pharmaceutical companies typically work on a large number of R&D projects at the same time. For example, Roche worked at the end of 2004 on 107 research projects and 79 development projects simultaneously. Thus, the out-licensing partners in the case study analysis are much smaller than an established pharmaceutical company. The major difference between the partner firms and the pharmaceutical companies is that the partners' focus on only a few development-related activities has made them highly dependent on getting compounds from the outside. Speedel, Intarcia, and Actelion all had to in-license their compounds under development.

Specialization and focus seem to pay off in pharmaceutical R&D. For example, Pfizer acquired in 2004 the company Esperion Therapeutics which had a sharp therapeutic focus and special development expertise in an underappreciated area. Esperion's tight business model demonstrated that specialization is very much likely to attract high attention by large pharmaceutical players. According to research by Evaluate Pharma and Defined Health (2004), specialty pharma companies seem to be much more efficient than the average established pharmaceutical companies in terms of operating margins as well as sales growth. While the compound annual growth rate (CAGR) of all big pharmaceutical companies for the period 1996 through 2004 has been around 8%, specialty pharma companies achieved an annual sales growth rate of 23% during the same time. The operating margin of the average specialty pharma company is also more than 5 percentage-points higher than the margin of the average big pharmaceutical company (see Fig. 47).

According to Thiel (2004), the necessary ingredients for a specialty pharma company to achieve this success include: the reputation, network and skills of the company's management team; a large amount of cash; and a willingness to look in unexpected places for new products. The success of most of the specialty pharma companies was primarily due to the fact that these companies were able to find underpromoted drug candidates at major pharmaceutical companies at conditions which seemed to be attractive to themselves. These underpromoted drug candidates are mostly drugs targeting niche-markets which would be considered to be too small by the large pharmaceutical companies. As they are nevertheless products which are most likely expected to be profitable, the specialty pharma companies might find them attractive. However, questions remain about the sustainability of this focused business strategy. This becomes particularly precarious as more and more companies are entering the specialty pharma markets which is expected to drive up prices for in-licensing opportunities. In addition, it is even expected that the big pharma-

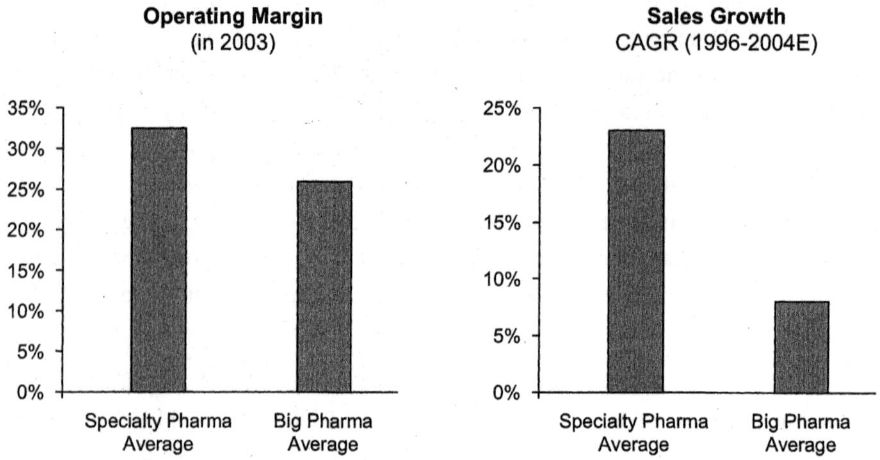

Source: Evaluate Pharma and Defined Health (2004)

Fig. 47. Industry performance of specialty pharma companies compared to established pharmaceutical companies.

ceutical companies are increasingly targeting smaller niche-markets providing severe competition for the specialty pharma companies. This competition might culminate in the point where both the specialty pharma and the traditional pharmaceutical company have to go to biotech companies for discovery assets. But right now, the competition could still be characterized as fairly modest. According to DeGiralamo (2004), the specialty pharma companies will be able to 'make a winner out of a damaged good' as long as they find a niche and an undersatisfied market need.

In summary, the partner firms that are most likely preferred by established pharmaceutical companies as licensees in an out-licensing deal are characterized by a strong focus on a few therapy areas and a relatively small portfolio of development projects (see Fig. 48). In contrast to most of the integrated pharmaceutical companies which pursue a rather broad R&D strategy, the preferred partner companies specialize only on certain R&D activities across selected R&D domains, which most likely center around clinical development. This is expected to lead to strong expertise and high efficiency gains in the execution of the respective R&D activities that are about to be conducted by the partner firm. Moreover, the partner companies seem to have a strong commitment to look at niche-markets with relatively small sales potential compared to the revenue expectations of the large pharmaceutical companies. These niche-markets are generally neglected by most traditional phar-

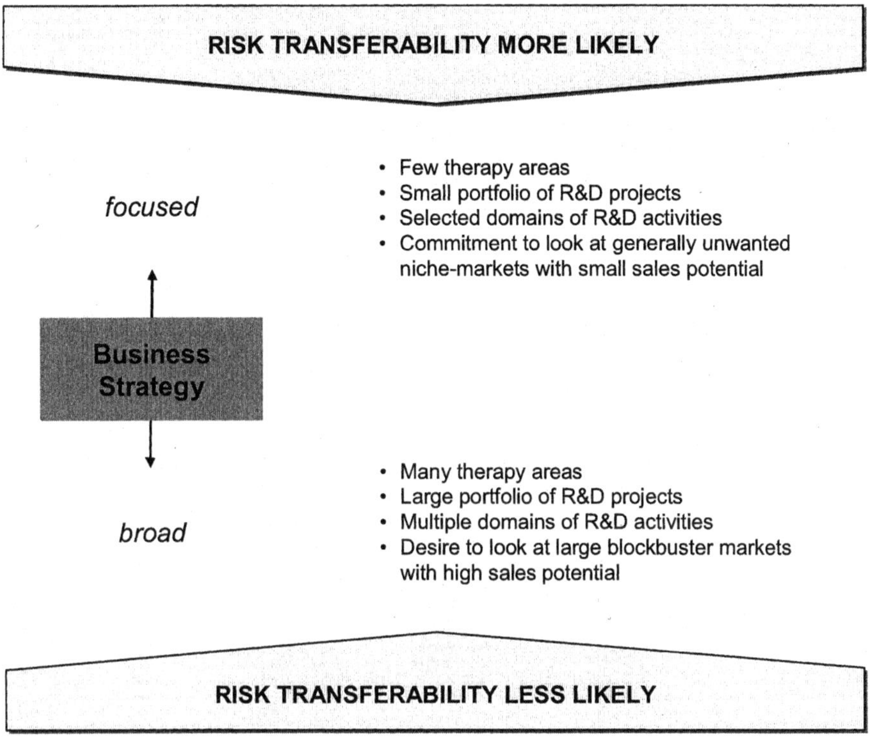

Fig. 48. Focused vs. broad business strategy of the licensee.

maceutical companies although they are likely to offer the opportunity of launching profitable products. Thus, the more focused the partner firm's business strategy, the higher its expertise and the more unique its positioning in the market. As a consequence, the partner firm is more likely capable to handle higher risks due to its special capabilities which in turn increases the risk transferability.

5.3.2 Corporate flexibility

As the partner companies in the case studies focus on in-licensing compounds from outside, they depend on other companies' research results simply by their nature. This requires them to think and act in a very process-oriented way. Barriers to external partners as well as between intra-organizational units have to be minimized. As the licensees not only rely on in-licensing of compounds, but also on working

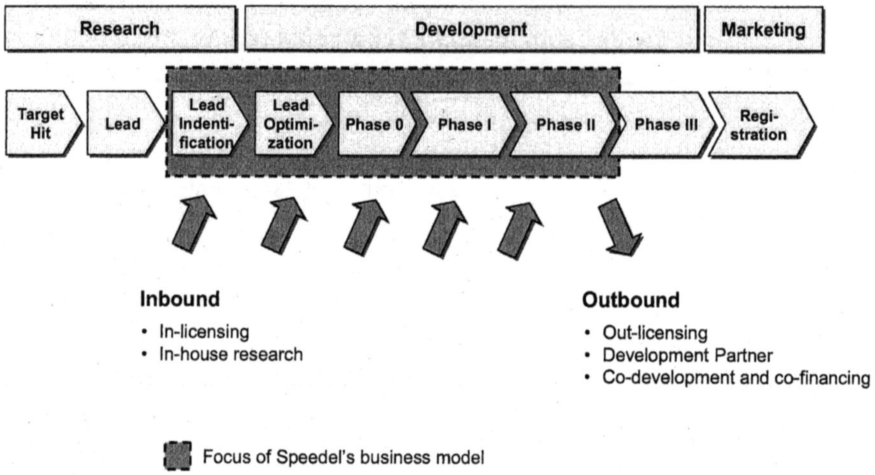

Source: Speedel (2004)

Fig. 49. Speedel's dependency and integration into other companies' innovation processes.

together with other companies on development and marketing issues, the partner companies are usually almost entirely integrated into the innovation process of other companies. This integration is illustrated by the case of Speedel in Fig. 49. Speedel in-licenses compounds at various stages of early development, such as the substance Aliskiren, and then partners during the late development stages and commercialization of the compound.

In addition, the partner firms' small size forced them to rely on external services for clinical trials. As a result, the partner companies as well as most other specialty pharma companies themselves use outsourcing to service providers, such as clinical research organizations (CROs) or clinical development organizations (CDOs). Thereby, their process-oriented structure predestines the specialty pharma companies to work well not only with licensors but also with outsourcing partners. The specialty pharma firm AlgoRx provides an example that illustrates the high dependency of specialty pharma companies on outsourcing.

AlgoRx Pharmaceuticals: Proactive use of outsourcing

The specialty pharma firm AlgoRx, based in Secaucus, NJ (USA), applies a strategic approach to outsourcing in order to lower its overall exposure to fixed costs and expensive investments in infrastructure. According to Thiel (2004), AlgoRx will be conducting half a dozen clinical trials in 2004, maybe even more. However, the firm only employs 14 people. The company does not need the lab space or personnel which are usually dedicated to basic research or other costly development activities. Instead, its efficient processes allow AlgoRx to have very low overhead costs.

The strong interaction with other companies during the R&D process requires not only the establishment of effective and efficient interfaces between the specialty pharma company and its partners, but also requires the specialty pharma company to have very efficient and flexible internal processes in place. Therefore, smaller pharmaceutical firms seem to be obliged to apply various technology platforms and adopt many different delivery mechanisms in order to bring their compound through clinical development.[39] This asks for a more flexible approach to drug development in the smaller firms compared to the larger firms. Despite their focus on speed and efficiency, the partner companies should ensure that their activities comply with the licensors' standards regarding quality and safety. If they do not comply, the licensor has to account for additional coordination and development efforts, which might compensate for the gains achieved by the licensee. In this context, the most frequently cited advantages of specialty pharma companies over traditional, fully integrated pharmaceutical companies include that the specialty pharmas usually are:

- unconstrained by a narrow commercial portfolio strategy;
- able to promote an innovative scientific culture rather than one based on process management and output quality;
- capable of specializing in complementary science areas, not only disease areas;
- not constrained on discovering blockbusters;
- less dependent to infrastructure in terms of lab space or personnel dedicated to basic research and discovery;

39 This finds support by research conducted by Guedj and Scharfstein (2004). The authors compared the strategies and performance of clinical trials between large, mature biopharmaceutical companies and smaller firms (which have not yet successfully developed a drug). In a sample of 235 cancer drug candidates that entered clinical trials during the perion 1990-2002 and were sponsored by public firms, the authors found that the smaller firms were more likely than the mature firms to advance from Phase I clinical trials to Phase II. However, the clinical results of their Phase II trials are less promising. The smaller firms were also less likely to advance to Phase III. Guedj and Scharfstein (2004) conclude that the evidence points to an agency problem between shareholders and managers of single-product smaller firms who seem to be reluctant to abandon development of their only viable drug candidates. By contrast, the managers of mature firms are more willing to drop unpromising drug candidates because they have other ones they can easily bring to clinical trials.

- able to serve a range of customers, rather than just one commercial group;
- capable of attracting investments from diverse groups.

As most of the specialty pharma companies do not represent a revolutionary approach to drug development, their focus on efficiency and flexibility seems to describe the most evident difference between specialty pharma companies and traditional pharmaceutical companies. Specialty pharma firms generally place great emphasis on development speed and try to get to late-stage drugs quicker. The company Speedel even incorporated the motto of 'speed in development' into its company name by combining the two words 'speed' and 'development'. Development speed ultimately benefits both parties of the collaboration because of the high importance of the time-to-market in breakthrough pharmaceuticals.

In summary, the partner companies' R&D activities do not materially differ from the activities of the licensors. However, due to their small size and strong focus, they are much more contingent upon both in-sourcing compounds and securing sufficient development and marketing capacities from outside partners than other pharmaceutical companies. This forces them to think and act in a more process-oriented way as well as to manage clear and efficient interfaces almost to an extent where they might be considered to be integrated into their partners' structures and processes. Moreover, the partner firms – like most other specialty pharma companies – are characterized by very flexible development structures. They are able to quickly give an in-licensed substance a new spin by either changing the compound's indication or applying a new delivery system. This highly efficiency-driven approach to drug development significantly speeds-up development performance (see Fig. 50). If the partner firm has a very strong commitment to development efficiency and flexibility, the pharmaceutical firm will consequently be better able to share R&D risks with its external partner. Therefore, the higher the licensee's corporate flexibility, the higher the transferability of R&D risks.

5.3.3 Entrepreneurial setting

Companies like Speedel, Intarcia, Actelion or many other specialty pharma firms are fairly young companies, but this type of firm is not entirely new to the pharmaceutical industry. There are several specialty pharma companies which have been founded already in the 1980s and early 1990s. Examples include Alkermes, Axca, Biovail, Connetics, Kos, Medicis Pharmaceuticals, Sepracor, Shire Pharmaceuticals, or Watson Pharmaceuticals. The inception of specialty pharma companies even goes back to the 1950s or 1960s, as illustrated by the cases of Forest Labs or Mylan.

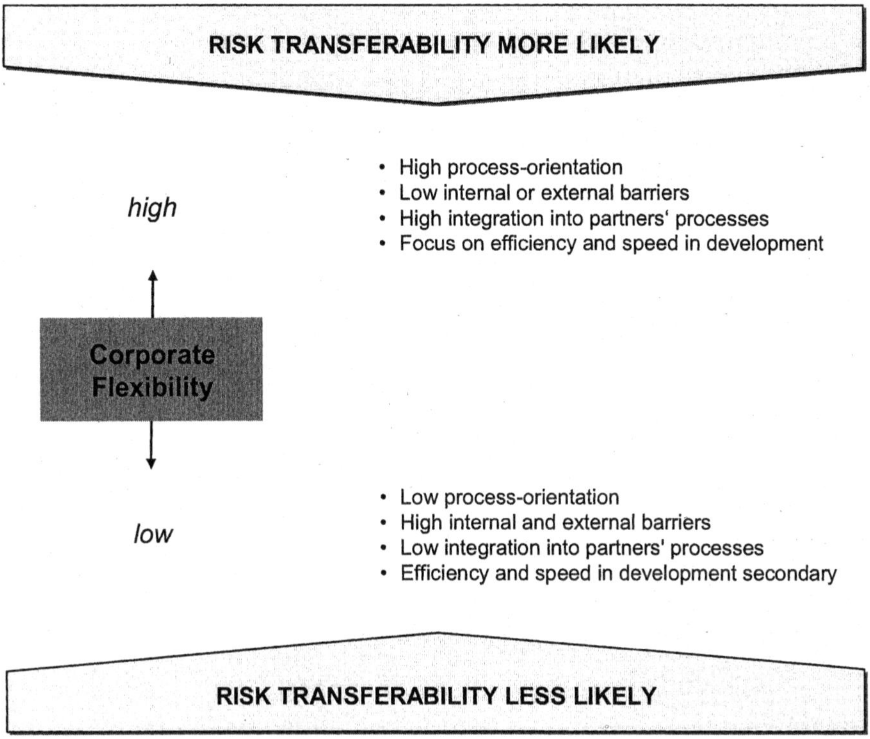

Fig. 50. High vs. low corporate flexibility of the licensee.

While there are only a few large specialty pharma companies which employ between 2,000 and 5,000 people, most of the specialty pharma companies are rather small and entrepreneurial. However, even the larger specialty pharma companies are still small compared to the large players in the pharmaceutical industry, such as Pfizer (122,000 employees), GlaxoSmithKline (103,000 employees) or Sanofi-Aventis (100,000 employees).

Another remarkable charateristic is that the partner firms in the analyzed case studies are all significantly funded by venture capital investors. Speedel secured about CHF 120 in venture capital, Intarcia around US$ 195 million, and Actelion CHF 66 million (Actelion raised another CHF 200 million by its IPO in 2000). The venture capital investors were willing to provide the capital for these high-risk endeavors and therefore, they ultimately represent the entities that carry the risk burden (see

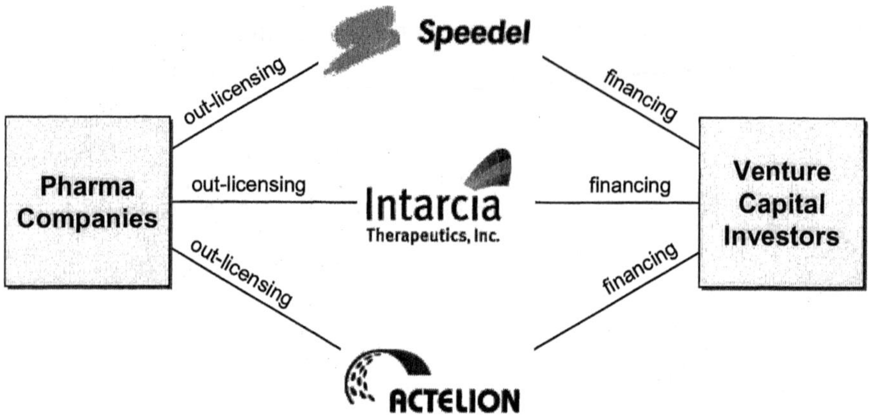

Fig. 51. Venture capitalists as providers of capital for high-risk development tasks.

Fig. 51). In addition, management usually owns a significant portion of the equity which links the employees' compensation to the success of the entire company.[40]

Speedel, Intarcia and Actelion do not represent isolated cases. There has recently been a significant boom of newly created companies which operate under the specialty pharma business model and are significantly funded by venture capital investors (see Table 8). However, it could have been observed that the newly founded companies in the specialty pharma segment – which are now also referred to as NRDOs (no-research-development-only companies) instead of specialty pharma companies – offer a new twist on the well known specialty pharma business model. Whereas old guard specialty pharma companies built their businesses primarily around products already approved – drugs with all or most of the technology risk behind them – today's NRDOs take on drugs at earlier stages, as early as clinical phase I or in some cases even pre-clinical development (see Thiel 2004). This implies that they proactively take on products with higher risks.[41] The emergence of this new generation of specialty pharma companies is due to the fact that today's

---

40 In this context, a study by Billings et al. (2004) reveals that that R&D productivity increases with the proportion of stock held by managers and directors of firms.

41 Venkataraman (1997) provides support for these findings by claiming that venture-backed startup companies typically face high levels of uncertainty.

market conditions in the pharmaceutical industry have created a positive environment for this type of specialized firms. The most important reasons for the surge in newly created NRDO companies include the following aspects:

- Big pharmaceutical companies have focused largely on blockbuster products to drive their sales growth. Many specialty markets have therefore been untapped due to their smaller size which made them unattractive for most of the large pharmaceutical companies to enter.
- Due to the wave of consolidation among major pharmaceutical companies, various compounds had to be divested due to strategic or antitrust reasons. This has resulted in attractive late-stage and commercial licensing candidates.
- Investors have recently been avoiding to invest in research and discovery-based biotech companies because they believe it takes too much time and costs for bringing new substances from discovery to the market. Instead, they prefer to invest in business models which are characterized by a shorter time-to-market of their products under development. By investing in specialty pharma companies, which in-license compounds in clinical stages, the fairly risky phases of the early discovery stages can be skipped. Investors may be able to receive a return on investment much earlier than in the case of a traditional biotech investment.

Table 8 provides a brief overview about some of the most recently established NRDO companies which focus on in-licensing drug candidates from major pharmaceutical firms.

Table 8. Selected newly-founded NRDOs.

Company	Focus, lead product or strategy	Year founded
Advancis Pharmaceuticals (formerly Advanced Pharma)	Anti-infective, including preclinical assets. In-licensed Eli Lilly's Keflex.	2000. IPO in October 2003
Angiogenix	Vascular therapeutics. Acquired nitrate products from NitrOSystems.	2002
Aspreva Pharmaceuticals	New indications for existing drugs. Rights to Roche's CellCept outside of organ transplantation.	2001
BioLineRx	Neurological disorders. In-licensed compounds from Tel Aviv and Bar Ilan Universities.	2003
CoTherix (formerly Exhale Therapeutics)	NDA pending for Ventavis (for pulmonary hypertension), in-licensed from Schering AG.	2000. IPO in registration

Table 8. (continued).

ESP Pharma	Approved or late-stage products. In-licensed products from Wyeth, including Cardene IV for hypertension.	2002
Hudson Health Sciences	Immunology or oncology. Novel antifolate from Dana Farber Cancer Institute in Phase I. Has preclinical assets.	2003
InterMune	Markets Actimmune for pulmonary fibrosis. In-licensed from Genentech: Infergen (for hepatitis C), and Amphotec (for certain fungal infections).	Formed in 1999 as a spin-off of Connetics
Novacardia	In-licensed Kyowa Hakko's adenosine A1 receptor antagonist.	2003
Peninsula Pharmaceuticals	Several antibiotic compounds in-licensed from Takeda.	2001
Rejuvenon	Cancer cachexia, Phase I in-licensed from Novo-Nordisk.	2000
Tercica	Endocrine. Insulin-like growth factor from Genentech, in Phase III.	2002. IPO in March 2004
Vanda Pharmaceuticals	Schizophrenia, iloperidone from Novartis in Phase III. Management formerly at Novartis.	2003

Source: adapted from Thiel (2004)

Many of these recently founded NRDOs have experienced great success on the capital markets by securing large amounts of venture capital as well as some successful IPOs. The best performing IPO in 2003 in any industry has been the NRDO Pharmion. Pharmion's stock price has risen more than 200% from its public offering until September 2004. Out of 28 therapeutics companies who made their IPO since 2003, 9 have cleaved closely to the NRDO model, and at least 2 more such firms are on deck at the time of writing (see Thiel 2004). The average specialty pharma company raised approximately US$ 100 million before going public (see Thiel 2004). These large investments are quite substantial when it is considered that the companies are funded at very early stages in their lifecycles. The 13 companies listed in Table 8 have an average age of 3 to 4 years at the time of writing (the average year of inception was in mid-2001). Sometimes, the newly venture-backed NRDO only had a management team but not even a compound. In Germany, the fairly young specialty pharma company Paion, which is headquartered in Aachen, went public in 2005. At the time of writing, Paion's IPO was the first and only IPO at a German stock exchange in 2005.

The new NRDO model: New start-up boom after the collapse of the technology bubble

Most venture capital investors are still burned by the aftermath of the genomics-driven stock bubble of 2000 (see Thiel 2004). As a result, they have started to shift their attention away from the traditional biotech investments which conduct early stage discovery-based research and have a time to market of their inventions of at least 13 to 15 years. Instead, investors prefer much shorter times to bring new substances to market in order to reduce the risk exposure of their own investments. Therefore, the NRDO model seems to have emerged as the Holy Grail for venture capital investors. Returns might be visible much earlier than before. It is therefore not surprising that many start-up NRDOs have been recently founded with a business plan and a management team but no product assets. Examples include Pharmion, Jazz Pharmaceuticals, The Medicines Company or AlgoRx. In March 2004, the NRDO Jazz Pharmaceuticals announced that it even secured a US$ 250 million Series B venture round. Some experts already say that this could be 'the ultimate sign of the space is getting a little overheated' (Thiel 2004).

In summary, there are many recently founded specialty pharma companies which have experienced great success in the marketplace. The overall market conditions in the pharmaceutical industry as well as the desire of investors to fund biopharmaceutical-related startups that show a shorter time-to-market of their products under development have created favorable market conditions for the surge in these companies. The analyzed partner firms in the case studies are characterized by a small size having between 35 and 840 employees which is negligibly small when compared to the sizes of the licensors which employ between 81,000 people (Novartis), 26,000 (Schering) and 65,000 (Roche). The significant venture capital funding in this area is an indicator for the fact that this business model represents an emerging trend in the pharmaceutical industry. As a consequence, the entrepreneurial setting of the partner firms can generally be described as rather strong (see Fig. 52). Therefore, an entrepreneurial atmosphere at the partner firm seems to be more likely to enable the partner firm to take on high-risk R&D projects. This in turn gives the pharmaceutical companies the opportunity to get involved in out-licensing deals with these spe-

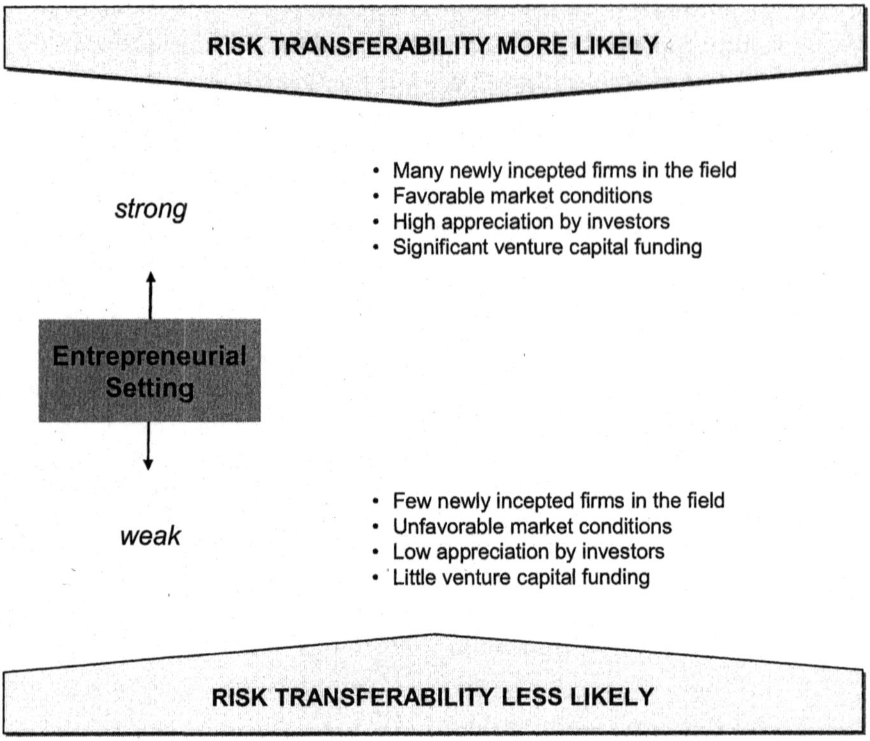

Fig. 52. Strong vs. weak entrepreneurial setting of the licensee.

cialized partner companies in order to share R&D risks. Therefore, a strong entrepreneurial setting of the partner firm is expected to increase the risk transferability of an out-licensing collaboration.

Conclusion: This chapter has observed the case studies from chapter 4 regarding the attributes of the licensees. The attributes of the licensees have been analyzed regarding their risk transferability. The following three attributes could have been identified which seem to have an impact on the risk transferability:

- Business strategy;
- Corporate flexibility;
- Entrepreneurial setting.

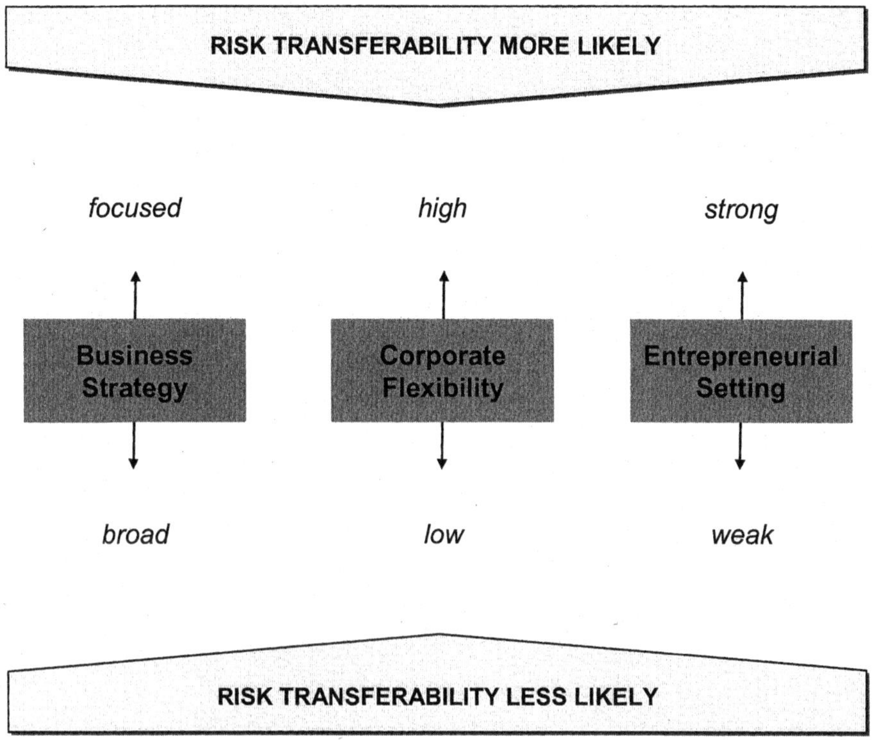

Fig. 53. Attributes of the licensee and their impact on risk transferability.

The risk transferability is more likely to be high if the attributes of the out-licensing partner meet the following criteria (Fig. 53):

- The business strategy should be focused;
- The corporate flexibility should be high;
- The entrepreneurial setting should be strong.

By contrast, the risk transferability is low for the opposite specifications.

5.4 Summary

This chapter has discussed characteristics of the out-licensing collaborations as introduced in the case studies in chapter 4 regarding their risk transferability. The risk transferability is expected to describe the pharmaceutical companies' ability to convey R&D risks to the external partner. The characteristics of the out-licensing collaborations could have been classified according to the three entities involved in the deal: the licensor, the license and the licensee. All entities are characterized by different attributes. The attributes of the licensor which have been considered to show a strong impact on the risk transferability included the out-licensing approach, the out-licensing organization as well as the out-licensing process. The attributes of the license centered around the appropriability regime, the bargaining range, and the compensation structure. The attributes of the licensee covered the business strategy, the corporate flexibility and the entrepreneurial setting.

Based on the case study analysis, the following summarizing statements about the risk transferability in out-licensing collaborations can be made: The pharmaceutical company's commitment towards out-licensing represents a basic requirement for an effective out-licensing strategy. This includes to adopt the mindset of an out-licensor and to establish a clear commitment towards out-licensing. Out-licensing should have dedicated resources and clear reporting structures which could include the assignment of profit and loss responsibilities. Moreover, the pharmaceutical company should not only be aware of the different tasks that have to be completed during an out-licensing deal, but it should have the respective methodologies, processes and guidelines in place which are necessary to successfully execute the out-licensing collaboration.

A license that enables a high risk transferability is typically characterized by an appropriability regime that offers a solid protection of intellectual property and reduces the unwanted outflow of information for the inventor (i.e. the pharmaceutical firm). Moreover, the appropriability regime should ensure a direct application potential of the license for the licensee. The bargaining range describes the value potential of the license by comparing the NPVs for both the licensor and licensee, and should ideally be large. This means that the licensee values the potential benefit of the compound to be much higher than its inherent risks – as compared to the licensor – which increases the likelihood of the deal to be closed. The compensation structure of the collaboration should tie the successes of the two partners together. Re-licensing rights and royalty revenue arrangements represent sound vehicles to link the partners' rewards and benefits which ultimately enables to share the risks of the joint activity.

It has shown that specialty pharma companies seem to be the most appropriate licensees preferred by large pharmaceutical companies. The partner firms in the analyzed case studies all covered only a few selected parts of the R&D process and pursued a very focused business strategy targeting only up to two therapy areas (Actelion does not pursue a strategy focusing on therapy areas. Instead the company seeks to offer treatments centering around one particular system – the endothelin). In addition, the partner firms were characterized by very flexible R&D structures due to their small size and a high dependence on partnering and outside innovation. All of the partners during the case studies as well as many additional companies in the specialty pharma industry segment are fairly recently established companies. These start-up companies even received their own classification by being referred to as NRDOs. Most of these companies are characterized by small functional teams, and are substantially backed by venture capital investors. This comparatively strong entrepreneurial setting allows these firms to take on risks which might be considered too high by established pharmaceutical companies.

Table 9 provides a brief summary about the specifications of all attributes for each of the analyzed case studies.

Table 9. Specifications of the attributes of the analyzed case studies.

	Novartis – Speedel (Aliskiren)	**Schering – Intarcia (Atamestane)**	**Roche – Actelion (Bosentan)**
Licensor			
Out-licensing approach	***passive*** (waiting for opportunities to arise)	***proactive*** (active commercialization of compounds)	***passive*** (waiting for opportunities to arise)
Out-licensing organization	***embedded*** (dedicated resources and defined responsibilities)	***embedded*** (dedicated resources and defined responsibilities)	***embedded*** (dedicated resources and defined responsibilities)
Out-licensing process	***structured*** (clear assignments and elaborated guidelines)	***structured*** (clear assignments and elaborated guidelines)	***structured*** (clear assignments and elaborated guidelines)
License			
Appropriability regime	***tight*** (same therapy area and same indication)	***tight*** (same therapy area but changed indication)	***tight*** (same therapy area but changed indication)
Bargaining range	***large*** (different preferences for project valuation)	***large*** (different preferences for project valuation)	***large*** (different preferences for project valuation)

Table 9. (continued).

Compensation structure	***success-based*** (call-back option and milestone payments)	***success-based*** (call-back option and/or co-selling agreement)	***success-based*** (call-back option and royalty revenues)
Licensee			
Business strategy	***focused*** (selected R&D activities across 2 therapy areas)	***focused*** (selected R&D activities across 2 therapy areas)	***focused*** (focuse on only one system, the endothelin)
Corporate flexibility	***high*** (dependence on partners and focus on efficiency)	***high*** (dependence on partners and focus on efficiency)	***high*** (at the time of the deal: dependence on partners)
Entrepreneurial setting	***strong*** (new, small and VC funded company)	***strong*** (new, small and VC funded firm, IPO to come)	***strong*** (start-up firm at deal closure; now mid-sized)

Fig. 54 aggregates graphically all three entities of the out-licensing collaboration and their respective attributes. The first step of every successful out-licensing arrangement includes that the pharmaceutical company (the licensor) shows a strong commitment and defines a clear strategy towards out-licensing. Thus, the inner circle in Fig. 54 shows the attributes of the licensor which represent the central origin of any out-licensing activity. They lay the foundation for any subsequent out-licensing activity of the pharmaceutical company. Only if out-licensing is well aligned within the overall corporate strategy of the pharmaceutical company, the entire collaboration can successfully be structured along the remaining two entities of the out-licensing arrangement: the product which is about to be exchanged (the license), and the partner firm which is expected to take on the risks of the product's further development (the licensee). The attributes of the remaining entities which complete the out-licensing agreement (the license and the licensee) are shown in the outer circle. The attributes of all entities involved in the out-licensing agreement have an impact on the transferability of risks during the collaboration.

The risk transferability regarding the *licensor* is most likely to be high if the out-licensing approach is proactive, the out-licensing organization is well embedded within the corporation, and the out-licensing process is structured. The risk transferability regarding the *license* is most likely to be high if the appropriability regime is tight, the bargaining range is large, and the compensation structure is success-based.

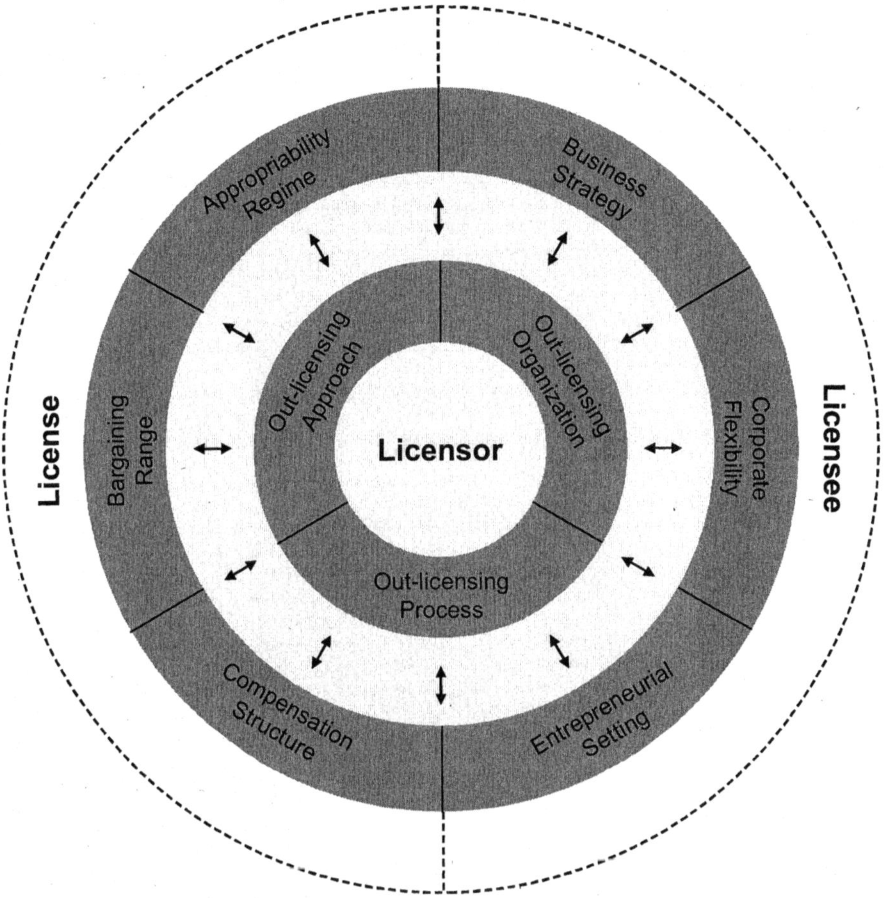

Fig. 54. Entities and their attributes involved in an out-licensing collaboration.

Finally, the risk transferability regarding the *licensee* is most likely to be high if the business strategy is focused, the corporate flexibility is high, and the entrepreneurial setting is strong.

6 Theoretical Basis for Risk-sharing in Pharma R&D Collaborations

Out-licensing deals have traditionally been done because of downstream concerns (see Cockburn 2004).[42] The case study analysis in the previous two chapters, however, has shown that the out-licensing firms (i.e. the pharmaceutical companies) own all assets which are necessary to successfully develop the licensed compounds. By contrast, the in-licensing firms (i.e. the partner companies) are relatively small and did not possess a track record of successful drug development at the time when the deals had been closed. Subsequently, it could be assumed that the pharmaceutical companies should ideally be the ones that develop the drug and not the smaller partners. In this context, Windhover (2000) claims that one of the most critical issues in out-licensing at established pharmaceutical companies includes that the partner firm must be able to convince the pharmaceutical company that it can execute the compound's development and help grow sales of their drugs, sometimes even before they have a marketing and sales track record. As a result, the pharmaceutical companies sell their licensing contracts to external partners although they do not seem to be able to ascertain the licensees' ability to successfully execute the compound's further development. As the licensees usually have more information about their own development capabilities than the licensors, out-licensing at established pharmaceutical companies is subsequently characterized by a fairly high asymmetric distribution of information.

The first scholars who discussed markets that are characterized by an asymmetric distribution of information have been Michael Rothschild and Joseph Stiglitz in 1976. Rothschild and Stiglitz (1976) define markets which are characterized by asymmetric information as all markets where the characteristics of the commodities exchanged are not fully known to at least one of the parties to the transaction. The authors conducted their research by looking at competitive insurance markets, and they described how these markets would behave when the buyers of insurance policies differ by risk levels (i.e. the likelihood of them being involved in an accident) but the sellers of the insurance policies are unable to distinguish among these risks. Rothschild and Stiglitz (1976) show that, if potential insurance buyers know their risk levels – and if they can keep that information from insurers – and if insurers are

42 This means that the out-licensing company usually has limited development capabilities and the in-licensing firm possesses the necessary capabilities to develop the licensed compound, such as (i) the expertise to deal with regulatory bodies, (ii) the competence to develop timely clinical testing, (iii) the ability to scale up manufacturing of a product for large quantities, and (iv) established marketing and distribution capabilities (see McCutchen and Swamidass 2004).

willing to offer any potentially profitable contracts, a process of sorting or self-selection might follow. As a consequence, the authors conclude that not only may a competitive equilibrium not exist, but when equilibria do exist, they may have strange properties. Rothschild and Stiglitz (1976) refer to this process of sorting as 'adverse selection'.

The market for out-licensing at large pharmaceutical companies seems to show many similarities with the competitive insurance markets described by Rothschild and Stiglitz (1976). The pharmaceutical company is about to offer a licensing contract to a potential partner firm (equivalent to the insurance company offering an insurance contract to a potential buyer). However, as the licensees are usually small companies which do not have a track record of successful drug development, the pharmaceutical company cannot differentiate among the potential licensees based on their ability to execute the compound's further development (equivalent to the different risk levels of the buyers of insurance contracts which are unkown to the insurance company). Especially if the pharmaceutical company sells the license to the partner firm as a straight license under a highly royalty-based contract, the nature of the out-licensing contract is similar to the nature of the insurance contracts as illustrated by Rothschild and Stiglitz (1976).[43] If the partner company is now unable to execute the compound's development (equivalent to 'the accident' in the insurance case), it is entitled to retain all intellectual property related to the license (equivalent to the 'insurance pay-out after the accident') although it has paid only a comparatively small amount to the pharmaceutical company (equivalent to 'the insurance premium').

Due to the similarities between the insurance market and the out-licensing market, applying the theory of adverse selection to the case of out-licensing might allow the transfer and utilization of some of the theory's insights already gained by Rothschild and Stiglitz (1976). This application could have a high relevance for pharmaceutical R&D managers in terms of locating equilibria in markets characterized by asymmetric information. Finding an equilibrium in the out-licensing market is necessary for closing an out-licensing deal which in turn represents a basic requirement

43 Under a straight license, the licensee becomes the full owner of all intellectual property covered by the license. The licensing deals in the case study analysis in chapter 4 were all straight licenses.

Under a highly royalty-based contract, the partner firm pays only a small fraction of the entire price as an upfront payment immediately upon closing the deal, and in return it will receive all of the intellectual property related to the license. The majority of the price is paid in terms of royalty revenues which accrue only if the partner firm successfully executes the compound's development and brings the drug to the market.

for being able to transfer R&D risks (as could have been illustrated in chapter 3.2). Understanding the emergence and existence of equilibria in the out-licensing market could ultimately help constituting a management framework for pharmaceutical companies regarding the manageability of out-licensing collaborations.

While chapter 6.1 briefly introduces the theory of adverse selection in the insurance markets as described by Rothschild and Stiglitz (1976), the subsequent chapter 6.2 applies the model of adverse selection to the case of out-licensing at established pharmaceutical companies. The goal of applying the model is to identify managerial areas of action which are considered to have an impact on finding an equilibrium in the out-licensing market. After these areas will have been derived, it can be determined how they have to be modified in order to reduce the asymmetric information and to find constellations which increase the likelihood of finding an equilibrium in the out-licensing market.

6.1 The Theory of Adverse Selection

The theory of adverse selection originates from research conducted in competitive insurance markets.[44] The theory represents an economical model that describes equilibria in markets where one party of a transaction does not have full information regarding the exchange of certain commodities (i.e. the market is characterized by an asymmetric distribution of information). Markets which are characterized by asymmetric information tend to show adverse selection processes when finding an equilibrium between supply and demand. Under quite plausible conditions, there might be no equilibrium in the market as long as there is asymmetric information.

The process of adverse selection works in stages. Rothschild and Stiglitz (1976) assume that the market begins with a single policy offered. If insurers cannot distinguish well among risk levels, the premium for the policy will be approximately 'community rated' (i.e. it will be similar for all potential buyers). However, if insurers are free to enter and if consumers know which risk type they are, such a situation cannot be an equilibrium. As high-risk consumers (i.e. the consumers who are more likely to be involved in an accident) value generous insurance benefits more than low-risk consumers do, there will always exist another policy on the market, less generous in effective coverage than the community-rated one, but lower in premium which will cause to split up the consumers with different risk levels. In the

44 If not otherwise mentioned, these chapters widely refer to Rothschild and Stiglitz (1976, pp. 630-638).

case of the two risk classes (i.e. high and low) there will always be a policy that the low-risks will prefer to the community-rated policy, while the high-risks will prefer to stick with the old policy at the old premium.

In the next stage, once that new policy is offered on the market and the low-risks switch, the old policy can no longer be profitably offered at its original premium. As the high-risks now overly represent the remaining consumers of the old policy, its premium subsequently will have to rise. Before that, the high-risk buyers caused externalities on the low-risk buyers (i.e. the low-risks subsidized the high-risks). As a consequence, the low-risk individuals are worse off than they would be in the absence of the high-risk individuals. However, the high-risk individuals are no better off than they would be in the absence of the low-risk individuals.

After the premium of the old policy will have increased, it might be possible that the high-risks will now also prefer the new policy, with less generous coverage to the old community-rated policy. At some point, the original policy might even disappear. Furthermore, Rothschild and Stiglitz (1976) show that this stage is not the end of the entire process. As will be described in chapter 6.2.6, there might be the situation that there may be no equilibrium at all; the market may move cyclically from one policy to another and never settles down because there will always be a new possible equilibrium after one equilibrium has been achieved.

6.2 Adverse Selection Applied to the Case of Out-licensing

As Rothschild and Stiglitz (1976) originally explained the model for insurance contracts in competitive insurance markets, this chapter highlights the specifications regarding the model's translation to the case of out-licensing in the pharmaceutical industry. Most of the argumentation is made by the analysis of a simple out-licensing example describing the behavior of a company that might become a potential buyer of a license ('the partner firm' or 'licensee'), whereas the license is sold by a large and established pharmaceutical company ('the licensor'). As shown earlier, this constellation is expected to be characterized by a fairly high level of asymmetric information.

Consider a partner company which projects its total revenues to be W. In order to meet its revenue projection, the firm has to come up with a sufficient number of new drug candidates that leave its R&D department and enter the market. Usually, the partner firm has only a limited number of R&D projects to reach the projected sales of W, especially if the partner company is a small firm. If the partner firm's

R&D department is – for any reason – not able to deliver the required number of compounds because the company cannot successfully execute the development of some projects, the partner firm experiences a decline in projected revenues of d. This would leave the partner company with total revenues of $(W - d)$.

However, the partner firm can 'insure' itself against this potential revenue decrease by purchasing a straight license from another company (in this case: the pharmaceutical company) under a highly royalty-based contract. Thereby, the partner firm pays only a small fraction of the entire price as an upfront payment immediately upon closing the deal (assumed to be α_1), and in return it will receive all of the intellectual property related to the license which is assumed to have the value $\acute{\alpha}_2$.[45] This assumption is reasonable because of two reasons. Firstly, pharmaceutical companies normally out-license only compounds that they have already terminated. Therefore, they do not believe that these compounds have a high value any more, and they are more likely to sell them for low upfront payments. Particularly if the partner firm is a smaller firm, the upfront payments are limited due to the partner's financial constraints (compare Windhover 2000). Secondly, the pharmaceutical companies are afraid to out-license a compound which might turn out to become a blockbuster later on (see Windhover 2000). Therefore, pharmaceutical companies typically prefer a large revenue participation over upfront payments.

Now assume that the partner company cannot successfully execute the licensed compound's development. This leaves the partner firm with the following situation. It only pays the pharmaceutical company the comparatively low upfront payment α_1, and is allowed to retain all intellectual assets inherent to the license valued at $\acute{\alpha}_2$. The remaining and comparatively large royalty revenue payments to the pharmaceutical company which are still outstanding do not have to be paid by the partner company any more because the compound's development has failed. While this situation seems to be a bargain for the partner company because it acquired a license for a relatively low amount, it has to be considered that the value of the compound's intellectual property rights usually drops to a certain extent in case the compound's development fails. However, the intellectual property rights that the partner firm is allowed to retain might lead to additional synergies, such as learning-effects, spillovers, process know-how or other forms of knowledge transfer to the partner company which have not been monetized in the upfront payment made to the pharma-

45 The majority of the price is paid in terms of royalty revenues which accrue only if the partner firm successfully executes the compound's development and brings the drug to the market.

ceutical company. Especially if the partner firm is a small and young company, this additional inflow of intellectual capital might have a comparatively high value for the firm. It is assumed that the value of these synergies – particularly for a small partner company – helps raise the value of the in-licensed product to approximately its initial value of $\acute{\alpha}_2$. Therefore, the partner firm's situation in this case would be $(W - d - \alpha_1 + \acute{\alpha}_2)$.

By contrast, if the partner company is able to execute the compound's development, the pharmaceutical company would – under a risk-sharing contract – most likely re-license the compound including its underlying intellectual property ($\acute{\alpha}_2$). However, it is assumed that a fair licensing deal is usually structured in a way that the payments by the pharmaceutical company for re-licensing the compound will allow the partner company to compensate for the decline in projected revenues (d) as well as potentially occurring milestone payments that had to be made by the partner firm. This would leave the partner company with the situation $(W - \alpha_1)$. If the deal terms of the licensing agreement would allow the partner company to retain the license (or if the pharmaceutical company would not execute its re-licensing rights), the partner company would usually have to reimburse the pharmaceutical company with royalty revenues or milestone payments. As the scope of these payments towards the licensor typically relates to the advancements of the compound (see Walton 2004), they might compensate for the value of $\acute{\alpha}_2$ which would leave the partner firm in the same position as if it had to return the intellectual assets of the compound to the pharmaceutical company.

Fig. 55 summarizes the partner firm's situation for the different states 'can execute the compound's development' and 'cannot execute the compound's development' for both cases: without having acquired a license and with having acquired a straight license under a highly royalty-based contract. Reflecting that the term $\alpha_2 = \acute{\alpha}_2 - \alpha_1$ describes the value of the license for the partner firm, the vector $\alpha = (\alpha_1, \alpha_2)$ completely describes the licensing contract.[46] On the out-licensing market, the licensing contracts (the α's) are traded. To describe how the market works, it is necessary to describe the supply and demand functions of the participants in the market. There are only two kinds of participants: licensees who buy licensing contracts and licen-

46 Actual licensing contracts are more complicated because a single contract will cover more than just the upfront payment paid by the licensee and the value of the intellectual property rights exchanged. In the scope of this model, however, it is assumed that the vector $\alpha = (\alpha_1, \alpha_2)$ sufficiently describes the entire licensing contract. For a more detailed explanation why the vector α can be used to portray the licensing contract, please refer to Rothschild and Stiglitz (1976, p. 630).

	Partner firm can execute	Partner firm cannot execute
without license	W	$W - d$
with license*	$W - \alpha_1$	$W - d - \alpha_1 + \acute{\alpha}_2$ = $W - d + \alpha_2$

* assumes a straight license under a highly royalty-based licensing contract.

Fig. 55. The partner firm's projected revenues in the case of out-licensing.

sors who sell them. The following sub-chapters describe in more detail the market for out-licensing contracts covering in particular (i) the demand for licenses, (ii) the supply of licenses, (iii) the information about probabilities that the licensee cannot execute the compound's development, and (iv) the existence of equilibria in the out-licensing market assuming both licensees with identical risk exposure as well as different risk exposure regarding the execution of the respective development tasks.

6.2.1 Demand for licensing contracts

Determining a partner firm's demand for licensing contracts is straightforward. The partner firm purchases a license to modify its pattern of projected revenues across different states of nature. Assume that W_1 denotes the projected revenues if the partner successfully executed the development, and W_2 describes the projected revenues if it could not execute. The expected utility theorem states that under relatively mild assumptions the partner firm's preferences for revenues in these two states of nature are described by a function of the form,

$$\hat{Y}(p, W_1, W_2) = (1-p)\, U(W_1) + p\, U(W_2) \qquad (1)$$

where $U(\ )$ represents the utility of projected revenues and p the probability that the partner firm cannot execute. The licensee's demand for licensing contracts may be derived from (1). A contract α is worth $Y(p, \alpha) = \hat{Y}(p, W - \alpha_1, W - d + \alpha_2)$. From all the contracts that are offered to the partner firm, the partner chooses the one that maximizes $Y(p, \alpha)$. As the partner firm always has the option of buying no license, the partner will purchase a license α only if $Y(p, \alpha) > Y(p, 0) = \hat{Y}(p, W, W - d)$. Reflecting the case of licensing in the pharmaceutical industry, it is assumed that all licensees are identical in all respects trying to avoid that their projected revenues do not meet expectations which means that they are generally risk-averse (i.e. the second derivation of their utility function is negative, $U'' < 0$); thus $Y(p, \alpha)$ is a quasi-concave curve.

6.2.2 Supply of licensing contracts

In contrast to explaining the demand for licensing contracts, it is less straightforward to describe how pharmaceutical companies decide which licensing contracts they should offer and to which potential partners. Thereby, it should be reflected that the return from a licensing contract is a random variable and it is assumed that the pharmaceutical companies are risk-neutral. After the pharmaceutical company has decided on the general strategy to sell its research results via licenses to external partner firms, they are concerned only with expected profits, so that the licensing contract α (when sold to a licensee who has a probability that it cannot execute the development of p), is worth

(2) $$\pi(p, \alpha) = (1 - p)\,\alpha_1 - p\,\alpha_2 = \alpha_1 - p\,(\alpha_1 + \alpha_2).$$

Even if the pharmaceutical companies are not expected to be profit maximizers, on a well-organized competitive market they are likely to behave as if they maximized equation (2).[47]

Pharmaceutical companies have financial resources such that they are willing and able to sell any number of licensing contracts that they think will make an expected profit. The market is competitive in a sense that there is free entry. Together, these assumptions guarantee that any contract that is demanded and that is expected to be profitable will be supplied.

---

47 For a more detailed derivation please refer to Rothschild and Stiglitz (1976, p. 631).

6.2.3 Probability that the licensee cannot execute

This chapter discusses how the pharmaceutical company and the partner firm (i.e. the licensee) come to know or estimate the parameter p, which plays a crucial role in both formulas (1) and (2). As mentioned earlier, the theory of adverse selection implies that the partner firms know the probability that they are unable to execute the development tasks, while the pharmaceutical companies do not know the parameter p. This assumption represents the basic requirement of the underlying information asymmetry. As the partner firms are identical in all respects and try to avoid that their revenues do not meet expectations, the result of this assumption is that the pharmaceutical companies cannot discriminate among the potential buyers of their licenses on the basis of their characteristics.

A pharmaceutical company may use its partner's market behavior to draw some conclusions about their probabilities of not being able to execute. Other things being equal, those partners with high probabilities of not being able to execute will demand licensing contracts with a higher coverage than those who are less prone to fail on the respective development tasks. Although possibly accurate, this is not a profitable way of finding out about buyer characteristics. Pharmaceutical companies want to know their licensees' characteristics upfront in order to decide on what terms they should offer to let them buy licenses. Information that accrues after the deal has closed may be used only for follow-on licensing deals but has no value for the current licensing deal.

However, it is often possible to force the partner firms to make market choices in such a way that they both reveal their characteristics and make the choices the pharmaceutical firm would have wanted them to make had their characteristics been publicly known (this process is also known as the mechanism of self-selection).

6.2.4 Definition of an equilibrium in the licensing market

It is assumed that the partner firms can buy only one licensing contract. This is an objectionable assumption because it implies that the seller of a license specifies both the prices and quantities of the licenses purchased. In most competitive markets, sellers determine only the price and have no control over the amount their customers buy. Nonetheless, Rothschild and Stiglitz (1976) believe that price and quantity competition is more appropriate for their model of the insurance market than traditional price competition. This assumption is also applicable in the case of out-licensing in the pharmaceutical industry for the following reason. Licensing contracts for pharmaceutical compounds are usually not handled in a way that buyers can easily decide about the amount they want to purchase. Each licensing contract typically involves a fairly long due diligence and negotiation process, which can last up to ten months as noted in the case study analysis.[48] Thus, it seems to be reasonable to assume that the seller (i.e. the pharmaceutical company) has control over both the price and quantity of the licenses.

By definition, equilibrium in a competitive licensing market is a set of contracts such that, when customers choose contracts to maximize expected utility,

- no contract in the equilibrium set makes negative expected profits, and
- there is no contract outside the equilibrium set that, if offered, will make a non-negative profit.

This notion of equilibrium is comparable to the Cournot-Nash equilibrium; each firm assumes that the contracts its competitors offer are independent of its own actions.

6.2.5 Equilibrium with identical licensees

Pharmaceutical companies are only exposed to imperfect information when the partner firms have different probabilities of not being able to execute the compound's development. This case is examined in the next chapter 6.2.6. However, to illustrate the mainly graphical procedure of finding an equilibrium in the market for out-licensing contracts, it is first analyzed how an equilibrium will be reached in a competitive licensing market with identical licensees. Thereby, the analysis is identical if the licensees (i.e. the partner firms) have different p's, but the pharmaceutical companies know the probabilities of their partners of not being able to execute. The market consequently splits up into several sub-markets – one for each different p represented. Each sub-market has the equilibrium as described now.

In Fig. 56, the horizontal and vertical axes represent the partner firms' projected revenues for the two states: can execute, and cannot execute. The point E with the coordinates $(\hat{W}_1, \hat{W}_2)$ is the typical state of a partner firm which did not acquire a license. Indifference curves are level sets of the function of equation (1). Purchasing the licensing contract $\alpha = (\alpha_1, \alpha_2)$ moves the partner firm from E to the point F $(\hat{W}_1 - \alpha_1, \hat{W}_2 + \alpha_2)$.

---

48 The case study analysis in chapter 4 provides a detailed description of out-licensing processes in the pharmaceutical industry including their duration and due diligence procedures.

Free entry and perfect competition will ensure that policies bought in competitive equilibrium make zero expected profits, so that if α is purchased,

$$\alpha_1 (1-p) - \alpha_2 p = 0 \qquad (3)$$

The set of all policies that break even is given analytically by equation (3) and graphically by the line *EF* in Fig. 56 which is sometimes referred to as the fair-odds line. The equilibrium policy α^* maximizes the partner firm's (expected) utility and just breaks even. Purchasing α^* locates the licensee at the tangency of the indifference curve with the fair-odds line. The license α^* also satisfies the two conditions of the equilibrium: (i) it breaks even, and (ii) selling any contract preferred to it will bring pharmaceutical companies expected losses.

As licensees are risk-averse, the point α^* is located at the intersection of the 45°-line (representing equal revenues in both states 'can execute' and 'cannot execute') and the fair-odds line. In equilibrium, each licensee buys complete licensing con-

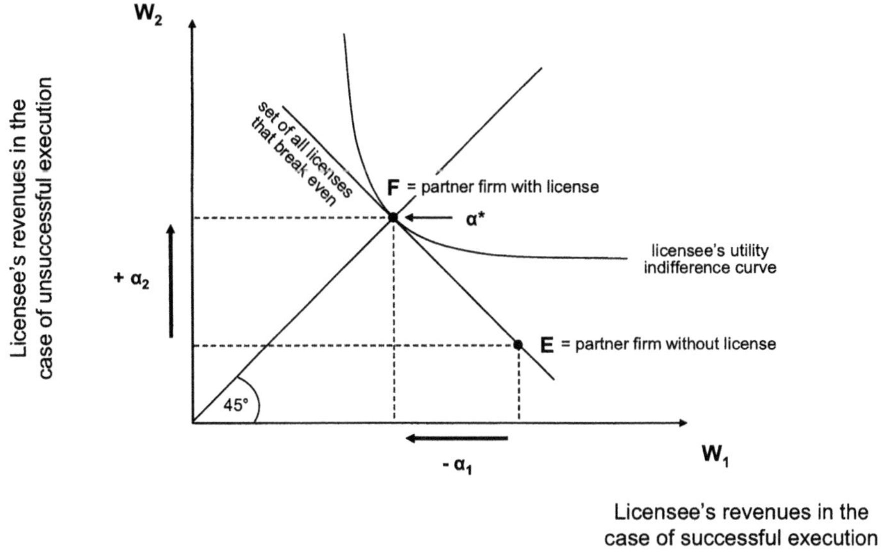

α^* equilibrium license (it maximizes the licensee's expected utility and breaks even)

Fig. 56. Equilibrium in the market for out-licensing with identical licensees.

tracts at actuarial odds. In order to see this, it can be observed that the slope of the fair-odds line is equal to the ratio of the probability of being able to execute the compound's development to the probability of not being able to execute $((1-p)/p)$, while the slope of the indifference curve (the marginal rate of substitution between revenues in the case that the partner could execute to revenues in the case that the partner could not execute) is $[U'(W_1)(1-p)]/[U'(W_2)p]$, which, when revenues in the two states are equal, is $((1-p)/p)$, and therefore independent of U.

6.2.6 Equilibrium with two classes of licensees

Now it is supposed that the market consists of two kinds of partner firms: licensees who are exposed to fairly low risks of not being able to execute a compound's development and licensees who are exposed to fairly high risks of not being able to execute. Subsequently, the low-risk licensees have a probability of not being able to execute of p^L, and the high-risk licensees have a probability of $p^H > p^L$. The fraction of high-risk licensees is λ, so the average probability of all licensees not being able to execute is $p^{average} = \lambda\, p^H + (1-\lambda)\, p^L$. This market can have only two kinds of equilibria: *pooling equilibria* in which both groups buy the same licensing contract, and *separating equilibria* in which different types of licensees purchase different licensing contracts.

A simple argument establishes that there cannot be a pooling equilibrium. The point E in Fig. 57 is again the initial endowment of all partner firms. Suppose that α is a pooling equilibrium and consider $\pi\,(p^{average}, \alpha)$. If $\pi\,(p^{average}, \alpha) < 0$, the pharmaceutical firms offering α lose money, contradicting the definition of equilibrium. If $\pi\,(p^{average}, \alpha) > 0$, then there is a licensing contract that offers slightly more coverage in each state of nature, which still will make a profit when all partner firms buy it. All will prefer this licensing contract to α, so α cannot be an equilibrium. Thus, $\pi\,(p^{average}, \alpha) = 0$, and α lies on the line EF (with slope $((1-p^{average})/p^{average})$).

It follows from (1) that at α the slope of the high-risk licensee's indifference curve through α, $\bar{U}^H$, is $(p^L/1-p^L)(1-p^H/p^H)$ times the slope of $\bar{U}^L$, the low-risk licensee's indifference curve through α. In Fig. 57, $\bar{U}^H$ (which represents the high-risk licensees' indifference curve as derived from the high-risk licensees' utility function U^H) is a broken line, and $\bar{U}^L$ (which represents the low-risk licensees' indifference curve as derived from the low-risk licensees' utility function U^L) is illustrated as a solid line. The curves intersect at α; thus, there might exist a contract, β in Fig. 57, near α, which low-risk licensees prefer to α. The high-risk licensees prefer α to β. Since β is near α, it makes a profit when the less risky buy it, $(\pi\,(p^L, \beta) \approx \pi\,(p^L, \alpha) >$

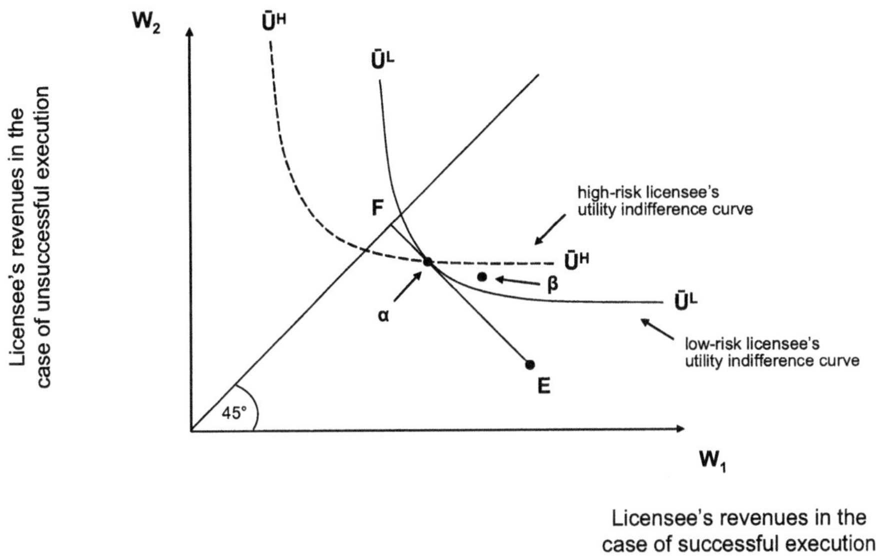

Fig. 57. Non-existence of a pooling equilibrium in the out-licensing market.

π $(p^{average}, \alpha) = 0)$. The existence of β contradicts the second part of the definition of equilibrium. Thus, α cannot be an equilibrium.

If there is an equilibrium, each type of licensee must purchase a separate contract. The arguments as mentioned above demonstrate that each contract in the equilibrium set makes zero profits. In Fig. 58, the low-risk licensing contract lies on the line *EL* (with slope $(1 - p^L) / p^L$), and the high-risk licensing contract on line *EH* (with slope $(1 - p^H) / p^H$). As shown previously, the licensing contract on *EH* that is most preferred by high-risk licensees gives complete coverage against the fact that the licensee is unable to execute the compound's development. This is α^H in Fig. 58; it must be part of any equilibrium. Low-risk licensees would, of all contracts on *EL*, most prefer contract β which, like α^H, provides complete coverage against the fact the licensee is unable to execute. However, β offers more coverage in each state than α^H, and high-risk licensees will prefer it to α^H. If β and α^H are marketed, both high- and low-risk licensees will purchase β. The nature of imperfect information in this model is that pharmaceutical companies are unable to distinguish among their potential buyers of licenses. All who demand β must be sold β. Profits will be negative; (α^H, β) is not an equilibrium set of contracts.

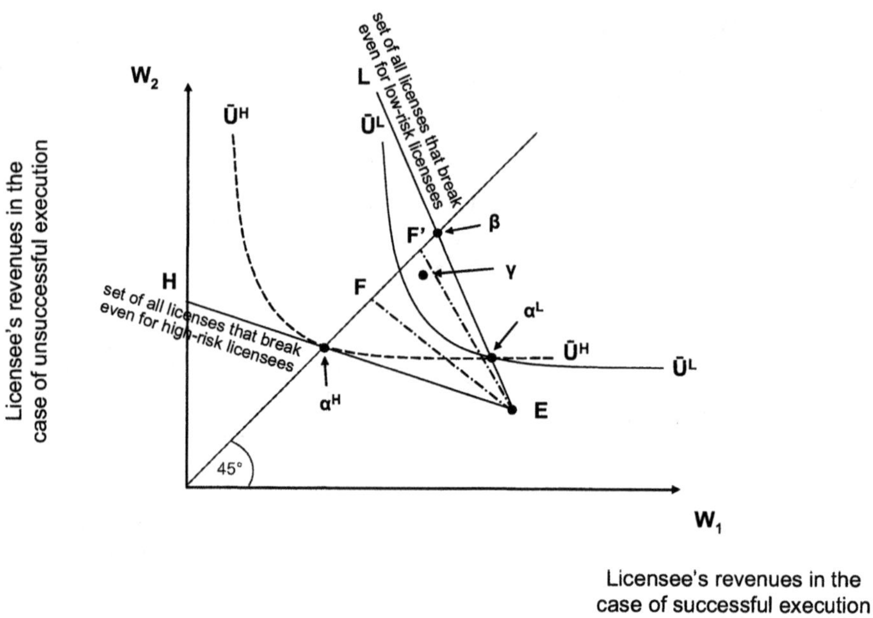

Fig. 58. Equilibrium in the out-licensing market with two classes of licensees.

An equilibrium contract for low-risk licensees must not be more attractive to high-risk licensees than α^H; it must lie on the 'southeast' side of $\bar{U}^H$, the high-risk licensees' indifference curve through α^H. Following the same argumentation as already deduced above, the one contract that low-risk licensees most prefer is α^L, the contract at the intersection of *EL* and $\bar{U}^H$ in Fig. 58. As a consequence, the set (α^H, α^L) is the only possible equilibrium for a market with low- and high-risk licensees.[49]

However, (α^H, α^L) may not be an equilibrium. Consider the contract γ in Fig. 58. It lies above $\bar{U}^L$, the low-risk licensees' indifference curve through α^L and also above $\bar{U}^H$. If γ is offered, both low- and high-risk licensees will purchase it in preference to either α^H or α^L. If it makes a profit when both groups buy it, γ will upset the potential equilibrium of (α^H, α^L). The profitability of γ depends on the composition of the market. If there are sufficiently many high-risk licensees that *EF* represents

49 Following Wilson (1976), this largely heuristic argument can be made completely rigorous.

market odds, then γ will lose money. If market odds are given by *EF'* (as they will be if there are relatively few high-risk licensees), then γ will make a profit. Since (α^H, α^L) is the only possible equilibrium, in this case the competitive out-licensing market will have no equilibrium. This consequently establishes that a competitive out-licensing market may have no equilibrium.

In their analysis of competitive insurance markets, Rothschild and Stiglitz (1976) could not find a simple intuitive explanation for this non-existence. However, the following observations by Hahn (1974) may be suggestive in explaining this pattern. The information that is revealed by a partner firm's choice of a licensing contract depends on all the other licenses offered; there is thus a fundamental informational externality that each licensing company, when deciding on which contract it will offer, fails to take into account. Given any set of contracts that breaks even, a firm may enter the market using the informational structure implicit in the availability of that set of contracts to make a profit; at the same time it forces the original contracts to make a loss. But as in any Nash equilibrium, the licensing firm fails to take into account the consequences of its actions, and in particular, the fact that when those policies are no longer offered, the informational structure will have changed and it can no longer make a profit.

As a consequence, the conditions under which an equilibrium does not exist can be characterized. An equilibrium will not exist if the costs to the low-risk licensee of pooling are low (because there are relatively few of the high-risk licensees who have to be subsidized, or because the subsidy per licensee is low, that is when the probabilities of the two groups are not too different), or if their costs of separating are high. The costs of separating arise from the licensee's inability to obtain complete coverage. Thus, the costs of separating are related to the licensee's exposure towards risk. Certain extreme cases make these propositions clear. If $p^L = 0$, it never pays the low-risk licensees to pool, and by continuity, for sufficiently small p^L it does not pay to pool. Similarly, if licensees are risk-neutral, it never pays to pool; if they are infinitely risk-averse with utility functions

$$(1') \qquad \hat{Y}(p, W_1, W_2) = Min\,(W_1, W_2)$$

it always pays to pool. One of the interesting properties of the equilibrium is that the presence of the high-risk licensees exerts a negative externality on the low-risk licensees. The externality is completely dissipative; there are losses to the low-risk licensees, but the high-risk licensees are no better off than they would be in isolation. If only the high-risk licensees would admit that they have high probabilities of not being able to execute the compound's development, all licensees would be made better off without anyone being worse off. The separating equilibrium as described may not be Pareto optimal even relative to the information that is available.

6.2.7 Discussion of the underlying assumptions

There are several assumptions made in the initial discussion of adverse selection by Rothschild and Stiglitz (1976). When applying the theory of adverse selection to the case of out-licensing, the assumptions have to be valid for the new circumstances as well. Otherwise, the theory's relevance for the observed coherencies cannot be legitimized. The major assumptions for the theory of adverse selection that have been made throughout the previous chapters including the explanation of their applicability to the case of out-licensing are listed in Table 10.

Table 10. Overview of underlying assumptions of the theoretical model.

Assumption	Description	Explanation
There are only two kinds of participants in the out-licensing market.	1. licensees who buy licensing contracts 2. licensors who sell licensing contracts	Licensing deals in the pharmaceutical industry are usually closed directly between the licensor and the licensee. It can reasonably be assumed that no third party intervenes in the deal.
No trade constraints of the licensing contracts.	The out-licensing market allows free trade of the licensing contracts (the α's)	Licensing contracts are generally free of any trade constraints. Only generally accepted rules, such as anti-trust regulations, apply.
The market begins with a single policy offered.	If providers of a good cannot distinguish well among risk levels, the premium for the policy will be approximately 'community rated' (i.e. it will be similar for all potential buyers).	Each licensing contract in pharmaceutical R&D is individually negotiated between the licensor and licensee. Thus, it can reasonably be assumed that the market might begin trading the licensing contracts with just one single policy offered.
The partner firms (licensees) are risk-averse.	The second derivation of their utility function is negative ($U'' < 0$).	While the licensees are taking over the risks of the compound's further development, it can be assumed that they are rather risk-taking than risk-averse. This becomes particularly eminent as most

Table 10. (continued).

		licensees are significantly venture capital funded which is a strong sign for a higher risk exposure of the firms' business. However, the risk-aversion in the context of this model does not relate to the licensees' business model but refers to the licensees' willingness to achieve their projected revenues *W*. As all licensees want to avoid failing to achieve their projected revenues, it is reasonable to assume that they are risk-averse.
The partner firms (licensees) are identical in all respects.	The licensees all try to avoid that their projected revenues do not meet expectations.	General business practice.
	In addition, the risk-aversion of all licensees is expected to be identical.	The licensees' level of risk-aversion is not affected by their differing probabilities of not being able to execute the compound's development.
The pharmaceutical companies (licensors) are risk-neutral.	The licensors are concerned only with expected profits.	Commonly applied assumption in business practice.
The return from a licensing contract is a random variable.		Commonly applied assumption in business practice.
Pharmaceutical companies are willing and able to sell any number of licensing contracts that they think will make an expected profit. The market is competitive in a sense that there is free entry.	Together, these two assumptions guarantee that any contract that is demanded and that is expected to be profitable will be supplied. Free market entry and perfect competition will ensure that policies bought in competitive equilibrium make zero expected profits.	Due to the existence of several potential sellers (big pharmaceutical companies) and the surge in new companies that could serve as potential buyers (e.g., specialty pharma companies), it can be assumed that the out-licensing market is competitive in a sense that there are no monopolistic or oligopolistic market structures in demand or supply.
The partner firms know the probability that they are unable to execute a compound's development, while the pharma firms do not.	The pharmaceutical companies cannot discriminate among the potential buyers of their licenses on the basis of their characteristics.	Due to the high complexity in pharmaceutical R&D it might be difficult for a pharmaceutical firm to judge the partner's probability of not being able to execute certain development activities.

Table 10. (continued).

		This is particularly true if the partner firm is a small company that is not listed on the stock market and is therefore not subject to certain reporting rules. This assumption represents the basis of the underlying information asymmetry.
The partner firms (licensees) can buy only one licensing contract.	The pharmaceutical firm can determine both: price and quantity of the licensing contracts.	Each licensing contract typically involves a fairly long due diligence and negotiation process. Thus, it seems to be reasonable to assume that the pharmaceutical company has control over both the price and quantity of the licenses.
Equilibrium in a competitive licensing market is a set of contracts such that, when customers choose contracts to maximize expected utility, (i) no contract in the equilibrium set makes negative expected profits, and (ii) there is no contract outside the equilibrium set that, if offered, will make a non-negative profit.	This definition of an equilibrium is comparable to the Cournot-Nash equilibrium.	The Cournot-Nash equilibrium applied to the case of out-licensing means that each pharmaceutical company assumes that the contracts its competitors offer are independent of its own actions. It can be reasonably assumed that this complies with general business practice.

Based on the descriptions in Table 10, it could have been shown that the major assumptions of the model of adverse selection apply for the case of out-licensing. Therefore, adverse selection seems to be an appropriate theory to deduce managerial recommendations for risk-sharing in pharmaceutical R&D collaborations.

6.3 Summary

This chapter has described the application of the theory of adverse selection to the case of out-licensing at large pharmaceutical companies. The theory of adverse selection was developed in markets characterized by asymmetric information and describes the emergence and existence of equilibria in those markets. As it could have been shown that the out-licensing market is characterized by a relatively high degree of information asymmetry, it could be deduced from the theory of adverse selection that an equilibrium might not exist if the risk exposure of the licensees regarding their capability to execute the compound's development is not fully known to the pharmaceutical company. The most common question at many pharmaceutical firms (after they have decided to adopt out-licensing as a strategy to share R&D risks and before they are about to decide about a particular out-licensing situation) is subsequently: *What* should we out-license for *how much* and to *whom*? By knowing about the possibility that there may be no equilibrium in the market for out-licensing, the licensor might take certain actions to reduce the underlying asymmetric information and eventually overcome the problem of adverse selection. This results in several implications.

Reflecting that an equilibrium can only exist at the intersection of the licensee's utility curve with the fair-odds line which represents the set of licenses that break even (the line *EF*), the pharmaceutical company has to structure the licensing arrangement in a way that the license is placed exactly at this intersection. Subsequently, obtaining an equilibrium in the out-licensing market depends on the features of the licensing-contract as well as the partner firm's probability of not being able to execute the compound's development. While the partner firm's probability of not being able to execute is p, the licensing contract α consists of the two elements α_1 and α_2, whereas $\alpha_2 = \acute{\alpha}_2 - \alpha_1$. Thus, there are in total three parameters which have a direct impact on finding an equilibrium in the out-licensing market:

$\acute{\alpha}_2$ Scope of the intellectual property rights that are subject to the license.
α_1 Upfront payment to be paid by the licensee for obtaining the license.
p Probability that the licensee will not be able to execute the compound's development.

Based on these parameters, the following managerial dimensions emerge which can actively be managed by the pharmaceutical company and could allow pharmaceutical R&D managers to reach an equilibrium in the out-licensing market:

- *Product coverage*: structuring the 'right' scope of the license;
- *Price setting*: determining the 'right' price structure for the license;
- *Performance presumption*: assuming the 'right' probability that the licensee can execute the compound's development.

By knowing about the three managerial dimensions including their underlying parameters, the pharmaceutical company can apply different strategies to influence these parameters in a way to possibly reach the desired equilibrium. After the equilibrium has been found, the out-licensing collaboration can take off, and only then, the risks can subsequently be transferred to the external partner company.

The following chapter describes the recommendations that could be given to pharmaceutical R&D management across the three dimensions 'product coverage', 'price setting', and 'performance presumption'.

7 Managerial Recommendations for Risk-sharing in Pharma R&D Collaborations

Based on the theoretical explanations about the phenomenon of adverse selection in the out-licensing market, this chapter derives recommendations for pharmaceutical R&D managers how to reduce the asymmetric information in the out-licensing arrangements to an extent where an equilibrium in the out-licensing market could be found. After having found an equilibrium, the out-licensing deal can be closed and the pharmaceutical company is able to transfer the risks to the external partner that it wanted to carry forward. The extent of the conveyable risks depends on the level of the collaboration's risk transferability. While these equilibria theoretically might not be stable, the goal is thus not to extend the current insights about the theory of adverse selection itself, but rather to illustrate how pharmaceutical R&D management can apply the insights of the theoretical model in order to approximate a (temporary) equilibrium. Consequently, the chapter's emphasis is to provide an understanding of the manageability of the out-licensing collaborations. This covers a detailed discussion of different management actions and their respective impact on the pharmaceutical company's ability to apporach an equilibrium. Thereby, the pharmaceutical company can exert an influence on the three managerial dimensions which have been deduced in the previous chapter (i.e. the product coverage, price setting and performance presumption).

The starting situation for the discussion of all three dimensions shall be as follows. The pharmaceutical company has decided to transfer certain risks by out-licensing a respective substance but does not know about the potential licensees' capability to execute the compound's development ('the asymmetric information'). As it has been shown in chapter 6, an equilibrium in an out-licensing market with different buyers who are reluctant to reveal information about their likelihood of being able to execute a compound's development might not exist. A temporary equilibrium might exist if the pharmaceutical company offers a separate contract for each type of licensee. However, due to the asymmetric information, the pharmaceutical company does not know how these separate contracts should look like (i.e. at which terms and price it should be offered to whom). In order to approximate a potential (temporary) equilibrium, the following discussion uses the 'community rated' license as a starting point. As explained in chapter 6, a 'community rated' license is a license that will be similar for all potential buyers. Based on the 'community rated' license, the pharmaceutical company can make adjustments along the three dimensions product coverage, price setting and performance presumption to increase the likelihood of finding an equilibrium, and subsequently to share the R&D risks.

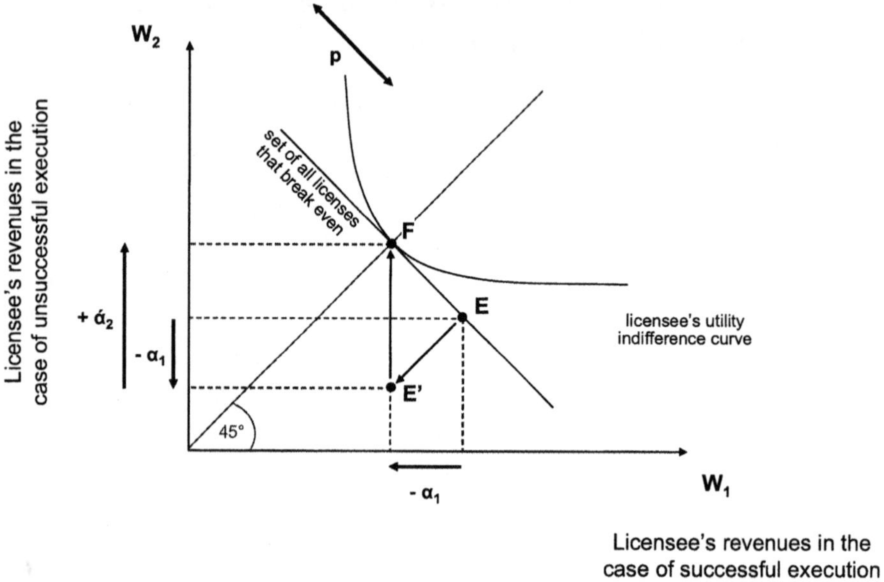

α_1: size of the upfront payment; $\acute{\alpha}_2$: license's coverage; p: risk exposure of the licensee.

Fig. 59. Parameters for finding an equilibrium in the out-licensing market.

The starting situation related to the 'community rated' license assumes the following situation (see Fig. 59). The pharmaceutical company initially believes that all licensees are identical regarding their probability of not being able to execute the compound's development. No licensee has acquired a license yet and the potential licensee is thus located at point *E*. At the time when the licensee purchases the license $\alpha = (\alpha_1, \alpha_2)$ from the pharmaceutical company, the licensee's position shifts from point *E* to *F*. Because the licensing contract consists of two parts α_1 and α_2 (whereas $\alpha_2 = \acute{\alpha}_2 - \alpha_1$), this transition is graphically illustrated in the figure as a two-step process $E \rightarrow E'$, and $E' \rightarrow F$. The first transition $E \rightarrow E'$ describes the impact of the license's price in terms of the upfront payment α_1 on the transition process. As the upfront payment α_1 is plotted on both axes as an amount that the licensee has to pay, this transition moves the licensee's state parallel to the bisecting line towards the origin. The second transition $E' \rightarrow F$ describes the impact of the license's coverage $\acute{\alpha}_2$ on the transition process. As the license's coverage $\acute{\alpha}_2$ represents the amount of intellectual property rights that the licensee is expected to receive, this transition moves the licensee's state straight upwards.

As it is still assumed that the licensee is risk-averse, this argumentation locates the licensee's new state *F* after having purchased the licensing contract, on the 45°-line. In order for an equilibrium to exist, the new state *F* must as well be located at the tangency of the fair-odds line with the licensee's utility indifference curve, whose shape and location are characterized by the partner firm's probability of not being able to execute the compound's development which is described by the parameter *p*. At the point where the licensee's new state *F* and the licensee's utility indifference curve meet, the equilibrium emerges. While this equilibrium might not be stable because it represents a 'community rated' license in a market with different sets of licensees, the following discussion analyzes the managerial actions that can be taken by pharmaceutical R&D management regarding the following three managerial dimensions in order to approximate a (temporary) equilibrium:

- Product coverage;
- Price setting;
- Performance presumption.

7.1 Product Coverage

In the case of out-licensing, pharmaceutical R&D management is able to decide about the characteristics of the commodity (the 'product') that is about to be exchanged in the licensing deal. In this context, the product coverage describes all aspects which characterize the scope of the commodity exchanged during the out-licensing agreement. The exchange of products via licensing deals generally requires the existence of intellectual property rights. Thereby, patents are the most prominent example of exchangeable intellectual property rights. Studies have shown that patents are the most effective means of appropriation in the pharmaceutical industry and it could be shown that 65% of pharmaceutical inventions would not have been introduced without patent protection, compared to a cross-industry average of 8% (Reuters 2002). By aggregating these patents to various bundles, it is possible to market different packages of intellectual property. The bundle of intellectual property rights defines the scope of the license and constitutes the product's coverage.

7.1.1 Relevant parameters

The patents exchanged in a licensing deal generally cover certain biotechnological processes (platform-technologies), exclusive know-how, or compounds (i.e. new molecular entities). The licenses mostly comprise databases or software modules, which contain the research results of the company that is selling the license (see Paetz and Reepmeyer 2003). According to IBM (2003), most of the licenses in out-licensing deals at major pharmaceutical companies cover new molecular entities (i.e. compounds).

As the out-licensing agreement entitles the licensee to receive the product which is subject to the license and expects the licensee to conduct the respective development activities, the coverage of the licensed product is an important factor for the overall success of the collaboration. The parameters that describe the product coverage thus receive a great emphasis in structuring the out-licensing deal. One of the most important and distinctive parameters that characterize an out-licensed compound includes the compound's stage in the R&D process. The commercial scope of a compound generally increases in later stages. However, the pharmaceutical company also has to put up significant amounts of money and related risks to bring that compound to a late stage in the R&D process. When deciding about the coverage of the offered product, the pharmaceutical company has subsequently to make a trade-off between minimizing costs/risks and maximizing the commercial scope.

Besides the stage of the compound in the R&D process, the compound's indication is another important parameter. In this context, it should be reflected that one compound can have multiple indications. According to Thiel (2004), pharmaceutical companies increasingly start to realize that their drugs are not always initially developed for the right indications and markets. A product can be on the market for decades before the research community discovers new and better uses. Several years after a drug's initial sales have declined, a minor product or me-too drug can gain sudden importance. Thus, a single compound can have various applications. A good example that illustrates the multifold application of a single substance to various markets is the case of thalidomide which – at one point in time – became known for tragic reasons.

Thalidomide: How one substance can be attractive for various markets

The story of the substance thalidomide, for all its tragedy, illustrates the fact that changes in a drug's profile can create new medical opportunities (compare Thiel 2004). First synthesized in 1953 by the German pharmaceutical company Ciba (which is now after various acquisitions part of the Swiss company Novartis), the compound's originators abandoned the further development after animal tests showed little discernable pharmacologic effect. Another German company, Chemie Grünenthal, initially studying the compound as a potential anticonvulsant, instead found that thalidomide acted as an effective sedative. Thalidomide hit the West German market in 1957 under the name Contergan, marketed as a sleep aid and eventually as a treatment for morning sickness. It was considered so safe that it was sold over-the-counter without prescription in many of the 42 countries that quickly approved its sale (thalidomide had never been approved in the US).

In 1961, a sudden spike in infant phocomelia – malformations of the limbs, hands, and feet – sent epidemiologists scrambling for a cause. They eventually found a common link to thalidomide, and Grünenthal stopped production in 1961. However, the product was still used sporadically, and in 1965, an Israeli doctor prescribed it as a sedative to a patient with leprosy, hoping to alleviate some of the discomfort caused by a painful skin condition known as erythema nodosum leprosum (ENL). Instead, the drug appeared to actually help the symptoms. Thus, thalidomide was quietly used for decades to help this tiny patient population.

The next major development occurred in 1991, when Gilla Kaplan, a Professor of cellular physiology and immunology at Rockefeller University in New York, published a study concluding that thalidomide selectively inhibits tumor necrosis factor-alpha, giving it a potential role as an anti-inflammatory. Although thalidomide itself had long been off patent, the company Celgene – based in New Jersey, USA – licensed Kaplan's new patents from Rockefeller University in 1992. In the years following, evidence indicating thalidomide might help AIDS-related complications such as cachexia (wasting syndrome) created a substantial demand for the drug in the US for the first time. Faced with 'buyer clubs' of AIDS patients importing thalidomide from South American and other manufacturers, the Food and Drug Administration (FDA) decided to work with Celgene to get the drug approved and manufactured in the US, where prescribing and distribution could be better controlled. After various clinical studies, the FDA approved thalidomide for ENL in 1998, fully realizing that the vast majority of its use would be off-label.

As better AIDS drugs made cachexia a less frequent complaint among patients with HIV, however, the market for thalidomide once again changed. After a pioneering 1999 study showed an impressive positive response rate in people with multiple myelome, the drug became widely used to treat this rare blood cancer. Sold under the brand name Thalomid, thalidomide reached sales of around US$ 290 million in 2004 in the US. The specialty pharma company Pharmion licensed most non-US rights from Celgene and is now selling the drug as much as US$ 56 million more in other markets. The total sales of thalidomide in 2004 are remarkably high when it is considered that the substance's indication had to change several times before it reached today's status, and the discovery of the initial drug was more than 50 years ago.

As illustrated by the case of thalidomide, renewing a compound's indication (also called repurposing, reprofiling or redirecting) might increase the commercialization potential of a drug candidate and therefore has a strong importance for defining the product coverage in an out-licensing deal. According to Intarcia, the strategy of redirected development is often the most efficient and cost effective means of advancing drugs rapidly into late stage development and commercialization.

Giving a compound a new spin might also affect its delivery system or formulation chemistries which improve bioavailability or reduce side-effects. Further parameters which describe the intellectual property bundle that is about to be exchanged in the licensing deal include the compound's efficacy, safety, compliance or administration. Oftentimes, these parameters interdepend with each other. According to Reuters (2003a), drug candidates offering only marginal improvements in efficacy in a certain target market may need to enhance their commercial prospects by other differentiating aspects, such as a better compliance. Alternatively, trials can be designed to target areas of unmet need, for example efficacy in specific patient subpopulations or improved dosage schedules. The interdependence of these parameters usually varies by therapeutic market and competitive environment.

In summary, there are various parameters which define the coverage of a product that is about to be sold in an out-licensing deal. The most important product parameters include:

- Position (stage) in the R&D process;
- Indication(s) of the substance;
- Formulation of the underlying chemical entity;
- Efficacy;
- Safety;
- Side effects;
- Delivery system;
- Compliance;
- Administration;
- Dosage;
- Changes in regulation or managed care;
- Possible spill-over effects.

The specifications of all these parameters not only define the product coverage but also the probability that the out-licensing deal will be closed which determines the pharmaceutical company's ability to transfer risks. The impact of the product coverage on the risk transferability is discussed in the next chapter.

7.1.2 Impact on risk transferability

Due to its dependence on intellectual property rights, the product coverage has strong ties to the collaboration's appropriability regime. According to Scherer and Ross (1990), the most important instrument of appropriability are patents. Other means include secrecy, lead time, moving quickly down the learning curve, superior sales or service efforts, and raising imitation costs or imitation time through making imitation more difficult for competitors (Scherer and Ross 1990).[50] Firms will patent more aggressively when (i) markets for technology are highly fragmented (i.e. the ownership rights to external technologies are widely distributed), (ii) firms make large investments in technology-specific assets, and (iii) the industry is under a strong legal appropriability regime, which is the case in the pharmaceutical industry (compare Ziedonis 2004). Therefore, by structuring the bundle of intellectual property rights that are expected to be sold during the out-licensing deal, the pharmaceutical company always exerts an influence on the appropriability regime of the underlying collaboration.

When configuring the bundle of intellectual property rights, the pharmaceutical company also has to tie the package of patents in a way that makes it most attractive to the potential licensee. Therefore, the product coverage not only exerts an influence on the collaboration's appropriability regime but also influences the selection of the potential licensee. For example, if the pharmaceutical company has decided to out-license a specific compound, it can only target a potential partner firm which serves a therapeutic area related to that compound. The licensee's therapeutic focus, in turn, is predetermined by its business strategy. Thus, by structuring the product's coverage, the pharmaceutical company narrows down or extends the pool of potential partner companies based on the nature of their business strategy.

Considering that the license's appropriability regime and the licensee's business strategy represent attributes that have an impact on the risk transferability during the out-licensing collaboration, the pharmaceutical company could modify the product coverage in order to exert an influence on the risk transferability of the collaboration. Reflecting the different states of the license's appropriability regime and the licensee's business strategy which are considered to enable a high risk transferability, the pharmaceutical company should review and analyze its offered product if (i) the

50 A number of researchers has tried to examine the effectiveness of different means of appropriability. For a detailed description refer to Levin et al. (1983, 1987), Teece (1986), Dosi (1988), Cohen and Levin (1989), European Patent Office and IFO Institute (1993).

applicability of the license at the partner company is tight enough, and (ii) the partner's business strategy is focused enough regarding the therapy area that the product is about to address, so that the partner company will most likely be willing to take the product for further development, and the pharmaceutical company will subsequently be able to share the underlying risks. If the partner firm considers the appropriability regime to be too loose, the pharmaceutical company should modify the product coverage along the different product parameters mentioned in the previous chapter in order to increase the product's applicability at the partner firm. At the same time, if the partner does not seem to be specialized or focused enough to successfully execute the compound's development, the pharmaceutical company could add or remove certain aspects of the product coverage to increase the match of the license with the partner firm's business strategy.

All of these modifications result in either a higher or lower product coverage compared to the initially offered 'community rated' licensing offer. Therefore, the managerial actions that can be taken by pharmaceutical R&D management to increase the likelihood of finding an equilibrium – and subsequently reaching the desired risk transferability – include increasing or reducing the product coverage. The managerial implications of making these adjustments to the product coverage are discussed in the following chapter.

7.1.3 Managerial implications

Based on the starting situation where the pharmaceutical company would offer a 'community rated' license, pharmaceutical R&D management can try to approximate an equilibrium by applying one of the following two alternatives regarding the product's coverage:

- *Increasing the product coverage.* The pharmaceutical company can increase the coverage of the bundle of intellectual property rights by extending existing intellectual property rights or adding additional rights.[51]
- *Reducing the product coverage.* The pharmaceutical company can reduce the coverage of the bundle of intellectual property rights by scaling down existing rights or removing certain rights.

---

51 Sometimes, a licensor might include additional substances into a licensing package which is then sold to a licensee in order to match a potentially perceived value gap in the licensing deal. Additional substances which are expected to close this value gap are also referred to as 'quids' (see Goebel 2004).

The following models describe the opportunities and effects of making these changes to the product coverage. It is assumed ceteris paribus that the other two parameters (the license's price α_1 and the partner firm's probability of not being able to execute the compound's development p) are initially unaffected by the changes in the product coverage $\acute{\alpha}_2$, and remain constant.

Increasing the product coverage

As illustrated in Fig. 60, the pharmaceutical company increases the product coverage $\acute{\alpha}_2$ by the amount x_1. Ceteris paribus, this moves the potential equilibrium F straight upwards. Accordingly, the fair-odds line which describes the set of all licenses that break even has to shift upwards as well due to the condition of the equilibrium derived from equation (3) which has been introduced in chapter 6.2.5 [$\alpha_1 (1 - p) - \alpha_2 p = 0$, whereas $\alpha_2 = (\acute{\alpha}_2 - \alpha_1)$]. As this change represents a move away from the initial equilibrium, the pharmaceutical company now has to take some managerial actions in order to reach an equilibrium again.

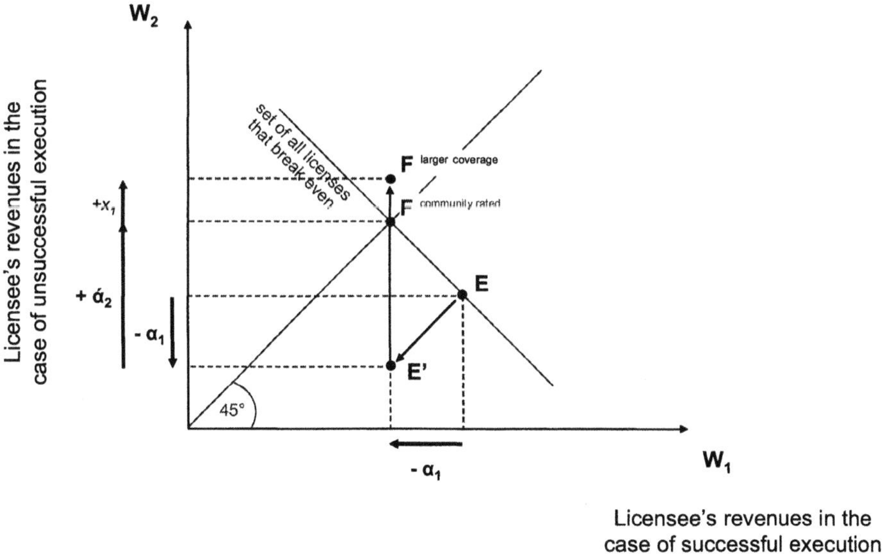

Fig. 60. Impact of increasing the product coverage on finding an equilibrium in the out-licensing market.

The necessary managerial actions can be derived analytically by equation (3) which illustrates the set of all licenses that break even, and thus represents a basic requirement for an equilibrium in the out-licensing market. An algebraic transformation of equation (3) leads to the following relation between the three parameters and provides the basis for deriving managerial actions:

(4) $$\acute{\alpha}_2 = \alpha_1 / p$$

As an increase in $\acute{\alpha}_2$ requires the ratio of (α_1 / p) to increase as well, the initial ceteris paribus assumption that both α_1 and p remain unchanged can no longer be sustained. In order to find an equilibrium, the pharmaceutical company can only increase the product coverage if it simultaneously adjusts the other two parameters as well. Accordingly, the ratio (α_1 / p) only increases under the following conditions:

- α_1 goes up, and p remains constant or decreases;
- α_1 and p go up, but α_1 increases by a proportionally larger extent than p;
- α_1 remains constant, and p goes down;
- α_1 and p go down, but α_1 decreases by a proportionally smaller extent than p.

Consequently, the managerial actions which should be taken by the pharmaceutical company to find an equilibrium after it has increased the product coverage include:

- Raise the upfront payment <u>and</u> target the same partner firm or a firm with a lower probability of not being able to execute the compound's development;
- Raise the upfront payment <u>and</u> target a partner firm with a higher probability of not being able to execute. However, the upfront payment has to grow proportionally more than the partner firm's probability of not being able to execute;
- Leave the upfront payment constant <u>and</u> target a partner firm with a lower probability of not being able to execute;
- Lower the upfront payment <u>and</u> target a partner firm with a lower probability of not being able to execute. However, the upfront payment has to decrease proportionally less than the partner firm's probability of not being able to execute.

As the strongest reaction in the ratio (α_1 / p) can be achieved if α_1 increases and p simultaneously decreases, the managerial action with the highest impact – after the product coverage has been increased – would be to raise the upfront payment <u>and</u> target a partner firm with a lower probability of not being able to execute the compound's development.

Reducing the product coverage

In contrast to increasing the product's coverage, Fig. 61 illustrates a reduction in the product coverage $\acute{\alpha}_2$ by the amount x_1. Under the same assumptions, the potential equilibrium F moves straight downwards. As this change also represents a move away from the initial equilibrium, the pharmaceutical company has to take managerial actions as well in order to reach the equilibrium.

Based on the same analytical derivation from equations (3) and (4) as illustrated in the previous paragraphs, a reduction of $\acute{\alpha}_2$ requires the ratio of (α_1 / p) to decrease. The ratio (α_1 / p) only decreases under the following conditions:

- α_1 goes down, and p remains constant or increases;
- α_1 and p go down, but α_1 decreases by a proportionally larger extent than p;
- α_1 remains constant, and p goes up;
- α_1 and p go up, but p increases by a proportionally larger extent than α_1.

Subsequently, the managerial actions which should be taken by the pharmaceutical company to find an equilibrium after it has reduced the product coverage include:

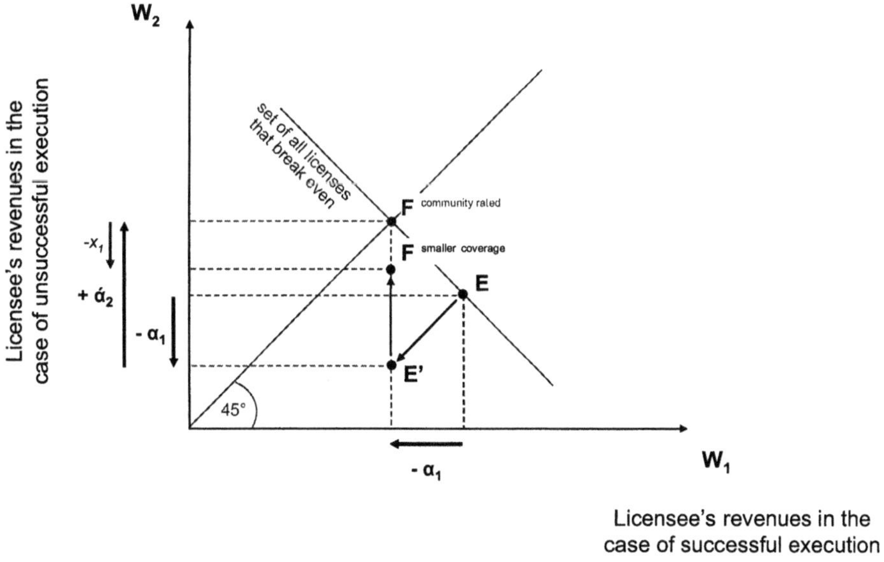

Fig. 61. Impact of reducing the product coverage on finding an equilibrium in the out-licensing market.

- Lower the upfront payment and target the same partner firm or a firm with a higher probability of not being able to execute the compound's development;
- Lower the upfront payment and target a partner firm with a lower probability of not being able to execute. However, the upfront payment has to decrease proportionally more than the partner firm's probability of not being able to execute;
- Leave the upfront payment constant and target a partner firm with a higher probability of not being able to execute;
- Raise the upfront payment and target a partner firm with a higher probability of not being able to execute. However, the partner firm's probability of not being able to execute has to increase proportionally more than the upfront payment.

As the strongest reaction in the ratio (α_I / p) can be achieved if α_I decreases and p simultaneously increases, the managerial action with the highest impact – after the product coverage has been decreased – would be to lower the upfront payment and target a partner firm with a higher probability of not being able to execute.

Conclusion: This chapter has analyzed the managerial relevance of modifying the product coverage on reducing the asymmetric information in the out-licensing arrangement in order to find an equilibrium in the out-licensing market. Due to its interdependence with the license's appropriability regime as well as the licensee's business strategy, the product coverage also impacts the risk transferability of the collaboration. Pharmaceutical R&D management could thus use its ability to change the product coverage in a way which increases the risk transferability to a level where the pharmaceutical company would be able to transfer the desired risks to the external partner. Fig. 62 illustrates graphically the consequences of increasing and reducing the product coverage compared to the initial 'community rated' situation.[52]

When modifying the product coverage, pharmaceutical R&D management should also keep in mind the following caveats. On the one hand, pharmaceutical R&D managers might be tempted to provide a rather generous offer (i.e. offering a product that has a higher coverage than the 'community rated' offer) in order to increase the probability that the partner company will be successful in executing the compound's development. On the other hand, the pharmaceutical company might be tempted to provide a fairly humble offer (i.e. offering a product that has a lower

52 As a change in the product coverage has an impact on the location of possible equilibria, it must be reflected that changes in the other two parameters (the price as well as the partner firm's probability of not being able to execute the compound's development) are required as well to reach an equilibrium.

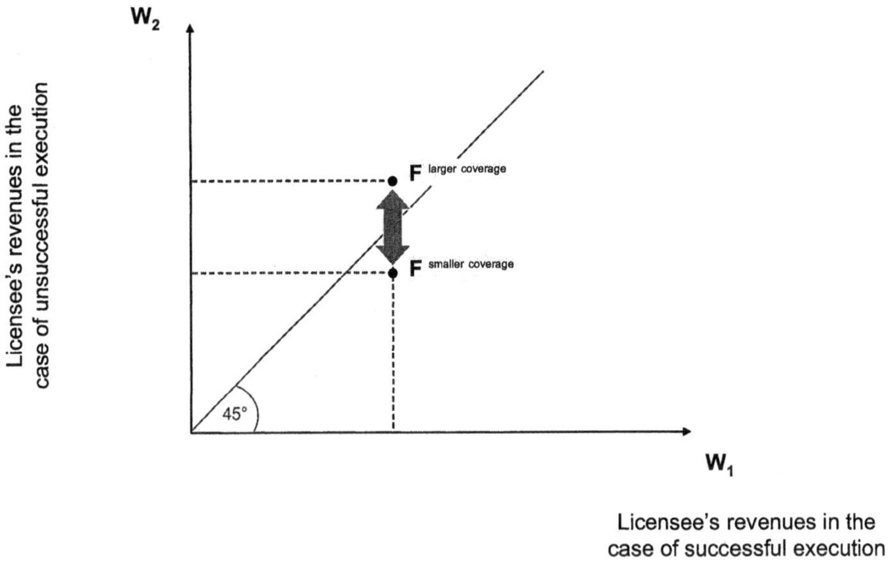

Fig. 62. Impact of changes in the product coverage on the ability to find an equilibrium in the out-licensing market.

coverage than the 'community rated' offer) because it could be exposed to giving up too much intellectual assets. This becomes particularly apparent under a straight licensing contract. If the partner firm fails to execute the compound's development, the partner firm will still be entitled to the intellectual assets of the license whereas the pharmaceutical company will most likely end up with only modest upfront payments and no royalty revenues. While the more generous offer will increase the chances of finding a partner, the less generous offer will reduce the downside risk of the collaboration but might also impede the closing of the out-licensing deal.

Thus, the 'right' product coverage always requires a trade-off between maximizing the likelihood that the partner firm agrees to in-license the product and minimizing the outflow of too much intellectual capital.

7.2 Price Setting

Pharmaceutical R&D management is not only able to decide about the product coverage that can be offered but also at which price the product should be offered to the potential licensee. While the parameter α_l describes the upfront payment that the licensee has to pay to the pharmaceutical company immediately after closing the deal, the price setting describes all aspects which relate to the entire price of the license (although the parameter α_l only reflects the size of the upfront payment). This could include payment elements which go beyond the upfront payment and are considered to have an indirect influence on the size of the upfront payment which has to be made by the partner company. As all payment elements in a licensing agreement interdepend with each other, a single analysis of just the upfront payment α_l would not provide a comprehensive illustration of the price setting that can be done by the pharmaceutical company.

7.2.1 Relevant parameters

The price setting describes all aspects related to the structure and amount of payments that are made between the pharmaceutical company and the partner firm. However, the resulting dimension which is relevant for the model is only the size of the upfront payment α_l. As the licensing deal will only take place if the partner considers the price setting appropriate, the parameters that constitute the price are an important element of the out-licensing deal.

In addition to upfront payments, there are many other parameters which characterize the price setting of a licensing deal and which might have an influence on the height of the upfront payments (see also Goebel 2004). They mostly relate to the structure and nature of the licensing deal and describe the timing and amount of payments which have to be made. One of the most important parameters which has a strong impact on the price setting in the out-licensing deal includes the re-licensing rights, particularly the call-back options. In case a call-back option is included into the licensing contract, the value of the license typically experiences a substantial discount from the perspective of the partner firm because the licensee will not be able to fully utilize the outcome of its R&D efforts. This might have a strong impact on the partner firm's willingness to pay upfront payments.

Besides re-licensing rights, royalty revenues represent another important price parameter which are also expected to have an impact on the price setting in the out-licensing collaboration. By agreeing on royalty revenue payments, the licensor might expect future cash-flows from the drug's market launch and is usually willing to sell the license for a lower upfront payment α_l. However, the royalty revenues are dependent upon a successful market introduction. If the product does not reach the market, no royalties will incur. Therefore, pharmaceutical companies could be tempted to demand higher upfront payments in order to make up for this risk. However, pharmaceutical companies usually prefer a fairly high proportion of royalty revenues (Windhover 2000).

Other compensation elements which are considered to have an impact on the price setting in an out-licensing deal include milestone payments. Milestone payments have to be made by the partner firm to the pharmaceutical company after specifically defined goals throughout the development process have been reached. The higher the milestone payments compared to the upfront payments, the lower the immediate cash flow that has to be paid by the partner company. While the licensee is consequently able to defer the payments to later stages of the development process, the pharmaceutical company would prefer to receive a higher proportion of upfront versus milestone payments. The following case example illustrates this pattern by comparing two constellations of upfront and milestone payments.

How the relation of milestone versus upfront payments influences a license's price setting

In order to illustrate the impact of the relation of milestone versus upfront payments in a licensing deal on the perception of the license's price, the following initial deal structure is assumed (compare Cook 2004):

Upfront payment:

US$ 14 million

Milestone payments:

Completion of Phase I: US$ 8 million

Completion of Phase II: US$ 9 million

Completion of Phase III: US$ 6 million

Approval: US$ 3 million

Now assume another deal with the following payment structure:

Upfront payment:

US$ 2 million

Milestone payments:

Completion of Phase I: US$ 4 million

Completion of Phase II: US$ 8 million

Completion of Phase III: US$ 13 million

Approval: US$ 13 million

The two deals illustrate that the partners in the licensing deal have different perceptions about the license's value. The second deal structure illustrates that the buyer of the compound's intellectual property rights (the licensee) is both less optimistic about the compound's odds and degree of success, and is also more risk averse than the seller (the licensor). Therefore, the second deal transfers financial risk from the licensee to the licensor. However, in the case of out-licensing, the pharmaceutical company is usually the entity that is interested in transferring risks. Thus, the pharmaceutical company would most likely prefer the first deal structure.

As illustrated by the case example, the price is perceived to increase from the perspective of the partner firm if the pharmaceutical company would demand a higher proportion of upfront versus milestone payments. However, the amount of upfront and milestone payments might be limited by the licensee's size. If the company is a fairly small company which cannot deliver high upfront payments, the pharmaceutical company might be willing to agree on a higher relative contribution of milestone payments.

Another group of parameters that influence the price setting includes additional resources which the pharmaceutical company might contribute to the collaboration but which are not directly monetized in the deal terms. This could include co-promotion / co-marketing arrangements or manufacturing agreements. As the pharmaceutical company is providing these resources to the collaboration, the price setting of the license will most likely be affected in a way that the price for the licensee will rise because the pharmaceutical company expects to be compensated for these resources. However, the impact on the size of the upfront payment depends on the individual structure of the deal. Other parameters which have an influence on the price setting and also depend on the individual negotiation of each deal include non-compete clauses, the existence of regional split-of-rights, sharing of R&D costs, loan facilities or equity stakes. Although equity stakes could have been observed in the out-licensing collaboration between Novartis and Speedel, they are not common elements in the compensation structure of an out-licensing collaboration.

In summary, there are various parameters which affect the size of the upfront payment in an out-licensing collaboration. The most important price parameters include:

- Call-back options;
- Royalty revenues;

- Milestone payments;
- Co-promotion/co-marketing arrangements;
- Manufacturing agreements;
- Non-compete clauses;
- Regional split-of-rights;
- Sharing of R&D costs;
- Loan facilities;
- Equity stakes.

The configuration of all price parameters not only defines the price setting but also the likelihood that the out-licensing collaboration can be closed which determines the pharmaceutical company's ability to transfer risks. The impact of the price setting on the risk transferability is discussed in the next chapter.

7.2.2 Impact on risk transferability

As the price setting determines the timing and amount of payments that have to be made during the collaboration, the price setting has a strong influence on both the license's bargaining range as well as compensation structure. The bargaining range compares the value of the license as perceived by both parties of the transaction. This requires the estimation of the pharmaceutical firm's NPV of the underlying project as well as the partner firm's NPV for the same project. By balancing the NPV projections for both sides of the collaboration, the license's price is ultimately the parameter that determines the difference in perceptions and subsequently the size of the bargaining range. As a result, the bargaining range describes the interval between the minimum and maximum price possible in the licensing deal. Therefore, by setting the price of the license, the pharmaceutical company always exerts an influence on the collaboration's bargaining range.

Due to its impact on structuring the timing and amount of payments for the collaboration, the price setting also influences the license's compensation structure. The constellation of the different price parameters as listed earlier directly translates into the compensation structure of the collaboration. According to Windhover (2000), the price setting by the pharmaceutical company should always bear in mind that the best deals are those that allow the partner company to acquire products at a price that permits for growth.

Considering that the license's bargaining range and compensation structure represent attributes that affect the risk transferability during the out-licensing collaboration, the pharmaceutical company could use its ability to modify the price setting to influence the risk transferability of the collaboration. Reflecting the different states of the license's bargaining range and compensation structure that enable a high risk transferability, the pharmaceutical company should review and analyze its price setting if (i) the price structure allows the partner firm to value the underlying project higher as the pharmaceutical company would value the project itself, and (ii) the deal terms of the licensing agreement are structured in a way which provides an incentive for the licensee to develop the substance while the pharmaceutical company is simultaneously able to retain the right to re-license the substance after initial risks could have been reduced. Only if the price setting considers these aspects, the partner firm will most likely be willing to take on the product and the pharmaceutical company will be able to share the risks inherent in the project. If the partner firm considers the bargaining range to be too small, the pharmaceutical company should modify the price setting along the different price parameters mentioned in the previous chapter in order to increase the perception of the license's value at the partner firm. If the partner firm believes that the compensation structure provides too little benefits, the pharmaceutical company could add or remove certain price elements to increase the incentives for the partner firm to in-license the compound.

All of these modifications in the price setting most likely result in either higher or lower upfront payments compared to the initially offered 'community rated' licensing contract. Therefore, the managerial actions that can be taken by pharmaceutical R&D management regarding the price setting of the license in order to increase the likelihood of finding an equilibrium – and subsequently reaching the desired risk transferability – include increasing or reducing the size of the upfront payment that has to be made by the partner firm (which could then have implications on the other elements of the price setting). The managerial implications of making these adjustments to the price setting are discussed in the next chapter.

7.2.3 Managerial implications

Based on the starting situation where the pharmaceutical company would offer a 'community rated' license, pharmaceutical R&D management can try to approximate an equilibrium in the out-licensing market by applying one of the following two alternatives regarding the price setting:

- *Increasing the size of the upfront payment.* The pharmaceutical company can increase the upfront payment by simply raising the amount that has to be paid by the licensee. This might go along with a modification of the deal structure affecting the other price parameters which are considered to have an indirect influence on the upfront payment. The modifications could include adding/dropping call-back options or lowering the relative contribution of royalty revenues or milestone payments.

- *Reducing the size of the upfront payment.* The pharmaceutical company can reduce the upfront payment by simply lowering the amount that has to be paid by the licensee. This might go along with a modification of the deal structure affecting the other price parameters which are considered to have an indirect influence on the upfront payment. The modifications could include adding/dropping call-back options or increasing the relative contribution of royalty revenues or milestone payments.

The following models describe the opportunities and effects of making these changes in the price setting. It is assumed ceteris paribus that the other two parameters (product coverage $\acute{\alpha}_2$ and the partner firm's probability of not being able to execute the compound's development p) are initially unaffected by the changes in the license's price α_1, and remain constant.

Increasing the upfront payment

As illustrated in Fig. 63, the pharmaceutical company increases the size of upfront payment α_1 by the amount x_1. As α_1 is plotted on both axes W_1 and W_2, this increase moves ceteris paribus the potential equilibrium F straight towards the origin of the coordinate system on the 45°-line. As this change represents a move away from the initial equilibrium, the pharmaceutical company now has to take some managerial actions in order to reach an equilibrium again.

According to equation (3) from chapter 6.2.5 which represents a fundamental requirement of the equilibrium, the necessary managerial actions can be derived from the following relation:

(5) $$\alpha_1 = \acute{\alpha}_2 * p$$

As an increase in α_1 requires the term ($\acute{\alpha}_2 * p$) to increase as well, the initial ceteris paribus assumption that both $\acute{\alpha}_2$ and p remain unchanged can no longer be sustained any more. The different constellations that allow an increase in the term ($\acute{\alpha}_2 * p$) are as follows:

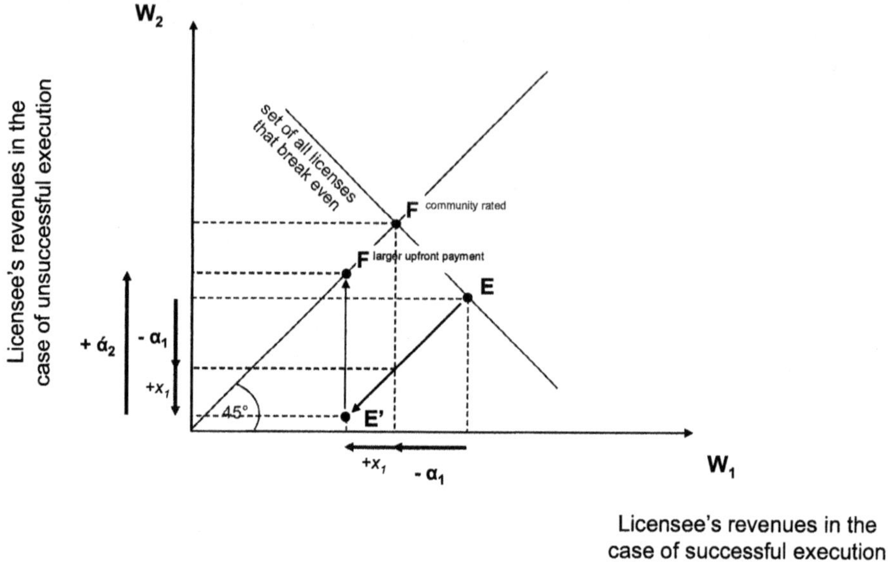

Fig. 63. Impact of increasing the upfront payment on finding an equilibrium in the out-licensing market.

- $\acute{\alpha}_2$ goes up, and p goes up as well or remains constant;
- $\acute{\alpha}_2$ goes up and p decreases, but $\acute{\alpha}_2$ increases by a proportionally larger extent than p decreases.
- $\acute{\alpha}_2$ remains constant, and p goes up;
- $\acute{\alpha}_2$ goes down and p goes up, but p increases by a proportionally larger extent than $\acute{\alpha}_2$ decreases.

As a consequence, the managerial actions which should be taken by the pharmaceutical company to find an equilibrium after it has increased the size of the upfront payment include:

- Raise the product coverage <u>and</u> target the same partner firm or a firm with a higher probability of not being able to execute the compound's development;
- Raise the product coverage <u>and</u> target a partner firm with a lower probability of not being able to execute. However, the product coverage has to grow proportionally more than the partner firm's probability of not being able to execute decreases;

- Leave the product coverage constant and target a partner firm with a higher probability of not being able to execute;
- Lower the product coverage and target a partner firm with a higher probability of not being able to execute. However, the partner firm's probability of not being able to execute has to increase proportionally more than the product coverage decreases;

As the strongest reaction in the term ($\acute{\alpha}_2 * p$) can be achieved if both $\acute{\alpha}_2$ and p increase, the managerial action with the highest impact – after the upfront payment has been increased – would be to raise the product coverage and target a partner firm with a higher probability of not being able to execute the compound's development.

Reducing the upfront payment

In contrast to increasing the size of upfront payment, Fig. 64 illustrates a reduction in the size of upfront payment α_1 by the amount x_1. Reflecting that the upfront pay-

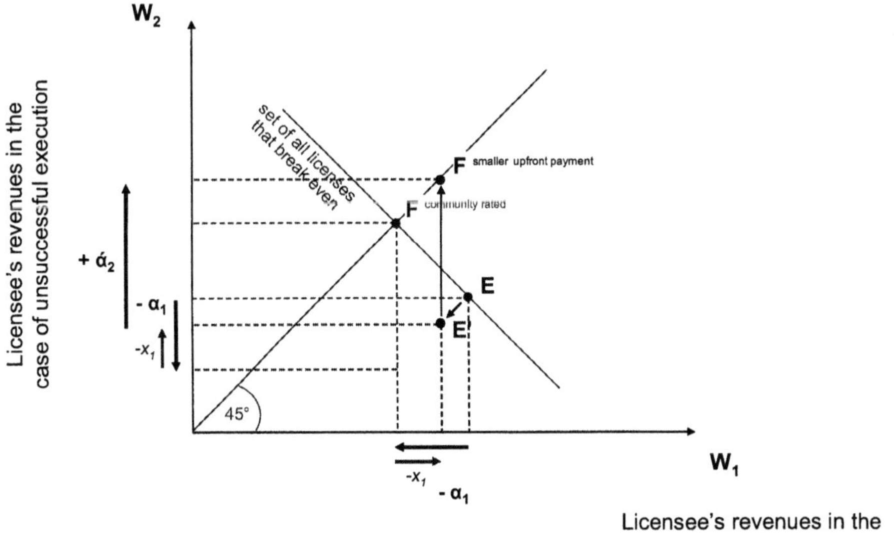

Fig. 64. Impact of reducing the upfront payment on finding an equilibrium in the out-licensing market.

ment appears on both axes W_1 and W_2, the potential equilibrium F moves away from the origin on the 45°-line. Similar to increasing the upfront payment, this change also represents a move away from the initial equilibrium. The pharmaceutical company has to take managerial actions as well in order to reach the equilibrium again.

Based on the same analytical derivation from equations (3) and (5) as illustrated in the previous paragraphs, a reduction of α_1 requires the term ($\acute{\alpha}_2$ * p) to decrease as well. The ceteris paribus assumption that both $\acute{\alpha}_2$ and p remain unchanged can no longer be sustained, and the term ($\acute{\alpha}_2$ * p) can only decrease under the following conditions:

- $\acute{\alpha}_2$ goes down, and p goes down as well or remains constant;
- $\acute{\alpha}_2$ goes down and p increases, but $\acute{\alpha}_2$ decreases by a proportionally larger extent than p increases.
- $\acute{\alpha}_2$ remains constant, and p goes down;
- $\acute{\alpha}_2$ goes up and p goes down, but p decreases by a proportionally larger extent than $\acute{\alpha}_2$ increases.

As a consequence, the managerial actions which should be taken by the pharmaceutical company to find an equilibrium after it has reduced the size of the upfront payment include:

- Lower the product coverage and target the same partner firm or a firm with a lower probability of not being able to execute the compound's development;
- Lower the product coverage and target a partner firm with a higher probability of not being able to execute. However, the product coverage has to decrease proportionally more than the partner firm's probability of not being able to execute increases;
- Leave the product coverage constant and target a partner firm with a lower probability of not being able to execute;
- Raise the product coverage and target a partner firm with a lower probability of not being able to execute. However, the partner firm's probability of not being able to execute has to decrease proportionally more than the product coverage increases;

As the strongest reaction in the term ($\acute{\alpha}_2$ * p) can be achieved if both $\acute{\alpha}_2$ and p decrease, the managerial action with the highest impact – after the upfront payment has been reduced – would be to lower the product coverage and target a partner firm with a lower probability of not being able to execute the compound's development.

Conclusion: This chapter has analyzed the managerial relevance of modifying the price setting – particularly regarding the size of the upfront payment – on reducing the asymmetric information in the out-licensing arrangement in order to find an equilibrium in the out-licensing market. Due to its interdependence with the license's bargaining range and compensation structure, the price setting impacts the risk transferability of the collaboration. Pharmaceutical R&D management could use its ability to modify the size of the upfront payment in a way which increases the risk transferability to an extent where the pharmaceutical company would be able to transfer those risks to the external partner which it would like to hand over. Fig. 65 illustrates the basic consequences of modifications in the size of upfront payment compared to the initial 'community rated' situation.[53]

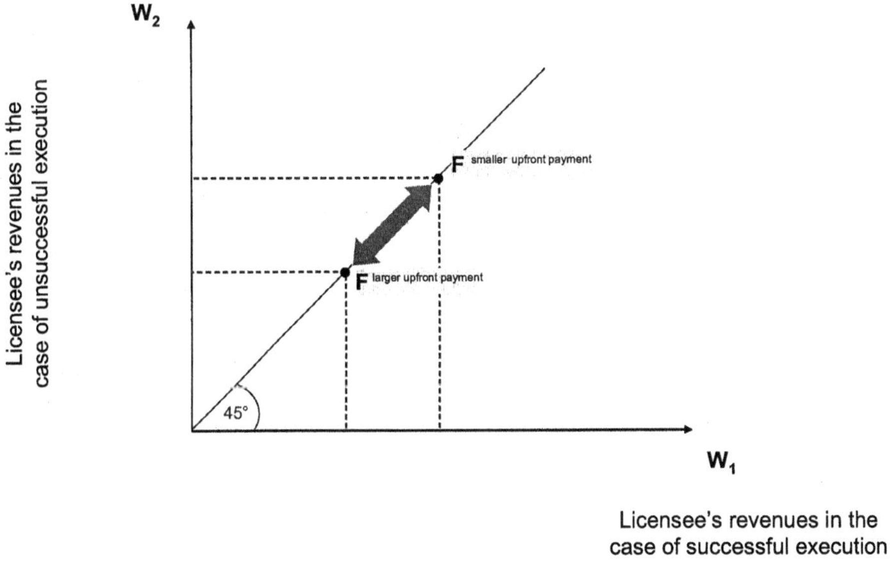

Fig. 65. Impact of changes in the upfront payment on the ability to find an equilibrium in the out-licensing market.

53 As a change in the size of the upfront payment moves the location of the possible equilibria towards or away from the origin, it has to be reflected that changes in the other two parameters (the product coverage as well as the partner firm's probability of not being able to execute the compound's development) are necessary as well to reach an equilibrium.

However, modifications in the price setting also bear some caveats which should be considered by pharmaceutical R&D management. The upfront payment represents only the first payment of the entire collaboration agreement. Most of the remaining payments are tied to the compound's successful development, such as royalty revenues or milestone payments. If the partner firm is unable to successfully execute the compound's development, the pharmaceutical company will end up with only a small fraction of the overall payments. In addition, the value of the call-back option usually drops significantly. Only if the partner firm can execute the compound's development, the pharmaceutical company could expect additional payments or might be tempted to exercise the call-back option. Therefore, the payments other than the upfront payment are all exposed to the risk that the partner cannot execute. This could lead to undesired and severe losses which would be attributable to the pharmaceutical company. An increase in upfront payments (compared to the 'community rated' terms) would result in a more immediate cash flow towards the pharmaceutical company, and would therefore be preferred by pharmaceutical R&D management. However, the partner firm might most likely not be willing to get involved in the licensing deal at these terms. In addition, the pharmaceutical company would have to give up some part of the potential to receive large royalty revenues in case the drug turns out to be a blockbuster. By contrast, a reduction in upfront payments (compared to the 'community rated' terms) would most likely increase the willingness of the partner to accept the deal, but would expose the pharmaceutical company to the risk to receive only a small fraction of the license's entire value if the partner firm cannot successfully execute the compound's development.

Therefore, the 'right' upfront payment always requires a trade-off between maximizing the potential payoff expected from the out-licensing deal and minimizing the risk of losing almost the entire value of the license.

7.3 Performance Presumption

When out-licensing a certain bundle of intellectual property rights, pharmaceutical R&D management is not only able to decide about the product coverage and price setting but also about the nature of collaboration that it would like to enter. The nature of the collaboration refers to the risk/benefit profile of the out-licensing deal. Assuming perfect competition in the out-licensing market, the pharmaceutical company has generally the choice to enter either into a collaboration which is more likely to succeed but would generate lower returns for the pharmaceutical company if the collaboration turns out to be successful or a collaboration which is less likely to succeed but would generate a higher return for the pharmaceutical company if the collaboration turns out to be successful. While the nature of the out-licensing collaboration is characterized by an asymmetric distribution of information, the pharmaceutical company, however, cannot discriminate among the potential partner companies on the basis of their ability to successfully develop the licensed compound. As the collaboration's performance potential represents highly relevant information for the pharmaceutical company's decision to engage in an out-licensing deal, pharmaceutical R&D management has to find a way to presume the nature of the collaboration and its inherent performance potential. In this context, the performance presumption refers to all aspects that allow the pharmaceutical company to draw conclusions about the collaboration's likelihood to succeed in terms of executing the out-licensed product's development.

7.3.1 Relevant parameters

There are several parameters that might help the pharmaceutical company to get an idea of the probability that the collaboration might turn out to be successful. These parameters usually relate to the partner's capabilities regarding the execution of the licensed product. One way for pharmaceutical companies to find out about the potential partners' development capability would be to look at their market behavior and to draw respective conclusions about their likelihood of being able to execute. However, Rothschild and Stiglitz (1976) argue that this is not a profitable way of finding out about buyer characteristics although it might possibly lead to accurate results. Information that accrues after the deal has closed may be used only for follow-on licensing deals but has no value for the current licensing deal because pharmaceutical companies want to know their licensees' characteristics upfront in order to be able to make decisions about the collaboration.

According to Rothschild and Stiglitz (1976), it is often possible to force the partner firms to make market choices in such a way that they reveal their characteristics and make the choices the pharmaceutical firm would have wanted them to make had their characteristics been publicly known. In order to force the partner firms to make market choices, the pharmaceutical company has to have at least some information about the potential partner's preferences to get involved in the licensing deal (i.e. their need to in-license a compound from the pharmaceutical company). The pool of potential partner companies that might feel the desire to in-license a compound is generally very large and consists of basically every company in the industry. The parameters that distinguish the potential partners among each other are usually related to the constitution of their R&D departments which in turn includes information about their resources, competencies and capabilities that enable the partner firm to successfully conduct the compound's development.

One of the most relevant parameters that determine the partner's likelihood to conduct the required development tasks includes the firm's experience with the R&D tasks that have to be completed. If the partner has already conducted several similar projects it will be more likely that the out-licensing collaboration might become a success than if the partner firm has never done any related job. Teoh (1994) supports this view by claiming that one of the most important factors for producing successful new chemical entities includes technological familiarity.

Another important parameter includes the expertise of the people working in the partner's R&D department. If the partner firm's employees are highly skilled in the respective therapy areas or technology platforms, the collaboration has a higher probability to be successful. In this context, Boerner (2002) figured out that one of the major success factors in the pharmaceutical industry includes internal clinical capabilities. Besides expertise of the company's employees, the partner firm's ability to execute will also most likely be affected by its employees' commitment towards the project as well as teamworking and management skills (Rautiainen 2001). Rautiainen (2001) further claims that human resources and the company's infrastructure represent other factors that describe a company's ability to successfully develop a new drug candidate. Moreover, networking and breaking down barriers between corporations are considered to be further important success factor which are related to the partner firm's ability to bring a compound successfully through the development stages (see Needleman 2001, Rautiainen 2001 or Boerner 2002).

Last but not least, the constitution of the partner's R&D portfolio also allows the drawing of some conclusions about the presumed likelihood of a collaboration's success. Parameters related to the R&D portfolio usually include the number and stages of R&D projects under development, the therapy areas served, the number and types of technology platforms applied, the number of issued and pending patents, the scope of conducted activities that describe which R&D stages/phase are covered, or the depth of activities highlighting the ratio of the firm's own activities vs. outsourced activities. If a partner deploys a rather large portfolio, applies several technology platforms and has already secured several patents in the respective area of development, this is usually a strong indicator for the company's ability to execute a compound's development. Hence, a collaboration will most likely turn out to be a success if the partner firm possesses a strong portfolio of relevant activities.

In summary, there are many parameters which are related to the likelihood that the collaboration turns out to be a success and which allow the pharmaceutical company to draw some conclusions about the presumed performance of the out-licensing deal. The most relevant parameters include:

- Experience with the respective R&D tasks;
- Technology familiarity;
- Expertise;
- Clinical capabilities;
- Commitment;
- Management skills;
- Human resources;
- Infrastructure;
- Networking;
- Constitution of R&D portfolio (number and stages of the R&D project, therapy areas served, technology platforms applied, patents).

The specifications of all these parameters not only allow the pharmaceutical company to draw conclusions about the potential partners' likelihood of being able to execute the development the licensed compound (which allows for presuming the performance potential of the collaboration) but also about the probability that the out-licensing deal will be closed which has an influence on the pharmaceutical company's ability to transfer risks. The impact of the presumption of the collaboration's performance on the risk transferability is discussed in the next chapter.

7.3.2 Impact on risk transferability

As the performance presumption relates to the partner's ability to execute the compound's development, it has a strong influence on the pharmaceutical company's decision about selecting the licensee. In this context, a study by Cambridge Healthcare & Biotech (2003) about the selection of partner firms in licensing deals in the pharmaceutical industry analyzed the most attractive partner characteristics in a licensing deal. The following six criteria were believed to be the most desirable 'soft' qualities that a licensor would like in a partner: (i) the partner has a high level of empathy with our objectives, (ii) the partner does not drive a very hard financial bargain, (iii) the partner is prepared to be flexible on the deal structure, (iv) the partner can move quickly when we need him to, (v) we can access the key decision makers directly, and (vi) the partner sticks to the sentiment of the agreement throughout the lifetime of the collaboration. Thus, the partner's attractiveness seems to be dependent on its adaptiveness to the requests and desires of the pharmaceutical company. Windhover (2000) supports this finding by claiming that the key of closing on out-licensing deals with large pharmaceutical companies will be creative deal structures. According to Hess and Evangelista (2004), the mid-sized biotech firm Abgenix is well known for pursuing and winning several licensing deals with large pharmaceutical companies by applying a creative and flexible approach to structure the deal in a way that it maximizes benefits not only for themselves but also for the pharmaceutical company. Abgenix' willingness to think outside the traditional alliance box earned the company a spot on many 'to-be-considered' lists in top therapeutic areas. Although Abgenix employs only around 400 people, it has built a network of partners that includes collaborations and technology licensing agreements with more than 50 commercial and academic organizations including large pharmaceutical companies, such as Amgen, Pfizer, AstraZeneca or Chugai. As the presumed probability of the collaboration's success seems to be higher if the partner firm is highly adaptive towards the pharmaceutical company, assessing the performance presumption of the collaboration leads to the situation that the pharmaceutical company narrows down or extends the pool of potential partner companies according to their corporate flexibility.

As the pharmaceutical company intends to use out-licensing as a means to share risks, the activities that are to be completed by the partner company are usually high-risk activities. Therefore, the collaboration's performance potential is presumably higher if the partner firm is not only adaptive but also willing and able to carry these high risks. A company's willingness to carry risks can best be described by its attitude towards innovation. Georgellis et al. (2000) argue that most literature equates the willingness to take risks with the existence of an entrepreneurial culture, and risk taking has long been a central theme of the entrepreneurship literature (compare Busenitz 1999 and Miller 1983). As entrepreneurs are often thought to engage in 'risky' events, they may be seen as more willing than average to take risks (Norton and Moore 2000). In addition, Miller (1983) highlights that a firm's degree of entrepreneurial orientation could be seen as the extent to which firms take risks, innovate and act proactively. In this context, the company's ability to take on risks can be deduced by having a look at the firm's capital structure. If a significant proportion of the company's capital can be classified as being positively associated with risk, the company's ability to carry risks is usually higher than if a significant proportion of the capital is not positively associated with risk. As venture capital investors proactively seek to make investments in high-risk endeavors because of their investment mandate, venture-capital backed firms seem to be more open towards risk.[54] By contrast, companies which base their capital structure on rather traditional funding sources tend to be more stable and incumbent firms that are comparatively less willing to get involved in high risk endeavors. Shin and Stulz (2000) analyzed different companies according to their risk profile, and they figured out that the standard deviation of the change in total risk is about four times larger for small firms than for large firms. This means that the companies which are exposed to lower levels of risks are usually larger firms. As illustrated by the examples of the case studies, it should be considered that significantly venture-backed companies might be able to take higher risks, and more stable and traditionally funded companies might have a limited ability to carry the required development risks.

Impact of the capital structure on a company's ability to carry risks

Novartis, Schering and Roche all agree that most out-licensing deals are preferably closed with smaller companies. They believe that smaller partner companies are better able to take higher risks due to their usually highly venture-backed capital structure. Novartis, Schering and Roche argue that the venture capital investors know about these high risks and intentionally invest in these companies because of their own investment mandate. By taking these high risks, the venture capital investors hope to receive a return on investment which is higher than the average return in the pharmaceutical industry. Therefore, it is not surprising that all partner firms in the analyzed case studies (Speedel, Intarcia and Actelion) were significantly venture capital funded companies.

As the presumed probability of the collaboration's success seems not only to be higher if the partner firm is higly adaptive but also characterized by an entrepreneurial climate, assessing the performance presumption of the collaboration also leads to the situation that the pharmaceutical company narrows down or extends the pool of potential partner companies according to their overall entrepreneurial setting.

Considering that the licensee's corporate flexibility and entrepreneurial setting represent attributes that have an impact on the risk transferability during the collaboration, the pharmaceutical company could modify its presumed performance regarding

54 Venture capitalists make high-risk equity investments in new entrepreneurial ventures (Callahan and Muegge 2002). Venture capital is an important internal factor in the early stages of a startup, and venture capital firms devote significant management resources to understanding new technologies and markets, finding promising startups in those spaces, providing them with financial resources, and coaching them through the early part of their lives (Davila et al. 2002).

the collaboration in order to exert an influence on the risk transferability. Reflecting the different states of the licensee's corporate flexibility and entrepreneurial setting which are considered to enable a high risk transferability, the pharmaceutical company should review its performance presumption for the collaboration if (i) the licensee is flexible enough, and (ii) the licensee's entrepreneurial setting is strong enough, so that the licensee will most likely be willing and able to in-license the compound for further development which would allow the pharmaceutical company to share the inherent risks. If the partner firm is not flexible enough to react according to the needs of the pharmaceutical company, the pharmaceutical company should target a more adaptive partner firm. Simultaneously, if the partner firm's entrepreneurial setting is not strong enough to run a high-risk development project, the pharmaceutical company could try to target a different partner who seems more likely capable to bring the compound successful through development.

All of these decisions relate to the partner firm's ability to execute the compound's development. Thus, the managerial actions that can be taken by pharmaceutical R&D management to increase the likelihood of finding an equilibrium – and subsequently reaching the desired risk transferability – include to target either a company with a higher or lower probability of not being able to execute a compound's development compared to the situation where the pharmaceutical company could not differentiate between the potential licensees. The managerial implications of making these choices are discussed in the following chapter.

7.3.3 Managerial implications

Based on the 'community rated' starting situation where the pharmaceutical company assumes that all licensees are identical, pharmaceutical R&D management can try to draw some conclusions about the partner's ability to execute the compound's development in order to approximate an equilibrium in the out-licensing market. Thereby, the pharmaceutical company can apply one of the following two strategies regarding the collaboration's presumed performance:

- *Targeting a partner who has a higher probability of not being able to execute.* The pharmaceutical company could proactively approach companies which seem to have a rather low experience, technology familiarity, expertise, clinical capabilities, management commitment and skills as well as only a limited infrastructure and network and an R&D portfolio which is fairly small and immature. Most likely, these firms are rather small and newly incepted companies that do not have a solid track record of successful development programs yet. However, the expected payoff attributable to the pharmaceutical company might be comparatively high if the partner can execute the compound's development.[55]

- *Targeting a partner who has a lower probability of not being able to execute.* The pharmaceutical company could proactively approach companies which seem to have a rather high experience, technology familiarity, expertise, clinical capabilities, management commitment and skills as well as a large infrastructure and network and an R&D portfolio which is quite large and well established. Most likely, these firms are rather large and established companies. However, the expected payoff attributable to the pharmaceutical company might be comparatively low if the partner can execute the compound's development.

The following models describe the opportunities and effects of approaching these different types of potential partner firms. It is assumed ceteris paribus that the other two parameters (the product coverage $\acute{\alpha}_2$ and the size of the upfront payment α_1) are initially unaffected by changes in the partner firm's probability of not being able to execute the compound's development p, and remain constant.

Targeting partners with a higher probability of not being able to execute

As illustrated in Fig. 66, the pharmaceutical company targets a partner firm with a higher probability p which is characterized by the indifference curve $\bar{U}^H$. The indifference curve $\bar{U}^H$ is located in the upper-left corner compared to the 'community rated' indifference curve. This has the reason that high-risk licensees are usually more willing to buy a licensing contract with a larger coverage in order to compensate for their higher exposure to the risk of not being able to execute the compound's development. In an efficient licensing market, the high-risk licensees have to pay a higher price for these licenses. As a result of receiving a higher coverage $\acute{\alpha}_2$ and paying a higher price (it is assumed that all price elements increase pro-rata, and therefore also the upfront payment α_1), their utility indifference curve moves to the left and upwards in the coordinate system.

As a result, the potential equilibrium F moves ceteris paribus to the upper left side compared to the initial 'community rated' situation. As this change represents a move away from the initial equilibrium, the pharmaceutical company now has to

55 While experience, expertise as well as management commitment are characteristics related to the employees, they are independent of the company's size because they might exist in small companies as well. However, it is difficult for an external pharmaceutical company do judge about these characteristics upfront without having no further information about the firm yet.

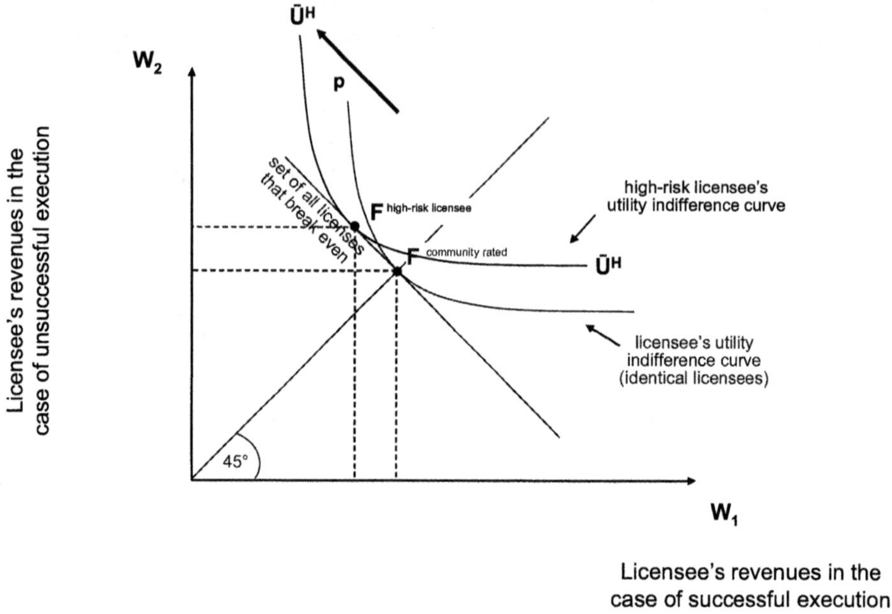

Fig. 66. Impact of targeting a high-risk licensee on the ability to find an equilibrium in the out-licensing market.

take some managerial actions in order to reach an equilibrium again. According to an algebraic transformation of equation (3) from chapter 6.2.5, the necessary managerial actions can be derived from the following relation:

(6) $$p = \alpha_1 / \acute{\alpha}_2$$

As an increase in p requires the ratio ($\alpha_1 / \acute{\alpha}_2$) to increase as well, the initial ceteris paribus assumption that both α_1 and $\acute{\alpha}_2$ remain unchanged can no longer be sustained. The constellations that allow an increase in the ratio ($\alpha_1 / \acute{\alpha}_2$) are as follows:

- α_1 goes up, and $\acute{\alpha}_2$ goes down or remains constant;
- α_1 goes up and $\acute{\alpha}_2$ goes up as well, but α_1 increases by a proportionally larger extent than $\acute{\alpha}_2$.

- α_1 remains constant, and $\acute{\alpha}_2$ goes down;
- α_1 goes down and $\acute{\alpha}_2$ goes down as well, but $\acute{\alpha}_2$ decreases by a proportionally larger extent than α_1.

As a consequence, the managerial actions which should be taken by the pharmaceutical company to find an equilibrium after it has targeted a partner firm with a higher probability of not being able to execute the compound's development include:

- Raise the upfront payment and lower the product coverage or leave the product coverage constant;
- Raise the upfront payment and raise the product coverage. However, the upfront payment has to grow proportionally more than the product coverage;
- Leave the upfront payment constant and lower the product coverage;
- Lower the upfront payment and lower the product coverage. However, the product coverage has to decrease proportionally more than the upfront payment.

As the strongest reaction in the ratio (α_1 / $\acute{\alpha}_2$) can be achieved if α_1 increases and $\acute{\alpha}_2$ simultaneously decreases, the managerial action with the highest impact – after a partner with a higher p has been targeted – would be to raise the upfront payment and to lower the product coverage.

Targeting partners with a lower probability of not being able to execute

In contrast to targeting a partner with a higher p, Fig. 67 illustrates the case that the pharmaceutical company targets a partner with a lower probability of not being able to execute. Following the same rational as in the previous paragraphs, the utility indifference curve of the low-risk licensees $\bar{U}^L$ will be found southeast of the initial 'community rated' situation. Low-risk licensees prefer to pay lower upfront payments in return for a lower coverage. Thus, the potential equilibrium F moves ceteris paribus to the lower right side in the coordinate system. As this change also represents a move away from the initial equilibrium, the pharmaceutical company has to take some managerial actions in order to reach an equilibrium again.

Based on the same analytical derivation as illustrated in the previous paragraphs, a lower p requires the ratio (α_1 / $\acute{\alpha}_2$) to decrease as well. The ceteris paribus assumption that both α_1 and $\acute{\alpha}_2$ remain unchanged can no longer be sustained, and the ratio (α_1 / $\acute{\alpha}_2$) can only decrease under the following conditions:

- α_1 goes down, and $\acute{\alpha}_2$ goes up or remains constant;
- α_1 goes down and $\acute{\alpha}_2$ goes down as well, but α_1 decreases by a proportionally larger extent than $\acute{\alpha}_2$;

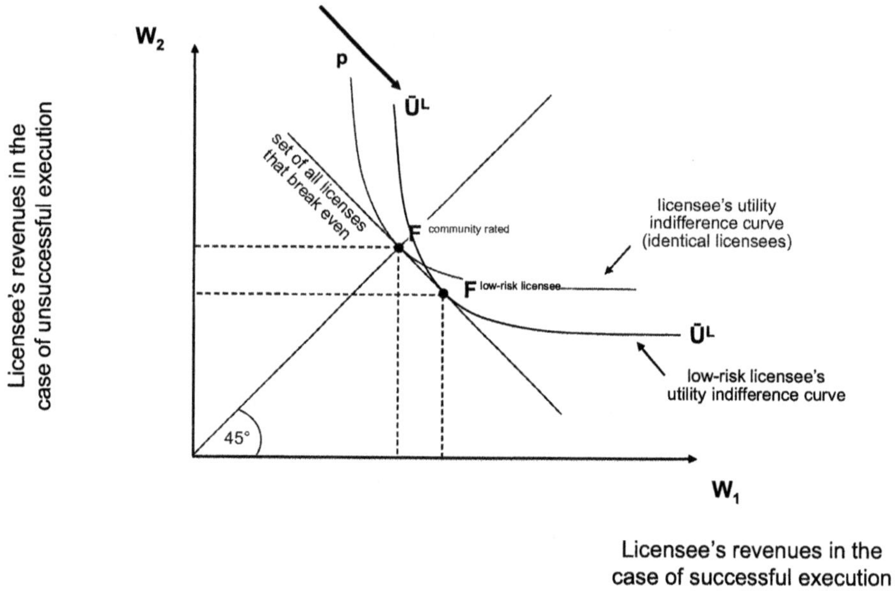

Fig. 67. Impact of targeting a low-risk licensee on the ability to find an equilibrium in the out-licensing market.

- α_1 remains constant, and $\acute{\alpha}_2$ goes up;
- α_1 goes up and $\acute{\alpha}_2$ goes up as well, but $\acute{\alpha}_2$ increases by a proportionally larger extent than α_1.

As a consequence, the managerial actions which should be taken by the pharmaceutical company in order to find an equilibrium after it has targeted a partner firm with a lower probability of not being able to execute the compound's development are as follows:

- Lower the upfront payment <u>and</u> raise the product coverage or leave the product coverage constant;
- Lower the upfront payment <u>and</u> lower the product coverage. However, the upfront payment has to decrease proportionally more than the product coverage;
- Leave the upfront payment constant <u>and</u> raise the product coverage;
- Raise the upfront payment <u>and</u> raise the product coverage. However, the product coverage has to increase proportionally more than the upfront payment.

As the strongest reaction in the ratio (α_1 / $\acute{\alpha}_2$) can be achieved if α_1 decreases and $\acute{\alpha}_2$ simultaneously increases, the managerial action with the highest impact – after a partner with a lower p has been targeted – would be to lower the upfront payment and to raise the product coverage.

Conclusion: This chapter has analyzed the managerial relevance of modifications to the presumed performance potential of the collaboration on reducing the asymmetric information in the out-licensing arrangement in order to find an equilibrium in the market for out-licensing. Due to its interdependence with the licensee's corporate flexibility and entrepreneurial setting, the performance presumption exerts an influence on the risk transferability of the collaboration. Pharmaceutical R&D management could thus make changes to its presumed performance of the collaboration in a way which increases the risk transferability to a level where the pharmaceutical company would be able to transfer the risks to the external partner which it would like to carry forward. Fig. 68 graphically illustrates the basic consequences of targeting different partner companies based on their likelihood of not being able to execute a compound's development compared to the initial 'community rated' situation.[56]

While it seems to be self-explanatory that a pharmaceutical company should try to approach a partner company with a lower probability of not being able to execute the compound's development (which equates to a higher probability of success for the project), it might also make sense that the pharmaceutical company should target a partner with a higher probability of not being able to execute. The lower probability of success could be overcompensated by the potentially occurring revenues and profits that the pharmaceutical might be able to expect. If the pharmaceutical company's risk-adjusted gains versus its costs regarding the out-licensing deal are higher for this type of partner company, it pays to target a partner firm with a higher probability of not being able to execute. The partners with a lower probability of not being able to execute the compound's development might only be willing to get involved in the licensing deal at deal terms that are most likely unattractive to the pharmaceutical company. Indeed, the managerial implications of targeting a partner with a lower probability of not being able to execute seem to be counterproductive

56 As a change in the target profile has an impact on the location of possible equilibria, it has to be reflected that changes in the other two parameters (the product coverage as well as the size of the upfront payment) are required as well in order to reach an equilibrium.

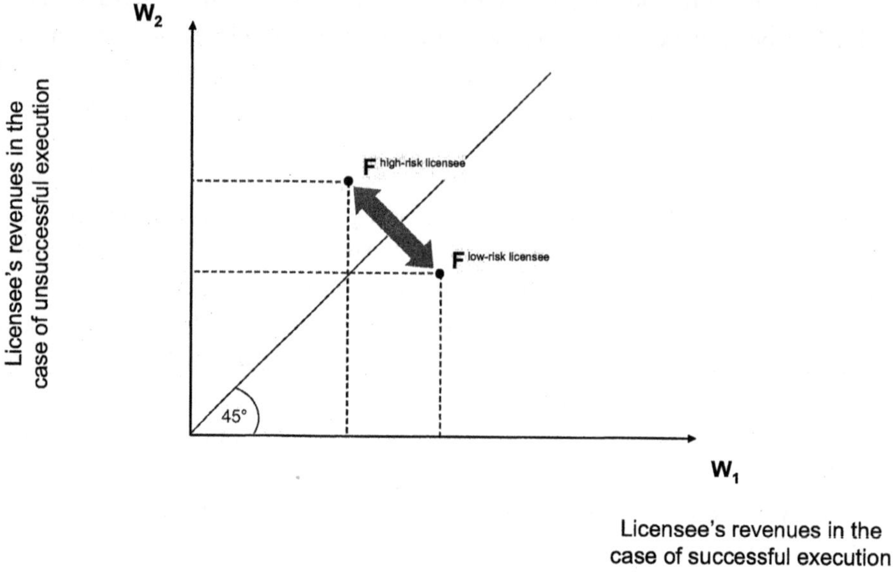

Fig. 68. Impact of changes in the performance presumption on the ability to find an equilibrium in the out-licensing market.

from an economic perspective. The model in the previous paragraphs suggests to always accrete the product coverage more in relative terms than the upfront payment. Compared to the initial 'community rated' offer, these changes always represent a degradation of the deal terms from the perspective of the pharmaceutical company. This degradation can only be overcompensated if the partner's probability of successfully executing the compound's development are over-proportionally higher than the declined deal terms.

Thus, the 'right' performance presumption always requires a trade-off between maximizing the probability that the partner firm is able to execute the compound's development and minimizing the risk that the partner firm retains too much of the joint project's benefits.

7.4 Summary

This chapter has deduced recommendations for pharmaceutical R&D managers about the managerial dimensions that exist in out-licensing collaborations. These managerial dimensions can be used to reduce the asymmetric information in the out-licensing arrangement which allows the approximation of an equilibrium in the out-licensing market. Thereby, the managerial recommendations have built upon insights from the economic theory of adverse selection as introduced in chapter 6. As the theory of adverse selection illustrates three parameters which are expected to influence the ability to find an equilibrium, the recommendations for pharmaceutical R&D management center around the corresponding three managerial dimensions 'product coverage', 'price setting' and 'performance presumption'.

It has been shown in chapter 6 that an equilibrium in the out-licensing market might not exist as long as there are different buyers who are reluctant to reveal information about their ability to execute a compound's development. Therefore, the managerial recommendations could not straightforward show how to find an equilibrium, but they rather illustrate potential avenues how to overcome the existence of asymmetric information and therefore the issue of adverse selection. As the pharmaceutical company will most likely not reach an equilibrium by offering a 'community rated' license, the pharmaceutical company can react accordingly and modify the product coverage, price setting or its performance presumption. These modifications might increase the likelihood of finding a (temporary) equilibrium. Although these equilibria theoretically might not be stable, the following management framework for risk-sharing in pharmaceutical R&D collaborations could have been deduced which might serve as a guideline for pharmaceutical R&D managers regarding the use of out-licensing collaborations as a means to share R&D related risks (Fig. 69):

1. As a first and central step, pharmaceutical R&D management has to incorporate a strong commitment towards out-licensing within the corporation (as illustrated by the inner circle in the management framework). Only a devoted dedication towards out-licensing sets the conditions for effective out-licensing collaborations. Out-licensing is well aligned within the overall corporate strategy and supports risk-sharing if the pharmaceutical company (i) adopts a proactive approach towards out-licensing, (ii) embeds out-licensing organizationally well within the corporation, and (iii) defines a structured out-licensing process.

2. After out-licensing has been incorporated, pharmaceutical R&D management can now modify the product coverage, price setting and performance presumption compared to the 'community rated' situation in order to approximate an equilibrium. As the product coverage, price setting and performance presumption have an influence on the attributes of the license and licensee, the pharmaceutical company might exert an influence on the risk transferability during the

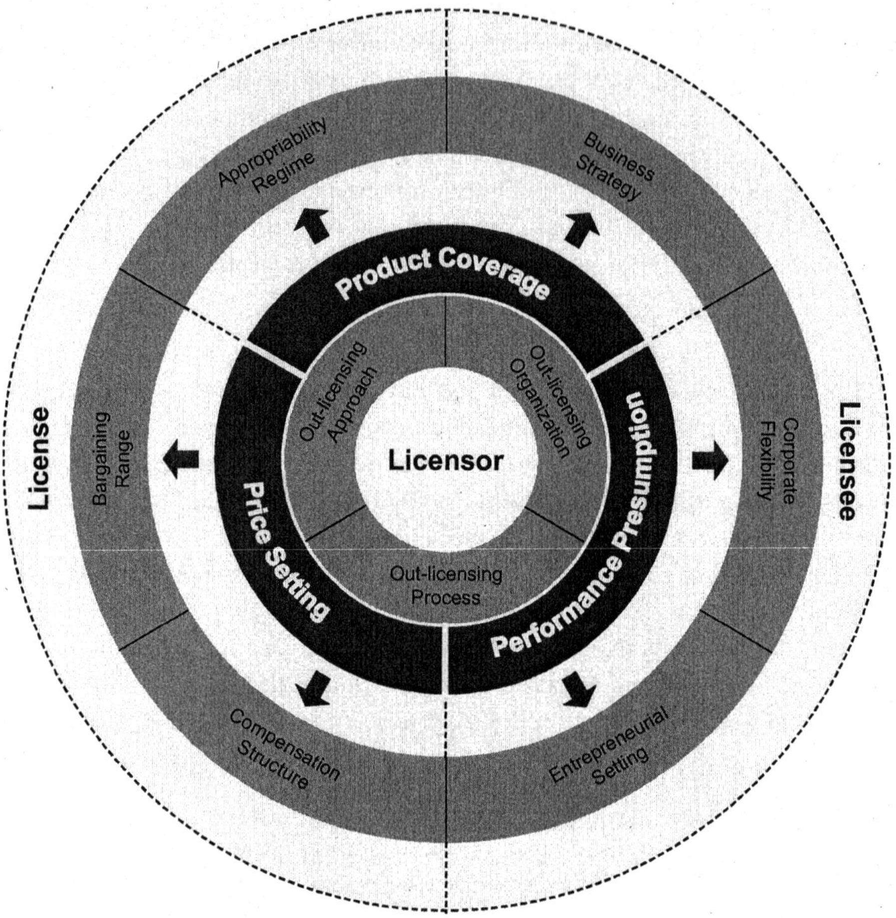

Fig. 69. Management framework for out-licensing as a method for risk-sharing in pharmaceutical R&D collaborations.

out-licensing arrangement. The interdependence between the managerial dimensions and the attributes of the license and licensee is as follows:

- *Product coverage.* The product coverage is expected to have strong ties to the license's appropriability regime and the licensee's business strategy;
- *Price setting.* The size of the upfront payment influences the license's bargaining range and compensation structure;

- *Performance presumption*. The performance presumption interdepends with the licensee's corporate flexibility and entrepreneurial setting.

By knowing about these coherencies, pharmaceutical R&D management can influence the risk transferability by directly modifying the product coverage, price setting or performance presumption in a way that the...

- the license's appropriability regime is as tight,
- the license's bargaining range is as large,
- the license's compensation structure is as success-based,
- the licensee's business strategy is as focused,
- the licensee's corporate flexibility is as high,
- the licensee's entrepreneurial setting is as strong...

as necessary so that the partner firm will most likely be willing and able to acquire the compound with its inherent risks and bring it successfully through development.

3. The managerial actions that can be taken by pharmaceutical R&D management regarding the product coverage, price setting and performance presumption compared to the initial 'community rated' situation which then exert an influence on the risk transferability respectively include:

- increase / reduce the product's coverage;
- increase / reduce the size of the upfront payment;
- target a partner with a higher / lower probability of not being able to execute.

The effects of these modifications compared to the initial 'community rated' situation are graphically summarized in Fig. 70. It has to be considered that any adjustment in one parameter represents a move away from the initial equilibrium under the 'community rated' situation which did not represent a stable equilibrium because of the assumption that there are two or more classes of licensees. In order to approximate a new equilibrium, pharmaceutical R&D management cannot only change one parameter, but has to simultaneously make adjustments along the other two parameters as well. Therefore, a hybrid construct of changes in all three parameters is usually applied when finding an equilibrium in the out-licensing market.

4. The following summarizing statements can be made about the adjustments in parameters when one parameter is about to be changed. The following remarks explicitly cover only those adjustments which are economically useful. As one of

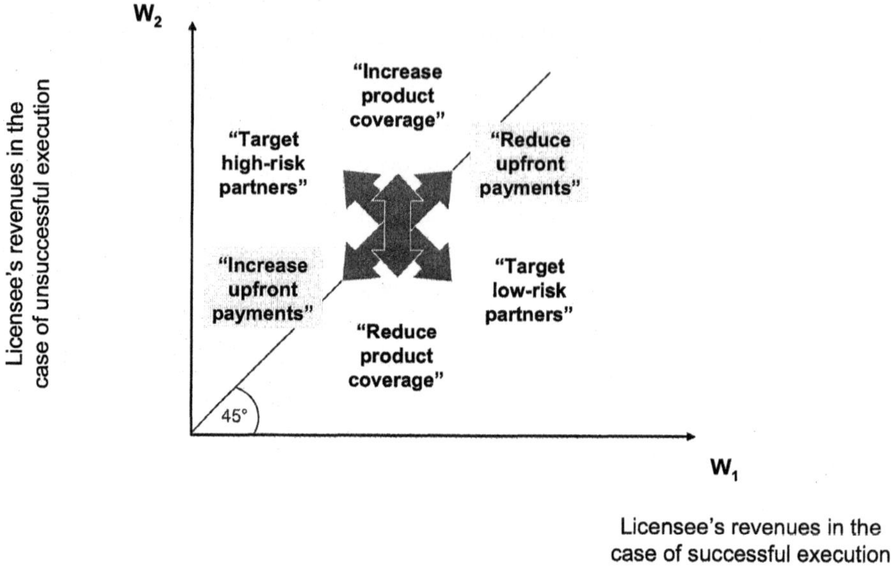

Fig. 70. Summary of changes in the product coverage, price setting and performance presumption on finding an equilibrium in the out-licensing market.

the basic assumptions of the model has been that the pharmaceutical companies are risk-neutral and only concerned with expected profits (thus, they sell any number of licensing contracts that they think will make an expected profit), no pharmaceutical company would be willing to offer a licensing contract that is economically non-rationale (e.g., no pharmaceutical company would offer a contract with a higher coverage at a simultaneously lower price as compared to the 'community rated' licensing offer). As a consequence, the managerial recommendations for making adjustments in the respective parameters can be reduced by the economically useless adjustments. Hence, if the pharmaceutical company would like to...

increase the product coverage, it also has to make the following adjustments:

- raise the upfront payment and target the same licensee or a lower-risk licensee;
- raise the upfront payment and target a higher-risk licensee (however, the up-

front payment has to grow proportionally more than the licensee's probability of not being able to execute);

reduce the product coverage, it also has to make the following adjustments:

- lower the upfront payment <u>and</u> target the same licensee or a higher-risk licensee;
- lower the upfront payment <u>and</u> target a lower-risk licensee (however, the upfront payment has to decrease proportionally more than the licensee's probability of not being able to execute);
- leave the upfront payment constant <u>and</u> target a higher-risk licensee;
- raise the upfront payment <u>and</u> target a higher-risk licensee (however, the licensee's probability of not being able to execute has to increase proportionally more than the upfront payment).

increase the upfront payment, it also has to make the following adjustments:

- raise the product coverage <u>and</u> target the same licensee or a higher-risk licensee;
- raise the product coverage <u>and</u> target a lower-risk licensee (however, the product coverage has to grow proportionally more than the licensee's probability of not being able to execute decreases);
- leave the product coverage constant <u>and</u> target a higher-risk licensee;
- lower the product coverage <u>and</u> target a higher-risk licensee (however, the licensee's probability of not being able to execute has to increase proportionally more than the product coverage decreases).

reduce the upfront payment, it also has to make the following adjustments:

- lower the product coverage <u>and</u> target the same licensee or a lower-risk licensee;
- lower the product coverage <u>and</u> target a higher-risk licensee (however, the product coverage has to decrease proportionally more than the licensee's probability of not being able to execute increases);

target a higher-risk licensee, it also has to make the following adjustments:

- raise the upfront payment <u>and</u> lower the product coverage or leave the product coverage constant;
- raise the upfront payment <u>and</u> raise the product coverage (however, the upfront payment has to grow proportionally more than the product coverage);
- leave the upfront payment constant <u>and</u> lower the product coverage;

- lower the upfront payment <u>and</u> lower the product coverage (however, the product coverage has to decrease proportionally more than the upfront payment).

target a lower-risk licensee, there are no economically useful adjustments to make. From an economic perspective, it can easily be argued that all activities related to targeting a firm with a lower probability of not being able to execute are counterproductive because the product coverage always has to be raised more in relative terms than the upfront payment.

8 Conclusion

Based on the findings of the previous chapters, this chapter derives the resulting implications for management practice and theory.

8.1 Implications for Management Practice

The implications for management practice initially cover a summary of the central statements and recommendations which have been made throughout the research. Afterwards, potential future directions and trends will be portrayed.

8.1.1 Central statements and recommendations

The central statements and recommendations refer to the practical problem in the pharmaceutical industry, the emerging potential to solve these problems, the characteristics of the empirical insights as well as the recommended solution for R&D managers regarding the management of risk-sharing in pharmaceutical R&D collaborations.

Key issues in managing pharmaceutical innovation

The foremost problem in pharmaceutical R&D management is the deteriorating R&D productivity. While R&D expenditures are escalating, the number of new drugs introduced to the market is declining or remaining constant at best. As a result, the average R&D costs per new drug approval have surged to about US$ 1 billion today. This trend leads to an increase in R&D related risks and is going along with a growing proportion of R&D activities that is conducted by external third parties.

- *Increase in R&D risks.* The growth in average R&D costs per new drug approval has caused the R&D related risks to reach unprecedented levels. Any failure of a newly developed substance during the R&D process can cause significant losses. The overall increasing R&D risks can be broken down into the following factors:
  - Risk of growth attainment;
  - Risk of increasing complexity;
  - Risk of technology investment;
  - Risk of high attrition;
  - Risk of blockbuster reliance;
  - Risk of market timing;

  - Risk of product differentiation;
  - Risk of regulative force.

  All of these risks represent a major threat to the successful execution of any R&D project. Indeed, many R&D projects today are terminated because of risk considerations.

- *Increase in R&D collaborations.* While pharmaceutical R&D has been a fully integrated process for many years, today's companies rely on vast networks with various types of external partners. These partnerships can have different forms and go far beyond the well known 'technology sourcing' strategies represented by the early pharma-biotech alliances. A fairly radical scenario even predicts that only lead finding, lead optimization and marketing will remain the core activities of pharmaceutical companies which have to be provided inhouse. All other activities of the pharmaceutical R&D process could potentially be done by external parties via various types of cooperation. The foremost reasons why pharmaceutical companies engage in R&D collaborations include intensive competition, access to markets, scarce own resources, lack of know-how, cost cutting or restructuring, growth aspirations, synergies and efficiencies, and last but not least risk reduction.

The increasing R&D risks have caused pharmaceutical R&D managers to put a large emphasis on vehicles and contractual arrangements in R&D collaborations that explicitly consider risk-sharing aspects. Risk-sharing arrangements have consequently become one of the most important key issues in pharmaceutical innovation management.

Risk-sharing as new paradigm in pharmaceutical R&D collaborations

As R&D risks have become increasingly unbearable, many pharmaceutical companies have started to contemplate using their outside partners to share some part of the risks. The nature of risk-sharing contracts is that each partner's success has to be based on the success of the joint project. Both companies gain or lose together, and each partner has to look at the other partner's success as its own success. Only if the partner possesses special capabilities or expertise that allow the development of the new drug candidate at a lower level of risk, a risk-sharing collaboration could effectively reduce the pharmaceutical company's exposure to the R&D risks. While there are some approaches to risk-sharing which have been applied for several years already, out-licensing represents a fairly novel type of risk-sharing.

- *Traditional approaches to risk-sharing.* The more traditional approaches to risk-sharing applied by pharmaceutical companies include:
  - Research alliance;
  - In-licensing;
  - Co-development.

  While research alliances and co-development refer to arrangements where the two partners conduct joint activities, in-licensing refers to the acquisition of intellectual property rights which have been invented by an external partner.

- *Out-licensing as novel approach to risk-sharing.* Many established pharmaceutical companies have traditionally been reluctant to apply out-licensing because they considered their research results to be their core assets. Selling them could lead to a disaster if the compound turns out to be a blockbuster later on. In addition, there was no downstream pressure for pharmaceutical companies to sell their compounds. Therefore, no company in the industry would usually belief that a compound which is sold by a large pharmaceutical company would be of any great value. However, most reasons why compounds become out-licensing candidates are usually not compound-specific problems but rather company-specific problems. At the same time, the potential for out-licensing is huge. As many R&D projects are stopped because of risk considerations, pharmaceutical companies have built up large portfolios of patents and other forms of valuable intellectual property which have not been commercialized yet. Out-licensing could thus not only help to dispose R&D risks but also to open and create new markets for the commercialization of internal research results. This form of utilization of research seems to be highly necessary reflecting the abysmal productivity in R&D. One of the most important tools which enables out-licensing to function as a risk-sharing approach includes the existence of re-licensing rights (e.g., call-back options). These rights allow licensing back a compound after the risks could have been reduced by the external partner. In summary, out-licensing not only increases the 'shots on goal' in pharmaceutical R&D but could also lead to additional revenues from initially terminated projects which would recoup at least some part of the tremendous amounts spent on R&D.

Characteristics of risk-sharing in pharmaceutical R&D collaborations

The case study analysis of out-licensing deals at Novartis, Schering and Roche provided information about the characteristics of all entities involved in an out-licensing collaboration. The entities include the seller of the license (the licensor), the license itself as well as the buyer of the license (the licensee). All entities are characterized by different attributes which were considered to have an impact on the risk transferability of the out-licensing collaboration.

- *Attributes of the licensor.* The licensor's attributes which are considered to have the most important impact on the risk transferability include:

  - Out-licensing approach;
  - Out-licensing organization;
  - Out-licensing process.

  The risk transferability is most likely high if the licensor's out-licensing approach is proactive, the out-licensing organization well embedded into the corporation, and the out-licensing process structured.

- *Attributes of the license.* The attributes related to the license which are considered to affect the risk transferability include:

  - Appropriability regime;
  - Bargaining range;
  - Compensation structure.

  The risk transferability is most likely high if the appropriability regime is tight, the bargaining range large, and the compensation structure success-based.

- *Attributes of the licensee.* The licensee's attributes which are considered to have a high impact on the risk transferability include:

  - Business strategy;
  - Corporate flexibility;
  - Entrepreneurial setting.

  The risk transferability is most likely high if the licensee's business strategy is focused, the corporate flexibility high, and the entrepreneurial setting strong.

The first step and central origin of every successful out-licensing collaboration includes a strong commitment by the pharmaceutical company towards out-licensing. Only if out-licensing is well aligned within the pharmaceutical company's overall corporate strategy, the out-licensing collaboration can be structured around the remaining two entities of the deal (i.e. the license and the licensee).

One of the most significant findings of the case study analysis included that most out-licensing deals of integrated pharmaceutical companies are preferrably signed with small and highly specialized partner firms. This type of collaboration reverses the traditional logic of out-licensing. While out-licensing is usually done because of downstream concerns, the analyzed cases show that the company which owns the necessary assets for further development (i.e. the integrated pharmaceutical company) sells the license to a firm (i.e. the small partner company) which has – at the time of the deal closure – no track record to prove its ability to successfully develop the compound. Because of the difficulty for the pharmaceutical company to distinguish among these small partner companies based on their ability to develop the compound, this type of risk-sharing collaboration is characterized by a fairly high asymmetric distribution of information.

Managerial recommendations for risk-sharing in pharmaceutical R&D collaborations

The managerial recommendations were based on insights derived from the theory of adverse selection which describes the existence of equilibria in markets that are characterized by asymmetric information. The managerial dimensions which evolve from the theory of adverse selection and which can proactively be influenced by the pharmaceutical company in order to reduce the asymmetric information and approximate an equilibrium in the out-licensing market include the 'product coverage', 'price setting' and 'performance presumption'.

- *Product coverage.* The product coverage describes all aspects which characterize the scope of the commodity exchanged during the out-licensing agreement. Due to its dependence on intellectual property rights, the product coverage has strong ties to the collaboration's appropriability regime. In addition, by structuring the bundle of intellectual property rights which are expected to be out-licensed during the collaboration, the pharmaceutical company narrows down or extends the pool of potential partner companies according to their business strategy. Therefore, modifications in the product coverage exert an influence on the risk transferability because of its interdependence with the license's appropriability regime and the licensee's business strategy. Compared to an initial 'community rated' situation (where the pharmaceutical company would offer a licensing contract that would be similar to all potential buyers), pharmaceutical R&D management has now the opportunity to either increase or reduce the product coverage in order to reach the desired risk transferability. However, changes in the product coverage require modifications of the other two dimensions (price setting and performance presumption) in order to find an equilibrium. In general, the 'right' product coverage requires a trade-off between maximizing the likelihood that the partner firm agrees to in-license the product and minimizing the outflow of too much intellectual capital.

- *Price setting.* The price setting primarily refers to the size of the upfront payment that has to be made by the partner firm to the pharmaceutical company. While there are several other payment elements (e.g., call-back options, royalty revenues, milestone payments, co-promotion/co-marketing arrangements, manufacturing agreements among others) which go far beyond the upfront payment and are considered to have an indirect influence on the size of the upfront payment, the price setting describes all aspects which relate to the entire price of the license. Due to its dependence on the structure and amount of payments that have to be made during the collaboration, the price setting has a strong influence on both the license's bargaining range as well as compensation structure. Due to the interdependence of these two attributes with the size of the upfront payment, modifications in the price setting exert an influence on the risk transferability. Compared to an initial 'community rated' situation, pharmaceutical R&D management has now the opportunity to either increase or reduce the upfront payment in order to reach the desired risk transferability. However, changes in the price setting also require modifications of the other two dimensions (product coverage and performance presumption) in order to find an equilibrium. In general, the 'right' upfront payment requires a trade-off between maximizing the potential payoff expected from the out-licensing deal and minimizing the risk of losing almost the entire value of the license.

- *Performance presumption.* While the asymmetric distribution of information does not allow the pharmaceutical company to discriminate among its potential partner companies on the basis of their ability to successfully develop the licensed compound, pharmaceutical R&D management can find ways to presume the nature of the collaboration and its potential performance. Assuming perfect competition in the out-licensing market, the pharmaceutical company can either enter into a collaboration which is less likely to succeed but would generate a higher return, or a collaboration which is more likely to succeed but would generate a lower return for the pharmaceutical company. In this context, the performance presumption refers to all aspects that allow the pharmaceutical company to draw conclusions about the collaboration's likelihood to succeed in terms of executing the out-licensed compound's development. Therefore, the performance presumption has a strong influence on the pharmaceutical company's decision regarding the selection of the licensee. Due to the interdependence between the performance presumption and the adaptiveness of the partner company to requests and desires of the pharmaceutical company as well as the entrepreneurial climate of the partner company, assessing the performance presumption leads to the situation that the pharmaceutical company narrows down or extends the pool of potential partner companies according to their corporate flexibility as well as entrepreneurial setting. Therefore, modifications in the performance presumption exert an influence on the risk transferability because of its interdependence with the licensee's corporate flexibility and entrepreneurial setting. Compared to an initial 'community rated' situation, pharmaceutical R&D management has now the opportunity to either target a potential partner with a higher probability of not being able to execute the compound's development or to target a partner with a lower probability of not being able to execute. This offers the pharmaceutical company the opportunity to approach the desired risk transferability which would allow the transfer of the risks that should be handed over to the external partner company. However, changes in the performance presumption require modifications of the other two dimensions (product coverage and price setting) in order to find an equilibrium. In general, the 'right' performance presumption requires a trade-off between maximizing the probability that the partner firm is able to execute the compound's development and minimizing the risk that the partner firm retains too much of the joint project's benefits.

Based on the comments about the three managerial dimensions ('product coverage', 'price setting' and 'performance presumption'), a management framework for risk-sharing in pharmaceutical R&D collaborations could have been deduced. The management framework might serve as a guideline for pharmaceutical R&D managers regarding the sharing of R&D-related risks during out-licensing collaborations and comprises the following aspects: After out-licensing has been incorporated within the pharmaceutical company and has been well aligned with the overall corporate strategy, pharmaceutical R&D management can modify the product coverage, price setting and performance presumption compared to the 'community rated' situation in order to approximate an equilibrium in the out-licensing market. As the product coverage, price setting and performance presumption have an influence on the attributes of the license (the appropriability regime, bargaining range and compensation structure) as well as the attributes of the licensee (the business strategy, corporate flexibility and entrepreneurial setting), the pharmaceutical company can exert an influence on the risk transferability during the out-licensing arrangement. This allows the pharmaceutical company to adjust the risk transferability to a desired level while the company is simultaneously approaching the equilibrium in the out-licensing market. The general managerial actions that can proactively be taken by pharmaceutical R&D management include increasing or reducing the product coverage, increasing or reducing the size of the upfront payment, as well as targeting a potential partner with a higher or lower probability of not being able to execute the compound's development. It has to be considered that not only one dimension can be modified, but the other two dimensions have to be adjusted simultaneously in order to reach an equilibrium. While there is generally no straight recipe for pinpointing the equilibrium, a hybrid construct of changes in all managerial dimensions is usually applied when finding an equilibrium in the out-licensing market.

8.1.2 Future directions and trends

The future directions and trends illustrate opportunities regarding the role of out-licensing at large pharmaceutical companies. These remarks go beyond the existing role that out-licensing is currently playing and shows potential approaches to manifest out-licensing as a vehicle to share risks in pharmaceutical R&D collaborations. The following comments on future directions and trends could have been derived:

- Most established pharmaceutical companies today use out-licensing because of tactical reasons. They only out-license compounds that did not make it into the company's top priority list. However, not only terminated compounds but potentially any compound that can be developed more efficiently by an external partner could become subject to an out-licensing agreement. In this context, the company Bayer strictly follows the principle "don't try to sell any left-overs" when it comes to selling intellectual property (see Gassmann et al. 2004). A more strategic approach to out-licensing could help improve not only the image of compounds that are out-licensed by large pharmaceutical companies but also the effectiveness of internal R&D. Pharmaceutical R&D management should constantly observe and analyze every R&D project in the pipeline if it might become an attractive out-licensing candidate. An out-licensing deal would pay off in every case where the expected benefits of the licensing deal that are attributable to the pharmaceutical company are greater than the risk-adjusted benefits of an internal development. Research by Kollmer and Dowling (2004) in the biopharmaceutical industry figured out that out-licensing brings comparable compensation for both not-fully and full integrated firms. Therefore, licensing seems to be an attractive commercialization strategy for fully integrated firms, where licensing would play the role of an additional commercialization channel. Elements which should be considered for the computation of the expected benefits include the revenues after the drug's market entry that are attributable to the pharmaceutical company (either via the company's own commercialization or on royalty basis), the costs incurred for the compound's development until the time of out-licensing, the upfront payments received by the licensee, eventually incurring milestone payments received by the licensee, eventually the price that has to be paid for re-licensing the compound, and any other benefit provided/received to/from the licensee.

- A more strategic approach to out-licensing goes along with a more aggressive commercialization of research results. Pharmaceutical R&D management should not only actively look for potential out-licensing candidates in its (usually large) inventory of intellectual property, but should actively create and customize bundles of intellectual property that can subsequently be marketed to potential licensees. Due to the increasing number of specialty pharma companies which might be tempted to acquire late stage projects without having the opportunity costs and risks at earlier stages, there are several companies that might have a particular need for the pharmaceutical company's intellectual assets although the pharmaceutical company did not see an application potential any more. The pharmaceutical company should not only regard these licensees as potential competitors who possibly 'steel' blockbuster revenues. Instead, these firms should be treated as customers and partners who help generate additional revenues and profits.
- Treating potential licensees as customers requires that the pharmaceutical company proactively creates markets for its own compounds. As selling a license in pharmaceutical R&D is usually a long-term process which can last up to ten months and involves a lot of uncertainty, a proactive marketing strategy of compounds requires a sophisticated sales approach which includes the potential customers at quite early stages. Once all information about a potential licensing candidate has been collected, it is important to convey these information to the target audiences. The target audience not only includes potential licensees but also key authorities which might have an influence on the drug's subsequent market launch, such as opinion leaders and high prescribing physicians. These intermediaries might spread the word in such a way that a product's benefits become clear, and the underlying compound might become an attractive object in the marketplace even long before the respective product enters the market. The proliferation of these information could be achieved via special events. For example, the company IBM successfully uses its 'Industry Solution Labs' to get key customers attracted early on to their latest technology inventions. IBM deploys two 'Industry Soluation Labs' worldwide. One is located in Hawthorne (US) and the other one in Zurich (CH). In its 'Industry Solution Lab' in Zurich,

IBM conducts about 300 events per year to show and communicate recent accomplishments in corporate research. These events are considered to be advanced marketing activities to demonstrate the latest innovations to prospective clients and interested parties. These labs are not considered a sales tool but rather a place of intensive exchange and ideation which is ultimately expected to speed up time-to-market of IBM's inventions. The labs' clients fill out visit request forms defining the customer and/or visitor level as well as the purpose of the visit. The success of the Industry Solution Labs is closely monitored with visitor feedback forms and customer satisfaction measurements. However, no systematic controlling of subsequently generated sales is being recorded. Pharmaceutical R&D management could structure and sponsor similar events (with a dedicated declaration) which would get potential licensees and other relevant parties interested in the company's achievements in research.

- A more progressive approach to the commercialization of research results could be implemented if the respective activities receive clear profit and loss responsibilities. Out-licensing could be organized as a profit center with a clear mission: To increase the utilization of corporate research. Schering was the only company in the case study analysis that started in fiscal year 2004 – for the first time ever – to incorporate out-licensing as an own item in the company's budget calculations. Being a pioneer in out-licensing, Eli Lilly is reported to have achieved around US$ 2 billion from its out-licensing activities over the last five years.
- The commercialization potential of the pharmaceutical company's research results increases not only with the quantity of substances under development. The quality of each substance is at least as important as the quantity. If pharmaceutical research focuses its attention on substances which can be applied for multiple indications, the value of the portfolio of total substances increases substantially. If the development of one substance fails, the substance's potential to find another application somewhere else is much higher if it could target various indications. As demonstrated by the cases of Roche and Schering, the out-licensed substances' indication has successfully been redirected after the licensing deals had been closed. For example, Schering's substance Atamestane initially targeted prostate cancer in men, but is now expected to become a drug against breast cancer in women.
- Besides focusing on substances with various indications, pharmaceutical companies could also proactively move into earlier phases with their out-licensing activities. While the IND approval has usually been considered to be the criterion for a substance to qualify as an out-licensing candidate, pharmaceutical R&D management could even try to market substances much earlier in the R&D proc-

ess. As the remaining R&D activities that have to be completed to bring these substances to market are much more comprehensive in these cases, the risks inherent in these substances are consequently much higher. However, the potential of these substances is also considered to be much higher. If the pharmaceutical company could find a partner firm which is eager to take on these higher risks in order to expect a higher performance, out-licensing deals could move into much earlier phases. Indeed, Thiel (2004) observed some signals for a trend towards earlier phases regarding out-licensing at established pharmaceutical companies.

- If the pharmaceutical company would out-license compounds much earlier in the R&D process, its substances would face intensive competition from biotech companies. As the biotech business model usually builds upon out-licensing early-stage compounds, there might be several substances on the out-licensing market fighting for the same potential licensees. Scott (2001) supports this view by claiming that out-licensing of early stage compounds has become much more competitive in recent years largely because of the explosion in activity by universities and start-up companies. Biotech firms are depending for several years on out-licensing because of their usually limited financial and clinical capabilities. This has led to the situation that biotech firms use their intellectual property rights not only to protect their inventions, but primarily as a marketing vehicle. In order to compete effectively, pharmaceutical companies could adopt a similar mindset and look at its intellectual property as a product that needs to be marketed in a highly competitive environment. This also has another positive side-effect. Due to the intense competition, pharmaceutical firms are forced to offer highly competitive compounds which not only increases the quality of their own compounds but also the likelihood of success of the out-licensing collaboration.
- The pharmaceutical company could even go one step further and set up a venture fund that proactively makes investments in entities which then could serve as an out-licensing partner. This approach has several advantages. Firstly, it significantly eases the ability to attract co-investments by other venture funds. As the pharmaceutical company is not the only company providing the high-risk capital for the underlying compound's development, the risks can effectively be shared with the other investors. Secondly, it proactively supports potential licensees who are characterized by a highly entrepreneurial culture which has shown to be a major factor related to the success of an out-licensing collaboration. Finally, it allows the gaining of a better understanding of the potential licensees' ability to execute the compound's development. Particularly in the case of Speedel, which received seed money from the Novartis Venture Fund, it seemed to have been very advantageous that Speedel's management has previously been working at

Novartis. As the mission of the Novartis Venture Fund is to also support entrepreneurial endeavors of the company's own employees, this has helped to drastically reduce the asymmetric information of the out-licensing deal because Speedel's management was already well known to Novartis. As the asymmetric distribution of information regarding the partner firm's ability to execute is considered to be the major reason why adverse selection processes might occur in out-licensing deals, having more in-depth knowledge about the potential partner firm because of its affiliation to the pharmaceutical company via a venture fund could ease the process of finding an equilibrium in the out-licensing market.

- As gaining information about the potential licensees' ability to execute a compound's development is an important issue for finding an equilibrium, the pharmaceutical company should try to gain as much information as possible about potential licensees. Therefore, pharmaceutical R&D management could set up an own intelligence unit which only deals with monitoring and scouting potential partners. This unit could deliver all necessary and relevant information about the out-licensing market which could reduce the asymmetric information. Particularly the surge in new specialty pharma companies requires a more profound segmentation of the market of potential licensees. As the theory of adverse selection has initially been developed in the insurance industry a few decades ago and insurance companies are quite experienced by now in terms of facing asymmetric information problems, there might be the potential that pharmaceutical companies could learn from insurance companies how to look for ways to reduce the information asymmetry. Insurance companies usually use sophisticated tools to segment the market of their clients who purchase their insurance contracts on the basis of their risk profile. If pharmaceutical R&D management could apply some of these approaches to segment the market of their potential clients, they might not only be able to reduce the issue of adverse selection but also to improve their out-licensing endeavors.

8.2 Implications for Management Theory

The implications for management theory first cover the book' contribution to research. Afterwards, all research questions which are still open are made explicit.

8.2.1 Contribution to research

The book' contribution to research primarily relates to the topic of 'risk-sharing in pharmaceutical R&D collaborations', particularly focusing on the case of out-licensing at large pharmaceutical companies. The contribution to research covers the following aspects:

- While risk-sharing in R&D collaborations has become an important issue in the pharmaceutical industry, no research has discussed pharmaceutical R&D collaborations from a risk management perspective so far. This is surprising because risks have been considered to be a primary reason for R&D collaborations in the pharmaceutical industry for many years. Several scholars have identified risk to be a driver for R&D collaborations, but no scholar has analyzed the management of these risks in the respective collaborations. Therefore, the underlying research addresses the absence of research related to this management issue by providing several novel insights about risk management in pharmaceutical R&D collaborations.
- Research on R&D collaborations in the pharmaceutical industry usually focuses on the traditional pharma-biotech collaborations. Particularly when it comes to licensing, most research discusses licensing deals where established pharmaceutical companies in-license products from biotech firms. Out-licensing at large pharmaceutical companies has been neglected in management research so far, although its importance is on the rise due to the necessity for pharmaceutical companies to improve their R&D productivity. While Kollmer and Dowling (2004) were among the first researchers who studied licensing as a commercialization vehicle of fully integrated companies in the biopharmaceutical industry, they only looked at this licensing approach from a superordinated perspective by comparing it with licensing deals of not-fully integrated firms. However, they did not analyze issues regarding the management of these licensing deals. By providing information about how out-licensing deals should be managed by large pharmaceutical companies, this book closes a gap in research which has not yet been discussed by management scholars.
- The explanations about the management of out-licensing collaborations have been based on the theory of adverse selection. While the adverse selection theory was initially developed in the insurance industry, this research has shown that the theory also finds acceptance in the case of out-licensing in the pharmaceutical industry. Particularly the similarities in the nature and structure of the insurance contracts and licensing contracts allowed the application of the theory of adverse selection to the case of out-licensing in order to constitute subsequent managerial recommendations. Based on the theory of adverse selection, this research is one of the first contributions to management research that explains the demand and supply of licensing contracts in the out-licensing market.

- While most prior research on licensing analyzes the performance or strategy of the deals, no research on licensing so far has paid attention to the coverage or price setting of the license. Although the theory of adverse selection supports that these parameters are expected to have a high importance on reaching an equilibrium, no research so far has taken into account that these parameters can proactively be influenced by the licensor. Therefore, this research is one of the first studies that considers possible changes in these two parameters and their impact on finding an equilibrium in the out-licensing market.
- In addition to the negligence of a differentiation among the license's coverage and price, no research so far has taken into consideration the licensee's ability to add value to a licensed product. While the theory of adverse selection also suggests that this attribute represents an unknown parameter in any licensing deal (although it is particularly important in the case of out-licensing at large pharmaceutical companies), the partner's likelihood to execute has never been part of any prior research on licensing. The research contributes to this lack of differentiation by introducing and discussing two classes of licensees (high-risk and low-risk licensees) and showing the effects of targeting each group of partner firms.
- In this way, the application of the theory of adverse selection has illustrated that the strategy to target low-risk licensees (i.e. licensees who have a lower probability of not being able to execute the compound's development) does not represent an economically useful approach for finding an equilibrium in the out-licensing market. This might be surprising, especially if it is considered that pharmaceutical companies are expected to be risk-neutral. Therefore, it should be assumed that they show similar preferences for both high-risk as well as low-risk licensees. The partners in the analyzed out-licensing collaborations were all small firms with a limited history of successful development programs and a fairly small R&D portfolio (i.e. they would typically qualify for a high-risk licensee). As no partner firm in the case studies could qualify as a low-risk licensee, the case study analysis seems to affirm the finding that low-risk licensees are less appreciated partner firms. Although a low-risk licensee would be more likely capable to bring the licensed compound successfully through development, the pharmaceutical companies in the case study analysis preferred high-risk licensees as their partners. According to the theory of adverse selection, targeting a high-risk licensee has the advantage that the upfront payment can always be raised more in relative terms than the product coverage by approximating an equilibrium. Thus, the research could illustrate that the price received by the pharmaceutical company might be a stronger indicator for closing an out-licensing deal than the coverage of the product which has to be given away.

- While the partner firms could be characterized as high-risk licensees, the research was also able to reveal that pharmaceutical companies try to limit their exposure to the negative side-effects which come along with targeting a high-risk licensee. In two out of three cases, the pharmaceutical companies knew the management team of the licensee well before the licensing contract had been signed because the teams comprised previous employees of the respective firms. Although the partner company itself would still qualify as a high-risk partner, the pharmaceutical company was much better able to decide if the partner firm would be able to complete the compound's development. In addition, all pharmaceutical companies retained re-licensing rights in the form of call-back options. As these rights enable the firms to get the intellectual assets back at any time during the collaboration, this gave them enough safety to limit their downside risk of targeting a high-risk licensee. Therefore, these observations might serve as an explanation of why the pharmaceutical companies preferred to out-license their compounds to licensees who could at first sight be characterized by a higher risk of not being able to execute the compound's development.
- Particularly the existence of call-back options has been critically discussed in management theory before (see also Brockhoff 1999, Zürcher and Blaser 2004). In this context, Helm and Kloyer (2004) conducted an analysis of the exchange risk perceived by the supplier in an R&D cooperation. The authors came to the conclusion that an option on later negotiation of an additional continuous innovation return sharing which is based on contractual hostages can lower the perceived exchange risk of the supplier. Such an option relies on contractual hostages, which allow the supplier to block or hinder the buyer from exploiting the R&D results through the production and marketing of final products (see Helm and Kloyer 2004). This research supports the work by Helm and Kloyer (2004) and was able to confirm that the existence of call-back options is essential for the pharmaceutical companies' willingness to get involved in an out-licensing deal and subsequently their ability to share risks.

8.2.2 Open research questions

During the course of the research, all research questions were able to be answered. However, some new questions have come up. The open questions which were not able to be answered within the scope of this research are as follows:

- While it could be shown that the theory of adverse selection can be applied to the case of out-licensing, there are, however, some differences in the theory's application in both cases. Particularly the pharmaceutical company's involvement during the due diligence of the licensing negotiations represents a major discrepancy to the insurance industry. Insurance companies usually offer their contracts with a certain policy at a certain premium, and the customer then purchases the contract or not; the due diligence for each individual insurance contract is mostly limited to some introductory questions that the customers are asked to answer, such as previous disease records in the case of health insurance. By contrast, the pharmaceutical company has the opportunity to gain a lot of information about its potential customer during the negotiation period which might even last for a couple of months. Therefore, the pharmaceutical company has the opportunity to draw some conclusions about the licensee's ability to execute the development of the licensed product (which represents the nature of the asymmetric information) well in advance of signing the licensing contract. While this opportunity seems to be a unique feature of the pharmaceutical industry, this opportunity is usually not given to insurance companies. Therefore, it could be questionable whether the extent of the information asymmetry is similarly high in both situations. Future research might take this into account and could pay more attention to the nature and extent of the information asymmetry.

- In addition, the research assumed that the partner firms are risk-averse. Although the risk-aversion in the context of the theory of adverse selection refers to the licensees' intention to achieve their projected revenues W and not to their general exposure towards business risk, the validity of this assumption might be questionable. While it can be reasonably assumed that the licensees are risk-averse in the sense that they try to avoid failing to meet their projected revenues, their risk exposure is generally higher than the pharmaceutical companies' risk exposure (which have been rated as risk-neutral). As the partner firms know about the high risks that they are about to acquire and which the pharmaceutical company is not willing to carry any more, it could be assumed that the partners should be more receptive to risks than the pharmaceutical firms. Thus, future research might analyze the situation that the partner firms are less risk-averse.
- Another assumption of the underlying model has been that there is free market entry and perfect competition in the out-licensing market. While the surge in new specialty pharma companies that focus on in-licensing compounds from major pharmaceutical firms justifies this assumption, out-licensing at large pharmaceutical companies still remains a fairly new phenomenon. Thus, it might be debatable if the hypotheses of free market entry and perfect competition are entirely fulfilled. A closer analysis of the nature of the out-licensing market could be subject to further research and might reveal the necessary information.

- The pharmaceutical company and the partner company usually have a different perception of the risks inherent in the development of the compound that is about to be licensed. However, the theory of adverse selection only takes into account the development risks related to the partner company (i.e. the partner company's ability to execute the compound's development). The development risks that the pharmaceutical company would be facing if it developed the substance by itself are not directly reflected by the model. Therefore, further research could also take into consideration risk management aspects which emanate from potentially occuring development activities within the pharmaceutical company in order to derive managerial recommendations for the pharmaceutical companies' R&D managers.
- The theory of adverse selection has initially been explained in the context of the insurance industry. Thus, the timing of payments is related to the conditions in the insurance industry. In particular, the theory of adverse selection does not take into consideration a potential time gap between the payment of the insurance premium and the insurance payout. By transferring the theory to the case of out-licensing in the pharmaceutical industry, the corresponding time period could span several years because of the long development times in the pharmaceutical industry. Thus, further research might take into account the time value of money by extending the current insights of the theory with the concept of discounting cash flows. In this way, the determination of an appropriate discount rate will be a critical aspect.
- The theory of adverse selection implies that the out-licensing market is characterized by externalities. The presence of the high-risk licensees exerts a negative externality on the low-risk licensees because there are theoretically losses to the low-risk licensees. However, these externalities seem to be completely dissipative because the high-risk licensees are no better off than they would be in isolation. Further research could tackle this issue and analyze in more detail the scope and degree of these externalities. If these externalities account for a large proportion of the deal value of an out-licensing collaboration, further insights about the practicability of out-licensing should be obtained.

In summary, this book addressed an area in both management practice and theory which is characterized by a high relevance for the industry but has been untapped by previous studies and scholars. While risk-sharing in R&D collaborations is one of the most prevalent issues in the pharmaceutical industry, out-licensing at established pharmaceutical companies has played only a minor role in the past. Some companies have only recently started to adopt this novel approach to lower their exposure to risks and still be able to bring their own compounds to the market. As these projects are generally not considered to be less profitable than out-licensing deals at biotech firms, they could offer a great commercialization vehicle of research results by large pharmaceutical companies. If pharmaceutical R&D management abandons the idea of letting their intellectual assets decay on their own shelves and adopts a more strategic and progressive approach to out-licensing, the company could not only reduce its exposure to R&D risks but also improve the productivity of its R&D investments.

A major concern for management research regarding the investigation of licensing deals is generally the fact that licensing represents one of the most sensitive activities of any company. Therefore, the extraction of sufficient data is always a serious problem which also represented a critical issue of this research. Nevertheless, this research allowed for the provision of several novel insights about risk-sharing in pharmaceutical R&D collaborations (particularly regarding the case of out-licensing) and concluded with a framework for managing out-licensing collaborations. While this framework might serve as a guideline for pharmaceutical R&D managers regarding the manageability of these collaborations, there are still some open questions which remain unanswered and could provide the starting point for future research on this highly relevant topic.

References

ACCENTURE (2002): *Commercial and R&D: Reinventing the relationship. Pharmaceuticals & medical products*. Accenture White Paper. 2002.

ACHILLADELIS, B; ANTONAKIS, N. (2001): The dynamics of technological innovation: the case of the pharmaceutical industry. *Research Policy*, Vol. 30, pp. 535-588.

ACTELION (2004a): Company press release as of 1 November 1998. http://www.actelion.com/uninet/www/www_main_p.nsf/Content/me+01+Nov+1998, accessed on 7 February 2005.

ACTELION (2004b): *Actelion's Marketed Products*. http://www.actelion.com/uninet/www/www_main_p.nsf/Content/Attachment+Marketed+Products+Fact+Sheet/$FILE/041026_Act_Fact_MarketProd.pdf, accessed on 7 February 2005.

ACTELION (2004c): *Actelion – Performance and Growth*. Company presentation as of September 2004. http://www.actelion.com/uninet/www/www_main_p.nsf/Content/ir+Events+29+Sep+2004/$FILE/040929_UBS_ConferenceNY_AJO_RH.pdf, accessed on 7 February 2005.

ACTELION (2004d): *Actelion – Growing beyond Tracleer®*. Company presentation as of February 2004. http://www.actelion.com/uninet/www/www_main_p.nsf/Content/ir+Events/$FILE/12%20Jan_04%20Feb_Company%20Presentation%2023Feb.pdf, accessed on 7 February 2005.

ACTELION (2005): *Actelion – Delivering Sustainable Growth*. Company presentation as of January 2005. http://www.actelion.com/uninet/www/www_main_p.nsf/Content/ir+Events+10+Jan+2005/$FILE/050110_CompanyPresentation_JPMorganconf.pdf, accessed on 7 February 2005.

ADAM, G. (2003): *Best Practices in Pharma Research*. Presentation held at First Tuesday Meeting on 20 May 2003 in Zurich by Dr. Geo Adam, Section Head Medicinal Chemistry, Hoffmann-LaRoche.

AGARWAL, S.; DESAI, S.; HOLCOMB, M.M.; OBEROI, A. (2001): Unlocking the value in big pharma. *The McKinsey Quarterly*, No. 2.

ALBERTINI, S.; BUTLER, J. (1995): R&D Networks in a pharmaceutical company: Some implications for human resource management, *R&D Management*,

Vol. 25, No. 4, pp. 377-393.

ALGER, I.; MA, C.A. (2003): Moral hazard, insurance, and some collusion. *Journal of Economic Behavior & Organization*, Vol. 50, pp. 225-247.

ALLEN, D.W.; LUECK, D. (1999): The role of risk in contract choice. *The Journal of Law, Economics & Organization*, Vol. 15, No. 3, pp. 704-736.

ALLEN, F.; GALE, D. (1999): Innovations in financial services, relationships, and risk-sharing. *Management Science*, Vol. 45, No. 9, pp. 1239-1253.

ANAND, B.; KHANNA, T. (1997): *Intellectual property rights and contract structure*. Harvard Business School Working Paper, No. 97-016.

ARROW, K.J. (1962): Economic welfare and the allocation of resources for invention, in: NELSON, R.R. (1962) (ed.): *The Rate and Direction of Incentive Activity: Economic and Social Factors*, Princeton: Princeton University Press, pp. 609-625.

ARROW, K.J. (1965): *Aspects of the Theory of Risk Bearing*. Helsinki: Yrjo Jahnssonin Saatio.

ARTHUR D. LITTLE; SOLVIAS (2002): *External synthesis services for research and development in the pharmaceutical industry*. Market Study of Arthur D. Little and Solvias AG, June 2002.

ASTEBRO, T. (2004): Key success factors for technological entrepreneurs' R&D projects. *IEEE Transactions on Engineering Management*, Vol. 51, Iss. 3, pg. 314.

AZOULAY, P. (2003): *Acquiring knowledge within and across firm boundaries: evidence from clinical development*. Working paper at Columbia Business School, 19 October 2003.

BADARACCO, J.L. (1991): *The Knowledge Link: How firms compete through strategic alliances*. Boston: Harvard Business School Press.

BATTERSBY, G.; GRIMES, C. (1996): *A primer on technology licensing*. Stamford: Kent Press.

BAYONA, C.; GARCÍA-MARCO, T.; HUERTA, E. (2001): Firms' motivation for cooperative R&D: an empirical analysis of Spanish firms. *Research Policy*, Vol. 30, pp. 1289-1307.

BAYONA, C.; GARCIA-MARCO, T.; HUERTA, E. (2004): Links between the characteristics of alliances and the applicability of research results. *The Journal of High Technology Management Research*, Vol. 15, Iss. 2, pp. 215-236.

BAZERMAN, M.H.; GILLESPIE, J.J. (1999): Betting on the future: the virtues of contingent contracts. *Harvard Business Review*, Sep-Oct 1999, pp. 155-160.

BCG (2001): *A revolution in R&D – how genomics and genetics are transforming the biopharmaceutical industry*. BCG Report. Boston, MA.

BEAMISH, P. (1996): *Note on international licensing*. Richard Ivey School of Business Working Paper, No. 9A96G008.

BECHMANN, G. (1993): Risiko als Schlüsselkategorie der Gesellschaftstheorie, in: Bechmann, G. (ed.): *Risiko und Gesellschaft*. Opladen.

BECKER, S.; KELLERMANN, C.; MENZ, W.; SABLOWSKI, T. (1999): *Struktur und Vernetzung der Biotechnologie-Industrie*. Arbeitsbericht des Projektes 'Vernetzung als Wettbewerbsfaktor'. Johann Wolfgang Goethe Universität, Frankfurt/Main.

BECKMANN, C.; FISCHER, J. (1994): Einflussfaktoren auf die Internationalisierung von Forschung und Entwicklung in der chemischen und pharmazeutischen Industrie. *Zeitschrift für Betriebswirtschaftliche Forschung*, Vol. 46, No. 7/8, pp. 630-657.

BERNOTAT-DANIELOWSKI, S. (2002): Portfolio Management zum Aufbau und zur Pflege eines wertschöpfenden, strategischen Produktportfolios, in: BREUER, R.; BECKER, W.; FIBIG, A. (eds.): *Strategien für das Pharma-Management – Konzepte, Fallbeispiele, Entscheidungshilfen*. Wiesbaden: Gabler, pp. 65-82.

BERNSTEIN, P.L. (1996): *Against the Gods*. Wiley: New York.

BIDAULT, F.; CUMMINGS, T. (1994): Innovating through alliances: expectations and limitations. *R&D Management*, Vol. 24, No. 1, pp. 33-45.

BILLINGS, B.A.; MUSAZI, B.G.N.; MOORE, J.W. (2004): The effects of funding source and management ownership on the productivity of R&D. *R&D Management*, Vol. 34, No. 3, pp. 281-295.

BLAU, G.E.; PEKNY, J.F.; VARMA, V.A.; BUNCH, P.R. (2004): Managing a Portfolio of Interdependent New Product Candidates in the Pharmaceutical Industry. *Journal of Product Innovation Management*, Vol. 21, Iss. 4, pp. 227.

BLEEKE, J.; ERNST, D. (1995): Is your strategic alliance really a sale? *Harvard Business Review*, Jan-Feb 1995, pp. 97-105.

BLEICHER, K. (1987): *Strategien der Unternehmensakquisition und -kooperation*, unpublished paper, University of St. Gallen.

BLEICHER, K. (1991): *Das Konzept Integriertes Management*, Frankfurt: Campus.

BOERNER, C.S.R. (2002): *New product development organization and performance: Theory and evidence from the pharmaceutical industry*. Dissertation at the University of California at Berkeley. UMI Number: 3063299. Spring 2002.

BOOZ ALLEN & HAMILTON (1997): *In vivo, making combinatory chemistry pay*. Booz Allen & Hamilton Report. New York.

BPI (1999): Die 'Innovationsschere' der pharmazeutischen Industrie, as cited in PROF. HOMBURG & PARTNER (2001): *Trends und Chancen in der Pharma-Branche*. Mannheim, April 2001.

BRACH, M.A.; PAXSON, D.A. (2001): A gene to drug venture: poisson options analysis. *R&D Management*, Vol. 31, No. 2, pp. 203-214.

BRANDER, J.A.; AMIT, R.; ANTWEILER, W. (2002): Venture capital syndication: improved venture selection vs. the value-added hypothesis. *Journal of Economics & Management Strategy*, Vol. 11, No. 3, pp. 423-452.

BRAUN, H. (1984): *Risikomanagement – eine spezifische Controllingaufgabe*. Darmstadt.

BROCKHOFF, K. (1991): Research and development cooperation between firms. A classification by structural variables. *International Journal of Technology Managment*, Vol. 6, No. 3-4, pp. 361-373.

BROCKHOFF, K. (1999): *Forschung und Entwicklung: Planung und Kontrolle* (5th ed.). Wien: Oldenbourg.

BROCKHOFF, K. (2003): Exploring strategic R&D success factors. *Technology Analysis & Strategic Management*. Vol. 15, Iss. 3, pg. 333.

BRUNNER, U. (2002): Neue Therapieoption bei pulmonaler Hypertonie. *Pharmazeutische Zeitung Online*. http://www.pharmazeutische-zeitung.de/pza/2002-25/pharm2.htm, accessed on 14 February 2005.

BUCHANAN, I.P.M. (2002): *R&D collaborations – a partners' perspective*. Vertex Pharmaceuticals. Presentation held in Zurich on 27 February 2002.

BUNCH, P.R.; SCHACHT, A.L. (2002): Modeling resource requirements for pharmaceutical R&D. *Research Technology Management*, Jan-Feb 2002, pp. 48-56.

BURGELMAN, R. A.; SAYLES, L. R. (1986): *Inside Corporate Innovation.*

BUSENITZ L.W. (1999): Entrepreneurial risk and strategic decision making: It's a matter of perspective. *The Journal of Applied Behavioral Science*, Vol. 35, No. 3, pp. 325-340.

BUSINESS WEEK (2002): Blazing Speed in Biotech – How Actelion marketed a breakthrough in record time. *Business Week*, as of 1 April 2002. http://www.businessweek.com/magazine/content/02_13/b3776145.htm accessed on 7 February 2005.

CABO, P.; DEGENAARS, G.; HUNCK-MEISWINKEL, A. (1998): *Industrial platforms in European biotechnology*. Paper presented at the 4th workshop on pharmaceutical and biotechnology innovation in the context of health care reforms on19 February 1998 in Brussels, Belgium.

CALLAHAN, J.; MUEGGE, S. (2002): *Venture capital's role in innovation: issues, research and stakeholder interests*. Working Paper at the Carleton University. November 2002. Carleton University, Ottawa: Ontario, Canada.

CAMBRIDGE HEALTHCARE & BIOTECH (2003): *Perceptions of in-licensing multinationals – The CH&B Licensing Survey*. http://www.chandb.com/ accessed on 1 February 2005.

CAMERON, K. S. (1986). Effectiveness as paradox: Consensus and conflict in conceptions of organizational effectiveness. *Management Science*, Vol. 32, pp. 539-553.

CAMPIONE, T.J. (2003): Making research collaborations succeed. *Research Technology Management*, Jul-Aug 2003, pp. 12-15.

CAP GEMINI ERNST & YOUNG (2001): *Perspectives on life science*. Issue 3, Fall 2001.

CARDINAL, L.B.; HATFIELD, D.E. (2000): Internal knowledge generation: the research laboratory and innovative productivity in the pharmaceutical industry. *Journal of Engineering and Technology Management*, Vol. 17, pp. 247-271.

CASSIMAN, B.; VEUGELERS, R. (2002): R&D cooperation and spillovers: some empirical evidence from Belgium. *The American Economic Review*, Vol. 92, Iss. 4, pp. 1169-1185.

CASSIMON, D.; ENGELEN, P.J.; THOMASSEN, L.; VAN WOUWE, M. (2004): The valuation of a NDA using a 6-fold compound option. *Research Policy*, Vol. 33, pp. 41-51.

CHAKRABARTI, A. K.; WEISENFELD, U. (1991): An empirical analysis of innovation strategies of biotechnology firms in the U.S. *Journal of Engineering and Technology Management*, Vol. 8, pp. 243-260.

CHATTERJI, D. (1996): Accessing external sources of technology. *Research & Technology Management*, March-April 1996, pp. 48-56.

CHEN, S.-H. (1997): Decision-making in research and development collaborations. *Research Policy*, Vol. 26, pp. 121-135.

CHESBROUGH, H.W. (2003): *Open innovation: The new imperative for creating and profiting from technology*. Harvard Business School Press. Boston, MA.

CHESBROUGH, H.W. (1999): The organizational impact of technological change: A comparative theory of national institutional factors. *Industrial and Corporate Change*. Vol. 8, Iss. 3, pg. 447.

CHESBROUGH, H.W.; TEECE, D.J. (1996): When is virtual vicious? *Harvard Business Review*, Jan-Feb 1996, pp. 65-73.

CHIESA, V.; MANZINI, R.; PIZZURNO, E. (2004): The externalisation of R&D activities and the growing market of product development services. *R&D Management*, Vol. 34, Iss. 1, pp. 65-76.

CHRISTENSEN, C.M.; MUSSO, C.S.; ANTHONY, S.D. (2004): Maximizing the Returns from Research. *Research Technology Management*, Vol. 47, No. 4, pp. 12-18.

COCKBURN, I.M. (2004): The changing structure of the pharmaceutical industry. *Health Affairs*, Vol 23, Iss. 1, pp. 10-22.

COCKBURN, I.; HENDERSON, R.M. (1998): Absorptive capacity, co-authoring behavior and the organization of research in drug discovery. *Journal of Industrial Economics*, Vol. 46, No. 2, pp. 157-182.

COCKBURN, I.; HENDERSON, R.M.; ORSENIGO, L.; PISANO, G. (1999): Pharmaceuticals and biotechnology, in: MOWERY, D. (Ed.): *U.S. industry in 2000:*

Studies in competitive performance. Washington: National Academy Press, pp. 363-398.

COCKBURN, I.M.; HENDERSON, R.M.; STERN, S. (2000): Untangling the origins of competitive advantage. *Strategic Management Journal*, Vol. 21, pp. 1123-1145.

COHEN, W.M.; LEVIN, R.C. (1989): Empirical studies of innovation and market structure, in: SCHMALENSEE, R.; WILLIG, R. (eds.): *Handbook of Industrial Organization*, Vol. 2. Amsterdam: North Holland.

CONNOLLY, C. (2001): Price tag for a new drug: $802 million. Findings of Tufts University Study are disputed by several watchdog groups. *Washington Post*, as of 1 December 2001. Page A10. http://www.washingtonpost.com/ac2/wp-dyn?pagename=article&contentId=A42120-2001Nov30&notFound=true, accessed on 1 March 2005.

CONTRACTOR, F.J.; LORANGE, P. (1988): Why should firms cooperate? The strategy and economics basis for cooperative ventures, in: CONTRACTOR, F.J.; LORANGE, P. (eds.): *Cooperative strategies in international business*. Lexington: Lexington Books, pp. 3-30.

COOK, A.G. (2004): *Let's make a deal: The contribution of licensing to portfolio strategy*. Presentation held at the 2004 PMSA Conference by Arthur G. Cook, ZS Associates.

DATAMONITOR (2003): *Licensing strategies: Benchmarking analysis of the top 20 pharmaceutical companies*. April 2003, pg. 52.

DAVILA, A.; FOSTER, G.; GUPTA, M. (2002): *Venture-capital financing and the growth of startup firms*. Working Paper University of Stanford and Washington University. August 2002. http://news-info.wustl.edu/pdf/gupta_ venture_capital.pdf, accessed on 2 February 2005.

DAVIS, S.; BOTKIN, J. (1994): The coming of knowledge-based business. *Harvard Business Review*, Iss. 5, pp. 165-170.

DE MEYER, A. (1999): Using strategic partnerships to create a sustainable competitive position for hi-tech start-up firms. *R&D Management*, Vol. 29, No. 4, pp. 323-328.

DECK, M.; STROM, M. (2002): Model of co-development emerges. *Research Technology Management*, May-June, pp. 47-53.

DEEDS, D.L.; ROTHAERMEL, F.T. (2003): Honeymoons and liabilities: the relationship between age and performance in research and development alliances. *The Journal of Product Innovation Management*, Vol. 20, pp. 468-484.

DEGIRALAMO, D.M. (2004): *Beyond the obvious: unmasking value and risk in specialty pharma opportunities*. Presentation prepared for the Specialty Pharma Corporate Development Global Summit. Princeton, NJ. September 2004.

DEMING, W.E. (1993): *The new economics*. Massachusetts Institute of Technology, Center for Advanced Engineering Study. Cambridge, MA.

DENNIS, C. (2004): *Getting started = internal marketing*. http://www.yet2.com/app/insight/insight/20010603_dennis, accessed on 15 October 2004.

DERCON, S.; KRISHNAN, P. (2003): Risk-sharing and public transfers. *The Economic Journal*, Vol. 113, pp. C86-C94.

DIMASI, J. (2001): *Tufts center for the study of drug development pegs costs of a new prescription drug at $802 million*. Press release, Tufts University, 30 November 2001.

DODGSON, M. (1993): *Technological collaboration in industry: strategy, policy and internalization*. London.

DOSI, G. (1988): Sources, procedures, and microeconomic effects of innovation. *Journal of Economic Literature*, Vol. 26, pp. 1120-1171.

DREWS, J. (1989): Research in the pharmaceutical industry. *European Management Journal*, Vol. 7, No. 1, pp. 23-30.

DUNNING, J.H. (1988): *Explaining international production*. London.

DUSSAUGE, P.; GARETTE, B. (1999): *Cooperative strategy – competing successfully through strategic alliances*. Chichester: Wiley.

DUTTA, J.; PRASAD, K. (2002): Stable risk-sharing. *Journal of Mathematical Economics*, Vol. 38, pp. 411-439.

ECKWERT, B.; ZILCHA, I. (2003): Incomplete risk-sharing arrangements and the value of information. *Economic Theory*, Vol. 21, pp. 43-58.

EHRBAR, T.J. (1993) (ed.): *Business International's guide to international licensing*. New York: McGraw-Hill.

EISENHARDT, K.; SCHOONHOVEN, C.B. (1996): Strategic alliance formation in entrepreneurial firms: Strategic needs and social opportunities for cooperation. *Organization Science*, Vol. 7 (in press).

EISENHARDT, K.M. (1989): Building theories from case study research. *Academy of Management Review*, Vol. 14, No. 4, pp. 532-550.

ERNST&YOUNG (2002): *Beyond borders – the global biotechnology report 2002*. Global Health Sciences. Ernst&Young Report.

EUROPEAN PATENT OFFICE; IFO INSTITUTE FOR ECONOMIC RESEARCH (1993): *Results and methods of economic patent research*. Proceedings of the 1st EPO-IPO Workshop on March 19-20. European Patent Office. Munich.

EVALUATE PHARMA; DEFINED HEALTH (2004): Data taken from DeGiralamo, D.M. (2004): *Beyond the obvious: unmasking value and risk in specialty pharma opportunities*. Presentation prepared for the Specialty Pharma Corporate Development Global Summit. Princeton, NJ. September 2004.

FARR, C.M.; FISCHER, W.A. (1992): Managing international high-tech cooperative projects. *R&D Management*, Vol. 22, No. 1, pp. 55-67.

FESTEL, G. (2004): Identifying and Realising the hidden value of intellectual property, in: PACL, H.; FESTEL, G.; WESS, G. (eds.): *The Future of Pharma R&D – Challenges and Trends*. Hünenberg: Festel Capital, pp. 123-128.

FORD, D. (1985): The management and marketing of technology, in: LAMB, R.; SHRIVASTAVA, P. (Eds.): *Advances in Strategic Management*, Vol. 3. Jai Press, London, pp. 103–134.

FREEMAN, C. (1991): Networks of innovators: A synthesis. *Research Policy*, Vol. 20, pp. 499-514.

GALLAGHER, R. (1952): Risk management: new phase of cost control. *Harvard Business Review*, Vol. 14, No. 5 (September-October), pp. 75-98.

GAMBARDELLA, A. (1995): *Science and innovation. The US pharmaceutical industry during the 1980s*. Cambridge, UK: Cambridge University Press.

GAMBARDELLA, A. (1992): Competitive advantage from in-house scientific research: the US pharmaceutical industry in the 1980s. *Research Policy*, Vol. 21, pp. 391-407.

GAREN, J.E. (1994): Executive compensation and principal-agent theory. *Journal of Political Economy*, Vol. 102, pp. 1175-1199.

GASSMANN, O. (1999): Praxisnähe mit Fallstudienforschung, *Wissenschaftsmanagement*, Vol. 3, pp. 11-16.

GASSMANN, O.; KOBE, C.; VOIT, E. (2001): *High-Risk-Projekte*. Heidelberg: Springer.

GASSMANN, O.; REEPMEYER, G.; VON ZEDTWITZ, M. (2004): *Leading pharmaceutical innovation – Trends and drivers for growth in the pharmaceutical industry*. Heidelberg: Springer.

GASSMANN, O.; REEPMEYER, G.; VON ZEDTWITZ, M. (2003): Analyzing structures of the pharmaceutical industry in Switzerland. *Journal of Health Care and Society*, Vol. 13, No. 2.

GASSMANN, O.; VON ZEDTWITZ, M. (1998): Organization of industrial R&D on a global scale. *R&D Management*, Vol. 28, No. 3, 147-161.

GAYNOR, M.; GERTLER, P. (1995): Moral hazard and risk spreading in partnerships, *RAND Journal of Economics*, Vol. 26, pp. 591-613.

GEORGELLIS Y.; JOYCE P.; WOODS A. (2000): Entrepreneurial action, innovation and business performance: The small independent business. *Journal of Small Business and Enterprise Development*, Vol. 7, No. 1, pp. 7-17.

GERYBADZE, A. (1995): *Strategic alliances and process redesign – effective management and restructuring of cooperative projects and networks*. Berlin: Gruyter.

GITTINS, J. (1997): Why crash pharmaceutical research? *R&D Management*, Vol. 27, No. 1, pp. 79-85.

GOEBEL, M. (2004): Mergers and acquisitions in the pharma industry, in: PACL, H.; FESTEL, G.; WESS, G. (eds.): *The future of pharma R&D – Challenges and Trends*. Hünenberg: Festel Capital.

GOMEZ-MEJIA, L.R.; WELBOURNE, T.M.; WISEMAN, R.M. (2000): The role of risk-sharing and risk taking under gainsharing. *Academy of Management Review*, Vol. 25, No. 3, pp. 492-507.

GRABOWSKI, H.; VERNON, J. (1990): A new look at the reutrns and risks to pharmaceutical R&D. *Management Science*, Vol. 36, No. 7, pp. 804-821.

GRABOWSKI, H.; VERNON, J. (2000): The determinants of pharmaceutical research and development expenditures. *Journal of Evolutionary Economics*, Vol.

10, pp. 201-215.

GREIS, N.P.; DIBNER, M.D.; BEAN, A.S. (1995): External partnering as a response to innovation barriers and global competition in biotechnology. *Research Policy*, Vol. 24, pp. 609-630.

GROSS, S.E.; DUNCAN, D. (1998): Case study: Gainsharing plan spurs record productivity and payouts at AmeriSteel. *Compensation and Benefits Review*, Vol. 30, No. 6, pp. 46-50.

GUEDJ, I.; SCHARFSTEIN, D. (2004): *Organizational scope and investment: Evidence from the drug development strategies of biopharmaceutical firms*. Working Paper. April 2004.

GULATI, R. (1995): Does familiarity breed trust? The implications of repeated ties for contractual choice in alliances. *Academy of Management Journal*, Vol. 38, pp. 85-112.

GULATI, R. (1998): Alliances and networks. *Strategic Management Journal*, Vol. 19, No. 4, pp. 293-317.

GULATI, R.; SINGH, H. (1998): The architecture of cooperation: Managing coordination costs and appropriation concerns in strategic alliances. *Administrative Science Quarterly*, Vol. 43, No. 4, pg. 781.

HAGEDOORN, J. (1990): Inter-firm partnerships and co-operative strategies in core technologies, in: Freeman, C.; Soete, L. (eds.): *New explorations in the economics of technical change*. London: Printer, pp. 3-37.

HAGEDOORN, J. (1993): Understanding the rationale of strategic technology partnering: interorganizational modes of cooperation and sectoral differences. *Strategic Management Journal*, Vol. 14, No. 5, pp. 371-385.

HAGEDOORN, J. (1995): Strategic technology partnering during the 1980s: Trends, networks, and corporate patterns in non-core technologies. *Research Policy*, Vol. 24, pp. 207-231.

HAGEDOORN, J. (1996): Trends and patterns in strategic technology partnering since the early seventies. *Review of Industrial Organization*, Vol. 11, pp. 601-616.

HAGEDOORN, J. (2002): Inter-firm R&D partnerships: an overview of major trends and patterns since 1960. *Research Policy*, Vol. 31, pp. 477-492.

HAGEDOORN, J.; LINK, A.N.; VONORTAS, N.S. (2000): Research partnerships. *Research Policy*, Vol. 29, pp. 567-586.

HAGEDOORN, J.; SCHAKENRAAD, J. (1992): Leading companies and networks of strategic alliances in information technologies. *Research Policy*, Vol. 21, pp. 163-190.

HAHN, F.H. (1974): *Notes on R-S models of insurance markets*. Mimeo, Cambridge University.

HALLER, M (1986): Risiko-Management – Eckpunkte eines integrierten Konzepts, in: JAKOB, H. (ed.): *Risiko-Management. Schriften zur Unternehmensführung*, Vol. 33. Wiesbaden.

HALLER, M (2002): Risikomanagement, in: DUBS, R.; EULER, D.; RÜEGG-STÜRM, J. (eds.): *Einführung in die Managementlehre*. Bern: Paul Haupt, pp. 991-1020.

HALLER, M. (1981): Risiko-Management und Versicherung, in: MÜLLER, L.; SCHMIDT, R. (eds.): *Allegemeine Versicherungslehre mit Grundzügen der Volks- und Betriebswirtschaftslehre*. Studienheft 13, Wiesbaden, pp. 515-557.

HALLIDAY, R.G.; DRASDO, A.L.; LUMLEY, C.E.; WALKER, S.R. (1997): The allocation of resources for R&D in the world's leading pharmaceutical companies. *R&D Management*, Vol. 27, No. 1, pp. 63-77.

HAMEL, G. (1991): Competition for competence and inter-partner learning within international strategic alliances. *Strategic Management Journal*, Vol. 12 [Special issue], pp. 83-103.

HÄNGGI, R. (1995): *Risikomanagement und simultaneous engineering*. Dissertation at the University of St. Gallen. Dissertation-No. 1782.

HARABI, N. (1995): Appropriability of technical innovations. An empirical analysis. *Research Policy*, Vol. 24, pp. 981-992.

HARRIGAN, K.R. (1986): *Managing for joint ventures success*. Lexington, MA: Lexington Books.

HARRIGAN, K.R. (1985): *Strategies for joint ventures*. Lexington, MA: Lexington Books.

HARRIGAN, K.R. (1988a): Strategic alliances and partner asymmetries, in:

CONTRACTOR, F.J.; LORANGE, P. (eds.): *Cooperative strategies in international business*. Management International Review, special issue.

HARRIGAN, K.R. (1988b): Joint ventures and competitive strategy. *Strategic Management Journal*, Vol. 9, pp. 141-158.

HARTMANN, M.; HASSAN, A. (2004): Real options for R&D portfolio evaluation, in: PACL, H.; FESTEL, G.; WESS, G. (eds.): *The future of pharma R&D – Challenges and Trends*. Hünenberg: Festel Capital, pp. 149-159.

HASTBACKA, M.A.; MCCARTHY, C. (1997): *Technology Licensing: A strategy for creating value*. Arthur D. Little Report, pp. 51-61.

HELM, R.; KLOYER, M. (2004): Controlling contractual exchange risks in R&D interfirm cooperation: an empirical study. *Research Policy*, Vol. 33, pp. 1103-1122.

HELTEN, E. (1994): Ist Risiko ein Konstrukt? Zur Quantifizierung des Risikobegriffs, in: *Risiko, Versicherung und Markt*. Festschrift for Walter Karten to his 60th anniversary. Karlsruhe.

HENDERSON, R. (2000): Drug industry mergers won't necessarily benefit R&D. *Research Technology Management*, Jul-Aug, pp. 10-11.

HERGERT, M; MORRIS, D. (1988): Trends in international collaborative agreements, in: CONTRACTOR, F.; LORANGE, P. (eds.): *Cooperative Strategies in International Business*. Lexington, MA: Lexington Books, pp. 99-109.

HERRLING, P.L. (1998): Maximizing pharmaceutical research by collaboration. *Nature*, Vol. 392, Supp. 30 April 1998, pp. 32-35.

HESS, J.; EVANGELISTA, E. (2004): *Pharma-Biotech Alliances – jockeying for position in the race to become 'partner of choice'*. http://www.contract pharma.com/Sep031.htm, accessed on 19 December 2004.

HILL, C.W.L. (1990): Cooperation, opportunism, and the invisible hand: Implications for transaction cost theory. *Academy of Management Review*, Vol. 15, pp. 500-513.

HIRSHLEIFER, J. (1965): Investment decision under uncertainty: choice-theoretic approaches. *Quarterly Journal of Economics*, Vol. 79, pp. 509-536.

HIRSHLEIFER, J. (1966): Investment decision under uncertainty: application of the state-preference approach. *Quarterly Journal of Economics*, Vol. 80, pp.

252-277.

HITZIG, R. (1978): Risk Management aus Sicht des Unternehmens. *Zeitschrift für die gesamte Versicherungswissenschaft*, pp. 99-113.

HOUSTON, J.G.; BANKS, M. (1997): The chemical-biological interface: developments in automated and miniaturised screening technology. *Current Opinion in Biotechnology*, Vol. 8, pp. 734-740.

HUXLEY, A. (2004): Man bewegt sich oft an der Grenze zur Vernunft. *io new management*, No. 7-8, pp. 54-57.

IBM BUSINESS CONSULTING SERVICES (2003): *A survey of strategic licensing practices in the pharmaceutical industry*. An IBM Institute for Business Value executive brief, available at http://www.ibm.com/bcs

IMS (2004): *IMS World Review 2004*. http://www.ims-global.com//insight/news_story/0403/news_story_040316.htm, accessed on 9 February 2005.

JAKOB, R. (2003): Eines von 47 Biotechunternehmen hat ein erfolgreiches Produkt. *io new management*, No. 3, pp. 10-13.

JARILLO, J.C. (1988): One strategic network. *Strategic Management Journal*, Vol. 9, pp. 31-41.

JONES, O. (2000): Innovation management as a post-modern phenomenon: The outsourcing of pharmaceutical R&D. *British Journal of Management*, Vol. 11, pp. 341-356.

JONES, O.; CONWAY, S.; STEWARD, F. (2000): Introduction: Social interaction and organisation change, in: JONES, O; CONWAY, S; STEWARD, F. (eds.): *Social interaction and organisational change: Aston perspectives on innovation networks*. London: Imperial College Press.

KALEMLI-OZCAN, S.; SORENSEN, B.E.; YOSHA, O. (2003): Risk-sharing and industrial specialization: regional and international evidence. *The American Economic Review*, Vol. 93, No. 3, pp. 903-918.

KATILA, R.; MANG, P.Y. (2003): Exploiting technological opportunities: The timing of collaborations. *Research Policy*, Vol. 32, pp. 317-332.

KIM, Y.J. (2004): An Analysis of the incentives to licensing in US information technology. *Journal of American Academy of Business*, Vol. 5, No. 1/2, pp. 31-36.

KLEINKNECHT, A.; REIJNEN, J.O.N (1992): Why do firms cooperate in R&D? An empirical study. *Research Policy*, Vol. 21, pp. 347-360.

KODAMA, F. (1992): Technology fusion and the new R&D. *Harvard Business Review*, July-August, pp. 70-78.

KOGUT, B. (1989): The stability of joint ventures. *Journal of Industrial Economics*, Vol. 38, pp. 1-16.

KOLLMER, H.; DOWLING, M. (2004): Licensing as a commercialisation strategy for new technology-based firms. *Research Policy*, Vol. 33, pp. 1141-1151.

KOSTOFF, R.N. (1996): Performance measures for government-sponsored research: Overview and background. *Scientometrics*, Vol. 36, No. 3, pp. 281-292.

KROMREY, H. (1995): *Empirische Sozialforschung – Modelle und Methoden der Datenerhebung und Auswertung*, 7th ed., Opladen.

KUBICEK, H. (1977): Heuristische Bezugsrahmen und heuristisch angelegte Forschungsdesigns als Elemente einer Konstruktionsstrategie empirischer Forschung, in: KÖHLER, R. (ed.): *Empirische und handlungstheoretische Forschungskonzeptionen in der Betriebswirtschaftslehre*, Bericht über die Tagung des Verbandes der Hochschullehrer für Betriebswirtschaft e.V., Stuttgart, pp. 5-36.

KUEMMERLE, W. (1999): Foreign direct investment in industrial research in the pharmaceutical and electronics industries - Results from a survey of multinational firms. *Research Policy*, Vol. 28, No. 2-3, pp. 179-194.

LADO, A.A.; BOYD, N.G.; HANLON, S.C. (1997): Competition, cooperation, and the search for economic rents: A syncretic model. *Academy of Management Review*, Vol. 22, Iss. 1, pg. 110.

LAMNEK, S. (1993): *Qualitative Sozialforschung*, Bd. 2: Methoden und Techniken. Weinheim: Psychologie Verlags Union.

LEHMAN BROTHERS (1999): *Pharmaceutical Outsourcing Digest*. 3 December 1999.

LELAND, H (1978): Optimal risk-sharing and the leasing of natural resources with application to oil and gas leasing on the OSC. *Quarterly Journal of Economics*, Vol. 92, pp. 413-437.

LEONE, A.J. (2002): The relation between efficient risk-sharing arrangements and firm characteristics evidence from the managed care industry. *Journal of Management Accounting Research*, pp. 99-117.

LERNER, J.; MERGES, R.P.; (1998): The control of technology alliances: an empirical analysis of the biotechnology industry. *Journal of Industrial Economics*, Vol. 46, pp. 125-156.

LERNER, J.; SHANE, H.; TSAI, A. (2003): Do equity financing cycles matter? Evidence from biotechnology alliances. *Journal of Financial Economics*, Vol. 67, pp. 411-446.

LEVIN, R.C.; KLEVORICK, A.K.; NELSON, R.R.; WINTER, S.G. (1983): *Questionnaire on industrial research and development*. Technical Report. Yale University.

LEVIN, R.C.; KLEVORICK, A.K.; NELSON, R.R.; WINTER, S.G. (1987): Appropriating the returns from industrial research and development. *Brookings Papers on Economic Activity*, pp. 783-821.

LIN, B.-W. (2001): *Strategic Alliances and Innovation Networks in the Biopharmaceutical Industry*. Institute of Technology Management, National Tsinghua University, Hsinchu, Taiwan.

LINK, A.; BAUER, L. (1989): *Cooperative research in U.S. manufacturing*. Lexington, MA: Lexington Books.

LINK, A.; TASSEY, G. (1989): *Cooperative research and development: The industry-university-government relationship*. Norwell, MA: Kluwer Academic Publishing, pp. vii–xxi.

LOCH, C.H.; BODE-GREUEL, K. (2001): Evaluating growth options as sources of value for pharmaceutical research projects. *R&D Management*, Vol. 31, No. 2, pp. 231-248.

LONGMAN, R. (2004): Jumpstarting research: Big pharma's out-licensing dilemma. Windhover Information Inc. *IN VIVO*, March 2004, A#2004800054.

LÜTHI, J.O.A. (2005): *Out-Licensing als Modell zur Risikoreduktion im pharmazeutischen F&E Management*. Master Thesis at the University of St. Gallen.

MANGEMATIN, V.; LEMARIÉ, S.; BOISSIN, J.-P.; CATHERINE, D.; COROLLEUR, F.; CORONINI, R.; TROMMETTER, M. (2003): Development of SMEs and heterogenity of trajectories: the case of biotechnology in France. *Research Pol-*

icy, Vol. 32, pp. 621-638.

MANSFIELD, E.; SCHWARTZ, M.; WAGNER, S. (1981): Imitation costs and patents: an empirical study. *The Economic Journal*, Vol. 91, Iss. 364, pp. 907-918.

MARTIN, R. (1988): Risk-sharing and franchising. *American Economic Review*, Vol. 78, pp. 954-968.

MCCULLY, M.G.; VAN BRUNT, J. (2004): *Late-Stage Deals Have Lots of Appeal. Signals Magazine – Recombinant Capital*. http://www.signalsmag.com/ signalsmag.nsf/0/9671BC1F7A6A7F5288256F3A007980ED, accessed on 16 November 2004.

MCCUTCHEN, W.W.; SWAMIDASS, P.M. (2004): Motivations for strategic alliances in the pharmaceutical/biotech industry: Some new findings. *Journal of High Technology Management Research*, Vol. 15, pp. 197-214.

MCGRATH, R.G.; NERKAR, A. (2004): Real options reasoning and a new look at the R&D investment strategies of pharmaceutical firms. *Strategic Management Journal*, Vol. 25, pp. 1-21.

MEDAD NEWS (2000): MedAd News, November 2000, as cited in: Accenture (2002): *Commercial and R&D: Reinventing the relationship. Pharmaceuticals & medical products*. Accenture White Paper. 2002.

MEGANTZ, R.C. (2002): *Technology Management – developing and implementing effective licensing programs*. New York: John Wiley and Sons.

MEHR, R.; HEDGES, B. (1963): *Risk management*. Illinois.

MENSCH, G. (1991): *Risiko und Unternehmensführung. Eine systemorientierte Konzeption zum Risikomanagement*. Frankfurt.

MILES, R.E.; SNOW, C.C. (1995): The new network firm: a spherical structure built on a human investment philosophy. *Organisational Dynamics*, pp. 5-17.

MILGROM, P.; ROBERTS, J. (1992): *Economics, organization and management*. Englewoos Cliffs, NJ: Prentice-Hall.

MILLER, D. (1983) The correlates of entrepreneurship in three types of firms. *Management Science*, Vol. 29, No. 7, pp. 770-791.

MILLSON, M.R.; RAJ, S.P.; WILEMON, D. (1996): Strategic partnering for developing new products. *Research Technology Management*, May-June, pp. 41-49.

MORDHORST, C.F. (1994): *Ziele und Erfolg unternehmerischer Lizenzstrategien.* Wiesbaden: Deutscher Universitäts-Verlag.

MOWERY, D.C. (1983): The relationship between intrafirm and contractual forms of industrial research in American manufacturing 1900-1940. *Explorations in Economic History*, Vol. 20, pp. 351-374.

MOWERY, D.C. (ed.) (1988): *International collaborative ventures in US manufacturing.* Cambridge, MA: Ballinger.

MOWERY, D.C.; TEECE, D.J. (1993): *Strategic alliances and industrial research.* Unpublished manuscript, Haas School of Business, University of California at Berkeley.

MUSCHICK, E.; MÜLLER, P. (1987): *Entscheidungspraxis. Ziele – Verfahren – Konsequenzen.* Berlin.

MYTELKA, L.K. (1991): *Strategic partnerships and the world economy.* London: Pinter.

NARULA, R.; HAGEDOORN, J. (1999): Innovating through strategic alliances: moving towards international partnerships and contractual agreements. *Technovation*, Vol. 19, pp. 283-294.

NEEDLEMAN, P. (2001): From a twinkle in the eye to a blockbuster drug. *Research Technology Management*, Nov-Dec, pp. 38-41.

NEFIODOW, L.A. (1990): *Der fünfte Kontradieff*, Frankfurt.

NELSON, R.R. (1990): US technological leadership: Where did it come from and where did it go? *Research Policy*, Vol. 19, pp. 119-132.

NICHOLSON, S.; DANZON, P.M.; MCCULLOUGH, J. (2003): *Biotech-pharmaceutical alliances as a signal of asset and firm quality.* NBER Working Paper 9007.

NIOSI, J. (2003): Alliances are not enough explaining rapid growth in biotechnology firms. *Research Policy*, Vol. 32, pp. 737-750.

NOHRIA, N.; GARCIA-PONT, C. (1991): Global strategic linkages and industry structure. *Strategic Management Journal*, Vol. 12 [Summer Special Issue], pp. 105-124.

NOOTEBOOM, B. (1999): *Inter-firm alliances – analysis and design.* London: Routledge.

NORTON, W.I.; MOORE, W.T. (2000): Entrepreneurial risk: have we been asking the wrong question? *Small Business Economics*, Vol. 18, No. 4, pp. 281-287.

NUENO, P. (1999): Alliances and other things. *R&D Management*, Vol. 29, No. 4, pp. 319-322.

OBERPARLEITER, K. (1930): *Funktionen- und Risikenlehre des Warenhandels*. Berlin: Spaeth&Linde.

OECD (1992): *Technology and the economy*. OECD, Paris.

OECD (2002): *Science, technology and industry outlook: drivers of growth: information technology, innovation, and entrepreneurship*. Special Issue of the STI Outlook. OECD, Paris.

OHMAE, K. (1985): *Macht der Triade*. Wiesbaden.

OSBORN, R.N.; BAUGHN, C.C. (1990): Forms of interorganizational governance for multinational alliances. *Academy of Management Journal*, Vol. 33, pp. 503-519.

OUCHI, W.; BOLTON, M. (1988): The logic of joint research and development. *California Management Review*, pp. 9-33.

PAETZ, O; REEPMEYER, G. (2003): *F&E-Allianzen in der Arzneimittelentwicklung*. Paper presented at doctoral seminar at the University of St. Gallen. June 2003, St. Gallen.

PARKHE, A. (1993): Strategic alliance structuring: A game theoretic and transaction cost examination of interfirm cooperation. *Academy of Management Journal*, Vol. 36, pp. 794-829.

PARR, R.L.; SULLIVAN, P.H. (1996) (eds.): *Technology licensing: corporate strategies for maximizing value*. 2nd ed. New York: John Wiley and Sons.

PERLMUTTER, H.V.; HEENAN, D.A. (1986): Cooperate to compete. *Harvard Business Review*, Vol. 86, Iss. 2, pp. 136-152.

PETER, C. (2002): *Unternehmerisches Risikomanagement*. Dissertation at the University of St. Gallen, Dissertation-No. 2525.

PFEIFFER, P. (2000): *Sicherung von F&E-Kompetenz in multinationalen Pharmaunternehmen*. Dissertation at the University of St. Gallen, Dissertation-No. 2362.

PFIFFNER, M.; STADELMANN, P.D. (1995): *Arbeit und Management in der Wissensgesellschaft*. Dissertation at the University of St. Gallen, Dissertation-No. 1674.

PHARMA INFORMATION (2002): *Swiss health care and pharmaceutical market*. Edition 2002. Basel: Interpharma.

PHARMACEUTICAL EXECUTIVE (2003): *PharmExec 50. Special Report*. May 2003. http://www.pharmexec.com/pharmexec/article/articleDetail.jsp?id=55215, accessed on 1 March 2005.

PHARMACEUTICAL EXECUTIVE (2004): *PharmExec 50. Special Report*. May 2004. http://www.pharmexec.com/pharmexec/article/articleDetail.jsp?id=95192, accessed on 10 February 2005.

PHRMA (2001): http://www.phrma.org, including information updated in 2001, accessed on 31 March 2003.

PHRMA (2003): *Pharmaceutical Research and Manufacturers of America – Annual Membership Survey*, 2003.

PHRMA (2004): *Pharmaceutical Research and Manufacturers of America – Industry Profile*, 2004.

PISANO, G. (1990): The R&D boundaries of the firm: an empirical analysis. *Administrative Science Quarterly*, Vol. 35, pp. 153-176.

PISANO, G. (1991): The governance of innovation: Vertical integration and collaborative arrangements in the biotechnology industry. *Research Policy*, Vol. 20, pp. 237-249.

PISANO, G. (1997a): *The Development Factory*. Boston, MA: HBS Press.

PISANO, G. (1997b): *R&D performance, collaborative arrangements, and the market-for-know-how: a test of the 'lemons' hypothesis in biotechnology*. HBS Working Paper 97-105.

PISANO, G.; SHAN, W.; TEECE, D. (1988): Joint ventures and collaboration in the biotechnology industry, in: MOWERY, D.C. (Ed.): *International collaborative ventures in US manufacturing*. Cambridge, MA: Ballinger, pp. 183-222.

POOLE, S.M.; VAN DE VEN, A.H. (1989): Using paradox to build management and organization theories. *Academy of Management Review*, Vol. 14, 562-578.

PORTER, M.E. (1985): *Competitive advantage: Creating and sustaining superior performance*. New York: Macmillan.

PORTER, M.E. (1990): *The competitive advantage of nations*. London: Basingstoke.

PORTER, M.E.; FULLER, M.B. (1986): Coalitions and global strategy, in: Porter, M.E. (ed.): *Competition in global industries*. Boston, MA.

POWELL, W.W.; KOPUT, K.W.; SMITH-DOERR, L. (1996): Interorganizational collaboration and the locus of innovation: Networks of learning in biotechnology. *Administrative Science Quarterly*, Vol. 41, No. 1, pp. 116-145.

PRATT, J.W. (1964): Risk aversion in the small and in the large. *Econometrica*, Vol. 32, pp. 122-136.

PRATT, J.W. (2000): Efficient risk-sharing: the last frontier. *Management Science*, Vol. 46, No. 12, pp. 1545-1553.

QUINN, R.; CAMERON, K. (1988): *Paradox and transformation*. Cambridge, MA: Ballinger.

RAUTIAINEN, T. (2001): Critical success factors in biopharmaceutical business. A comparison between Finnish and Californian businesses. *Technology Review* 113/2001. TEKES. 24 p.

RAZGAITIS, R. (1999): *Early-stage Technologies: Valuation and Pricing*. New York: John Wiley and Sons.

RECOMBINANT CAPITAL (2005): *Analyst's Notebook. Trends*. http://www.recap.com /consulting.nsf/ANB_tab_trends?openform, accessed 11 February 2005.

REUTERS (2002): *Pharmaceutical innovation – An analysis of leading companies and strategies*. Reuters Business Insight, Healthcare.

REUTERS (2003a): *The blockbuster drug outlook to 2007: Identifying, creating and maintaining the pharmaceutical industry's growth drivers*. Reuters Business Insight, Healthcare.

REUTERS (2003b): *Patent protection strategies: Maximizing market exclusivity*. Reuters Business Insight, Healthcare.

REUTERS (2003c): *Pharmaceutical R&D outsourcing strategies – An analysis of market drivers and resistors to 2010*. Reuters Business Insight, Healthcare.

ROBBINS-ROTH, C. (2001): *Zukunftsbranche Biotechnologie*. Wiesbaden: Gabler.

ROBERTS, E.; BERRY, C.A. (1985): Entering new businesses: selecting strategies for success. *Sloan Management Review*, Spring 1985.

ROBERTS, E.; MIZOUCHI, R. (1989): Inter-firm technological collaboration: the case of Japanese biotechnology. *International Journal of Technology Management*, Vol. 4, No. 1, pp. 43-61.

ROTERING, C. (1990): *Forschungs- und Entwicklungskooperationen zwischen Unternehmen*, Stuttgart.

ROTH, G. Y. (2004): *Contract pharma – Glossary of terms – A lexicon of pharma & biopharma industry words and acronyms*. http://www.contractpharma.com/images/Glossary.pdf, accessed on 10 July 2004.

ROTHAERMEL, F.T. (2001): Complemetary assets, strategic alliances, and the incumbent's advantage: an empirical study of industry and firm effects in the biopharmaceutical industry. *Research Policy*, Vol. 30, pp. 1235-1251.

ROTHAERMEL, F.T.; DEEDS, D.L. (2004): Exploration and exploitation alliances in biotechnology: a system of new product development. *Strategic Management Journal*, Vol. 25, pp. 201-221.

ROTHSCHILD, M.; STIGLITZ, J. (1976): Equilibrium in competitive insurance markets: an esssay on the economics of imperfect information. *Quarterly Journal of Economics*, pp. 629-649.

RUH, H.; SEILER, H. (eds.) (1993): *Gesellschaft – Ethik – Risiko*. Proceedings of a poly-project-workshop on 23-25 November 1992 in Basel.

SAFTLAS, H. (2001): *Industry surveys healthcare: Pharmaceuticals*. 27 December 2001, New York: Standard & Poors, p. 32.

SAKAKIBARA, M. (1995). *Cooperative research and development: Theory and evidence on Japanese practice*. Doctoral thesis. Harvard University, Cambridge, Massachusetts.

SAKAKIBARA, M. (2001): Co-operative research and development: who participates and in which industries do projects take place? *Research Policy*, Vol. 30, pp. 993-1018.

SCHERER, F.M.; ROSS, D. (1990): *Industrial market structure and economic performance*. 3rd ed. Boston: Houghton Mifflin.

SCHLEE, E.E. (2001): The value of information in efficient risk-sharing arrangements. *The American Economic Review*, Vol. 91, No. 3, pp. 509-524.

SCHMIDT, U. (1999): Efficient risk-sharing and the dual theory of choice under risk. *The Journal of Risk and Insurance*, Vol. 66, No. 4, pp. 597-608.

SCHON, D.A. (1963): Champions for Radical New Inventions. *Harvard Business Review*, Vol. 40, March-April.

SCOTT, D. (2001): *Out-Licensing – laying the groundwork for a successful deal.* http://pharmalicensing.com/features/disp/1007462302_3c0ca79e79f67, accessed on 19 December 2004.

SCOTT, J.T. (1989): Historical and economic perspectives of the National Cooperative Research Act, in: LINK, A.; TASSEY, G. (eds.): *Cooperative research and development: The industry–university–government relationship.* Norwell, MA: Kluwer Academic Publishing, pp. 65-84.

SHAN, W.; VISUDTIBHAN, K. (1990): Cooperative strategy in commercializing an emerging technology. *European Journal of Operational Research*, Vol. 47, pp. 172-181.

SHARMA, A.; LACEY, N. (2004): Linking product development outcomes to market valuation of the firm: The case of the U.S. pharmaceutical industry. *Journal of Product Innovation Management*, Vol. 21, Iss. 5, pg. 297.

SHERIDAN, C. (2003): Speedel Group raises CHF 52.1m through debt, equity financing. *BioWorld International*, 9 July 2003, via http://www.findarticles.com, accessed on 5 January 2004.

SHIN, H.-H.; STULZ, R.M. (2000): *Firm value, risk, and growth opportunities.* Working paper at Ohio State University. June 2000. 37 pages.

SIGNAL MAGAZINE (1997): How the elephants dance Part 2; as cited in Accenture (2002): *Commercial and R&D: Reinventing the relationship. Pharmaceuticals & medical products.* Accenture White Paper.

SINHA, D.; CUSUMANO, M. (1991): Complementary resources and cooperative research: A model of research joint ventures among competitors. *Management Science*, Vol. 37, No. 9, pp. 1091-1106.

SMITH, G.V.; PARR, R.L. (1993): *Intellectual property: licensing and joint venture profit strategies.* New York: John Wiley and Sons.

SOVEREIGN (2005): *Actelion.* http://www.sovereign-publications.com/actelion.htm, accessed on 7 February 2005.

SPEEDEL (2004): *Introducing the Speedel Group*. Company presentation. http://www.speedelgroup.com, accessed on 10 September 2004.

STUART, T.E. (2000): Interorganizational alliances and the performance of firms: A study of growth and innovation rates in a high-technology industry. *Strategic Management Journal*, Vol. 21, No. 8, pp. 791-811.

TAPON, F.; THONG, M.; BARTELL, M. (2001): Drug discovery and development in four Canadian biotech companies. *R&D Management*, Vol. 31, No. 1, pp. 77-90.

TAPON, F.; THONG, M. (1999): Research collaborations by multi-national research oriented pharmaceutical firms: 1988-1997. *R&D Management*, Vol. 29, No. 3, pp. 219-231.

TAYLOR, C.T.; SILBERSTON, Z.A. (1973): *The economic impact of the patent system. A study of the british experience*. Cambridge, UK: Cambridge University Press.

TEECE, D.J. (1986): Profiting from technological innovation: Implications for integration, collaboration, licensing and public policy. *Research Policy*, Vol. 15, pp. 285-305.

TEECE, D.J. (1989): Competition and cooperation: Striking the right balance. *California Management Review*, Vol. 31, No. 3, pp. 25-37.

TELESIO, P. (1979): *Technology licensing and multinational enterprises*. New York: Praeger.

TEOH, P.-L. (1994): Speed to global market success: An empirical prediction of new product success in the ethical pharmaceutical industry. *European Journal of Marketing*, No. 11, pp. 29-49.

THIEL, K.A. (2004): Good-bye Columbus! New NRDOs forego discovery. *Nature Biotechnology*, Vol. 22, No. 9, pp. 1087-1092.

TIDD, J. (1997): Complexity, networks and learning: Integrative themes for research on the management of innovation. *International Journal of Innovation Management*, Vol. 1, No. 1, pp. 1-19.

TOMCZAK, T. (1992): Forschungsmethoden in der Marketingwissenschaft. *Marketing Zeitschrift für Forschung und Praxis* 2, pp. 77-87.

TORRES, A. (1999): Unlocking the value of intellectual assets. *The McKinsey Quarterly*, No. 4, pp. 28-37.

TOWNSEND, R. (1994): Risk and insurance in village India. *Econometrica*, Vol. 62, pp. 539-591.

TRAJTENBERG, M.; HENDERSON, R.; JAFFE, A. (1992): *Quantifying basicness and appropriability of innovations with the aid of patent data: A comparison of university and corporate research.* Paper presented at the INSEE Seminar on Technological Appropriation. Paris, June.

TYCELOTE, A. (2004): Hybrid corporate governance and its effects on innovation: a case study of AstraZeneca. *Technology Analysis & Strategic Management*, Vol. 16, Iss. 1, pg. 97.

ULRICH, H. (1981): Die Betriebswirtschaftslehre als anwendungsorientierte Sozialwissenschaft, in GEIST, M; KÖHLER, R. (eds.): *Die Führung des Betriebes*, Stuttgart: Poeschel, pp. 1-26.

ULRICH, H.; KRIEG, W. (1974): *St. Galler Management Modell*, 3rd ed., Bern: Paul Haupt.

VENKATARAMAN, S. (1997): The distinctive domain of entrepreneurship research: An editor's perspective, in: KATZ, J.; BROCKHAUS, R. (eds.): *Advances in entrepreneurship, firm emergence, and growth.* Greenwich, CT: JAI Press.

VINOD, H.D.; RAO, P.M. (2000): R&D and promotion in pharmaceuticals: A conceptual framework and empirical exploration. *Journal of Marketing Theory and Practice*, Vol. 8, Iss. 4, pp. 10-21.

VÖLKER, R. (2001): Planung und Steuerung von Entwicklungsprojekten in der Pharmabranche, in: GASSMANN, O.; KOBE, C.; VOIT, E. (eds.): *High-Risk-Projekte*. Heidelberg: Springer, pp. 231-247.

VON ZEDTWITZ, M.; GASSMANN, O.; REEPMEYER, G. (2003): *International pharmaceutical innovation – the example of swiss companies*. Paper presented at the R&D Management Conference, Manchester, UK, 7-9 July 2003.

WALTON, F. (2004): In- and Out-licensing, in: PACL, H.; FESTEL, G.; WESS, G. (eds.): *The Future of Pharma R&D – Challenges and Trends*. Hünenberg: Festel Capital, pp. 107-122.

WEISENFELD, U.; REEVES, J.C.; HUNCK-MEISWINKEL, A. (2001): Technology management and collaboration profile: virtual companies and industrial platforms in the high-tech biotechnology industries. *R&D Management*, Vol. 31, No. 1, pp. 91-100.

WGZ BANK (2002): *Branchenanalyse Life Science*. WGZ Report, October 2002. Düsseldorf.

WHITE, E. (1997): *Licensing – A strategy for profits* (2nd ed.). Alexandria: Licensing Executives Society.

WHITTAKER, E.; BOWER, D.J. (1994): A shift to external alliances for product development in the pharmaceutical industry. *R&D Management*, Vol. 24, No. 3, pp. 249-260.

WILSON, C.A. (1976): *Equilibrium in a class of self-selection models*. PhD Thesis, Universitiy of Rochester.

WINDHOVER (2000): Opportunism knocks. *Windhover's Review of Emerging Medical Ventures*. Vol. 5, No. 4, pp. 32. http://www.windhover.com/ contents/monthly/exex/e_2000900064.htm, accessed on 19 December 2004.

WINDHOVER (2003): In-licensing: Still a difficult model. *Windhover's Review of Emerging Medical Ventures*. Vol. 8, No. 10. http://www.windhover.com/ contents/monthly/exex/e_2003900172.htm, accessed on 19 December 2004.

WINTER, S.G. (1987): Knowledge and competence as strategic assets, in: TEECE, D.J. (ed.): *The competitive challenge*. Cambridge, MA: Ballinger Publishing Company, pp. 159-185.

WOOD MACKENZIE (2003a): As cited in presentation by F. Humer, CEO of Hoffmann-La Roche, June 2003.

WOOD MACKENZIE (2003b): As cited in company presentation by Speedel, February 2004.

WSJE (2003): Speedel makes its mark guding drugs through testing stages. *Wall Street Journal Europe*, as of 8 May 2003.

YAARI, M. (1965): Convexity in the theory of choices under risk. *Quarterly Journal of Economics*, Vol. 79, pp. 278-290.

YEOH, P.-L.; ROTH, K. (1999): An empirical analysis of sustained advantage in the US pharmaceutical industry: impact of firm resources and capabilities. *Strategic Management Journal*, Vol. 20, pp. 637-653.

YIN, R.K. (1994): *Case study research: design and methods*, 2nd ed. Thousand

Oaks: SAGE Publications.

ZAMBROWICZ, B.P.; SANDS, A.T. (2003): Knockouts model the 100 best-selling drugs – will they model the next 100? *Nature Reviews Drug Discovery*, Vol. 2, pp. 38-51.

ZANETTI, P.; STEINER, U. (2001): *Sektorstudie Pharma Europa – Biotech als Hoffnungsträger*. Zürich: Leu Investment Research.

ZIEDONIS, R.H. (2004): Don't fence me in: Fragmented markets for technology and the patent acquisition strategies of firms. *Management Science*, Vol. 50, Iss. 6, pp. 804-821.

ZIMMERMANN, H.; JAEGER, S.; STAUB, Z. (1995): *Asset- und Liability-Management: Erfolgsstrategie für Banken*. Zurich.

ZÜRCHER, J.; BLASER, M. (2004): *Cornerstones for Biotech Success. Swiss Biotech Report 2004*. Basel: Ernst & Young, pp. 20-21.

List of Abbreviations

ACE	Angiotensin-converting enzyme
AIDS	Acquired Immune Deficiency Syndrome
APV	Arbeitsgemeinschaft für Pharmazeutische Verfahrenstechnik
AZ	AstraZeneca
BD	Business development
BD&L	Business development & licensing
BMS	Bristol-Myers Squibb
CAGR	Compound annual growth rate
CDO	Contract development organization
CMO	Contract manufacturing organization
CML	Chronic myelogenous leukaemia
CNS	Central nervous system
CRO	Contract research organization
CSO	Contract service organization
ENL	Erythema nodosum leprosum
eNPV	Expected net present value
ERA	Endothelin receptor antagonist
ET	Endothelin
FDA	Food and Drug Administration
GSK	GlaxoSmithKline
HIV	Human Immunodeficiency Virus
HTS	High-throughput screening
IND	Investigational new drug
IP	Intellectual property

IPO	Initial public offering
J&J	Johnson & Johnson
M&A	Merger(s) & acquisition(s)
MIT	Massachusetts Institute of Technology
NCE	New chemical entity
NDA	New drug application
NME	New molecular entity
NPV	Net present value
NRDO	No-research-development-only
OECD	Organisation for Economic Co-Operation and Development
OPAC	Operating profit after capital charges
OTC	Over-the-counter
PAH	Pulmonary arterial hypertension
PDM	Product Development Meeting
Phase I	Clinical development phase I
Phase II	Clinical development phase II
Phase III	Clinical development phase III
PhRMA	Pharmaceutical Research and Manufacturers of America
SEC	Securities and Exchange Commission
SMEs	Small and mid-sized enterprises
SMO	Site management organization
SWX	Swiss Stock Exchange
UHTS	Ultra high-throughput screening

List of Figures

List of Tables

GPSR Compliance

The European Union's (EU) General Product Safety Regulation (GPSR) is a set of rules that requires consumer products to be safe and our obligations to ensure this.

If you have any concerns about our products, you can contact us on ProductSafety@springernature.com

In case Publisher is established outside the EU, the EU authorized representative is:

Springer Nature Customer Service Center GmbH
Europaplatz 3
69115 Heidelberg, Germany

Batch number: 10725973

Printed by Printforce, the Netherlands